PARANOIA AND MODERNITY

PARANOIA AND MODERNITY

Cervantes to Rousseau

John Farrell

Cornell University Press
Ithaca and London

Publication of this book was made possible, in part, by a grant from Claremont Colleges.

First published 2006 by Cornell University Press

Printed in the United States of America

Library of Congress Cataloging-in-Publication Data

Farrell, John.
  Paranoia and modernity : Cervantes to Rousseau / John Farrell.
    p. cm.
  Includes bibliographical references and index.
  ISBN-13: 978-0-8014-4410-4 (cloth : alk. paper)
  ISBN-10: 0-8014-4410-1 (cloth : alk. paper)
  1. Civilization, Modern— Psychological aspects. 2. Paranoia
—Philosophy. 3. Paranoia in literature. 4. Agent (Philosophy)
5. Personality and culture. I. Title.
  CB358.F37 2005
  909'.09821'019— dc22   2005017717

Cloth printing   10 9 8 7 6 5 4 3 2 1

To Blanford Parker

"Remember, Sancho," said Don Quixote, "that wherever virtue exists in an eminent degree, it is persecuted."
—DON QUIXOTE

Shall I believe that I am nothing? Shall I believe that I am God?
—BLAISE PASCAL

Contents

Acknowledgments

This study was completed with the help of a year-long fellowship from the National Endowment for the Humanities and grants from the Aurora Institute and the Gould Center for Humanistic Studies. I especially wish to thank Wight Martindale, the director of the Aurora Institute, Jonathan Petropoulos, the director of the Gould Center, Nicholas Warner, its interim director, and Richard Drake, its assistant director, for their kindness and consideration. I have incurred many personal and scholarly debts in the course of this project. I am especially grateful to Fred Crews and Louis Sass for their advice and support. I owe debts too numerous to mention to colleagues at Claremont McKenna College, and especially to my colleagues in the Department of Literature. My friends Bob Faggen, Jeff Ferguson, Maureen McLane, John Plotz, Chuck Henebry, and Eleanor Courtemanche provided much stimulation on the issues addressed in these pages; parts of the manuscript benefited from the keen scrutiny of Audrey Bilger, Fred Crews, and Bill Ascher. The work would have been accomplished far less efficiently without the assistance of Anne Palmer, Mary Flannery, Ivan Lincir, and Angela Jacquez. Connie Bartling was invaluable at every stage. Finally, I am grateful for the sustaining friendship and intellectual companionship of Yoon Sun Lee, Doron Weber, Martha Bayles, Annie Maccoby, John Rabinowitz, Jackie Geller, Ching Lim, Gary Siperstein, Charles More, Pia Sorenson, Kal Applbaum, Ingrid Jordt, Claudine Frank, David Venturo, Tony Kemp, and Karen Gross. And to my family I owe, as usual, the greatest debt.

J.F.

PARANOIA AND MODERNITY

Introduction

This book attempts to explain the surprising centrality and, at times, dominance of the paranoid character in modern Western culture by tracing portrayals of agency—freedom and responsibility, power and control—from the late Middle Ages to the mid-eighteenth century. Paranoia is a psychological tendency in which the intellectual powers of the sufferer are neither entirely undermined nor completely cut off from reality, but rather deployed with a peculiar distortion.[1] Paranoid thinking can be a concomitant of schizophrenia; it can become a psychosis on its own; or it can appear in people who function relatively normally but whose thinking exhibits what may be described as a "paranoid slant," a penchant for over-estimating one's own importance, for feeling persecuted, being morbidly preoccupied with autonomy and control, or finding hostile motives in other people's behavior. Paranoid characters hold long grudges. They can be aloof and secretive or ironical and superior. In cases that go beyond a mere "slant," the paranoid discovers plots forming around him, enemies interfering with his life, hidden significance in facts or occurrences that to the unaffected mind seem insignificant. His sense that he is the focus of sinister attention may be accompanied by delusions of grandeur, and it may be held in place by a far-flung system of interpretation. For the paranoid mind, the neutral distinction between appearance and reality slips easily into the insidious distinction between truth and lie.[2]

[1] Women suffer from paranoia as often as men, but paranoia in the period covered by this study has entirely to do with male authors and characters, with women at times in the role of enemies. Therefore I have adopted the masculine pronoun when referring to the paranoid figure, while maintaining gender-neutral usage elsewhere.

[2] For the classic use of *paranoia* as a term of cultural analysis, see Richard Hofstadter, *The Paranoid Style in American Politics and Other Essays* (New York: Knopf, 1965). For the symp-

For the paranoid, nothing is accidental; anything and everything can be about him. The fact that the world does not overtly show its hostility only certifies its duplicity and malice. Friendliness makes him suspicious; hostility reassures him of the truth of his delusions even while it stimulates genuine fear. He feels unappreciated, resisted, embattled, oppressed. It may be his livelihood that is threatened or his life, the possession of a love object or the recognition of his genius. The enemies may be local, a family member or a colleague; they may be chosen from among minority groups that are frequently the targets of social resentment; they may be supernatural beings or creatures from another planet, or earthly powers like states or multinational corporations. The resentful, suspicious, and grandiose behavior of the paranoid often earns him the hostility and mockery he fears. The motives of his tormentors may remain mysterious even to him, but this does not mean he cannot marshal the evidence for their workings with cogency or convey it with eloquence. Paranoia is a disease of justice, and it demands a hearing. Having real power does not free the paranoid from his imaginary enemies, as the examples of Hitler and Stalin would suggest.[3]

Among the commanding figures of modern culture since the sixteenth-century, paranoid psychology appears with remarkable frequency. In some cases the tendency is only one dimension of a many-sided personality. In the life of René Descartes, for example, we can see an extraordinary caution and fearfulness of others, a taste for exile and disputes about priority,[4] yet his philosophical stance does not necessarily lead to suspicion. In other cases the paranoid cast of mind seems inseparable from the author's essential logic, rhetoric, and worldview. Thomas Hobbes, whose thought plays an important role in these pages, remarked at the end of his life that his "Mother Dear/ Did bring forth Twins at once, both Me, and Fear."[5] Many aspects of his life and thought bear out the claim. For Martin Luther, the focus of hostility upon a reliable cast of enemies, and the sense of self-confirmation and self-

---

toms of paranoia, see Robert S. Robins and Jerrold M. Post, M.D., *Political Paranoia: The Psychopolitics of Hatred* (New Haven: Yale University Press, 1997). Ronald K. Siegel, in *Whispers: The Voices of Paranoia* (New York: Crown, 1994), provides an illuminating set of case histories, though in a somewhat Quixotic spirit.

[3] On the history of *paranoia* as a diagnostic term, see Aubrey Lewis, "Paranoia and Paranoid: A Historical Perspective," *Psychological Medicine* 1 (1970):2–12. The recent trend has been to make a strong separation between a non-delusory paranoid "slant" (Paranoid Personality Disorder) and the psychotic formation of fixed, often lifelong delusions (Delusional Disorder), of which persecution and grandiosity are among the range of clinically observable themes. Alistair Munro, *Delusional Disorders: Paranoia and Related Illnesses* (Cambridge: Cambridge University Press, 1999). For the present diagnostic landscape, see the *Diagnostic and Statistical Manual of Mental Disorders (DSM-IV-TR)*, 4th ed., text revision (Washington, DC: American Psychiatric Association, 2000).

[4] Stephen Gaukroger, *Descartes: An Intellectual Biography* (Oxford: Oxford University Press, 1995), 18.

[5] This is from an anonymous translation of Hobbes' autobiographical Latin poem included in *The Elements of Law Natural and Politic,* ed. J. C. A. Gaskin (Oxford: Oxford University Press, 1994), lines 27-28.

justification that come from hostility and denunciation, constitute important motives of his work. And in two of the most influential figures of advanced modernity, Jean-Jacques Rousseau and Friedrich Nietzsche, we can observe the progress from a hostile and suspicious worldview to manifest psychosis. Nietzsche's megalomania was a phase on the way to dementia and silence, while Rousseau waged a long struggle to integrate his delusions of persecution with reality, to convince others of their truth, and to make peace with his isolated and frustrated condition.

Though paranoia is a modern concept, the paranoid character can already be glimpsed in the literature of antiquity; Sophocles' *Ajax* provides a striking example. In modern literature, the figure of the paranoid becomes the very type of the hero. Don Quixote is the first great modern paranoid adventurer, and Cervantes' treatment of him, with its astonishing minuteness and delicacy of observation, remains the most penetrating and influential portrait of madness in Western literature. Grandiosity, suspicion, and persecution define the characters of Swift's Gulliver, Stendhal's Julien Sorel, Melville's Ahab, Dostoyevsky's Underground Man, Ibsen's Masterbuilder Solness, Strindberg's Captain (in *The Father*), Kafka's K., and Joyce's autobiographical hero Stephen Dedalus.[6] Paranoia in an enlarged social form is a central imaginative impulse in American literature since World War II. The all-encompassing conspiracy has become almost the normal way of representing American society and its institutions in this period, giving impetus to heroic plots and counter-plots in a hundred films and in the novels of Burroughs, Heller, Ellison, Pynchon, Kesey, Mailer, DeLillo, and others.[7]

Obviously there are powerful sociological factors at work in this tendency to see ourselves as controlled by hidden forces from without. Every one of us in modern consumer society is indeed the daily target of vast and anonymous agencies deploying images and information—partial information, misinformation—with the aim of shaping our political and economic behavior. And the forces of social change that shape this intrusive environment, forces which were only beginning to be visible in the eighteenth century, seem to become ever more pressing and dynamic, so that it is almost natural to feel

---

[6] Not all of these authors, however, take the same view of their paranoid heroes. *The Father* seems to be less a play about a paranoid character than a paranoid play about an authentic victim of conspiracy. With Joyce, however, a considerable degree of satiric distance is evident even in *A Portrait of the Artist as a Young Man*. Though Stephen's three weapons, "silence, exile, and cunning," were at least for a time Joyce's own, in *Ulysses* Stephen's grandiose and suspicious character is transcended by the humorous, tolerant, and mature Leopold Bloom.

[7] More and more recent books have focused upon paranoia as a powerful force in modern culture and a way of making sense of the contemporary world. See, for instance, *Transparency and Conspiracy: Ethnographies of Suspicion in the New World Order*, ed. Harry G. West and Todd Sanders (Durham: Duke University Press, 2003); *Conspiracy Nation: The Politics of Paranoia in Postwar America* (New York: New York University Press, 2002) and *Conspiracy Culture: American Paranoia from Kennedy to the "X-Files"* (New York: Routledge, 2001), both edited by Peter Knight; and *Paranoia within Reason: A Casebook on Conspiracy as Explanation*, ed. George E. Marcus (Chicago: University of Chicago Press, 1999).

caught in a system with a logic and intentions of its own. As we operate within this vast network, the effects of our own actions, as well as those of others, become incalculable. To borrow Nicholas Cusanus's description of God, we are part of an order whose circumference seems to be everywhere but whose center is nowhere.

Yet sociology will take us only so far in understanding the prominence of suspicion and paranoia in modern culture, for our ways of interpreting the pressures of multinational capital are crucially determined by the intellectual outlook we bring to them. When we acknowledge, for instance, that there are real-world forces threatening the freedom and autonomy of real people, we are implying that it is possible for real people to have freedom and autonomy. We are implying that they can be agents in a substantial sense and that their actions can be guided by notions of truth and value that are more valid than paranoid delusions. These premises, essential to daily life, are difficult to account for in any model, but modern intellectuals have tended to make their renunciation into a virtue and a point of pride. Especially during the period when the paranoid imagination has flourished in American culture, those critics of literature and film who might have tried to grasp the meaning of this phenomenon in broad intellectual terms have themselves overwhelmingly shared the suspicious attitudes of Pynchon, Heller, Kubrick, and Kesey, often without the humorous reserve of the "catch-22."

These literary critics, of course, took as their masters a generation of postwar French intellectuals who, under the broad banners of Nietzsche, Marx, and Freud, carried the suspicion of society to new depths: Jean-Paul Sartre, for whom the "gaze" of others imposes a fundamental experience of alienation; Louis Althusser, for whom the discourse of responsibility is a primary instance of ideology; Jacques Lacan, for whom language itself is the source of our unnatural submission to the Father; and Michel Foucault, who speaks in terms of an unlocatable and alien *power* that infiltrates every particle of social being. When these notions become dominant, we have passed the point at which it is possible to make a distinction between paranoia and anything else to which the term could be meaningfully opposed. The sense that we are being manipulated and controlled cannot be labeled false because we are indeed, according to this view, the victims of social relations of unfathomable and inescapable manipulative power; nor can it be labeled true because that would be to fall back into the myth of the plenitude of metaphysical discourse that is one of the effects of power itself.

Rather than providing a satisfactory analysis of the attractions of paranoid narrative, therefore, literary criticism in the post-sixties period largely participated in the trend.[8] Its major critical models seek to describe forms of

---

[8] An exception is Timothy Melley, *Empire of Conspiracy: The Culture of Paranoia in Postwar America* (Ithaca: Cornell University Press, 2000). Melley's treatment of paranoia in postwar American culture focuses upon broad questions of agency (paranoia as "agency panic") and brings imaginative, sociological, and critical works into a single frame of analysis. I agree

agency, teleology, or intentionality—discourse, capital, power—that are at once all-encompassing and alien, totally intimate yet totally other. There is a deterministic element here, but freedom and responsibility are not eliminated as one would expect, only displaced to an unfixable and unaccountable locus of control, a kind of phantom limb of intentionality and purpose the resistance to which sustains the moral urgency of the analysis. There remains in the critical practice of the time an animating sense that things could and should have been different, that somewhere decisions have been made but that responsibility remains difficult or impossible to locate.

It will be evident that I am using the term *paranoia* in two different senses. First, I distinguish the purely psychological tendency toward suspicion, grandiosity, persecutory delusions, and systems of interpretation described above, a tendency which seems to be one of the besetting aberrations of the human character. In chapter 3, I use the analysis of Cervantes' character Don Quixote as an opportunity to exemplify the standard clinical list of symptoms as they apply to individual psychology. Second, I use *paranoia* to describe those accounts of the human situation, such as the ones mentioned above, that aim to undermine our ability to distinguish our thought from coherent delusion or manipulative contrivance; in doing so, they make the assumptions that underlie paranoia, in the restricted personal sense, into normative or universal ones. We might call this second sense of *paranoia* a metaphorical extension of the first, and even think of its use as a satiric way of declining the invitation to paranoia implicit in the intellectual habits to which it refers. The descriptive value of this second, generalizing sense, however, and its historical validity as a term of analysis become evident when we consider that the satiric application of madness as a general category was itself one of the typical gestures of the culture I am trying to illuminate. The emergence of the clinical term *paranoia* after the period covered by this book, applying to an intellectually coherent and meaningful delusion, only enhanced the possibilities for heroic self-deflation. A salient example is the irony with which Freud makes his brilliant coinage *narcissism,* the psychological root of paranoia, into a general term for intellectual activity. The self-heroizing wit with which Freud admits his likeness with the paranoid schizophrenic Judge Schreber, for instance, was part of a rhetorical game he learned from Swift and Cervantes.[9] Freud saw himself in Oedipus's crime, in Narcissus's mirror, in the antics of Quixote, and in Schreber's delusions, and he made a grandiose point of pride out of his ability to accept these distorted

---

with his central claim that "agency panic" is connected with the problems of liberal individualism, though I offer a different view of what that entails.

I have also benefited much from Gabriel Josipovici's elegant book *On Trust: Art and the Temptations of Suspicion* (New Haven: Yale University Press, 1999), though the story I tell is a different one from his.

[9] I have explored Freud's heroically self-ironizing rhetoric and his relation with Cervantes, Swift, and Schreber in *Freud's Paranoid Quest: Psychoanalysis and Modern Suspicion* (New York: New York University Press, 1996).

reflections as his own. In his usage, *paranoia* becomes a comic self-reflection that one cannot repudiate.

Pynchon's bitter recognition of paranoia, then, as the only alternative to chaos or emptiness, has a deep background. What makes for the plausibility of this type of thinking, which so ostentatiously undermines its own premises and its own dignity even as it is being posed? The explanation, I argue, has to do with the history of the problem of agency itself in the intellectual development of the West, a history that shows the principled denial of agency and its displacement to be two of the deeply rooted impulses in modern culture as it emerged out of the medieval framework. I will attempt to show that the development of modernity since Luther has been marked by a series of struggles about the definition of human agency—struggles about freedom and the possibility of choice, human access to valid ideals, authority and control, the good or evil in human nature, and the relation of the individual to society. Each of the protagonists of my narrative offers a favored image of human agency, while also addressing a specific image of the agent he wishes to exclude. Part 1 of the book provides a sketch of the medieval model of agency (chapter 1) and two key literary examples, *Sir Gawain and the Green Knight* and *Don Quixote* (chapters 2 and 3), showing how paranoid psychology is contained or marginalized within that model. Part 2 moves to the broad-based attack on the medieval conception of agency and the emergence of its successor model in discourses across the spectrum of intellectual concern—in Luther's religion and that of his Reformed successors (chapters 4 and 5), in Bacon's science (chapter 6), and in the political writings of Hobbes (chapter 8), while Descartes represents an important mixed example (chapter 7). In part 3, I show the deepening of the assault on agency, its gradually developing autonomy with respect to religious motives, and some of the range of its aesthetic potential in the writings of Pascal (chapter 9), La Rochefoucauld (chapter 10), and Swift (chapters 11 and 12). Part 4 begins with an attempt to assess the effect of the countervailing model of Enlightenment optimism, its rejection of the suspicious stance, and the new belief in society as a natural system, which, we will see, offers its own invitation to paranoia. Locke, Shaftesbury, Pope, Hume, and Adam Smith are among the authors discussed (chapter 13). In chapters 14 and 15, I conclude by showing the reversal of this already twice-inverted model by Jean-Jacques Rousseau, who may be said to have detonated it from within. When we talk about the disappearance of Nature in the postmodern context, it is Rousseau's conception of Nature that is relevant, and when Nature disappears, it is the exploded shell of his system that remains. I conclude with an epilogue that attempts to cast a new light on the disappearance of Nature in contemporary literature and theory and the arrival of postmodernist paranoia, with Michel Foucault, Fredric Jameson, and Thomas Pynchon as key points of reference.

The observation that provoked my study was a psychological one—the surprising visibility of the paranoid character among the heroes of modern culture. That does not mean, however, that my method is primarily psychological. Psychology lends not so much the method of explanation as the object to be explained. For psychology has great limitations as a mode of historical understanding. The psychological trends visible in history call for historical, not just psychological explanation, and the imperatives of individual psychology cannot be isolated from other dimensions of thought: from shared intellectual assumptions, foundational metaphors, and rhetorical habits. Even where we can glimpse common psychological themes across historical distances, there remains the question of the meanings locally attached to them. Psychological analysis tends to emphasize passivity and subjectivity, and the nature of my topic would seem to point in that direction, for paranoia is defined by the sense of being controlled or frustrated by others. I have assumed, nevertheless, that accounts of agency, while they may emerge out of the psychological needs of their creators, can yet become powerful social and political instruments. Assertions of agency are themselves forms of agency. Even to deny agency is a form of agency, although it is a risky one, for that which you deny to your opponents, you yourself must do without, and too radical a disclaimer of your own responsibility may leave the power of action entirely elsewhere. One of the peculiarities of the modern mind is how much more easily it conceptualizes the power of others and what They, collectively or individually, can do to Us as opposed to agency considered from the first-person point of view.

While the sequence of historically contested notions of agency provides, then, the heart of my narrative, the psychology of individuals remains of considerable importance. Luther and Rousseau, the inaugurating figures of the two most important conceptions of agency I discuss, display the full range of clinical manifestations of paranoia, but they could never have gained their enormous sway over the development of the modern intellect had they not expressed their personal imperatives in intellectually, theologically, and politically persuasive terms. They were men of great force, and their desperate view of the individual human situation in relation to the other powers of the world gave remarkable glamour to their ideas. Even more striking is the charm of that imaginary hero Don Quixote. Insanity made him an object of laughter to his creator, yet in the later annals of modernity, he became the very image of the modern hero facing his inevitable fate. This could only have happened as the result of changes that made his peculiar habits of mind come to seem not only typical but valuable.

Reducing everything to psychology is one of the ways in which paranoia comes to seem like a norm. Excluding psychology is another one, for to exclude the psychological dimension completely is to lose sight of the ethical individual. Paul de Man, in a well-known essay, poses a choice between two methods of analyzing the thought of Jean-Jacques Rousseau—to see it, on the one hand, in the manner of Jean Starobinski, as an expression of paranoia, grounded in the habits of feeling peculiar to Rousseau's nature, or to see it, on the other hand, in the manner of Jacques Derrida, as typifying problems central to Western metaphysics and its "ontology of presence." For de Man, only the latter can be a valid approach to Rousseau's work. "In his relationship to language," de Man writes, "Rousseau is not governed by his own needs and desires, but by a tradition that defines Western thought in its entirety."[10] In de Man's own later analysis, Rousseau's oeuvre becomes a highly self-conscious working out of the problematics of language as metaphor, the richest and most systematic expression of a point of view later embodied more explicitly in Nietzsche's essay "On Truth and Lie in an Extra-Moral Sense."[11] The critic's task, therefore, is not to contextualize or demystify Rousseau but to free him from readers more naïve than himself. In de Man's view, Rousseau's suspicion is of such a refined and sophisticated sort that it cannot be compatible with the mythologies of Nature, truth, and freedom ostensibly advanced in his work.

In de Man's way of thinking, then, there is a psychological dimension, which is meaningless, and an intellectual one, which is dominant. There is no middle ground. "Tradition" is all-determining—there is no outside on the basis of which Rousseau's doctrine can be questioned. Curiously, with the exclusion of individual psychology, Rousseau's "metaphysical" outlook, or de Man's interpretation of it, becomes normative for everyone. Paranoia becomes the norm of the Western intellect.

It is a strange dichotomy that compels us, in interpreting an author's work, to choose so radically between feeling and thinking, between psychological experience and intellectual commitment, as if these were two entirely separate parts of our mental life. Mere psychological reduction deprives intellectual activity of its significance and makes its influence into nothing more than a satiric spectacle in which later authors reiterate routines that originally served a private emotional need. The intellectual hermeticism of de Man, by contrast, posing Rousseau's oeuvre as the truth of Western metaphysics, makes the shortcomings of Rousseau's outlook into necessary and inevitable elements of our own.[12] My approach tries to locate a historical middle ground that is neither the inevitable march of Western metaphysics nor the random exfoliation of individual eccentricity. The models of agency

[10] Paul de Man, *Blindness and Insight: Essays in the Rhetoric of Contemporary Criticism*, 2nd ed., rev. (Minneapolis: University of Minnesota Press, 1983), 114. The history of French critical judgments on Rousseau's mental and other illnesses is reviewed in Claude Wacjman, *Les jugements de la critique sur la "folie" de J.-J. Rousseau: représentations et interprétations 1760– 1990* (Oxford: Voltaire Foundation, 1996), esp. 48–60.

[11] See part 2 of *Allegories of Reading: Figural Language in Rousseau, Nietzsche, Rilke, and Proust* (New Haven: Yale University Press, 1979).

[12] In the case of Rousseau, it is de Man who would lead us further astray. Although his account of Rousseau and language is plausible as an interpretation of the *Essay on the Origins of Language*, it is a professional projection of the most blatant kind to make language into as central an issue for Rousseau as it was to become for philosophers and literary critics of the twentieth century. Starobinski gives a far less misleading account in spite of his psychoanalytic assumptions, which are lightly applied. See especially *L'oeil vivant: Corneille, Racine, La Bruyère, Rousseau, Stendhal,* edition augmentée (Paris: Gallimard, 1999), 129–230.

I describe are shared intellectual constructions that express personal psychology and resonate with others who find them psychologically congenial. They partake of the arbitrariness and questionableness of all human constructions, and stem from some of the weakest and most distorted human impulses. At the same time, these historically significant models of agency strive toward one of the fundamental goals of Western culture, the articulation of a coherent and persuasive view of human action. Their failure is one of the crucial legacies of modernity. Moreover, while they differ from each other, they work largely with a common vocabulary, its elements rearranged or revalued but rarely discarded. The breaks between models are not arbitrary in the manner of Thomas Kuhn's "paradigms" or Foucault's "epistemes." Rather, they stand in a dialectical relation to one another as a set of historically situated answers to universalizing questions.

It is important to emphasize that I am neither offering a complete history of modernity up to the eighteenth century, nor do I claim that that the tendencies of modern culture I have highlighted are the only important ones.[13] Nevertheless, readers who accept my account should come away with a different view of some of the central figures and issues in modern culture and will perhaps return to some basic philosophical questions with a renewed sense of their political and cultural importance, chief among them the challenge of formulating a persuasive account of human action compatible with modern views of ontology and knowledge. I hope, also, that literary critics of the present will find it instructive to clarify the deep historical origins of some of their most reflexive assumptions. Perhaps the most important lesson of this study, finally, is that while intellectuals since the seventeenth century have been acutely aware of our tendency to project a sense of the ideal onto the actual world, and have developed a healthy skepticism about the Baconian "Idols of the Mind," they have been astonishingly credulous about our opposite capacity—for degrading the objects of intellect and building systems of suspicion. Suspicion may have been our greatest naïveté. These two opposite, over-confident tendencies of the mind, the idealizing and the suspicious, have more in common than a first glance would suggest. Both offer gratifying simplicity in their posture toward the world. Both understand the actual world as though it were configured the way someone would like it to be, the idealist finding his own wish there, the paranoid someone else's. The two modes often depend upon each other, and each should carefully be distinguished from the balanced skepticism and methodological caution that fruitful inquiry demands.

---

[13] The potential richness of nineteenth and twentieth-century English culture for this subject has recently been shown by David Trotter in *Paranoid Modernism: Literary Experiment, Psychosis, and the Professionalization of English Society* (New York: Oxford University Press, 2001). Trotter's book takes up the story of modern paranoia just about where I leave off, but his way of conceiving the subject is almost entirely different from mine.

Part 1

THE PARANOID TEMPTATION

1

Agent and Other

Before an intentional action can be performed by a human agent, it is necessary for that agent to have attained some grasp of an existing state of affairs, to have conceived another state of affairs preferable to it, and to have a sense of the capacity to bring the second state out of the first. Anything less than this fails to qualify as ground for a true action, and behavior that is not preceded by or grounded in such deliberation does not qualify as morally significant. Only in such cases are we willing to judge and be judged.[1] This does not mean, of course, that such deliberation occurs every time we act. On most occasions we rely upon established procedures and habits. The more harmoniously integrated and efficient our behavior, the less we have to think about it. Yet we know that we may be called upon to justify what we are doing at some point, and we normally proceed with some justification in mind. This might be a standard of rationality or of practical fitness, or a reference to established sources of guidance such as authority, tradition, or professional expertise. It is in the context of such a process that our actions can be judged deficient; they may not only be inadequate but completely negligent of or adverse to the demands of the situation or the principles that should govern it. Both the existing state of affairs, then, and the action taken to address it are held up in the light of what should be.

The sense of Is and Ought and the choice that moves between them, em-

[1] Donald Davidson sums up a long tradition of thought about moral reasoning this way: "When a person acts with an intention, the following seems to be a true, if rough and incomplete, description of what goes on: he sets a positive value on some state of affairs (an end, or the performance by himself of an action satisfying certain conditions); he believes (or knows or perceives) that an action, of a kind open to him to perform, will promise or produce or realize the valued state of affairs; and so he acts (that is, he acts *because* of his value or desire and his belief)." *Essays on Actions and Events* (Oxford: Clarendon, 1980), 31.

bedded in the very form of moral judgment, permits categories of agency that extend beyond the performance of a single action. We see our behavior as defining us broadly and substantially in ethical terms, investing us with a moral identity that carries beyond the moment or situation. This identity is shaped in the performance of roles that have been devised to accomplish the variety of ends proper to society. What we call character is the sum of what we establish about ourselves in choosing and performing these roles. Our character is vitally determined, then, by the range of existing practices that society can offer and the prestige and meaning it accords their performance.

There are also categories of ethical evaluation still more comprehensive than that of the individual character or even of a whole human life. We recognize collective persons or agencies, objects of moral judgment defined by race, religion, nation, class, gender, institutional function, or historical position ('modernity' as it is commonly defined would be an example of the latter). A good deal of the conflict and dispute in the modern world centers upon categories of this sort, all of which can be taken to provide a horizon of interpretation for our actions, usually in the context of some religious, political, or historical narrative. The widest of these categories is that of humanity itself: one's general conception of a human being has a great effect upon the manner in which one holds individuals up to a moral standard and, of course, the kind of standard or standards to be applied.

I believe that every reader will recognize these features of our life—the Is, the Ought, and the sense of agency. All three of them have, in the history of thought, been theorized and hypostatized in a variety of ways—in such terms, for instance, as the Ideal, Reality, the Subject, or Human Nature. In the following, I will frequently adopt terms of this kind, along with the more neutral term "agent," to stand for the ways in which these elements of moral consciousness appear in the literature and thought of the past (without, however, implying any commitments about their ultimate bases). Along with them I will introduce one more element of the moral situation: the role of the other. To the degree that others share the ideals that motivate our actions, we may join with them in a common agency. Yet, however broadly we conceive the moral agent, there are always others, agents that remain outside of the moral position we occupy. Even the human species as a whole, considered as a moral entity, typically stands over against others—God, the devil, Nature. Others often constitute the most important dimension of the reality that an agent attempts to work upon, resist, or change. There are times, also, when others come between us and the goals we have chosen for ourselves in a way that we recognize as a violation of shared ideals and responsibilities. In some cases the agency of others can step into the moral space between ideal and actual and supplant our own agency, so that we are no longer able to sustain the sense of autonomy necessary to feel responsible for our actions. If in such cases we are not what we feel we should be, if there is a discrepancy between Is and Ought, we may hold some other to blame. This is the nature of at least one important type of claim to injustice, that the moral space of our own agency has been violated so that we cannot act as we would like, or as we feel we have a right to do.

To flesh out these brief remarks about moral judgment would require a volume in itself. I do not intend, however, a contribution to ethics or the philosophy of action, only a set of terms that will help identify some of the prominent features of moral intelligence.[2] It is not, however, the details of the model that are likely be the first objects of concern to many contemporary readers, but the premise of the whole. Even though I have tried to employ the moral vocabulary in a descriptive and neutral way, my account tacitly assumes that moral judgment is a valid activity, circumscribed though it may be with great difficulties, and its vocabulary full of political consequence. In modern culture, however, there are important trends at work to make this point of view seem less than persuasive.

The difficulty as we experience it was trenchantly stated in a classic essay by Isaiah Berlin: the validity of moral judgment demands that, when a person acts in a certain way, he or she could have acted otherwise; yet, given the deterministic premises now dominant in our modern, secular worldview, the possibility of having acted otherwise has become extraordinarily difficult to accept.[3] The reason is simple: accounting for things has come precisely to mean ruling out the possibility that they could have been otherwise. We explain our personal and communal choices and actions by seeking external, extra-moral sources of determination, which provide us with terms of analysis that can only be applied in a reductive spirit—psychology, biology, history, economics, culture. In the process, the Ought threatens to collapse into what merely Is. The vocabulary of moral judgment, grounded in the possibility of doing and being otherwise, comes to look like a tissue of naive mistakes, a crude shorthand, a "folk psychology," or even a form of delusion to which we have become unwisely enthralled—an indefensible remnant of idealism joined to a stubborn habit.

In spite of this reductionist tendency, however, the habit of idealism remains. For all of us, the striving toward psychological and moral integrity necessarily involves being able to achieve a sense not only of who and what we are but of whom and what we might become, defined in the light of our capacities, of our social and, sometimes, historical expectations, and of human nature. Without a notion of what should be, even the simplest action can make no sense; without the possibility of doing and being otherwise, political critique becomes a self-mocking fantasy, and even the most irrepressible moral judgment has no grounds. And so, as Berlin suggests, we go on employing forms of interpretation and judgment that cannot in principle be

---

[2] For a demarcation of the issues pursued in this field, see the introduction to *The Philosophy of Action*, ed. Alfred Mele (New York: Oxford University Press, 1997).

[3] Isaiah Berlin, "Historical Inevitability" (1953), in *Four Essays on Liberty* (New York: Oxford University Press, 1969), 41–117. Not all philosophers share, of course, Berlin's assumption that determinism and freedom are incompatible.

sustained with the intellectual resources at hand. We understand the actual while we remain uncomfortably in the grip of the ideal.

It is within this context that I raise the conundrum of paranoia in the modern world. In the figure of the paranoid we see a moral agent whose view of himself is so severely distorted on the side of ideality and perfection that his tenuous grasp of the actual can only be sustained by means of a self-aggrandizing persecutory delusion. It is not the claim to being besieged and controlled that defines the paranoid, for he has that in common with the truly persecuted. Nor is it simply in being wrong about a claim of persecution that paranoia lies, for anyone can sometimes err about such a thing; shirking the blame is one of our most constant temptations. But a compulsive habit of seeking others whom we can hold responsible for our own failures, especially when these failures themselves originate from an inflated and illusory sense of self, this is the disease of justice we call paranoia.

The paranoid blames others for his failure to correspond with his image of himself; his purchase on the ideal comes at the price of debilitating suspicion. Yet modern culture, in spite of its anti-idealistic cast, has seen itself profoundly reflected in the image of this figure from the time of the seventeenth century to the present, and people who take up the paranoid stance have enjoyed extraordinary influence. The grandiose and suspicious personality of paranoid characters is obviously not a deterrent to their influence but one of its causes. This is owing to the way paranoia resonates with the problem of moral intelligence, of the actual and the ideal, which has become acute in modern intellectual culture; it arises from the difficulty of formulating a coherent ethics in light of the prevailing views of ontology and knowledge.

Modern people identify with the paranoid character in part because they too feel the indispensability and attraction of moral and political idealism, even though they frequently fear that these things may turn out to be nothing more than archaic forms of delusion or mechanisms of social control. Like the paranoid, they feel the need to account for their individual and collective failures, to set their own lives meaningfully in the context of their moral relations with others. This necessarily involves them in questions of justice and the fixing of blame, another set of modern habits that has stubbornly outlasted its traditional intellectual foundations. In spite of our modern skepticism toward moral judgment, the tendency to attach responsibility to others, and especially to collective others—institutions, classes, races, genders—has never been more pronounced. Unable to live out the consequences of absolute, amoral reductionism, our thinking has become *relatively* reductionist—moving away from categories of individual responsibility toward group categories that remain morally significant even while they fit into the naturalizing vocabulary of social science. Our skepticism about moral idealism, then, on the level of the individual seems oddly to have strengthened the credibility of collective blame, the idealistic sense that institutions, or even whole cultures, should have done or been otherwise, or that they should now change for the better. The thinking of the Right, with its emphasis upon individual responsibility, and of the Left, with its emphasis upon collective action, share an idealistic sense of agency that is increasingly paradoxical and difficult to sustain in the intellectual climate of modernity.

From the standpoint of secular modernity, the medieval moral system, with its strong investment in the ideal, looks like a form of communal self-indulgence, a collective version of paranoid excess. It must be the symptom of an unwillingness, inability, or unreadiness to make the greater concessions to reality that define modern culture. This was the view, for example, of Sigmund Freud; his attitude has antecedents going back to Francis Bacon.[4] Yet there is a difficulty here, one that in its general, logical form has been much dwelt upon in the last thirty years under the influence of Nietzsche: in subjecting the medieval worldview to this kind of moral and intellectual critique, the modern intellectual is participating in a form of that very activity he or she is attempting to renounce. The intellectual resources and the rhetoric that make religion look like paranoia come from within the religious tradition itself. The prophets of modernity share the language of renunciation, humility, adherence to truth, and attribution of blame that belonged to their Christian precursors. Nietzsche was particularly aware of, and infuriated by, the paradox that, in his terms, nihilism, the recognition that there is no truth, is the final, most tenacious, and most puritanical expression of the "will-to-truth."[5] The stance from which this recognition can be articulated is at once as anti-idealistic and as perfectionistic as could be. Out of a disdain for all motives of sacrifice, it demands a total sacrifice. Nietzsche condemns but cannot escape the religion he calls nihilism, the religion of suspicious self-scrutiny and exemplary renunciation, the religion that falls down on its knees, as he puts it, to "worship the question mark."[6]

Adopting this historical perspective, we seem to have returned immediately to the same uncomfortable impasse that we reached in our initial consideration of moral thinking in the light of modern reductionism. First, our reductionist instincts tell us that moral ideals, which we cannot actually abandon, have no more objective validity than paranoid fantasies or the self-indulgent mass delusions of religion; then, our historicist instincts tell us that our desire to renounce all self-indulgent delusions is yet one more form of that very self-indulgent fantasy that we wished to avoid. Starting from the materialist side, we cannot escape our ideals; starting from the historicist side, we cannot actually become materialists, for the moment we do so we find ourselves delivering a sermon in the style either of Geneva or of Basel. The more passionately we insist upon the limits of the actual, the more rad-

---

[4] I have outlined Freud's view of paranoia and modernity in the opening chapter of *Freud's Paranoid Quest: Psychoanalysis and Modern Suspicion* (New York: New York University Press, 1996), and in chapter 4 I have shown the extent of his affiliation with Bacon.

[5] See, for instance, sections 24 and 25 of the third essay of *On the Genealogy of Morals*, trans. Walter Kaufmann and R. J. Hollingdale (New York: Vintage, 1967), 148–56.

[6] Nietzsche, *Genealogy of Morals*, 156.

ically we depart into the ideal. The more we try to avoid paranoia, the more paranoid urgency we betray.

It is curious that when fidelity to religion is an ideal it is difficult to achieve, but when it becomes an embarrassment it is difficult to avoid. Perfectionism remains intrinsically difficult, whether its goals are saintly, satanic, or secular. In both medieval and modern culture we see a striving toward perfection and a struggle with excess. It just so happens that, for the modern type, the form of excess that is envisioned is frequently the medieval ideal itself. This fact only assures us of the intimate connection between the two.

Our relation with the ideal, then, remains a complex one. Idealism evokes great suspicion and it holds great attraction. It is an irresistible excess, and, like it or not, the power to blame, to hold responsible, is something that we cannot do without. Both in the excess of idealism, then, and in the habit of blame, the paranoid is a too typical and commanding figure. My assumption will be that every culture needs the means of coping with the inevitable discrepancy between the way its occupants feel things ought to be and the way they are, but that our special dilemma can only be understood in the context of its local origins—in the context, in other words, of post-medieval Western culture.[7] The story I will attempt to tell begins, then, with the functioning of moral intelligence in pre-modern, Western, Christian culture and follows the transformations of Is, Ought, agency, and other as they shift and realign up to the late eighteenth century, at which point we can see the outlines of present attitudes largely in force. At the beginning of the story, the figure of the paranoid is a laughable aberration; at its climax, with Rousseau, we find an intellectual system that at once is dictated by the needs of a clearly psychotic character and yet manages profoundly to shape the canonical language of agency in a way that makes paranoia difficult to disclaim, the sense of being controlled and victimized having become almost inseparable from intellectual self-consciousness per se.

Agency and the Catholic Church

For the philosophical culture of the pre-modern West, the distinction between Is and Ought was embedded in the structure of reality itself. In the Platonic system, to take a canonical example, the imperfections of earthly existence and of human action were thought to arise from the discrepancy between becoming and being, between the profusion of contingent, transitory creatures and things that constitute this world and the true, eternal, and

---

[7] In fact, though no attempt at cross-cultural comparisons will be made here, my study has shared aims with what Marshall Sahlins calls the "native anthropology of western cosmology" and gives particular emphasis to the factors he stresses, the dominance of the Augustinian influence and the definition of "man" as a creature separate from society. See Marshall Sahlins, "The Sadness of Sweetness: The Native Anthropology of Western Cosmology," *Current Anthropology* 37, no. 3 (June 1996): 395–428.

unchanging patterns of reality, the forms. The objects of our experience are mere copies of these exemplary ones—including Truth, Justice, and the Good. If human action is imperfect, it is because we have only a distant and difficult access to these guiding notions. This world of transitoriness, of becoming, to which we ourselves largely belong, fatally separates the intellect from the ideal. Plato, making the Is and the Ought virtually into separate worlds, created the possibility of an infinite aspiration.

In the thought of Plato, divinity emerges from the examination of the soul, whereas in Christian philosophy the point of departure is God. The existence of imperfection in the cosmos inevitably preoccupied Christian theology because the notion of a perfect and all-powerful God, responsible for the creation of human beings and the world *ex nihilo,* makes a paradox out of evil, irregularity, and defect. The Church Father Augustine achieved a solution to the problem that was to be decisive for a thousand years and that, with profound appeal, continues to exert its hold on the modern psyche: it is the human will that is responsible for evil, the will of each individual separated from the good of its nature by an original sin and so operating in a fallen world. The "will itself," Augustine puts it, "or man himself, insofar as his will was evil, was, as it were, the corrupt tree which brought forth the evil fruit of those evil deeds."[8] Augustine's solution preserves Plato's realm of ideas, now located in the mind of God, and his realm of contingency, the post-lapsarian cosmos, but responsibility devolves upon the human being living in the City of Man, which is the community of those dedicated to the love of the fallen self. If Man is not utterly lost, it is only because God's grace operates to heal his rift with truth.

Augustine's model succeeds in giving scope to the depravity of this world while it preserves the possibility of the ideal. Indeed, it is the vehicle of a high moral demand—that one should relinquish the place of one's birth and seek the City of God. In the seventeenth century, when Augustinian Christianity faced its most formidable and perplexing intellectual challenge, mounted not from within another religious perspective but from the standpoint of incipient modernity, its greatest apologist, Pascal, pointed to the doctrine of original sin and the Fall as the one empirically indispensable element of Christian dogma; no other explanation but this story of before and after could cope, he argued, with the ever-perplexing duality of human nature—its abject depravity and its divine awareness of its condition. It was at this same moment that John Milton chose to reassert the central myth of the Fall in its grandest, most comprehensive and syncretic form.

The Augustinian-Platonic synthesis was not, of course, without rivals in Christian orthodoxy; the trend of its scholastic modifications, beginning with Anselm of Canterbury at the end of the eleventh century, was to ascribe greater and greater freedom and responsibility to the human agent. The Aris-

---

[8] Augustine, *The City of God against the Pagans,* bk. 14, chap. 11, trans. R. W. Dyson (Cambridge: Cambridge University Press, 1998), 604.

totelianism of Thomas Aquinas, for instance, represents a radical shift in the understanding of being and the human creature from that of Augustine. For Thomas, the imperfection of a thing arises not from its lack of correspondence with an ideal pattern but rather from a failure to actualize the indwelling potential, or essence, without which it would not be a being at all. A thing *is,* we might say, just insofar as it becomes what it ought. But only God is pure reality, pure actualization of potential. Only for Him is existence identical with essence. Lower beings achieve reality by participation in Him, each creature aiming at such perfection as may constitute its nature. Though infinitely far from God's perfection, humankind stands midway down the hierarchy of beings that participate in him each to its proper degree.

The philosophy of Thomas departs from the alienation, the sense of crippled being, that distinguishes Augustine; yet on moral grounds he is broadly faithful to his precursor. The emphasis upon the fallen will remains. Though the will is naturally inclined toward its ultimate good, which is God, it is free to choose otherwise. It can easily be distracted by secondary goods. Like the intellect, its guide, it is involved with the things of sense and subject to the imperfections of physical existence. Without the help of God and of the church it would fail to attain even the degree of perfection to which it is properly given. Later scholastic developments enhanced Augustine's emphasis upon the will, but with a more optimistic bent, insisting not only on the absolute freedom of God's will but also granting relative independence to the human will. The farthest movement away from the pessimism of Augustine occurred in the later Middle Ages under the influence of William of Ockham. The nominalist school tended to deny to the intellect any access to the principles that underlie creation considered as what for God would have been absolutely possible. What is apparent to us is only God's actual, or ordained, creation, *de potentia ordinata,* and the concepts that we use to grasp it are not God's but our own. In the ordained creation, however, the will has a power of independent choice that approaches what Pelagius, Augustine's great opponent, originally claimed for it.[9] Freedom and responsibility inhere in the will and it has a certain power of good.[10]

If good belongs to God and, in part, to human beings, the agency of evil

[9] Readers of Heiko Augustinus Obermann's *The Harvest of Medieval Theology: Gabriel Biel and Late Medieval Nominalism* (Durham, N.C.: Labyrinth, 1983) will know how dauntingly complex is the task of clarifying, even for one figure, the moral and theological implications of late scholastic nominalism. For a succinct overview, see Donald J. Wilcox, *In Search of God and Self: Renaissance and Reformation Thought* (Boston: Houghton Mifflin, 1975), 153–66.

[10] This is not to say that nominalism, with its voluntaristic tendencies, did not make an important contribution to modern views of agency. See pt. 2, "Theological Absolutism and Human Self-Assertion," in Hans Blumenberg, *The Legitimacy of the Modern Age,* trans. Robert M. Wallace (Cambridge: M.I.T. Press, 1983), and Louis K. Dupré, *Passage to Modernity: An Essay in the Hermeneutics of Nature and Culture* (New Haven: Yale University Press, 1993), 120–28.

too has its place in medieval thinking in the figure of Satan. From a mytho-graphic point of view, the medieval cosmos was a battleground between the powers of God and Satan, and Satan took a vivid role both in the preaching and religious art of the time. But the overwhelming tendency of the ortho-dox tradition was toward the belief that Satan is not responsible for human downfall. He provides merely the occasion of temptation and offers little danger to those who have not already embraced him. According to Augus-tine, the sin of Adam and Eve would not have occurred had not the parents of humankind already given way to pride in their hearts.[11] Furthermore, evil both in men and angels, though it does not come from God, is nevertheless part of his plan for the cosmos. God creates evil men and angels only in ser-vice to the good, with foreknowledge "thereby adorning the course of the ages like a most beautiful poem set off with antitheses" (472).

Satan, therefore, plays a necessary role in the poem of God's greater good. He is often a figure of contempt, as he appears at the center of Dante's *In-ferno*. The devil of medieval fancy is not an integral being but a grotesque, a congeries of distorted features, signifying not only a comical lack of power but, more importantly, a lack of participation in being. Evil is privation, the absence of being; it has no true agency or substance of its own. The struggle with evil is the struggle with our own vocation for nothingness.[12] And evil and nothingness, especially for the late medieval imagination, were con-fronted most immediately not in the figure of the devil but in the soul's strug-gle with the body. The imperative to control bodily desire spread out from the monasteries in the high Middle Ages and produced an intense cult of as-cetic heroism in response to a growing worldliness.[13]

The belief in the power of the devil did not for the most part set a limit upon the sense of human agency. It was not Satan's urgings but the fact of God's omnipotence that imperiled the significance of human action. The at-tempt to articulate the Christian sense of agency in the light of God's power posed many of the same problems of determinism that have arisen in the modern context: theological and materialist conceptions of causality present equally difficult obstacles to the autonomy of the human agent. Yet the me-dieval synthesis succeeded as a working model of ethical understanding by assimilating the limits upon human power and freedom to the effects of pre-vious, prelapsarian action, so that these very limits could be made to testify in favor of the meaningfulness of human responsibility. Its very conscious-ness of limit was thus empowering. Christian psychology struck a balance

[11] *City of God*, bk. 14, chap. 13, 608.

[12] See Jeffrey Burton Russell, *Lucifer: The Devil in the Middle Ages* (Ithaca: Cornell Univer-sity Press, 1984).

[13] On the late medieval culture of heroic self-culpabilization and self-denial, see Jean Delu-meau, *Le peché et la peur: la culpabilisation en Occident, XIIIe–XVIIIe siecles* (Paris: Fayard, 1983), and also Caroline Walker Bynum, *Holy feast and holy fast: the religious significance of food to medieval women* (New York: St. Martin's Press, 1990).

between the recognition of sinfulness and the power to act rightly, between the aspiration to perfection and the avoidance of pride. Nor did it leave the human powers unaided in the attempt to be faithful to the ideal, for it provided a crucial agent of mediation in the person of Christ, present to all believers through the church and the sacraments.[14]

[14] Of course the displacement of responsibility onto others implicit in the doctrine of the Fall might also be seen as illegitimate, an evasion of blame or an inadmissible qualification of agency. This is how it looked to philosophical protestants of a later age—to Kant, for instance, in *Religion within the Limits of Reason Alone* and Kierkegaard in *The Concept of Anxiety.*

2

The Responsible Knight

The central aim of Christian moralism was to dampen the temptation to exaggerate one's own worth or to blame others for one's own failures. It emphasized that the individual soul is the locus of responsibility yet discouraged the notion that the soul could achieve perfection without the aid of the church. The dangers of self-inflation, of self-reliance, and of the excess of perfectionism always posed the most important threat to salvation. Among the deadly sins pride was deadliest to the soul. It might even seem as if the Christian moral system had been designed with the paranoid's temptation in mind, and in a sense it was, for the inability to accept blame or responsibility for failure was the besetting foible of the moral system of pagan aristocracy, which Christianity throughout its history struggled to contain. The moral stance of the pagan hero is a militant perfectionism that cannot concede a point of honor and will stop at no expedient to displace blame. *The Iliad* is a living anatomy of its vicissitudes. Sophocles's *Ajax* shows the extremity of its moral dynamic. The hero Ajax, having lost the award of Achilles' shield to Odysseus, finds himself unable to bear the shame of his dishonor without lapsing into persecution mania. Shrouded in a punitive delusion by Athena, he turns his violence upon a herd of cattle, which he mistakes for a troop of his rivals. Recognizing this further humiliation, Ajax's only option is suicide. The heroic character cannot take failure or blame upon himself and live. If he cannot punish the perpetrators or witnesses of his shame, he must suffer the consequences.

Ajax provides a stark example of the heroic character undone by the inflexibility of its virtues. In spite of his passion and blindness, though, Ajax remains noble and admirable; in choosing death he devotes himself to an eternity of solitude and smoldering hatred in a way that remains heroic. The playwright enhances our sense of the grandeur of his character by contrast with the pettiness and short-sightedness of his opponents. Ajax clearly and correctly sees that fate has led him to his death and he accepts that fact with bravery. There is no thought of renouncing the heroic ideal. Sophocles does offer, though, a note of hope, a note that sounds only at the end of the play. It comes from an unexpected source, the pragmatist Odysseus, who in the last scene calls a halt to the chain of vengeance against Ajax's kin out of awe at what the gods can do to mortals. Remonstrating with Ajax's enemies, he strikes a note that Bernard Knox describes as "tolerant and tragic humility."[1] The groundwork for Odysseus's surprising action has been laid earlier when he reacts soberly to the sight of Ajax's humiliation at the hands of Athena:

> Yet I pity him,
> His wretchedness, though he is my enemy,
> For the terrible yoke of blindness that is on him.
> I think of him, yet also of myself;
> For I see the true state of all of us that live—
> We are dim shapes, no more, and weightless shadow.[2]

In this moment the common vulnerability of the human condition becomes a bond between men, putting a stop to the cycle of violence and shame. But this can only occur when the incensed hero himself no longer poses a threat, for Sophocles' Ajax would never accept the friendship of Odysseus any more than Homer's Ajax would speak to Odysseus in the underworld.

The tragedy of Sophocles and the moral psychology of Augustine represent the beginning and the midway phases of the long struggle with the vicissitudes of the heroic ethos that preoccupied Western culture up to the time of the Enlightenment. Christian teaching worked a partial transvaluation upon its pagan precursor. The ancient virtues, to recall the phrase imputed to Augustine, took on the aspect of "splendid vices." But medieval Christianity did not attempt to draw an absolute distinction between itself and its predecessor. It did not seek a wholesale renunciation of aristocracy. Rather, it lived in tension with and to a degree absorbed the heroic worldview. The culture of the Middle Ages remained infused with an aristocratic ethos that set a high value upon social dignity and personal distinction. The church drew largely from its strength: many of the principal Christian teachers, including Augustine and Aquinas, originated from within the aristocratic class.[3] Aristocratic privilege had its place even in monastic life. Heroism preoccupied the vulgar literature of the Middle Ages, either as hagiography or

---

[1] Bernard Knox, *Word and Action: Essays on the Ancient Theater* (Baltimore: Johns Hopkins University, 1979), 151.

[2] *Ajax*, 121–26, trans. John Moore, in *Sophocles II, The Complete Greek Tragedies*, ed. David Grene and Richmond Lattimore (Chicago: University of Chicago Press, 1957).

[3] On the upper-class origins of medieval saints, see Alexander Murray, *Reason and Society in the Middle Ages*, pt. 4 (Oxford: Clarendon, 1978).

in the more secular form of chivalric romance, and in Dante's *Inferno,* the pilgrim is told that "L'onrata nominan," "worldly fame" of the heroic kind, "wins grace in heaven" (4:76–78). Despite the orthodox disapproval of the heroic ethos, the poetry of honor and glory could not be suppressed.[4]

The genius of the courtly romance in its mature phase was to stage the drama of the pagan virtues within a Christian framework. The action that it portrays is martial but its meaning is moral: the faithful knight should be able to endure any extremity of persecution and manipulation, any degree of interference from the other, without the loss of autonomy. Nothing can touch him to the core while he possesses the goodness of his soul, but much of his success will depend on holding to this truth. It is when he fails that the paranoid temptation can arise. We will take as our example *Sir Gawain and the Green Knight,* an anonymous fourteenth-century poem written in the English West Midlands.[5] The hero of this poem makes for himself an extraordinary claim to perfection, expressed in the form of an ornamental pentangle inscribed on his shield and designed to signify that his virtues are as integrally linked as the interlocking lines of a geometric figure. In the center is an image of Mary identifying Gawain as her knight. To test his assertion of identity, Gawain finds himself beset with a series of challenges by malevolent powers. First he must defend the honor of King Arthur's court by participating in a beheading game with a mocking green giant who, after the first blow, picks up his severed head from the floor and uses it to deliver the details of the return match. Then, as Gawain searches for the place where he is pledged to the rematch, he is entertained in a magically perfect castle, Hautdesert, by a host with a daringly seductive wife. When the lady of the castle finds that her charms cannot induce the knight to fall, she offers him a charm to protect him from the blow he expects to take.

So far Gawain has lived up to his image as a perfect knight, but now he abandons the sponsorship of Mary for that of the host's wife and ties on her girdle like a champion's garter. At the rendezvous with the Green Knight, Gawain stands up to his ordeal. The fearsome challenger takes three passes at his neck with a giant ax, but gives him only a nick to signify the quality of his performance. Then the giant announces that he is himself the host and that the girdle Gawain is wearing is his property. Gawain has endured a difficult challenge but is guilty of deception, and the fault is especially embarrassing because he had pledged to exchange with the host any winnings he might obtain at the castle. He has egregiously violated the code inscribed on his shield, whose governing notion is "trawthe," truth in the broad Middle

---

[4] See Maria Rosa Lida de Malkiel, *L'idée de la gloire dans la tradition occidentale: antiquité, moyen-age occidental, Castille,* trans. Sylvia Roubaud (Paris: Librairie C. Klincksieck, 1968); French translation of *La Idea de la Fama en la Edad Media Castellana* (Mexico: Fondo de Cultura Económica, 1952), 89–150.

[5] Except where otherwise indicated, quotations are from Marie Borroff, *Sir Gawain and the Green Knight: A New Verse Translation* (New York: Norton, 1967).

English sense that includes faith, honesty, and loyalty.[6] No longer Mary's knight, he has been fighting under the banner of pagan magic.

Here, as in the *Ajax,* we find heroic perfectionism confronted with actual failure; however, in the sequel both the self-punitive and the paranoid temptations are comically contained. The process is complex and has several stages. At first, Gawain is humiliated and throws down the girdle, disclaiming his part in it and making symbolic restitution. The host, Bercilak, comparing Gawain with other knights, accounts him nearly perfect—not a thief, only a man who loved his life a little too much. It is all the more galling for Gawain to be justified by this qualified standard, which is beneath his pride. His heart shakes with a "grim rage," the blood of his body burns in his face, and he accuses himself in the blackest terms, confessing his fault in a manner that imitates the sacrament of penance. Bercilak discounts the fault and offers Gawain the girdle as the token of his adventure, and Gawain finally accepts it as a "sign of excess," a sign of the "faults and the frailty of the flesh perverse."

With the tying on of the girdle, Gawain's struggle to adjust to his new identity would seem to be over, for the girdle has become a symbol of his character, with all its mixed glories and faults. Gawain has made a good confession. There is a hitch in it, though, and one that shows it is not so easy for a hero like Gawain to accept blame. In an interlude before he ties the girdle back on, Gawain launches a tirade against womankind. As Larry Benson puts it, we are suddenly and unexpectedly "treated to the diverting spectacle of one of the most famous lovers in medieval literature breaking into monkish anti-feminism."[7] Gawain is only the latest of women's victims, which proceed in a line—Solomon, David, Samson—all the way back to Adam:

> "And one and all fell prey
> To women that they had used;
> If I be led astray,
> Methinks I may be excused."
> (2425–28)

It is only after uttering his tirade that Gawain accepts the girdle and ties it on so that it will permanently replace the pentangle as the symbol of his renown. Gawain's outburst strikingly violates the form of confession, in which it was forbidden to mention the name of any other person in connection with one's sins.[8] The reason for this prohibition is evident: the point of confession is to take responsibility upon oneself, not to share the blame with others. In fact, we see Gawain, who has just been heaping abuse upon him-

---

[6] On the meaning of "trawthe," see J. A. Burrow, *A Reading of Sir Gawain and the Green Knight* (New York: Barnes & Noble, 1966), 43.

[7] Larry D. Benson, *Art and Tradition in Sir Gawain and the Green Knight* (New Brunswick: Rutgers University Press, 1965), 240.

[8] Thomas N. Tentler, *Sin and Confession on the Eve of the Reformation* (Princeton: Princeton University Press, 1977), 93.

self and is about to do so again, suddenly shifting responsibility onto the other sex. The gesture is both exculpatory and self-aggrandizing: for a moment Gawain can accept his participation in the common doom of humanity, but only as a member of the honor roll of victimized heroes. If he has deviated from the perfection he has taken as an ideal, it is because some other agent beside himself has intervened in the space of action between Is and Ought. An other is to blame.

It is important to note that, when he lapses into this temptation, Gawain has available to him a ready made ideology of blame; the anti-feminist content of his defamatory impulse is no private aberration but one of the broader ideological elements of medieval culture. Yet it is a tendency that the poem discourages and even mocks. Mary's knight, man of courtesy and devoted servant of womankind, is at his most ridiculous when he becomes the adversary and accuser of all women.[9]

It would be too much to expect that Gawain, in the moment of his humiliation, should be able to take the tolerant and knowingly humorous attitude toward his own performance that Bercilak does, for, as I have observed, this tolerance and humor are in a sense a rebuke to Gawain's former pretensions and to his pride. But what of his attitude when he returns to the court of Camelot? By then many more adventures have come between him and his disgrace; the "penance" cut into his neck has healed, suggesting that he has had time to adjust to the consequences of his discoveries; he now wears the green girdle as his "sign of excess." But he is still bitterly ashamed; the blood still burns in his cheeks when he thinks of his fault. His moral wound has not healed. We see Gawain behaving toward the court, as he does at the beginning of the poem, with an excess of self-deprecation; but whereas on the first occasion he spoke with sinuous courtly aplomb, here he releases a long pent self-reproach:

> "Behold, sir," said he, and handles the belt,
> "This is the blazon of the blemish that I bear on my neck;
> This is the sign of sore loss that I have suffered there
> For the cowardice and coveting that I came to there;
> This is the badge of false faith that I was found in there,
> And I must bear it on my body till I breathe my last.
> For one may keep a dark deed, but undo it no whit,
> For where a fault is made fast, it is fixed evermore."
> (2505–12)

---

[9] Howard R. Bloch, in *Medieval Misogyny and the Invention of Western Romantic Love* (Chicago: University of Chicago Press, 1991), argues that the rhetoric of misogyny in the middle ages was indissolubly linked with its opposite, the idealization of women (61). We can see in this case how Gawain's shift from one of these modes to the other is motivated by the pressure that has been applied to his own idealized identity. Gawain's outburst exemplifies Virginia Woolf's observation that derogating women in general gives psychological comfort to individual men. Chap. 2 in *A Room of One's Own* (New York: Harcourt, 1929).

These are Gawain's final words, and they are troubling ones. Given a straight-forward theological interpretation, they constitute a rejection of the possibility that sin can be forgiven. Under these terms Gawain could never be shriven of his cowardice or his coveting. Such skepticism toward the healing power of the sacraments would be a sin in itself. That seems, however, far too literal a way of apprehending Gawain's last words. Rather, what Gawain seems to be lamenting is that he can never leave behind the significance of what he has learned about himself, which is that he is capable of faults. He is still a perfectionist, though no longer perfect. It is now the perfection of the judge that he assumes, upholding the verdict upon his own crimes. He has gone from egotism to superegotism. Gawain is still making a claim for himself as a being of extraordinary moral significance, though that significance is as a sinner, not a hero, and he is still erecting the elaborate symbol of his worth, even though his worth has turned from positive to negative. In the opening scene of the story, Gawain had taken up the quest with exemplary, in fact excessive, humility, but now we can measure his hypocrisy. Even at this moment, Gawain suffers from an excess of self-involvement, and we might wonder for a moment if he will not become a perennial nuisance at the court, oscillating between the egotism of exemplary self-flagellation and the temptations of victimhood.

But this is not how the story ends. Rather, the king and court comfort the knight, and with a loud laugh they graciously agree that henceforth the knights will wear a belt of bright green as a badge of honor for Gawain's sake (2515–21). By accepting the girdle and making it a social rather than a personal symbol, the king and his companions have almost magically transformed its significance and given Gawain a lesson in humility. With a single deft touch of humanity Gawain is deprived both of the shame of his fault and of his claim to distinction. His girdle is now a mark of honor belonging to the entire court. At the same time, it implies a recognition of the common fallibility of mortal creatures. And this doubleness can be accepted all at once—thus the laughter, a sign of the humorous conjunction of honor and flaw. The court together laughs away Gawain's excess. Laughter is what can cure it and the treatment it deserves.

Now there is a sense in which, if ever a man had reason to be paranoid, it was Gawain. His whole adventure has been constructed out of false appearances and deceptions. He has been the object of supernatural manipulations involving a magical green giant, an enchanted castle, and a false lady. He has been made to play Christmas games with his life at risk and without a proper understanding of the stakes. And he is about to discover that he was merely a pawn in Morgan le Fey's campaign against Guinevere—caught in a war of opposing feminine superiors. And yet, even taking all of this into account, Gawain comes to recognize that he would have been safe had he not given in to a sinful intention. He put the safety of his body above that of his soul, which is the only thing that truly matters. That is why he is so upset with himself and why he is looking for others to blame. It is ultimately the reason why he accepts the girdle as a mark of sin.

Several elements of the situation are crucial to the achievement of this acceptance. First, there had to be present an objective structure of judgment in the poem and a somewhat adequate judge. Bercilak is in a position to judge Gawain, because he has magically orchestrated all that has taken place both at Camelot and at Hautdesert and even directed Gawain on his travels. In point of knowledge and in point of power, Bercilak stands virtually in the position of God. His willingness to spare Gawain's life combines justice with mercy in a manner of divine forbearance.[10] Added to this is the perfect exactitude with which Bercilak's way of dramatizing his judgment fits Gawain's response to the temptation—the ax passes him three times, giving, on the final swing, a slight nick signifying Gawain's single fault during the lady's three visits to his chamber. The judgment is the perfect image of the act—not poetic justice but a poetic enactment of actual justice. In all respects, then, the poet has ingeniously contrived a situational equivalent of the day of doom. Gawain feels himself authoritatively judged and he accepts the judgment—accepts it, indeed, with too great a zeal, with typically heroic self-importance. Second, though Gawain is judged according to his deed, the significance of this deed is ultimately interpreted not in ideal terms but in terms of what can be expected from fallen humanity. There is a middle term, in other words, between Is and Ought, a term that recognizes the limited degree of perfection attainable by mortal agents. Third, the evaluation of Gawain's behavior takes place within a kind of institutional framework, the framework of confession, which provides it with the means of dramatization and ritual cleansing. Even though there is not a formal confession here, we see Gawain and Bercilak, confronted with the fact of Gawain's fault, falling naturally into the habits of narration, evaluation, contrition, consolation, and forgiveness; the process is repeated when Gawain returns home to the court. Such habits, of course, belong to everyday life, probably at all times and places, but here they have a ritual, public dimension, and we see them functioning in the exploration and resolution of Gawain's exemplary guilt. Finally, it is essential that even the egotism of Gawain's exaggerated self-reproach is contained by the Round Table when its members tie on the girdle. In doing so, they underline the belief that sin is not exceptional but the common mortal condition. Thus Gawain is relieved of his stigma. This sense of corporate responsibility greatly softens the temptation to blame others. Others *are* to blame—the pride of the court belonged to all. At the beginning of the poem not one of the other knights was as willing to risk his life as Gawain. But the fact that others are to blame does not diminish one's own responsibility. The community is held together by a common sense of responsibility and limit that applies to all of its members.

[10] See Burrow, *A Reading of Sir Gawain*, 140–42.

It is this final element, social solidarity, that seems to me the most crucial, though it depends upon the others for its value. "A hero ventures forth from the world of common day into a region of supernatural wonder: fabulous forces are there encountered and a decisive victory is won: the hero comes back from this mysterious adventure with the power to bestow boons on his fellow men."[11] If this is the true pattern of the course of the hero (framed by Joseph Campbell), "a separation from the world, a penetration to some source of power, and a life-enhancing return" (35), then Gawain's deviation from it is striking. His encounter with "fabulous forces" results in a loss of power, and he returns to his community unable to "bestow boons." Rather, he is in need of them. An orthodox mythological interpretation would emphasize that the consolation offered to Gawain at the end of the story is drawn from that "source of power," or, in this instance, grace, laid up for human beings by a precursor hero, Christ, in his "life-enhancing return" from the dead. It is impossible to exclude such a reading, impossible to detach the vocabulary of the poem from the implicit assumptions of the Christological myth. But the transfer of power through grace that is implicit in confession does not seem to carry the weight of closure for the story, nor does it seem to be psychologically decisive. What is emphasized is not the sacrificial aspect of Christian redemption but the socially integrative power of the myth of the Fall. The recognition that all human beings are fallen is what makes Gawain no longer an exception at the end of the story. He is neither a perfect being nor an irredeemably ruined one. Of course it takes charity on the part of Arthur's courtiers to admit their kinship with Gawain, even though they know that the kinship is truly honorable. But it is primarily by truth, and the laughter it causes, rather than by power that Gawain is delivered from his second temptation.[12]

The *Gawain*-poet expresses his view of life in a way that exemplifies his skepticism toward absolutes of innocence and guilt in human experience. The effect of the narrative is first to emphasize and then to undermine the apparent contrasts between otherness and self, between surface glamour and hidden corruption. The open-endedness of the narration, its strategic reserve, and the space it leaves for interpretation with regard to Gawain's fault signal the poet's awareness of the epistemic limits of human moral understanding. This permits great freedom in dramatizing the vicissitudes of Gawain's journey toward self-knowledge. The story begins with an episode

---

[11] Joseph Campbell, *The Hero with a Thousand Faces* (Princeton: Princeton University Press, 1949), 31.

[12] Though in later times the blame-displacing temptation will always be the primary tendency of the Quixotic idealist, the self-punitive aspect of grandiose pride also plays its part in modern literature. The best example is Conrad's *Lord Jim*, in which the failure and guilt of the title character push him into further and further efforts at heroic self-confirmation, leading finally to self-extinction. To Marlow, the narrator, Jim looks like "one of us," but his breach of solidarity, unlike Gawain's, cannot be healed, leaving him instead to suffer a more dignified version of the fate of Ajax.

that makes an impression of radical strangeness—the Green Knight and his challenge. Gawain becomes involved with this power and so becomes separated morally and then physically from the community of the Round Table. The further he pursues his adventure, the more starkly appearance and reality seem to diverge. When he arrives at Hautdesert, everything is suddenly too perfect, too hospitable and idyllic. There must be something behind this illuminated surface. The poet renders all of this in a manner beautifully calculated to make the audience share Gawain's interpretive situation, to be confronted with a teasing proliferation of seemingly significant details, an unfocussed sense of threat, an aura of strangeness.[13] The poem is distinctive for the way that the protagonist of the quest becomes its object, so that the whole is experienced from the perspective of the hunted rather than that of the hunt. Had it not been lost to English literature for six hundred years, we would undoubtedly be able to cite *Gawain* as one of the incipient gestures of literary perspectivalism, a practice closely linked with the subject of paranoia.

When Gawain is finally made aware of all that has been lurking behind the appearances at Hautdesert, his view of his experiences is not rectified; rather, it is converted into the opposite extreme. Moving from innocence to suspicion, Gawain now has access to all of the hints of darkness that have intrigued the reader. While there is obvious justification for this reversal, Gawain's adventure seems generally well devised to exploit and dramatize his special tendency to separate things into pure categories of good and evil, a tendency that is an element of his pride. At the end of the poem the sense of the radical otherness of Gawain's opponents is deflated by Bercilak's revelations, and Gawain is challenged to accept a view of himself and others that is integrally mixed. His first response, as we have seen, is a swing to the opposite extreme, both in his view of himself and in his view of women. This is where the laughter comes in, both Bercilak's laughter and that of the court, a laughter signifying familiarity with human doubleness and incongruity. Cowardice, covetousness, even "untrawthe" can no longer be thought of as foreign.

Further, the poem's elaborate pattern reinforces the significance of its final, familiarizing note. Up to this point the complex plot, with games within games and hunts within hunts, and the many formal parallels and repetitions of the narrative itself—two speeches of humility, two beheadings, two vestings in armor, two confessions—have served to focus the irony of Gawain's situation, making a spectacle of his naiveté and self-regard. Now, however, with the tying on of the garter, there is a rapid convergence between scene and background pattern. Long-submerged pressures are released and everything comes to the surface to be greeted by the knowing and tolerant laughter of the court, a laughter that is not superior or ironic but self-inclusive.

---

[13] Cf. John Ganim, *Style and Consciousness in Middle English Narrative* (Princeton: Princeton University Press, 1983), 76–77.

Laughter is a central motif of the story, harsh and heroic in the opening confrontation, falsely hearty and gay at Camelot, sown with hidden threat at Hautdesert, but now finally transparent and simple; it is a laughter that dismisses rather than conceals and is no longer a sign of otherness but of rueful self-recognition. Sophocles's insight would have been just as apt here as in the *Ajax*—a recognition of "the true state of all of us that live." But in this story the hopeful note does not come too late.

3

The Knight Errant

The moral conflict in Gawain's adventure arises from a point of incompatibility between the Christian and the chivalric ethos. It is not that these two cannot be embraced in a single code of conduct, for the tension between Christian and martial virtues is hardly felt in the poem. There is tension, however, about the manner in which one is entitled to assert one's worthiness in relation to one's ideals. Aristocratic values certify aristocratic excellence in comparison with unennobled humanity, whereas Christian values impose an ideal, universal demand that can never entirely be met by any human being. The aristocrat's claim to be superior to others must be crucially qualified under a Christian dispensation, which ideally forbids comparison. To claim aristocratic perfection in spiritual terms is to be supremely guilty of pride, and the inability to accept one's imperfections as part of humanity makes one supremely vulnerable to the temptations of paranoia and blame. This is one of the culturally specific problems that *Gawain and the Green Knight* attempts to dramatize. It is not just the hero but the chivalric code itself that is subject to the irony of the poem.

And yet, as the poet's outlook would lead us to expect, this irony itself is restrained and limited. As Larry Benson puts it, "*Sir Gawain* is at once a brilliant affirmation and a comic rejection of the life that was romance."[1] Assertions of heroic value, having been tested and found wanting, are not to be eradicated but disciplined, tempered with humility, and made subject to education. One cannot be *perfectly* free even from pride. To expect so would be to commit another error on the side of perfectionism. Gawain's excess of humility is an error of just this kind, and the hysteria of his self-reproach

---

[1] Larry D. Benson, *Art and Tradition in Sir Gawain and the Green Knight* (New Brunswick: Rutgers University Press, 1965), 211.

produces the final dramatic complication of the story. Such fits of scrupulosity were a matter of great concern to medieval moralists and theorists of confession.[2] The *Gawain*-poet distinguishes his own stance from that of the hero by striking a fine balance between the questioning of chivalric idealism and the acceptance of human folly.

This balance between irony and sympathy is also exemplified in the poet's relation to romance as a literary form. Not only is the chivalric code of the Round Table subject to question from the point of view of Christian moralism; it is also glaringly antique, for by the fourteenth century the trappings of the solitary knight-errant, with his perfect, otherworldly virtue, had already the quality of a wholesome fiction. Marie Borroff compares the code of chivalry to the Boy Scout's code, "similarly viable and similarly subject to ridicule, in our century."[3] Arthurian courtliness has about it an earnestness and a punctiliousness that, while not quite ludicrous, show more than a touch of literary fancy in the days of Boccaccio, Chaucer, and Froissart.[4] In this poem we find, therefore, an element of generic critique, a movement from romance to satire upon romance.

It would be easy, however, to overemphasize this dimension, for the *Gawain*-poet has kept his satiric impulses carefully in check. If it is true, as one scholar has suggested, that the two most notable sources of the poem are ones that treat Gawain in proto-Quixotic burlesque,[5] the author has done everything possible to mute this aspect of his treatment. He defuses the satiric attitude toward the Round Table, for instance, by making a point of Arthur's youthfulness. And, as if to prevent the setting of the Round Table from seeming too flatly ideal, too much like the castle of Hautdesert, "cut of paper, for a king's feast" (802), the poet adds a sinister historical resonance to the background: in the opening and concluding stanzas of the poem, the story of Gawain's adventure emerges from and recedes into the matter of the founding of Britain, part of the cycle of "wrack and blunder" that began with the treacherous fugitives from Troy. This lineage of treason resonates with

[2] Thomas N. Tentler, *Sin and Confession on the Eve of the Reformation* (Princeton: Princeton University Press, 1977), 75–77 and passim.

[3] Marie Borroff, *Sir Gawain and the Green Knight: A New Verse Translation* (New York: Norton, 1967), vii.

[4] "The sophisticated man of the fourteenth century had only to look about him to see that the romance ideal no longer fit the life he knew. The 'crusades' of this century have nothing but the name in common with the great enterprises of the High Middle Ages, and the few examples of chivalric conduct that Froissart admiringly cites are glaring exceptions in his chronicles of a cruel and greedy era. In England, France, and the Low Countries the peasants were asserting themselves in a way that showed clearly that the old feudal order was dying, while the Great Schism and the rise of heresy showed that even the church was not as secure as it once seemed, and plague and famine threatened the existence of society itself, while those who wished to revive the good old days busied themselves with founding ceremonial orders of knighthood that only preserved in an overelaborate fashion the forms of a previous, mainly fictional age." Benson, 244–45.

[5] D. D. R. Owen, "The Burlesque Tradition in *Sir Gawain and the Green Knight*," *Forum for Modern Language Studies* 4 (1968): 124–45.

the Christian motif of the Fall. We are reminded of the seriousness of a breach of "trawthe" and of the primitive necessity of this virtue for civilization. Such minor effects of chiaroscuro, deftly applied to the shiny lacquered surface of the work, give the tale of Gawain the seriousness of comedy rather than the detached mirth of satire.

Like Sir Gawain, the hero of *Don Quixote* holds himself up to the highest standards of the chivalric ideal as represented in the literary institution of romance, but his world, so to speak, differs from Gawain's in that this ideal is no longer in force. His efforts, therefore, to put it mildly, aim at an object even more problematic than Gawain's, more problematic than that of any of his own heroic models—not merely to live up to a superhuman code of conduct but to restore it from its merely literary state to a present reality. We see here in evidence a sense of historical difference far more radical than what is betokened by the moderate irony directed toward the conventions of romance in *Sir Gawain*. Quixote is a revolutionary in the original sense of the word. His motivation is closely bound up with the rhetoric of historical pathos and loss. He wants to turn the world back to an earlier time of purity and perfection, a golden age when "all things were in common; to win the daily food no labor was required of anyone save to stretch forth his hand and gather it from the sturdy oaks that stood generously inviting him with their sweet ripe fruit." This paradise is not merely natural but moral. "Fraud, deceit, or malice had then not yet mingled with truth and sincerity. Justice held her ground. . . . Maidens and modesty . . . wandered at will alone and unattended" (74–75).[6]

It is evident that Quixote's quest is of a truly grandiose dimension. He aims not only at personal glory but a redemption of the modern world, a reversal of the Fall (in its classical version), a rejection of the necessity of moral imperfection in human beings and in society. Through the force of his own agency he will overcome the ontological and, as he sees it, historical discrepancy between what is and what ought to be. And this entails, of course, a marvelous enhancement of his powers and personal destiny: "Friend Sancho, know that I by Heaven's will have been born in this our iron age to revive in it the age of gold, or the golden as it is called. I am he for whom perils, mighty achievements, and valiant deeds are reserved. I am, I say again, he who is to revive the Knights of the Round Table, The Twelve of France, and the Nine Worthies" (132). All this, of course, is madness, but it is important to see that it does not involve a complete departure from reality. Quixote does recognize that he must prove himself in his new identity, and show his prowess to the world in the hope that it will be recognized. Only in the moments of greatest enthusiasm, when some novel encounter allows his imag-

[6] *Don Quixote: The Ormsby Translation*, ed. and rev. by Joseph R. Jones and Kenneth Douglas (New York: Norton, 1981). I have treated the subject of this chapter from a different angle in chapter 5 of *Freud's Paranoid Quest: Psychoanalysis and Modern Suspicion* (New York: New York University Press, 1996), where I have acknowledged my indebtedness to sources that would otherwise have been mentioned here.

ination to conjure up one of those fearful adversaries he longs to vanquish, does Quixote's mind actually give way to delusion.

Quixote suffers, then, from the paranoid's most egregious symptom, grandiosity; yet this does not mean he contents himself with the fantasy of power. It is the nature of his condition to insist upon the realization of his delusion and to endure, therefore, the mortifications of failure. No irony can relieve the thwarted hero. Though he often laughs at Sancho, he can never laugh at himself; that, of course, is for the reader. Quixote's part, rather, is to suffer every form of indignity, humiliation, debacle, and defeat. Early in the story his powers of rationalization insulate him to some extent from failure: knights-errant must expect to encounter "a thousand dangers and reverses" (102). His delusion permits only a skewed and selective accounting of his adventures, and he is further protected, at least in part 1, by a bizarre capacity to be satisfied with a merely ideal object of courtly adoration. Nevertheless, Quixote is sufficiently attuned to reality to be sensitive to failure, and the pattern of frustration in his experience is so clear that even he cannot avoid recognizing it. His environment resists his efforts, and he personalizes this resistance, transforming it in his imagination into a concerted hostility.

The frustrations of Quixote's adventures give rise to the next key element of the paranoid stance: the myth of persecution. If Quixote's adventures do not achieve a satisfactory outcome, it is not his fault but the fault of evil enchanters—first one, then a whole "swarm." The displacement of blame, which for Gawain is a momentary reflex of humiliation, becomes for Quixote the indispensable expedient of his distorted identity. Others are to blame for his failure, and their preoccupation with him testifies to his importance. The face-saving and even self-congratulatory facility of the enchanters becomes evident the first time Quixote evokes them, after the adventure of the windmills, when he tells Sancho that "the sage Frestón" had "turned these giants into mills in order to rob me of the glory of vanquishing them, such is the envy he bears me" (59–60). Again, after the adventure of the sheep, which he takes for soldiers, Quixote insists that "this malignant being who persecutes me, envious of the glory he knew I would win in this battle, turned the squadrons of the enemy into flocks of sheep" (123). The poor knight's greatness is his undoing, just as his undoing is his greatness.

The introduction of the persecutory agency brings with it the final accessory of paranoia, the interpretive system of suspicion. Unable to tolerate the real discrepancy between his conceptions of Is and Ought, Quixote would logically be forced either to relinquish his sense of reality or his ideal were it not that the agency of the enchanters permits him a new way of keeping them together in a coherent framework. Now Is and Ought are to be arranged as surface and depth, or appearance and reality, a contrivance that makes logically contradictory beliefs psychologically compatible. Quixote's illusions remain significant and meaningful for him as the false appearances that testify to his peculiar truth, the truth of his greatness and persecution. His ontological and intellectual problem is thus solved by introducing a duplicity that is both epistemological and moral. Reality, which corresponds with the Ought of his imagination, is hidden behind a false surface of appearances, and the falsity of this surface becomes, in his view, the mask through which he must strike in order to recover his true self. It is in fact, however, a mask that he must hold in place in order to preserve his grandiose delusion. Only by doing so can he persist in his belief that behind the busy and banal life of the Spanish roadside there lurks a multitude of enemies and that the agency of these enemies explains all of the bizarre disjunctions of Quixotism. "Is it possible," he asks Sancho,

> "that all this time you have been going about with me you have never found out that all things concerning knights-errant seem to be illusions and nonsense and ravings, and to be done topsy-turvy? And not because it really is so, but because there is always a swarm of enchanters around us who change and alter everything with us and turn things as they please, and according as they are disposed to aid or destroy us. Thus what seems to you a barber's basin seems to me Mambrino's helmet, and to another it will seem something else." (179–80)

The dialectic of enchantment and disenchantment becomes for Quixote a general rule of experience. Even favorable developments can be attributed to the supernatural interventions of benevolent magicians. After the passage quoted above, Quixote continues, "And rare foresight it was in the sage who is on my side to make what is really and truly Mambrino's helmet seem a basin to everybody, for since it is held in such estimation, all the world would pursue me to rob me of it. But when they see it is only a barber's basin, they do not take the trouble" (180). On rare occasions the enchanters do intervene in reality, as when they cause Quixote to be transported home in a cart by a crew that to Sancho's unromantic eye seems to have been conscripted from Quixote's home village. This episode is borrowed directly from the books of chivalry, though Quixote finds in it an enchantment "of a sort that transcends all I have ever read of in all the histories that deal with knights-errant that have been enchanted" (380). In a later episode, Quixote manages to divide the world of enchanters into warring elements who are responsible for the favorable and unfavorable alterations of circumstance (590). For the most part, though, the enchanters do not alter facts, only appearances. Quixote keeps the imperatives of his inner necessity from coming absolutely into contradiction with external fact by means of a suspicious fiction.

It is fascinating to observe that in part 2, where, we shall see, Quixote's paranoid system suffers a gradual loss of energy and coherence resulting from his loss of confidence in his adventures, there is also an important change in the way he interprets the activity of enchantment. In part 1, the enchanters undo Quixote's heroic efforts by causing his enemies to appear in comical disguises—armies as sheep, giants as windmills, and so on. In part

2, however, Quixote acquires a different view of enchantment when he mistakes the action of a puppet theater for reality, leading to a heroic intervention and slaughter of the innocents. In this case, the madman, seeing the havoc he has caused, actually takes partial responsibility for his error and agrees to pay for it. Quixote announces,

> "Now I am fully convinced of what I have many a time before believed. The enchanters who persecute me simply put figures like these before my eyes and then change them into whatever they please. In very truth I assure you gentlemen now listening to me that everything that has taken place here seemed to me to take place literally. Melisendra was Melisendra, Don Gaiferos Don Gaiferos, Marsilio Marsilio, and Charlemagne Charlemagne. That was why my anger was roused, and to be faithful to my calling as a knight-errant I tried to aid and protect those who fled. These good intentions of mine produced what you have seen. If the exact opposite has occurred, the fault is not mine, but that of the wicked beings who persecute me. Nevertheless, I am willing to shoulder the expenses of this error of mine, though no ill will lay behind it." (574–75)

Now, instead of having real adventures interfered with by enchantment, the adventures themselves have become false, conjured up entirely by his true enemies. About the enchanted mills on the Ebro, which Quixote had at first mistaken for a "castle or fortress" surely containing "some oppressed knight or ill-used queen or infanta or princess," he observes, "I did not mean to say that [the enchanters] really changed them from one form to another, but that it seems as though they did. . . ." (588). Quixote is close to recognizing that his entire experience has been nothing more than a puppet fantasy. Yet the malignant source behind this fantasy preserves its heroic significance.

"'Remember, Sancho,' said Don Quixote, 'that wherever virtue exists in an eminent degree, it is persecuted'" (436). In appealing to the enchanters, Quixote is of course drawing upon the stock resources of the romance tradition, where enchanters are already a means of accommodating the perfection of knighthood with the vicissitudes necessary to plot. They serve as the kind of agent that can furnish insidious superhuman dangers to knights too powerful to be challenged in martial encounters by ordinary mortals. In this way they provide the element of dramatic conflict, as in *Sir Gawain*. It is interesting that Quixote does not invent the enchanters himself. That is left to his niece, who, in order to cover up her own intervention in Quixote's affairs, blames the disappearance of Quixote's library on "'a magician who came on a cloud one night after the day your worship left here'" (56). In fact, the library has been subjected to a therapeutic purge by the priest and the barber. The niece's convenient displacement of blame becomes the first component in a far-flung system of rationalizations. Her vivid invention, meant to flatter and pacify her uncle, gives his paranoid system a capacity for lim-

THE KNIGHT ERRANT   39

itless development, for she has found, in her humorous, off-handed way, the logically compatible and generically appropriate assumption that will permit Quixote's delusion to flourish.

Paranoia distorts ordinary moral intelligence, but not beyond recognition. The fact that Quixote's delusion mimics a public form of culture means that it is so much the easier for others to participate with him in its construction. So we find the character Dorotea, at a heated point of the narrative, making excuses for Sancho's unwillingness to cooperate with Quixote's fantasies: he has been enchanted (362). And Sancho himself, disclaiming an irreverent faux pas (having put curds in Quixote's helmet): "they persecute me as a servant and part of your worship" (512). The enchanters have become a repository for all blame. And here we must also take note of a fact of the narrative that cannot be accommodated to realistic understanding but must be dealt with in other terms: the readers of part 1, armed with the license of the enchanters, swarm through the pages of part 2, ready to enter into the mirth of Quixote's deluded adventures and making a number of his enchantments come true, though never in a way so unfaithful to the spirit of part 1 that Quixote can derive any lasting satisfaction from them.

It is the special genius of Cervantes' tale, however, and in keeping with his satiric design, that, even with the help of a horde of enchanters, along with the many other resources of selective and partial judgment he employs with regard to himself and his adventures, Quixote hardly ever manages to achieve confidence in his mission. He remains a scrupulous madman, and his story hovers in a sly region of consciousness between what he half knows and what he is willing to acknowledge. In chapter 20 of part 1, Quixote tells Sancho confidentially, "as yet I do not know how chivalry will turn out in these wretched times of ours" (141). Not long after this we see his acute shame when confronted with the consequences of his interference with the chain gang—the misdeeds of the prisoners he released: "Don Quixote changed color at every word, not daring to say that it was he who had liberated those worthy people" (228–29). Deep into part 2, when his aristocratic stage managers, the duke and duchess, have arranged a reception for Quixote fitting with the dimensions of his inner need—servants shouting "Welcome, flower and cream of knight-errantry," while sprinkling scented water upon him—we are told that "this was the first time that he thoroughly felt and believed himself to be a real knight-errant and not an imaginary one, now that he saw himself treated as he had read of such knights being treated in days of yore" (595). The pleasure of this recognition turns out to be short-lived. The more actively others are able to enter into his scheme and manipulate his folly, the more galling becomes the yoke of enchantment.

It is not, however, the duke and duchess, nor any of the other readers in part 2, amusing themselves with Quixote as with a toy, whose contrivances cause him the most pain, but rather his increasingly agile and clever protectors and therapists. First Sancho, obliged to bring his master into the presence of the fair Dulcinea, substitutes an enchanted Dulcinea who appears to

Quixote like a homely and foul-smelling peasant lass, divested of her beauty and distinction. Quixote later asks the duke,

> Who could it be but some malignant enchanter of the many that persecute me out of envy—that accursed race born into the world to obscure and bring to naught the achievements of the good and glorify and exalt the deeds of the wicked? Enchanters have persecuted me, enchanters persecute me still, and enchanters will continue to persecute me until they have sunk me and my lofty chivalry in the deep abyss of oblivion; and they injure and wound me where they know I feel it most. For to deprive a knight-errant of his lady is to deprive him of the eyes he sees with, of the sun that gives him light, of the food whereby he lives. (606)

The knight is rapidly losing hope, his "lofty chivalry" is weakening, and it is a great blow to his delusory system when, near the end of the story, Dulcinea fails to return from the kingdom of enchantment even after Sancho has finally performed the obligatory three thousand three hundred lashes. As much as the enchanters may persecute him, and as improbable as their persecutions become, they can never truly discourage the madman, for their efforts remain a testimony to the reality of his quest. But when the rules of enchantment are broken, as in this case, then Quixote's vision suffers. In fact, that vision has already at this point been inflicted with a mortal wound in a defeat carried out strictly within the rules of chivalric delusion. The blow is administered by Quixote's neighbor, Samsón Carrasco, when, disguised as the Knight of the White Moon, he challenges and unseats Quixote, and, as a forfeit, sends him back to his village for a year's forced idleness. This adventure has no falsity to it. It cannot be disenchanted since it takes place entirely within Quixote's delusory system. He must, then, accept responsibility. When Sancho advises patience and tries to put the blame on fortune, Quixote answers,

> You are very philosophical, Sancho . . . But I can tell you there is no such thing as Fortune in the world, nor does anything which takes place, be it good or bad, come about by chance, but by the special preordination of heaven; and hence the common saying that "each of us is the maker of his own Fortune." I have made mine, but not with the proper amount of prudence, and my presumption has therefore made me pay dearly; for I ought to have realized that Rocinante's feeble strength could not resist the power and size of the Knight of the White Moon's horse. (792)

There is still, obviously, a self-protective element in this confession. It was Rocinante's lack of strength, not Quixote's, that was at fault. But imprudence and, above all, presumption are grave knightly admissions, and Quixote's sense of the exact accountability of knightly conduct is as absolute as Gawain's in his final self-reproach.

During the sad journey home, as if to augment this self-punitive trend, Cervantes administers some particularly harsh drubbings to his hero, and Quixote is left to reflect finally upon the magnitude and completeness of his failure and upon its incompatibility with his heroic identity. He remarks to Sancho on his loss of appetite, not just for food but for life itself, and the envy he feels toward Sancho's attachment to life is poignantly evident:

> "Eat, Sancho my friend," said Don Quixote. "Sustain your life, which is of more consequence to you than [mine is] to me, and leave me to die from my worries and the pressure of my misfortunes. I was born, Sancho, to live dying, and you to die eating, and to prove the truth of what I say, look at me, printed in histories, famed in arms, courteous in behavior, honoured by princes, courted by maidens; and after all, when I looked forward to palms, triumphs, and crowns, won and earned by my valiant deeds, I have this morning seen myself trampled, kicked, and crushed by the feet of unclean and filthy animals. This thought blunts my teeth, paralyzes my jaws, numbs my hands, and robs me of all appetite for food, so much so that I have a mind to let myself die of hunger, cruelest death of all deaths." (750)

The discrepancy between desire and fact stands out fully for Quixote as the sting of defeat brings him slowly back to his senses. He is now giving credit to their testimony without invoking any enchanters. Shortly afterwards, closer to home, Quixote and Sancho, through no fault of their own, are overrun by a drove of pigs. Sancho wants to kill some of them, but Quixote restrains him.

> "Let them be, my friend," said Don Quixote. "This insult is the penalty of my sin; and it is the righteous chastisement of heaven that jackals should devour a vanquished knight and wasps sting him and pigs trample him under foot." (802)

In this scene the typical roles of the knight and squire have been comically reversed, for it is Sancho who finds enemies where there are none, and Quixote who sees things as they are. What is more, Quixote now takes responsibility for what is mere chance. As in the case of Gawain after his failure, Quixote retains an excessive sense of self-importance even though its valence has shifted to the negative. Whereas in the past Quixote disclaimed all of the significance of his failures, now he finds significance where there is none to be found. But the mere recognition of failure has brought him distinctly closer to sanity. When he and Sancho stop at an inn near the end of their journey, the narrator remarks that Quixote does not take it to be a "castle with moat, turrets, portcullis, and drawbridge; for ever since he had been vanquished, he talked more rationally about everything" (816). "Talking more rationally" in this case means admitting imperfection and the ordinary into a consciousness from which they have been long estranged. The effect, however, is by no means salutary. At this point the old man cannot bring himself to eat and has to depend pathetically upon his squire. "I'm in no condition to give crumbs to a cat," he tells Sancho, "my judgment is so confused and upset" (794). His first act upon returning home is to take permanently to his bed. "The doctor's opinion was that melancholy and depression were bringing him to his end" (826). Quixote returns entirely to his senses only at the cost of his life. The resources of suspicion have finally been exhausted. Reality has battered its way into his state of delusion and deprived him both of glory and excuse.

In the opening chapter of part 2 of *Don Quixote,* the barber, who along with the priest is attempting to test the recovery of their unfortunate neighbor by engaging him in polite conversation, tells him the story of a madman of Seville who strove by means of rational persuasion to convince his jailers that he was sane. Near the climax of the story, when it seems that the madman is about to be released, he announces to his fellows that "all this madness of ours comes of having the stomach empty and the brains full of wind." "I know I am cured," he adds a moment later, "and that I shall not have to do penance again" (429). This madman's thinking contains an interesting combination of elements: on the one hand, he dismisses insanity as a mere physical aberration; on the other hand, he thinks of his imprisonment as a kind of penance. The connection of madness and sin arises again when Alonso Quixano, the true perpetrator of Don Quixote's adventures, awakens unexpectedly from his insanity, giving praise to God for the restoration of his wits. We have seen that as Quixote he has already been moving in the direction of self-reproach. Now the blame that, in his delusion, became attached to the failure of his adventures gives way, in the state of sanity, to the shame that he has undertaken them at all. With this shame comes a penitent remorse. This turn of the story has given perplexity to many readers who find themselves in sympathy with Sancho, the priest, and the barber, hoping to keep Quixote alive by inciting him to further follies. But the hero will have none of it:

> "Sirs, not so fast," said Don Quixote. "'In last year's nests there are no birds this year.' I was mad, now I am in my senses; I was Don Quixote of La Mancha, I am now, as I said, Alonso Quixano the Good. And may my repentance and sincerity restore me to the esteem you used to have for me." (828)

In this spirit, Quixano makes a good death, and we can see that in its final pages the soul of Don Quixote crosses the divide between paranoid self-exaltation and Christian responsibility. Grandiose and persecuted pride is finally converted to repentance, even though it takes a shift from one identity to another for the hero to accomplish it. By the end of the story he is as much of an enemy of the books of chivalry as his creator. In this way the drama of madness is finally contained in a traditional moral framework, though only barely, for while the interest of Quixote's repentance sustains just two pages, his comic persecution has taken up several hundred.

There is a nice irony in the manner of old Quixano's death, for the seriousness and dignity with which he renounces his charade makes a fine rebuke to all of those who would prefer to keep him alive as a madman rather than see him die as a Christian. Once again the comparison with the story of Gawain is instructive. Gawain is saved from the temptations of paranoia and self-rebuke by the willingness of his peers to admit their participation in his fault and by the mechanism of a corporate fault itself. Quixano, however, is rescued from delusion and neglect primarily because others are interested enough in his fantasy for its own sake to want to enter it, if only for the fun of an imaginary joust. They do participate in Quixote's folly, but with irony and detachment, as a mere amusement. And this is naturally quite fitting, for while the old man's folly may be testimony to the frailty of human nature, it is not, after all, an inevitable result of it, not one that others must share in. It does not stem from anything so inescapably human as Gawain's love of life, but only from follies that should be entirely avoidable. Thus Quixano cannot make the transition from satiric victim to comic hero; the ending of the novel is Christian but not comic, for the hidalgo's aberration, in spite of its public origins and social significance, remains a private and arbitrary one. Coming finally to his senses, he is left to reproach himself in moral solitude, and dies in a sober state.

An Author's Victory

Having established that the story of Cervantes' great character Don Quixote is a marvelously observant study in the psychology of paranoia—its origins and construction, its logic and dynamics, its eventual deterioration and collapse—it might seem as if we had gone quite a long way toward achieving one of the objects of this work, which is to show that paranoid logic is close to the center of modern intellectual culture. For Cervantes' character has certainly found his way to the heart of that culture. The book in which he appears has been considered Spain's most significant contribution to world literature and even a determining factor in its national outlook. As Byron put it, "Cervantes smiled Spain's chivalry away."[7] More than that, *Don Quixote*

---

[7] "Cervantes smiled Spain's chivalry away;/A single laugh demolish'd the right arm/Of his own country;—seldom since that day/Has Spain had heroes. While Romance could charm,/The world gave ground before her bright array;/And therefore have his volumes done such harm,/That all their glory, as a composition,/Was dearly purchased by his land's perdition." *Don Juan*, 13:11. *Byron: Poetical Works*, ed. Frederick Page, corrected by John Jump (New York: Oxford University, 1970), 810.

has been held up as the inaugural example of that quintessentially modern literary and intellectual institution, the novel, the lodging place of the transcendentally homeless modern soul, standing, as Georg Lukács has it, "at the beginning of that time in which the God of Christendom began to forsake the world; in which man becomes lonely and can find meaning and substance only in his own homeless soul."[8] Quixote becomes in this view the first great portrait of that soul experiencing its alienation in a disenchanted world, a world no longer confidently reflecting back to the mind its own comfortably self-centered cosmos. Equally strange, Quixote's pathetic idealism has been refashioned, only half humorously, into the modern image of a suffering Christ who, in the words of Miguel de Unamuno, lost his wits "for our sake." Thus Cervantes' character was much too good for the author who created him: "If Our Lord Don Quixote were to rise from the dead and return to this Spain [of 1905], they would seek out the ulterior motives behind his noble extravagance."[9] Whether seen as deracinatedly modern or divine, Don Quixote has been given full credit for the idealism to which he in his delusion makes claim. Among modern readers his impossible dream of universal admiration has come true.[10]

The glorification of the paranoid Don Quixote by his interpreters is indeed profoundly important for our study, but the subject must be treated with caution, for the figure that has been embraced by so many admirers does not actually appear in the pages of Cervantes. The sanctified Quixote of later readers is, rather, a paranoid who has been justified against his enemies and detractors, including even the author of his adventures. This is not to deny, of course, that the invention of Quixote was a founding gesture of the modern novel. Whether this gesture was generically original or merely gave new impetus to what had been a marginal form of narrative, there is no doubt that Cervantes steered the postmedieval imagination in a distinctive and fruitful direction. As the Welsh critic Ioan Williams observes, Cervantes had discovered an ingenious, extraordinarily fruitful way of combining the preexisting literary elements of romance and realism.[11] Romance and realism should stand in contradiction to each other, but here we can see the literary advantage of Quixote's deviant psyche: just as the paranoid character's interpretive system of suspicion permits him to keep Is and Ought psychologically in force at the same time through the epistemological contrivance of

---

[8] Georg Lukács, *Die Theorie des Romans: Ein geschichtsphilosophischer Versuch über die Formen der großen Epik* (Neuwied: Luchterband, 1963), 103.

[9] Miguel de Unamuno, *Our Lord Don Quixote: The Life of Don Quixote and Sancho with Related Essays*, vol. 3 of *Selected Works of Miguel de Unamuno*, trans. Anthony Kerrigan (Princeton: Princeton University Press, 1967), 9.

[10] On Quixote's glorification see Anthony Close, *The Romantic Approach to 'Don Quixote': A Critical History of the Romantic Tradition in 'Quixote' Criticism* (New York: Cambridge University Press, 1977).

[11] Ioan Williams, *The Idea of the Novel in Europe, 1600–1800* (New York: New York University Press, 1979), 3.

appearance/reality, so Cervantes is able keep romance, the genre of Ought, and realism, the genre of Is, in force at the same time—one as psychology, the other as "true history." So powerful was this literary innovation that the first post-Cervantine century of the novel was largely populated with imitations of *Don Quixote*.[12]

Still, there is nothing in Cervantes' treatment of the Quixote character to justify the fantastic idealization that was bestowed upon him in art and criticism after the late eighteenth century, nothing to suggest that the picture of the paranoid given by Cervantes should have come to represent the typical human condition, or that the character is justified in his world-redemptive insanity. Cervantes was no revolutionary. He shared neither the paranoid psychology nor the intellectual assumptions of his creation. He put Quixote forward not as a representative of the highest possibilities of the human soul but rather as a laughable lunatic, "the most amusing madman in the world" if the author can get his way. Quixote's plight is not evidence of cosmic insecurity or transcendental homelessness on the part of its creator but rather of an extraordinary moral and intellectual security as well as artistic bravado. Cervantes and his audience stand in comic wonder before the follies of the paranoid, who is nothing better than a humorous aberration.[13]

In insisting upon the satiric purpose of Cervantes' great portrait of madness, I do not mean to deprive the character of all the admirable qualities to which later readers have been drawn. Alongside Quixote's grandiosity there is an undeniable generosity that is also part of his character and cannot be entirely eclipsed by his madness. Further, in the latter half of part 2, as the relation between Quixote and Sancho develops, a special form of intimate courtesy grows up between them as they negotiate together about the conduct and meaning of their adventures. Sancho works within the limits of Quixote's delusion and Quixote works within the limits of Sancho's ignorance, each in his own way feeling superior to the other yet each becoming tender of the other's failings. It is a touching display of charity, but none of it means that Quixote's heroic vision can be justified or that it can provide a satiric counterpoint to the life going on around it. Cervantes' madman is quite the opposite of the Holy Fool, who is wise precisely because of his folly, showing the world around him to be foolish in its seeming wisdom. Quixote is wise only *in spite of* his folly, and even then only in lucid intervals. Unlike the Erasmian wisdom of Folly, the ideas that come from his delusion are foolish in the simple sense, and they make him into a laughingstock. It will be impossible to understand the true significance and pathos of later incarnations of paranoia justified without having first grasped these satiric origins.

It is important for us, then, to clarify the meaning of the satiric distance

---

[12] Williams, *Idea of the Novel*, 26–68, 84–90, and passim.

[13] I espouse the "hard" view of *Don Quixote* expressed most succinctly in Oscar Mandel's classic article, "The Function of the Norm in *Don Quixote*," *Modern Philology* 35 (Feb. 1956): 154–63.

that separates Cervantes and his character. In the foregoing section I attempted to analyze Quixote's psychology according to the scheme of Is, Ought, and agent, with the foreign agency of the enchanters playing the role of the other who is responsible for Quixote's failure. For the paranoid, an other takes the place of the agent in the position of responsibility. This, however, is still to understand the matter from a point of view somewhat too close to Quixote's. From the viewpoint of his creator, things look rather different. Long before he had a chance to fail, Quixote had already been victimized, not by enchanters but by the authors of the books of chivalry who furnished him with his ideal. The ideal itself, then, is in this case the creation of an other. It is, in fact, a public hoax, and Quixote's very strivings are the mark of his enslavement to it. To the extent that he is an idealist, he is already a victim. Where Quixote experiences contingent failures, the reader witnesses inevitable absurdity because the very notion of Quixote's heroism is insane, imported from a social form of madness, the books of chivalry. Part 1 of Cervantes' novel is the story of how Quixote was first captured by a false ideal, of the mystifications that he and others devised in order to sustain his belief in it, and of the way his friends eventually came to manipulate him for his own benefit by means of that ideal. Part 2 is the story of how Quixote's delusion itself magically became a public commodity through the dissemination of part 1, and how, with the help of this commodity, "idle readers" like the duke and duchess were able further to manipulate the paranoid, diverting themselves with his adventures as with a toy, flattering and humiliating him by turns, and becoming a Providence to him just as his author had originally been.

Paranoia, we have seen, embodies a claim of injustice: others are keeping me from being what I should be, what I truly am. In form it is indistinguishable from what might be a responsible and reasonable complaint of victimization. Others, after all, individually or in groups, can and often do keep us from becoming what we should be, what we would be except for their interference. Cervantes, in writing *Don Quixote,* was himself making a complaint of a certain kind—that the life of Spain, and particularly his own life as an author, would have been much better off without the writers of the books of chivalry. Quixote's absurd claim to victimization is the instrument and comic deformation of Cervantes' humorously grandiose but nevertheless sincere and plausible complaint about the literary culture of his day. Both Quixote and his creator were warring against the evils of enchantment, but whereas Quixote's enchanters were impossible to locate outside the world of books, the enchanters who became the targets of Cervantes' attack were all too real. He tells us again and again from the first page to the last that the purpose of his work was nothing other than to attack the books of chivalry that had foisted such nonsense upon the readers of the world. His grudge against these authors is evident. The tide of their intellectual detritus threatened to swamp the productions of more fastidious wits like himself, making him long for the offices of a censor who would properly educate the reading public (379). There is more than a touch of neglected greatness in the complaint, not quite persecuted but unfairly put-upon and calling for redress.

The books of chivalry were to Cervantes' age what television and murder mysteries are to our own, a ubiquitous influence disdained and patronized by intellectuals and ordinary folk alike.[14] It would have been an easy feat to parody them by lifting one of their stock heroes out of his original setting into a modern one. It was by a stroke of genius, though, that Cervantes realized the possibilities latent in the idea of an obsessed and distracted reader who, in a fit of delusion, could embody the folly of all of those who occupy themselves with the tales of chivalry. Such stories represent for him the essence of vulgarity, for the feats of heroism that they narrate with a straight face are of such a kind as only the ignorant could take seriously, a point that the educated priest in Quixote's village makes more than once. They are all, he says, "fictions, fables, falsehoods, and dreams held by men asleep, or rather, still half asleep" (431). Nor could these productions be defended on literary grounds. The literary merits to which some of the older and more sophisticated versions could lay claim was, in the view of Cervantes, altogether lacking in their contemporary imitations, which went on, in the manner of popular culture, copying in a servile way forms that have outlived, or should have outlived, their interest among literate readers. In Quixote's febrile enthusiasm there is no distinction between the witty romances of Ariosto and last week's potboilers. Quixote's heroism, it seems, is revolutionary only in virtue of being vulgar, socially pretentious, and out of date.[15] It has often been held to be, as Lukács put it, "the first great battle of interiority against the prosaic vileness of external life."[16] In fact, it is the interior life of Quixote that has been degraded—not by "prosaic vileness" but by vile and vulgar prose.

So it was an act of literary and social criticism, an attempt at freedom from false influence, that brought the paranoid Quixote into the world to exemplify a disease of reading. In the onset of Quixote's illness, it was especially the passages of ceremony and praise, the "outpourings of adulation and courtly challenges," that inspired him to fervid imitation. There were times when he "felt the urge to take up the pen and finish" earlier stories. Rhetoric is what incites Quixote's insane passion—it is a fantasy of language that he longs to satisfy. The motive of this insanity, and of Cervantes' pride, is not an eccentric one in the context of the time. To have one's fame borne upon winged words constituted the defining aspiration of heroic culture, an aspiration that was honorable even when pursued nearly to the point of madness.

The literary aspect of Quixote's derangement, too, represents a perversion

[14] See Martin de Riquer, "Cervantes y la caballeresca," in *Suma cervantina*, ed. J. B. Avalle-Arce and E. C. Riley (London: Tamesis Books, 1973), 273–92; rptd. as "Cervantes and the Romances of Chivalry," in *Don Quixote: The Ormsby Translation*, trans. Joseph R. Jones, 895–913.

[15] See Farrell, *Freud's Paranoid Quest*, 109–13.

[16] Lukács, *Theorie*, 104.

of deep habits of medieval and Renaissance intellectual culture, in which to read a book was to make it a part of oneself, to take it into one's memory and unite it with one's character. It was a culture for which rhetoric was a fundamental part of education and considered an essential social adhesive. To respond to the rhetoric of praise was to allow one's soul to be shaped in a common intellectual pattern and drawn toward the highest objects of desire. There was no inhibition, of course, about the social uses of rhetoric, about flattery or self-display, or about making claims to aristocratic worth or social dignity. Merit deserved and demanded to be constantly, publicly admired. The hunger for tribute of this kind sends the hidalgo Alonso the Good, a down-at-heels aristocrat of the lowest rank, into his self-heroizing psycho-rhetorical excess. What he desires is a genuine good, but he has fallen in love with a false image of it. The pretentiousness of Quixote's fantasy was flagrantly obvious to his audience, and what made it so very funny as long as aristocratic dignity had its day.

It is a splendid part of the joke that, in Samsón's account, the "common people" see the knight as completely crazy, whereas the noble orders take his ambitions more seriously and respond to the social claims he makes for himself (436). They are a little touched with his madness and so can understand it. This is why they love to entertain themselves with Quixote's follies, and some of the most distinguished of his hosts in part 2 carry their jokes far enough so that they themselves look to the narrator like fools (810). Quixote has indeed been an eloquent proponent of social mobility, not of hidalgos, though, but of knights-errant (148–49). The forward-looking theme of social mobility, which would become the staple subject of the novel, makes its appearance here, then, but only to provide the pleasure of seeing the upwardly aspiring hero comically humiliated.

There is, of course, another side to the Quixote figure, the side that talks lucidly, learnedly, and eloquently on all subjects aside from his idée fixe. In speech he is as noble and wise as in action pretentious and absurd. Time and again he justifies and defends his inanities with reasoning that would be remarkable sense applied to any behavior but his own.[17] Quixote's fluent wit marks him as the image of his creator, displaying the powers of discrimination, judgment, and taste that justify Cervantes' own claim to dignity and merit.

Thus the character serves two functions for his author: both to embody the folly of the books of chivalry and to provide an example of the proper judgment that is missing from them. The coexistence of these two incongruous qualities in the behavior of a single person makes the vulgarity of the books of chivalry all the more obvious and the felicity of Cervantes' language all the more striking. He loses no opportunity to emphasize the tastelessness of Quixote's aristocratic charade by immersing it in the vulgar world it pre-

---

[17] A fine example is Quixote's beautiful Aristotelian self-defense after the Adventure of the Lions (517).

tentiously denies, represented, of course, by the uninhibitedly creaturely figure of Sancho. So arises the humor of a hundred undignified situations and
bodily embarrassments. And while Sancho is the perfect audience and foil
for Quixote's slapstick misadventures, Cervantes also brings onto the scene
a host of educated, respectable witnesses who have the judgment to appreciate the remarkable qualities of his speech. It was an article of faith of the
time that breadth of knowledge, wit, and refinement in matters of language
were indicative of social worth. The Quixote figure is a living contradiction
of this attitude, but Cervantes presents the contradiction as an uncanny one
and makes the humorous appreciation of it the touchstone of merit in the
world of the novel. He thus affirms the value of true refinement and certifies
his own.

Decent men and women of Cervantes' time felt no scruple in laughing at
the deranged behavior of the mad or in putting them on show for entertain-
ment. In the novel, even Quixote's well-meaning friends like the barber and
the priest go into fits of laughter watching him be beaten to a pulp in the pursuit of one of his fantasies (397). That Quixote's lunacy takes a coherent
form derived from literature, that it has so clear a social significance, and
that its egoistic shrewdness is so blatantly evident, all of this only intensifies
the generic amusement of lunacy itself. This is the heart of Cervantes' comic
achievement, to have invented a dramatically intelligible and socially meaningful spectacle of the mad. For the purposes of satire, Cervantes imagined
in the figure of a lunatic the form that the modern psyche would eventually
assume for itself: inner self-idealization and romance projected outward onto
a hostile and resistant reality.

Delmore Schwartz is said to have remarked that "even paranoids have
real enemies." His plea on behalf of paranoids was a little beside the point,
for paranoids just about always have real enemies, though not always the
ones they have imagined. Their hostile and aggressive behavior earns them
the resistance from the social environment that they expect to find, and their
unwillingness to trust their senses can make them all the easier to manipulate and mislead. No paranoid could hope for a more widespread, resource
ful, or energetic conspiracy than the one that besets poor Don Quixote once
his adventures have begun. This story of derision and manipulation is in
many ways a cruel one, full of endless hard knocks, and even some of Cervantes' contemporaries, the text of part 2 informs us, apparently "would
have been glad if the author had left out some of the countless beatings that
were inflicted on Señor Don Quixote in various encounters" (439).[18] Such
beatings, however, did not keep the novel from being considered, for a hundred and fifty years or so, the most delightful and humane of entertainments,
the least harmful and most enjoyable book ever written. Actual persecution
does not verify Quixote's fantasies or his complaints because he cannot identify his true tormentors. The crucial fact of the novel is that its hero never

[18] So Quixote himself is informed by Samsón Carrasco at the beginning of part 2.

manages, until the last pages, either to question the books of chivalry or to see behind the illusions and tricks that have been set to beguile him. No matter how elaborate are the plots designed to mock him, he is always the most important contributor to his own deception.

Only at the very end of the novel, when Quixote finally assumes responsibility for his enthrallment to a false ideal, does his perspective fuse with that of the author. Here we must consider a final complication, one that has a crucial effect upon the ending. Before Cervantes had come to write the conclusion of part 2, he found himself outflanked by a rival enchanter, the author Avellaneda, who had taken up the use of his main character and even criticized Cervantes' handling of him. The strings of his marvelous puppet were being taken out of the author's hands. The public source of the madness in his work, which had made it intelligible and significant in the first place, also made it peculiarly vulnerable to copying; the very attachment to the books of chivalry that had made Quixote susceptible to the manipulations of his readers came to threaten Cervantes as well. And so he had to show Don Quixote "finally dead and buried" at the end of part 2 "so that no one may dare bring forward any further evidence against him" (417).

This motive gives to the ending of the story a peculiar double thrust, for the very gesture of self-abnegation and self-reproach that frees Alonso the Good from the infatuations of pride and from the manipulations of his local audience also secures Cervantes' possession of him and certifies the author of this work as the only valid judge of Quixotic misadventure. From early on in part 1, Cervantes has been using the device of a fictitious Arab historian, Cid Hamete Benengeli, as a comic screen for his own authorial activity. Cid Hamete is at first a figure of contempt, a mechanism borrowed from the books of chivalry themselves. Before long, however, Cervantes has become fond of him as a vehicle for his own wit, and when Cid Hamete's and his own authorial possession of Don Quixote are challenged by Avellaneda, they turn as one toward this new enemy. Not only has it become impossible to tell the author and the narrator apart, but now they merge comically into a oneness of literary being with their central character: "For me alone was Don Quixote born, and I for him; it was his to act, mine to write; we two together make but one, notwithstanding the pretended Tordesillesque writer who has ventured with his great, course, ill-trimmed ostrich quill to write the achievements of my valiant knight" (830). The tone is whimsical, valetudinarian. It seems to participate in Quixotic folly by its very absorption with its subject, but that gives it, at the closing of the book, so much the greater air of self-possession. It has been a beautiful joke, and now it is over. Justice has been done; a comic version of Providence has been brought to fulfillment. While Quixote, alias Alonso the Good, dies sadder and wiser than he was, his creator remains a merry witness of his follies, untainted by their excess.

The paranoia of Cervantes' comic hero is both the instrument and the deformed satiric image of his own claim to and execution of justice against the

vulgar productions of his literary rivals, and it is Cervantes' belief in the distinction between actual justice and delusions of victimization that entitles
him to mock. His satiric perspective is, not surprisingly, a socially conservative one and, in intellectual terms, largely traditional. In the course of my
analysis, I have touched upon a number of elements of his work that do seem
to look forward to modern attitudes and preoccupations. In every case, however, the sense of anticipation is equivocal or must be crucially qualified.
There is, for instance, the employment of class comedy, but a class comedy
that is not yet approached from the bourgeois point of view. There is Cervantes' clinical interest in the curiosities of psychology, decidedly like the
modern except that mental illness remains here an aberration, not a privileged model for the analysis of normal thinking as it was later to become for
authors such as Freud. While Cervantes depicts delusion, habitual error, and
perspectival deformation in every variety, there remains nevertheless the
dominant perspective of the people of good sense who laugh with a good
heart at Quixote's folly.

Further, though there may be Pyrrhonistic inspiration in the staging of
Quixote's adventures, we do not see here the general perspectivalism of
some later novelists.[19] Neither can the linguistic self-consciousness of Don
Quixote be taken as a mark of irony of the postmodernist kind. While the
story becomes an ever more dense mesh of fictitious inventions contrived by
readers sane and insane, narrators and editors of varying perspective, and
even rival authors confronted and vanquished, we are dealing with a phase
of culture that had not yet developed the norms of sincerity and novelistic
realism, the suspicion about and wish to escape from rhetoric, that were to
characterize modern culture.[20] For this earlier way of thinking, neither the
rhetorical constructedness of "histories," to use the Renaissance term, nor
the "self-fashioning" of authors, could appear as a scandal. The outlook I
am describing is pre- rather than postmodern. The great amusement that it
takes in the confusions of reality and rhetoric has a moral basis, the privilege of good sense laughing at failures of perception, judgment, and taste that
could and indeed should have been avoided. I have also, perhaps, fallen into
anachronism in calling Quixote's system of dividing appearance from reality an "epistemology," for it partakes of none of the methodological caution
or skepticism of that later-seventeenth-century development. It is rather a
comic manifestation of the psychology of suspicion, a humorous credulity
about hidden causes and agencies that is ultimately moral rather than intellectual in its origins.

Finally, all of the equivocally forward-looking aspects of Quixotism co-

[19] Cf. Leo Spitzer, "Linguistic Perspectivism in the *Don Quijote*," in *Linguistics and Literary History: Essays in Stylistics* (Princeton: Princeton University Press, 1948), 43–85.

[20] Michel Foucault's brilliant but elusive pages on *Don Quixote* exaggerate the book's modernity. See Michel Foucault, *Les mots et les choses: une archéolgie des sciences humaines* (Paris:
Gallimard, 1966), 60–64.

exist quite easily in Cervantes' imagination with elements of culture that are more obviously traditional. If Cervantes casts doubt, for instance, on the credibility of the books of chivalry, he remains faithful to the conventions of romance more properly deployed in the high Renaissance mode exemplified by the fiction of Sir Philip Sidney or Honoré d'Urfé, or by his own *Persiles and Sigismunda*.[21] Part 1 of *Don Quixote* itself has been intercalated with a series of romances—not in the chivalric vein but modernized up to their day—narrating, therefore, the complex fates of beautiful and good gentlemen and ladies tested by the vagaries of fortune until finally brought to the rewards they deserve.[22] A providential justice lies behind the action, and there are even times when Quixote's ridiculous doings make him the unwitting instrument of Providence uniting parted lovers and other victims of fortune.

It must be remembered, too, that the ending of *Don Quixote* represents a very traditional judgment upon its central character. Cervantes may have been impelled by market forces to take his hero out of circulation, but he could have sent him to his grave with all his imperfections on his head. Instead he brought him to his senses so that he could pronounce his own denunciation. In my own adolescent reading of *Don Quixote,* I imagined that the hero would end his life like Rostand's Cyrano, with a final, spell-binding, desperately heroic death-bed oration. Such a reading misses the interest of the long trajectory from madness and exhilaration to sanity and penitence that constitutes part 2. Quixote is not by any means wrong, in the view of the author, to reproach himself with pride and foolishness, or to prefer a remorseful sobriety to the exhilarations of madness. But this does not mean that Cervantes ends the novel on the same chastened note as his character, for as we have seen, the death of Don Quixote merely completes the great providential scheme of Cervantes' authorial jest.

Don Quixote, for all of its irony, perspectival wit, and rhetorical mimicry, remains securely within the religious and intellectual ambit of late medieval culture and partakes of its central intellectual habits and preoccupations. It

---

[21] The comparison within this "framework of sensibility" belongs to Williams, *Idea of the Novel,* 2. He notes that Sidney and d'Urfé were, like Cervantes, both soldiers and novelists (2, n. 2). The production of Shakespeare's romances between the publication dates of parts 1 and 2 of *Don Quixote* suggests that this form of imagination was not by-gone but at its height.

[22] Overlooking the seriousness with which Cervantes takes the traditional forms and values of the culture of romance has misled his later readers to overvalue the protagonist of Cervantes' satiric romance. Quite recently, for instance, Ian Watt sums up his treatment of Cervantes's novel by saying that "the shared enterprise of Don Quixote, Sancho Panza, and their ungainly but lovable quadrupeds . . . answered the need to express how the association of values of a long-gone world with the rewards of human fellowship in a common purpose could endure even amid the insoluble contradictions and brutalities of their contemporary world." Watt is right about the "human fellowship," though Cervantes does not sentimentalize it, but his attribution of a sense of loss and contradiction seems to me an anachronism. *Myths of Modern Individualism: Faust, Don Quixote, Don Juan, Robinson Crusoe* (Cambridge: Cambridge University Press, 1996), 89.

was a culture that could allow its members to acknowledge their part in imperfection and sin, their kinship with a figure like Gawain, yet to laugh with only venial complicity in the "shrewd lunacy," the social pretentiousness and folly, of Quixote, a folly all the more shameful, amusing, and wonderful combined with such qualities of intellect and social refinement as his own. In making his indictment against the authors of the books of chivalry, Cervantes does not resemble the paranoid Quixote because his indictment of these books is arguably justifiable, while Quixote's accusations against the enchanters are a comic shadow of an indictment, a complaint that is actually an indulgence and an excuse. It was thus entirely permissible as well as enjoyable to regard the paranoid as a hapless and laughable other.

In the Catholic culture of the medieval and early modern era, then, the excess of perfectionism leads most readily to laughter in one of two forms: either the wise laughter of acceptance and rueful self-recognition that we see in response to Gawain's folly or the jubiliantly derisive hilarity that greets Quixote. We shall have to inquire into later developments to discover how the figure of the self-idealizing victim, once mocked with such hearty good conscience, came to acquire its pathos, charm, and mesmerizing sway over the Western imagination.

Part 2

THE ALIENATION OF AGENCY

4

Luther and the Devil's World

It is Quixote's fate to have fallen under the spell of an ideal that is actually the manipulative tool of an exploitative alien agency, an other. As I have tried to suggest, his plight can be attributed to faults that are contingent and special to him. Extraordinary personal and social imperatives made him susceptible to a false idealism. In the mind of the author, he could and indeed should have behaved otherwise, for there were in his possession true ideals, ones that, had he remained faithful to them, would have been the basis of a meaningful life, perhaps good fortune on earth, and certainly the expectation of eternity. At the end of the story he takes responsibility for his failure. When we mark, however, the transition from the late medieval framework of thought in which Cervantes was still operating to the onset of modernity, the persuasiveness of such ideals in the minds of many intellectuals largely vanishes after a prolonged and many-sided attack on the validity of ideals themselves. This attack reduces the forms of idealism to projections of delusion or to instruments of manipulative agencies, or both. It is not just social and religious ideals that are undermined but, eventually, all possible ideals except those paradoxical reflexes of the will-to-truth that drive us to renounce idealism and truth itself in the name of some still more scrupulous discipline.

Medieval culture had achieved the means of drawing a limit to the dangers of suspicion by articulating a coherent doctrine of freedom and responsibility under the auspices of the church. The solution was not merely an intellectual one; it depended upon the legitimacy, credibility, and power of the institution that sustained it. In the subsequent period of theological and political struggle, this institution itself became the focus of extraordinary suspicion and blame. The dishonor of the church was in proportion to the magnitude of the claims it had made for itself: as the avatar of the savior, its role was to be nothing less than the incarnation of an ideal order of life, a marriage between Christ and Christians. By the end of the thirteenth century, the corruption of this order, the crass venality of its agents, and the enslavement of its policy to temporal interests all became matters of obsessive concern for medieval intellectuals. The monastic orders were a particular object of derision, as no reader of Dante, Boccaccio, or Chaucer can be unaware. Reform had long been in progress; medieval history is nothing so much as a protracted sequence of attempts to renew the bond between the institutions of religious life and its ideals. But the corruption of Rome and the papacy itself from the fourteenth century onward made a stubborn obstacle to the renewal of the church. Papal legitimacy became especially difficult to credit after the Schism of 1378–1415, when popes and antipopes began to proliferate. Though the crisis was temporarily resolved at the Council of Constance, the solution remained indissolubly connected in memory with the burning of the Bohemian proto-Reformationist, Jan Hus. Only with the help of further violence would Rome be able to defend the universal hegemony and temporal power it had so long struggled to acquire; moreover, the church was gradually losing the authority and legitimacy such means required. Martin Luther's visit to the papal city in 1510–11 left an indelible impression of moral squalor upon the young monk who was struggling to achieve a sense of his own fitness for salvation under the arms of the church. Later he was grateful for having had the chance to witness the scene of corruption firsthand.[1]

The medieval church that Luther challenged six years later held title to universal authority in matters of the spirit resting upon the claim of an unbroken succession from the apostle Peter. Christ's vicar in Rome had the power to bind and loose in heaven and on earth, and the church served as a mediating agency between Christian life and God's judgment. With the sacrament of confession it could relieve human souls of their guilt before God. It had access as well to a special treasure, the fund of grace accumulated by the collective sacrifice and prayers of the monastic orders, a fund that could be dispensed in exchange for money, with no more sign of penitence on the part of the buyer than his or her willingness to purchase. As Leopold von Ranke put it, not without irony, "There is a fantastic sublimity and grandeur in the conception of the church, as a community comprehending heaven and earth, the living and the dead; in which all the penalties incurred by individuals were removed by the merit and the grace of the collective body. What a conception of the power and dignity of a human being is implied in the belief that the pope could employ this accumulated treasure

---

[1] Conversation occurring between 28 March and 27 May 1537. Martin Luther, *Table Talk,* ed. Theodore G. Tappert, vol. 54 of *Luther's Works,* American edition (St. Louis: Concordia Publishing House; Philadelphia: Fortress Press, 1955–86), 237. All further references (abbrev. *LW*) will be to this edition. I have removed the citations for biblical references provided by the editors.

of merits in behalf of one or another at his pleasure!"[2] In a fuller and wider sense than the usual one, then, the church had taken responsibility upon itself. Without its help there was no deliverance from sin or hope of perpetual reward. The imperative to reform, then, could not have been more urgent for the medieval Christian, whose spiritual fate lay in the hands of an institution that had strayed from its original ideals.

Luther's response to the corruption of the church was not, however, a reform in the proper sense, one that held the church up to its animating principles.[3] It was instead a radical reorientation of the believer's relation to God, to Christian ideals and institutions, and especially to the church itself. Luther did not repudiate the moral corruption of the church; he accepted it as an expression of human impotence, of our inability to resist the power of Satan, saying, "Life is bad among us, as it is among the papists, but we don't fight about life and condemn the papists on that account."[4] What he did condemn and repudiate was present church doctrine, especially the doctrine that human agency can be considered responsible for the actions that lead to salvation or damnation. Equally abhorrent was the correlate assumption that human institutions can presume to mediate or affect in any way the will of God. For Luther, both the freedom and the efficacy of human agency are illusions, snares of the devil. The church's claim to mediate between God and Christians on the basis of human works represents a mark of demonic presumption and conceit. The notion that Christians can uphold God's law as presented in the Old Testament is an absurdity: the law, as Paul taught, was given to us precisely in order to show us our impotence. While there is value in our struggle to uphold it, it is sheer madness to think that we could succeed.[5] In this world, law is a tool of Satan, and even the saints were sinners (161–76). The scriptures display the flaws of even the best human beings in order to mortify human pride: "No one is certain that he is not continually committing mortal sin, because of the most secret vice of pride."[6] Human beings must recognize their absolute helplessness before God, their utter inability to choose the good and save themselves.

These words of Paul: "All have turned aside, the whole world is guilty, there is none righteous," are mighty rolls of thunder and piercing light-

---

[2] Leopold von Ranke, *History of the Reformation in Germany,* ed. Robert A. Johnson, trans. Sarah Austin (New York: Dutton, 1905), 152.

[3] As Heiko A. Oberman observes, Luther considered himself "preacher, doctor, or professor and was all of these," but reform belonged to God; Luther was no "inspiring idealist" but a prophet of apocalypse. *Luther: Man between God and the Devil,* trans. Eileen Walliser-Schwarzbart (New Haven: Yale University Press, 1989), 79.

[4] *Table Talk,* LW, 54:110.

[5] "The entire good of the work is that although sin is in us, still we fight with ourselves so that it will not govern, and so that we will not obey its lusts." *Against Latomus* (1521), trans. George Lindbeck, LW, 32:212.

[6] See Luther's defense of this condemned teaching in the *Defense and Explanation of All the Articles* (1521), trans. Charles M. Jacobs and George W. Forell, LW, 32:91.

ning flashes, and in truth the very "hammer that breaks the rocks in pieces," as Jeremiah calls it, by which everything that exists is shattered, not only in one man or some men or some part of them, but in the whole world and all men without a single exception, so that at these words the whole world ought to tremble, fear, and take to flight. What stronger or graver terms could have been used than that the whole world is guilty, all the children of men are turned aside and worthless, no one fears God, no one is not wicked, no one understands, no one seeks for God?[7]

This is Luther's essential note, a fearful, tempestuous outrage before the fact that his fellow Christians do not see their complete unfitness to uphold the moral ideals of Christianity and do not share the absolute suspicion about and despair of human nature that alone would set them in proper relation to God. "The whole world is guilty" and subject to condemnation, guilty not just of sin, for that is unavoidable, but of believing that human beings have power of their own, of refusing to see that the only righteousness within their hope is an "alien righteousness," bestowed upon them by Christ for reasons beyond mortal grasp.[8] Their faults are "alien" too, evidence of the devil's power. Human beings live entirely under the control of alien forces, good or ill: "The human will is placed between [God and Satan] like a beast of burden. If God rides it, it wills and goes where God wills. . . . If Satan rides it, it wills and goes where Satan wills."[9] For such creatures, only an absolute self-humiliation and surrender to the power of the good will permit them to escape the force of evil and give them the hope of being among the "elect," God's chosen—if they happen already to belong to God:

> No man can be thoroughly humbled until he knows that his salvation is utterly beyond his own powers, devices, endeavors, will, and works, and depends entirely upon the choice, will, and work of another, namely, of God alone. For as long as he is persuaded that he himself can do even the least thing toward his salvation, he retains some self-confidence and does not altogether despair of himself, and therefore he is not humbled before God, but presumes that there is—or at least hopes or desires that there may be—some place, time, and work for him, by which he may at length attain to salvation. But when a man has no doubt that everything depends on the will of God, then he completely despairs of himself and chooses nothing for himself, but waits for God to work; then he has come close to grace, and can be saved. (62)

---

[7] *The Bondage of the Will* (1526), trans. Philip S. Watson and Benjamin Drewery, *LW,* 33:256–57.

[8] *Two Kinds of Righteousness* (1519), trans. Lowell J. Satre, *LW,* 31:297.

[9] *Bondage, LW,* 33:65.

This passage shows Luther working against the psychological temptations that keep the unconverted from accepting the truth. His insistent manner of enumerating the aspects of human agency—"powers, devices, endeavors, will, and works"—betrays the preacher's eagerness to uncover all the poses under which the presumption to agency can be disguised. Luther would leave no place to hide. He knows the secret conceit that resists his doctrine. Those who disagree condemn themselves. They cannot be humble before God and therefore they cling to an exaggerated view of their own powers.

In attempting to grasp the original and personal stamp of Luther's thought, it is important to recognize that, from a merely doctrinal point of view, it is not his stand against free will and the individual's power to merit salvation by his or her own means that sets him decisively apart from the established tradition. On this question, Luther did find himself in opposition to Erasmian humanism and to late scholastic nominalism, both of which recognized the soul's ability to act in such a way as to determine salvation or damnation. This emphasis, though, was itself a relatively innovative one, reflecting developments of the fourteenth century and after. Luther's position, stressing election and predestination, hewed much closer to that of Augustine and Aquinas and to the official theology of the church even as it existed up to the time of the Council of Trent, than did that of Erasmus.[10] Only in the seventeenth century, under the initiative of the Jesuits, would belief in the freedom of the will with regard to matters of salvation be promoted to the status of church doctrine. Nor can we take Luther's expressions of contempt for the world and for the Christian's involvement as a novelty in the context of tradition. The medieval rhetoric of *contemptus mundi* was already so elaborate and extreme that there was little to be added.[11] Luther did importantly extend the scope of contempt. Where Catholic writers, faithful to their Augustinian and Neoplatonic sources, inveighed against the senses and their power to entangle the soul in the trammels of the flesh, Luther condemned both body and soul to the Pauline category of "flesh," in contrast to the "spirit," which was wholly from God. If Luther's teaching seems sometimes to relax the medieval contempt for the body, it is only because its antithesis, the soul, has been deprived of its title to a higher nature (33). The Lutheran demotion of the soul relative to the body was the first step in the long recuperation of the body that has preoccupied modern culture.

It is particularly when Luther denies the value of human agency itself, severing all connection between action and salvation, that he undermines the

---

[10] Leszek Kolakowski observes that, up to the time of the Council of Trent, the church's tendency was as much to absorb as to oppose Reformed teaching. "What is striking in the final Tridentine codification of the doctrine of justification is that it seems to be harder on Pelagian errors than on the horrifying new heresy of the Reformation." *God Owes Us Nothing: A Brief Remark on Pascal's Religion and on the Spirit of Jansenism* (Chicago: University of Chicago Press, 1995), 53.

[11] Jean Delumeau, *Le peché et la peur: la culpabilisation en Occident, XIIIe–XVIIIe siècles* (Paris: Fayard, 1983), 15–33.

very basis of medieval culture, a culture that was grounded in the heroism of saints and martyrs, the "imitation of Christ," and the mediating power of the church.[12] Medieval teaching proclaimed the benefits of moral perfection, the renunciation of sin, and the higher life, as far as mortals could attain it. Christians were encouraged to set themselves apart from others according to their virtue, to display their spiritual aspirations, and to dramatize their love of God through symbolic actions—alms, fasting, silence, self-mortification, pilgrimage.[13] These symbolic demonstrations took place in the context of a spiritual community embracing the living and the dead. Christians were active seekers of the good of life as they understood it, however excessive or corrupt their practices and institutions might have become. And while the most exacting formulations of official theology might have tended to emphasize God's grace rather than the choices made by men and women as the key element leading to salvation or damnation, it was still action, and not mere faith, that would signify the difference. Nor was the primacy of God's agency a significant pastoral theme. The emphasis was upon what the sinner could accomplish with God's grace, and even teachers like Bernard of Clairvaux who powerfully defended the sovereignty of God in matters of salvation did not deny the freedom of the will as Luther did.[14] God had established his law, and it was for to humankind to live up to it.

In the most characteristic medieval teaching, the soul is a *viator* moving between this world and the next, between salvation and damnation, searching for a middle state as near to perfection as possible, while avoiding the temptations of pride and despair. Its fate is always uncertain, hinging upon future action, but the movement is upward, away from the body in the direction of the soul and God. Luther's way, however,, is downward—to plumb the depths, passing through despair into hopefulness. But if it is only when "being humbled and brought back to nothingness" that one can attain the righteousness of Christ ("wait[ing] for God to work"), one acquires, nevertheless, at the moment of "self-despair," a righteousness that is as complete and as perfect as Christ's. Suddenly the law no longer exerts its sway upon us, ideals of conduct are no longer relevant to salvation, and our inability to satisfy their dictates no longer subjects us to the devil. God has forgiven

---

[12] *Imitatio Christi* was an increasingly important late medieval theme from the time of Wycliffe: "The imitation of Christ was the true rule of life, which would bring salvation to all who followed it (meaning, of course, the predestined). The example of Christ was the most familiar and the most reliable of all, and 'every action of Christ is an instruction to us.'" Jaroslav Pelikan, *Reformation and Church Dogma (1300–1700)*, vol. 4 of *The Christian Tradition: A History of the Development of Doctrine* (Chicago: University of Chicago Press, 1978), 36–37.

[13] It was a form of heroism that was often accessible to women as well as men, as Carolyn Walker Bynum shows in *Holy feast and holy fast: the religious significance of food to medieval women* (Berkeley: University of California Press, 1987).

[14] As Pelikan observes, the well-known maxim of Bernard, "Take away free will, and there is nothing that needs to be saved; take away grace, and there is nothing to save it," seeks to preserve grace and free will together in an "erudite" fashion. *Reformation and Church Dogma*, 144.

us. He has made us as righteous as himself. When a man has been "truly humbled and reduced to nothing in his own eyes," when he "finds in himself nothing whereby he may be justified and saved," then all that he sought by trying to obey the law he will "accomplish quickly and easily through faith."[15]

Here, then, is the turn in Luther's moral drama, the vision of the great reward, when, as the apostle says, "power is made perfect in weakness" (355). All unworthiness is overcome by the condescension of Christ, and the symbolic relation of marriage with Christ that formerly belonged to the church now becomes the blessing of the individual (352). Luther's faith is the other extremity of his despair. Having subjected the human image to a withering barrage of contempt, he now exalts the redeemed soul. Having surrendered its will and emptied itself to nothingness, the redeemed soul comes to possess all things. Physical possessions, of course, are not in question here— "such power belongs to kings, princes, and other men on earth" (354).

> The power of which we speak is spiritual. It rules in the midst of enemies and is powerful in the midst of oppression . . . a truly omnipotent power, a spiritual dominion in which there is nothing so good and nothing so evil but that it shall work together for good to me, if only I believe. . . . Lo, this is the inestimable power and liberty of Christians. . . . Who then can comprehend the lofty dignity of the Christian? By virtue of his royal power he rules over all things, death, life, and sin, and through his priestly glory is omnipotent with God because he does the things which God asks and desires. (355)

Luther excoriates his opponents for arrogating to human power the ability to choose about the things of eternity, an ability that he reserves exclusively to the divine;[16] but in his own account the faithful and properly submissive soul acquires a divinity of its own. The soul gains "a truly omnipotent power" for itself in union with a will that is beyond comprehension. This union with God is not a substantial or mystical one; it is part neither of being nor experience. Luther's God remains hidden. Rather, all is accomplished by the spirit infused through a proper understanding of the scripture. The soul's bliss derives from the conviction that one would not be able to achieve an absolute surrender to God without being moved by God's power. Considered in oneself, one is utterly wretched and helpless; considered in relation to God, one is justified in all of one's squalor, being properly aligned with his will.

Now it might seem that my account of Luther, emphasizing his thoroughgoing negation of human powers, would naturally put him in the camp

---

[15] *The Freedom of a Christian* (1520), trans. W. A. Lambert and Harold J. Grimm, *LW*, 31:348–49.

[16] *Bondage, LW*, 33:107.

of the skeptics, and, indeed, Luther's urge to humiliate the human image did extend to questions of knowledge. He largely shared Paul's suspicion of and contempt for philosophy, and whereas Augustine, Luther's theological guide among the fathers of the church, maintained the Platonist's belief in our access to the independent reality of intellectual truth, imparted to us by illumination from the mind of God, Luther had been schooled in the Ockhamist doctrine that truth was a contingent product of God's will. There is no knowledge we can grasp outside of God's ordination, nothing objective about the world beyond the fact that God has chosen it. God is the author of all.

And yet, in spite of his "divine monergism," as Jaroslav Pelikan calls it,[17] Luther is no skeptic, and his attack upon the human image is carried out not with a skeptic's caution but with an overmastering sense of command. The ground of this command is the existence of one area of intellectual activity where human powers, properly guided by the spirit, find themselves adequate to their task—interpreting the scriptures. Those who seek knowledge of God in the order of the world will be disappointed—that is the devil's portion;[18] but in the scriptures we have direct access to God's Word. It provides us with the "supreme consolation of Christians in all adversities, to know that God does not lie, but does all things immutably, and that his will can neither be resisted nor changed nor hindered."[19] The "soul which clings to [the words of scripture] with a firm faith," Luther tells us, "will be so closely united with them and altogether absorbed by them that it not only will share in all their power but will be saturated and intoxicated by them."[20] Such rhetoric would not be out of place in a mystical treatise describing ecstatic union with God.

On the basis of this spiritually inspired certainty, Luther looks behind all the false facades, the divine masks of this world, to find the hidden truth. The position of the skeptic, we have seen, is quite a different one, resting upon methodological caution and an unwillingness to go beyond what the evidence strictly allows, especially if the moral or political consequences might not be desirable. The contrast of dispositions between Luther and the skeptic is apparent in his debate with Erasmus on free will. Erasmus proclaims from the outset his "inner temperamental horror of fighting." Rather than delighting in contentious "assertions," he would rather "take refuge in the opinion of the Skeptics" wherever scripture would allow. He goes on to

---

[17] Pelikan, *Reformation and Church Dogma*, 145.

[18] Luther's attitude toward natural theology softened as he grew older, and he became interested in what the mind can know of God unaided by scripture. It was knowledge of an anxious kind, as Pelikan describes it. "Without the aid of revelation, the mortal man can know that there is a judgment hanging over him, he can brood over death, and he can stand in awe of his fate." Jaroslav Pelikan, *From Luther to Kierkegaard: A Study in the History of Theology* (Saint Louis: Concordia, 1950), 22–23.

[19] *Bondage, LW,* 33:43.

[20] *Freedom of a Christian, LW,* 31:349.

imply that Luther is infatuated with his own ideas.[21] Erasmus's disclaimer about "assertions" refers pointedly to the title of an earlier work of Luther's that includes a discussion of this subject.[22] The humanist is unwilling to put philosophical over moral considerations; his "refuge" among the skeptics is predicated upon the sense that the current orthodoxy is an acceptable one, which our reason gives no grounds to overthrow. Erasmus therefore cautions Luther ominously about the "secret places in the Holy Scriptures into which God has not wished us to penetrate more deeply" (38). We should contemplate such matters as the freedom of the will with that "mystic silence" we preserve for God himself (39). Accusations of pride and presumption are Luther's favorite rhetorical tools, but here Erasmus tries to turn the tables on him. Now Luther's confidence in interpreting the scripture puts him in the position of the one who makes a positive claim for human powers. By this method Erasmus seeks to contest Luther's hold on the proper grounds of humility.

It was poor strategy, for in his reply Luther boldly refuses the gambit altogether, willingly embracing as a virtue every one of the faults of which Erasmus implicitly or explicitly accuses him. "A man," he says, "must delight in assertions or he will be no Christian. And by assertion—in order that we may not be misled by words—I mean a constant adhering, affirming, confessing, maintaining, and invincible persevering."[23] Erasmus's willingness to persist in uncertainty betrays for Luther a damnable lack of concern about essential matters of the spirit: "Anathema be the Christian who is not certain and does not grasp what is prescribed for him! How can he believe what he does not grasp?" (23). For Luther, taking God's promise seriously will be impossible without a knowledge of his will. Erasmus, it seems, prefers the diffidence of a skeptic to Christian knowledge; he will emerge from skepticism only insofar as he is forced to do so by the authority of scripture or of the church, as if to be enlightened by these sources were against his will—"What Christian would talk like that?" (22).

> By such tactics you foster in your heart a Lucian, or some other pig from Epicurus' sty who, having no belief in God himself, secretly ridicules all who have a belief and confess it. Permit us to be assertors, to be devoted to assertions and delight in them, while you stick to your Skeptics and Academics till Christ calls you too. The Holy Spirit is no Skeptic, and it is not doubts or mere opinions that he has written on our hearts, but assertions more sure and certain than life itself and all experience. (24)

[21] Desiderius Erasmus, *On the Freedom of the Will*, trans. E. Gordon Rupp and A. N. Marlow, in *Luther and Erasmus: Free Will and Salvation* (Philadelphia: The Westminster Press, 1979), 36–37.

[22] *An Assertion of All the Articles of Martin Luther Condemned by the Latest Bull of Leo X* (1520).

[23] *Bondage*, LW, 33:20.

Here we see the Lutheran bravado and sarcasm on full display, as he speaks unhesitatingly for the Holy Spirit. The final clause in this paragraph bears special emphasis. The truth of scripture is *more certain than life itself and all experience*. It puts our understanding of *life itself and all experience* aside, suspends our view of the surface, and causes us to look behind, toward the "substance of things not seen." One could get no further from the skeptic's reserve, and, while the version of skepticism propounded by Erasmus is no doubt a shallow one, Luther would have answered Montaigne or Bayle in the same terms.

It was futile for Erasmus to suggest the virtues of caution or the benefits of peace. In Luther's eyes, scripture and the world that is available to our knowledge are specular opposites, as perfectly opposed to each other as his position was to that of the church. It is hardly likely, according to such a view, that the message of scripture will bring peace to the world. On the contrary, "it is the most unvarying fate of the Word of God to have the world in a state of tumult because of it." The gospel has come into the world to combat the devil, the god of this world, and Luther often uses "the Word of God" as a metonymy for the movement he had created, dividing the world between friends and enemies of "the Gospel": "For the Word of God comes, whenever it comes, to change and renew the world" (52). It is a mark of the gospel's truth that the devil resists it, a fact that constantly encouraged Luther in his struggles against the pope. And so we can understand how it came about that Erasmus should defend an elevated view of the freedom of the will on the timid and tepid ground of skeptical orthodoxy while Luther annihilated human powers with revolutionary confidence.

Confession with the Devil

The transformation that occurs between the theology of the church and that of Luther on the issue of human agency is a remarkable one, a true and deliberate transvaluation. Whereas in the former it had been a deadly temptation for human beings to refuse responsibility, now it was an even more deadly temptation for them to claim it. All responsibility was in God's hands. All faith was to be invested in him, with no need either for works or for the mediation of the church. Those who promoted moral ideals or sacred rituals as the way to salvation were agents of Satan, attempting to lure the soul away from God. God's church had become a trap for sinners and its teachings on responsibility the most visible instantiation of sin. It was not simply that Luther, by reinstating the absolute character of God's will, abolished human power. It was precisely to abolish the illusion of human power that Luther took up his cause.

For this reason, freedom and responsibility remained the central issues of the Reformation and the sacrament of confession the crux of Luther's revolt against the church. The campaign began with an attack on the sale of indulgences, incited by a particularly venal papal initiative, launched in tandem with the Fuggers, to extort money from the German states for a fictitious crusade against the Turks. In an astonishingly short time, Luther extended his critique to embrace every phase of Christian life. The attacks against him only increased the boldness and the scope of his critique, inciting him to push his reasoning further and further toward its logical conclusions and to find support and encouragement from among powerful interests. By 1520 the miner's son from Erfurt was advising German princes virtually to scrap the great panoply of Church tradition and observance. Justified souls, who had become not only Christ's "brethren, co-heirs, and fellow-kings, but also his fellow-priests,"[24] would have little need of ceremonies or exemplary works. Luther's program, laid out in great detail in the "Advice to the German Nobility," was implemented with a thoroughness that few reformers have achieved. As Steven Ozment relates,

> In the first half of the sixteenth century cities and territories passed laws and ordinances that progressively ended or severely limited a host of traditional beliefs, practices, and institutions that touched directly the daily life of large numbers of people: mandatory fasting; auricular confession; the veneration of saints, relics, and images; the buying and selling of indulgences; pilgrimages and shrines; wakes and processions for the dead and dying; endowed masses in memory of the dead; the doctrine of purgatory; Latin Mass and liturgy; traditional orders; the sacramental status of marriage, extreme unction, confirmation, holy orders, and penance; clerical celibacy; clerical immunity from civil taxation and criminal jurisdiction; nonresident benefices; papal excommunication and interdict; canon law; papal and episcopal territorial government; and the traditional scholastic education of clergy.[25]

This was reformation on a grand scale, a great stripping away of the ritual life of the church, its institutional and moral substance, and its intellectual foundations. The unintended consequences were a thoroughgoing internal renewal of the church—a "counter-reformation"—and almost two hundred years of sectarian violence, adding testimony to Luther's dark view of human nature and his sense of God's mystery.

The fact that Luther was able to carry out his reform, that he was not handled by the church in the same way that Hus and other heretics had been handled, was owing, of course, in large part to the divided political state of Europe. Luther himself understood his conflicts with the church in terms of opposing German and Italian interests, and he was altogether justified in do-

[24] *Freedom of a Christian, LW,* 31:355.
[25] Steven Ozment, *The Age of Reform, 1250–1550: An Intellectual and Religious History of Late Medieval and Reformation Europe* (New Haven: Yale University Press, 1980), 435.

ing so.[26] From the beginning, his theological criticisms were taken up for their political and economic ramifications, so that the humble monk, "a despised, inferior person," as he put it, was lifted onto the stage with cardinals and princes to play the role of a peculiarly mordant jester (123). The original and vital impulse of Luther's critique, however, was not political any more than it was a simple response to the corruption of the church. It was the outcome, rather, of his own struggle to find the hope of salvation within that corrupt institution.

All that we know of Luther's early life suggests the character of an extraordinarily anxious perfectionist who could never be certain that he was worthy of salvation in God's eyes and whose anxiety about the state of his soul led him through repeated crises. In later life, Luther saw his decision to enter the monastery as partly incited by the rigors of discipline imposed on him at home as a child.[27] As for so many gifted young men and women in the history of Christian culture, the pursuit of ascetic or monastic perfectionism became an avenue of independence from his parents. The monastery was to him a liberation as much as a confinement. Luther's decision to become a monk had been triggered by a warning from God about the state of his soul, which came in the form of a bolt of lightening that almost killed him. In the monastery Luther was free to concentrate entirely upon his spiritual development, but the fearfulness that plagued him only intensified. At the celebration of his first mass as a priest, he was so awed and intimidated by the power of God that he wanted to flee the altar (156).

The struggle for moral perfection in the sight of such a terrifying God was too much for Luther. Finally he was released from it by a spiritual insight that came to him in a tower of the monastery. It was the turning point in his life, the guiding moment he was to recount again and again to his family and companions in later years. He describes it in the brief preface to the Latin edition of his works, written just two years before his death.

> Though I lived as a monk without reproach, I felt that I was a sinner before God with an extremely disturbed conscience. I could not believe that he was placated by my satisfaction. I did not love, yes, I hated the righteous God who punishes sinners, and secretly, if not blasphemously, certainly murmuring greatly, I was angry with God, and said, "As if, indeed, it is not enough, that miserable sinners, eternally lost through original sin, are crushed by every kind of calamity by the law of the decalogue, without having God add pain to pain by the gospel

---

[26] "They think that those half-witted Germans will always be gullible, stupid fools, and will just keep handing over money to them to satisfy their unspeakable greed." *To the Christian Nobility of the German Nation concerning the Reform of the Christian Estate* (1520), *LW,* 44:144.

[27] "My parents kept me under very strict discipline, even to the point of making me timid. For the sake of a mere nut my mother beat me until the blood flowed. By such strict discipline they finally forced me into the monastery; though they meant it heartily well, I was only made timid by it." *Table Talk, LW,* 54:235.

and also by the gospel threatening us with his righteousness and wrath!" Thus I raged with a fierce and troubled conscience. Nevertheless, I beat importunately upon Paul at that place, most ardently desiring to know what St. Paul wanted.

At last, by the mercy of God, meditating day and night, I gave heed to the context of the words, namely, "In it the righteousness of God is revealed, as it is written, 'He who through faith is righteous shall live.'" There I began to understand that the righteousness of God is that by which the righteous live by a gift of God, namely by faith. And this is the meaning: the righteousness of God is revealed by the gospel, namely, the passive righteousness with which merciful God justifies us by faith, as it is written, "He who through faith is righteous shall live." Here I felt that I was altogether born again and had entered paradise itself through open gates.[28]

In the light of this new understanding, Luther instantaneously revised his view of the scriptures in such a way as to overcome the remoteness of God, so that each of God's formerly terrifying attributes could now be seen as accessible to humanity; indeed, a "totally other face of the entire Scripture" showed him that God's power and wisdom were already working though human agency, making it possible (337). By this means Luther's spiritual crisis was resolved. Suddenly God's power, wisdom, salvation, and glory were Luther's too. He had been endowed with a "passive" righteousness, alien yet his own, assuring him of justification before God. The distance between himself and his ideal, so troubling to him in his former state, had now collapsed; the space of the ethical, insofar as it related to salvation, simply vanished. Whereas in his unenlightened state no imperfection had been too small to threaten the repose of Luther's conscience, now he found himself in possession of a certainty that no crime or worldly contingency could shake. It was no longer up to him to save his soul; God had already done it.

Thanks to this theological and psychological breakthrough on the part of Martin Luther, the corrupt mediation of the church could be thrown off with a denial of all human mediation or agency in matters of salvation. Human fate for many in western Europe was placed entirely in the hands of an absolutely remote and incomprehensible being, a being defined by its otherness from humanity. Now this being, of course, was still "God," and, therefore, by nature good and worthy of trust, which is what keeps Luther's view of life from being mere cosmic paranoia. But this God is good in a way that is not only inaccessible to human understanding but in complete violation of it. In fact, it is the discrepancy between the human and the divine sense of justice that makes for the very challenge of faith.

Faith has to do with things not seen [as the apostle Paul had written]. Hence in order that there may be room for faith, it is necessary that

---

[28] "Preface to the Complete Edition of Luther's Latin Writings," LW, 34:336–37.

everything which is believed should be hidden. It cannot, however, be more deeply hidden than under an object, perception, or experience which is contrary to it. Thus when God makes alive he does it by killing, when he justifies he does it by making men guilty, when he exalts to heaven he does it by bringing down to hell. . . . Thus God hides his eternal goodness and mercy under eternal wrath, his righteousness under iniquity. This is the highest degree of faith, to believe him merciful when he saves so few and damns so many, and to believe him righteous when by his own will he makes us necessarily damnable, so that he seems . . . to delight in the torments of the wretched and to be worthy of hatred rather than of love. If, then, I could by any means comprehend how this God can be merciful and just who displays so much wrath and iniquity, there would be no need of faith.[29]

It becomes apparent in these words why Luther had so much difficulty believing in the mercy of this God until he finally left the burden of responsibility entirely to God himself. For God is a being whose very existence, from the mortal point of view, is paradox; he is both good and responsible for evil to an absolute degree.[30] When the paranoid Don Quixote was confronted with evidence that threatened his sense of perfection, he resorted to a hermeneutic system of transformations by which the obvious meaning of his experience could be converted into its opposite. Evil became appearance, good reality. Here we see Luther doing the same, preserving the excellence and goodness of the creator with whom he identifies by converting evil appearances into their opposites: they are all part of God's ultimate plan. This is suspicion with the values reversed: the appearance of fault masks a hidden good, apparent hostility conceals hidden love. For the benevolent other is now the hidden one, while no appearance of earthly good is to be trusted.[31]

[29] *Bondage, LW,* 33:62–63.

[30] Even Luther occasionally shrinks from the absolute denial of human responsibility, not because of the demeaning implications for human effort but, rather, on account of the implication that God must be responsible for evil. "Since, then," he writes, "God moves and actuates all in all, he necessarily moves and acts also in Satan and ungodly man. But he acts in them as they are and as he finds them. . . . It is like a horseman riding a horse that is lame in one or two of its feet; his riding corresponds to the condition of the horse, that is to say, the horse goes badly. But what is the horseman to do? . . . It is the fault, therefore, of the instruments, which God does not allow to be idle, that evil things are done, with God himself setting them in motion." *Bondage, LW,* 33:176.

[31] Donald J. Wilcox observes that the early Luther was still operating with the dichotomy between ideal and fallen worlds that he derived from the German mystics and that, we have seen, goes back to Plato. In his later thought he adopts the nominalist division of worlds developed in the works of Ockham and Biel. Here the distinction is between not ideal and fallen worlds but between the world God actually created, the "ordained world" (or *ordo ordinata*), and the "absolute world" (or *ordo absoluta*) that might be said to embody the infinite possibilities of creation which were open to him, limited only by the law of noncontradiction. Luther adopted the view that human beings exist in both of these worlds—in the actual, ordained world, where we are mixed creatures, imperfectly deploying our active judgment, and in the absolute world,

Luther was not, of course, original in taking this transient world to be the screen of a truer and higher one. For Plato and Augustine, as for Paul, we see "through a glass darkly." But for them what we see in the darkened glass is a genuine reflection; it does participate in the truth. The City of Man is an imperfect image of the City of God, but it is an image of it, just as human beings were created in God's image. For Luther, however, the apparent order is an inversion of the true and the good. Entirely fallen, its reflection of God's image is inverse and corrupt. As an image of justice, it is no less ironic and contradictory than the good is simple and pure. The relation of appearance to reality in the eyes of Luther becomes neither epistemological nor ontological, but simply moral. The opposite of truth is not simple falsehood, error, or appearance, but lie. This world looks like a lie, and God looks like a liar, a malicious persecutor and killer.. In order not to make him such, one must hold the world of appearance in complete suspicion, refrain from judgment, and have faith.

To accept perfect injustice, then, as if it were perfect justice, becomes both the humiliation and the pride of the redeemed Christian.[32] To validate his paradox, which is God's, Luther resorts to the interpretation of scripture and to personal testimony, bringing to bear all the magisterial confidence of his titanic personality, the confidence of a man who has come through his trial and can imagine no other way. The difficulty of believing the articles of faith becomes just one more proof of how deadly was the danger from which God had removed him and how great the extent of divine mercy. It is also, of course, the ground of his superiority over his adversaries, who succumb in commonsensical conformity with the evil of what exists, while Luther sees behind it. His heroism is grounded in and nourished by the power of suspicion.

Even after his experience in the tower, though, and his formulation of "justification by faith," Luther continued to struggle with God and the devil. He had made faith and suspicion the polar coordinates of religious consciousness—perfect suspicion of oneself and all creation, perfect faith in the hidden God—but it was hard to maintain these stances with unflinching consistency. "My temptation is this," he is reported as saying, "that I think I don't have a gracious God."[33] All sins for Luther now amount to unbelief, to "mak[ing] God a liar."[34] Trust had become the fundamental virtue, the

---

where we may passively enjoy perfection through God's judgment alone. *In Search of God and Self: Renaissance and Reformation Thought* (Boston: Houghton Mifflin, 1975), 297–99.

[32] "Admittedly, it gives the greatest possible offense to common sense or natural reason that God by his own sheer will should abandon, harden, and damn men as if he enjoyed the sins and the vast, eternal torments of his wretched creatures, when he is preached as a God of such great mercy and goodness, etc. It has been regarded as unjust, as cruel, as intolerable, to entertain such an idea about God, and this is what has offended so many great men during so many centuries. And who would not be offended? I myself was offended more than once, and brought to the very depth and abyss of despair, so that I wished I had never been created a man, before I realized how salutary that despair was, and how near to grace." *Bondage, LW,* 33:190.

[33] *Table Talk, LW,* 54:82.

[34] *Freedom of a Christian, LW,* 31:350–51.

one thing needful, but it remained difficult to trust in the absolute condescension of an infinitely remote God, to accept all of existence as a necessary
part of his will, and neither to wish even for a moment that God could have
done or been otherwise nor to fear that one's own moral imperfections might
jeopardize one's salvation. Sin was palpable all around; it permeated Luther's
consciousness, in spite of God's gracious redemption, while God remained
hidden.

What permitted Luther to tolerate this heroic level of inner tension and
cognitive disorientation was the fact that, while it was impossible to understand the disposition of the world as an expression of God's will, it was easy
to understand it as a tool of Satan's. With God's withdrawal behind the
mask, Satan steps forward as an explanatory principle of vast importance.
Satan is the prince of this world, and without God's grace, human beings
would be without the slightest power to defend themselves against him. His
presence explains our tendency to waver in relation to God. If our hearts resist the force of scripture, a single word of which would otherwise overcome
us at the first hearing, it is owing to the power of Satan.[35] Even our thoughts
are not our own but, often, his. When our sins come to accuse us of unworthiness, it is not God, threatening to forsake us, but Satan, attempting to in-
still suspicion of the Word, to "make the law out of the gospel."[36] Satan
attacks us when we are alone and visits us in our dreams (89–90). Only by
believing that he has no power over us can we maintain our slender hold on
God's good will. And even then we remain physically in Satan's control. He
can inflict all the torments of Job. When we are sick or sad or frightened, it
is his doing.

Life, then, is nothing less than a constant personal struggle against Satan
and his legions, devils without and within. The attenuated spirit of evil that
had represented nullity and nonsense for the Middle Ages became for Luther
an agent of terrifying reality, a principle rivaling God in significance: "The
Devil and God are two enemies. Therefore, while God loves life, the devil
hates life" (34). In passages like this one, Luther sounds like a Manichean.
At times of temptation, God and the devil seem both to become his enemies
(34). The threat of the devil in the mind of Luther was serious and constant.
His tendency to become angry with God, to dispute with God over blame,
remained with him, and the devil was always there to exploit it.[37] Repeatedly he advises friends and visitors that "'No man should be alone when he
opposes Satan. The church and the ministry of the Word were instituted for

[35] *Bondage, LW,* 33:100.
[36] *Table Talk, LW,* 54:106.
[37] "When I'm troubled by thoughts which pertain to political questions or household affairs,
I take up a Psalm or a text of Paul and fall asleep over it. But the thoughts which come from
Satan demand more of me. Then I have to resort to more difficult maneuvers before I extricate
myself, although I easily get the upper hand in thoughts of an economic or domestic character.
However, when I'm angry with God and ask him whether it's he or I who's wrong, then it's more
than I can handle." *Table Talk, LW,* 54:7.

this purpose, that hands may be joined together and one may help another" (78).[38] In this advice we can see part of the motivation for Luther's flight from the spiritual dangers of monastic solitude.

If Luther's struggle with the devil was never-ending, it also clearly became for him something of a relief from his powers of self-torment, from the flaying of his soul in prostration before God. It is the devil who is now to blame when his conscience bites and his spirits sink before his judge. Like Quixote with his swarm of enchanters, an other is constantly available to take the responsibility for Luther's fault. And as with Quixote, Luther's struggle with his hidden enemy takes place in the domain of the comic and the excremental:

> Almost every night when I wake up the devil is there and wants to dispute with me. I have come to this conclusion: When the argument that the Christian is without the law and above the law doesn't help, I instantly chase him away with a fart. The rogue wants to dispute about righteousness although he is himself a knave, for he kicked God out of heaven and crucified his Son. (78)

From this passage one would have guessed that the devil was not only a free agent in his quarrel with God but that he had carried it out successfully, "kicked God out of heaven." Satan takes the blame both from Luther and from God. It may seem that Luther's indignant farting represents a loss of nerve in his confrontation with the Adversary, a lapse in his conviction or in his powers of argument; in fact, however, the fart is apropos, for it tells the devil that, in tempting Luther to blame himself, he is asking the man to look for purity and grace where only flatulence and absurdity can be expected. As long as Luther can maintain this comical contempt both toward himself and toward the devil, he can come to no harm. It was, we may say, his personal form of exorcism, and the ritual proved efficacious time and again.

> I am in a different mind ten times in the course of a day. But I resist the devil, and often it is with a fart that I chase him away. When he tempts me with silly sins I say, "Devil, yesterday I broke wind too. Have you written it down on your list?" When I say to him, "You have been put to shame," he believes it, for he does not want to be despised. (16)

The devil in this comedy plays the role of the confessor, listing sins for examination and penance. But none of Luther's sins is now any more significant than a fart. That is the measure of value in this filthy devil's world, and Luther accepts it with brave self-mockery.

Much psychoanalytic effort has been expended on interpreting the "anality" of Luther's diabolism, incited in part by the speculation that his tower

[38] *Table Talk, LW,* 54:78.

experience may have taken place on the privy.[39] The valuable point to emerge from these discussions is the reminder that the devil had always been associated with excrement. The association was not special to Luther, for, as he himself observes, "The painters paint the devil black and filthy."[40] Black masses, consecrated to the devil, typically involved excrement instead of the eucharist (207): where God gives his body as food for his people, the devil gives them filth. And since the tempter's very substance is of the lowest things, when Luther consigned this world entirely to the devil, he was able to dramatize this gesture with a rhetoric of filth and contempt that did not have to be invented. It was an important part of Luther's contribution to have elevated the figure of Satan, imparting to modernity its peculiar obsession with demonic presence.[41] Luther's stance, however, retained a hint of medieval merriment that was not to be recovered until Goethe. There was undoubtedly an overactive awareness of filth, as of fallenness, connected with Luther's perfectionistic character, but once his illumination had come, he could revel in the fallen and filthy world of the devil and even match farts with him without being tainted; he could touch pitch and not be *further* defiled. Death, the ultimate corruption of Nature, could no longer threaten him, and more than one observer has reported Luther's satisfaction in describing his nearness to death: "It's as I've often said: I'm like a ripe stool and the world's like a gigantic anus, and so we're about to let go of each other."[42] This complacent obscenity shows how much at home Luther could sometimes make himself in the fallen world, how fully he could accept his part in it.[43] In the paradoxical logic of his faith, to accept his affinity with filth and corruption wholeheartedly was the means of being nearest, "most beautiful," to God.[44]

---

[39] For Erik H. Erikson, Luther's flair for excremental drama is part of his contribution to the modern capacity for receptiveness to inner experience, a "truly Renaissance approach" (209). *Young Man Luther: A Study in Psychoanalysis and History* (New York: Norton, 1958), 204–6 and 244–50. For Norman O. Brown, by contrast, Luther's demonic and excremental vision heralds the increasing force of the death instinct in the Protestant era, which was to bloom into the demonic agency of capitalism. *Life against Death: The Psychoanalytic Meaning of History* (Middletown: Wesleyan University Press, 1959), 202–33. But if Luther is a precursor of Freud, as both these authors take him to be, it is rather to Freud the conjuror of hidden demonic forces, wielder of reductive and satiric rhetoric, ingenious diagnostician of his enemies, and purveyor of suspicion, as I have tried to show him in *Freud's Paranoid Quest: Psychoanalysis and Modern Suspicion* (New York: New York University Press, 1996).

[40] Quoted in Brown, *Life against Death*, 207.

[41] Oberman, *Luther*, 104.

[42] *Table Talk, LW*, 54:448.

[43] Luther continued, nonetheless, to experience bouts of extreme spiritual angst; he suffered particularly intense depression and disturbance of mind in connection with a severe physical illness in 1527–28. Oberman, *Luther*, 320–24.

[44] According to the Psalmist, Luther concluded, "It is not he who considers himself the most lowly of men, but he who sees himself as even the most vile, who is most beautiful to God." *D. Martin Luthers Werke: Kritische Gesamtausgabe* (Weimar, 1883–), 3:287–92. Quoted and translated in Ozment, *Age of Reform*, 243.

In his private struggles with the devil in his conscience, then, Luther could at times be bumptious and brazen, at times vulnerable and anxious. In his stance toward the external world, however, his universal perception of the demonic inspired him with exuberance, conviction, and violent eloquence. The inner confrontation with God and devil, once resolved in his favor, led him outward toward the sins of others. The dialogue with the confessor-devil that I have just quoted continues:

> Afterward, if I engage him in further conversation, I upbraid him with the pope and say, "If you do the same as he does, who is your pope that I should celebrate him? Look what an abomination he has prepared, and it continues to this day!" Thus I remind myself of the forgiveness of sin and of Christ and I remind Satan of the abomination of the pope. This abomination is so great that I am of good cheer and rejoice, and I confess that the abomination of the papacy after the time of Christ is a great consolation to me. Consequently those who say that one should not rebuke the pope are dreadful scolds. Go right ahead and inveigh against the pope, especially if the devil disturbs you about justification. He often troubles me with trivialities. I don't notice this when I'm depressed, but when I feel better I recognize it easily.[45]

It is with a surprising but typical candor that Luther admits the satisfaction he takes in the corruption of his enemies. Throughout his writings he unburdens himself in their direction. The pope is antichrist, and all who assist him are devils, swine, madmen, fools. Luther emits his animus with a naïve lack of inhibition. There is no straining for effect, not even a desire to wound, but a simple fitness of description to object, a fitness so natural and inevitable that it overrides circumlocution or decorum. Scatology and invective on the tongue of Luther are no more tendentious than a proper name, and there is no need to be measured or moderate while addressing a world that God has already and condemned to the rewards of its pride.

No one who has read more than a few pages of Luther's controversial writings will need an example of his polemical contempt. "As you see in my books," he admits, "I despise my adversaries. I take them for fools" (93). The most interesting of his tirades are the ones in which he tries, against the imperatives of his nature, to mix diplomacy with correction, as we can see in his dispute with Erasmus, whose biblical scholarship and erudition he respected, or in his letter to Leo X, a document that represents one of his last attempts to heal his breach with the church. But even on these occasions Luther simply cannot contain his vituperative spirit. This is the description he gives Leo of his debate with Johann Eck at Leipzig in 1519, an event that

---

[45] *Table Talk, LW,* 54:16.

brought Luther out of the silence he had assumed after his first round of attacks on the papacy. When Luther had returned peacefully to his studies,

> Satan opened his eyes and then filled his servant Johann Eck, a notable enemy of Christ, with an insatiable lust for glory and thus aroused him to drag me unawares to a debate, seizing me by means of one little word which I had let slip concerning the primacy of the Roman church. Then that boastful braggart, frothing and gnashing his teeth, declared that he would risk everything for the glory of God and the honor of the Apostolic See. Puffed up with the prospect of abusing your authority, he looked forward with great confidence to a victory over me. He was concerned not so much with establishing the primacy of Peter as he was with demonstrating his own leadership among the theologians of our time. To that end he considered it no small advantage to triumph over Luther. When the debate ended badly for the sophist, an unbelievable madness overcame the man, for he believed that it was his fault alone which was responsible for my disclosing all the infamy of Rome.[46]

It is natural for modern readers to interpret a passage such as this one figuratively, and there are indeed parts of it that perhaps can be taken as rhetorical exaggerations: while there is every reason to think that Eck was a "boastful braggart," it is not likely that Luther believed he was actually "frothing and gnashing his teeth" at Leipzig. That is a violent cliché. The claim that "Satan opened his eyes," however, while it is anthropomorphic, is meant to indicate a literal inspiration, or possession, by the devil. Such demonic possession for Luther would not imply that a person's will had been supplanted by another, demonic one, but merely that, as with all sinners, the will through its own impulse had given in to and was under the control of Satan. For Luther all of us are in a real sense possessed all of the time, either by God or Satan or both. In Eck, Luther was confronting a directly inspired agent of Satan puffed up with the pride that is the devil's perennial resource. Luther is always fighting the devil or his boobies; they are his only opponents, so he has no reason to stay his hand.

It is interesting to note, also, that having defeated this opponent Luther goes on to make a diagnosis of his spiritual fate: Eck was driven to madness with the thought that he alone was responsible for Luther's devastation of the church. For Luther, Eck has been caught in the ruse of responsibility, that oscillating pattern of pride and despair that typifies for him the pre-Reformation psychology of the will. We may again be reminded of Gawain in his tirade against himself, moving from an excess of innocence to an excess of guilt, or of Quixote finally taking responsibility, to a mortal degree, upon himself. This is the trap that Luther believes he has escaped, and the process has given him an unmatched battery of resources for confronting his foe. His

---

[46] From the "Open Letter to Leo X" prefixed to *The Freedom of a Christian, LW,* 31:338.

attacks and denunciations are never mere expressions of feeling but recognitions of reality, inseparable from the framework of his thought and, thus, from God's judgment.

Essential to the support of Luther's uncomplicated stance toward the world around him is the fact that, in his mental universe, everything has already been settled. Christ has given his promise and those who will not heed it must be damned like the devil who tempts them. The world is divisible into saved and damned. It is not a matter of what they do but of who they are.[47] God's unaccountable prejudice in favor of some and against others must be respected. And although God's will is in theory unknowable, Luther easily consigns all who oppose him to the devil's filth and flames; he does not even spare fellow champions of the gospel like Zwingli and Œcolampadius, once they have deviated from the path. When necessary he condemns sinners to their own death and perdition, as in the Peasants' Revolt of 1525, when he exhorted the authorities to recognize the rebellious peasants as demons.[48] Luther presumes in this case to decree that all who die opposing the peasants with a proper Christian seriousness will receive a martyr's reward from God, while all the peasants will be "lost in body and soul" (53). He exhorts his readers to treat the peasants who would not surrender their demands as if they were mad dogs: "let everyone who can, smite, slay, and stab, secretly or openly, remembering that nothing can be more poisonous, hurtful, or devilish than a rebel."[49] As many as a hundred thousand people died in the outcome. Luther's attempt to explain his "harsh book" against the peasants shows not a trace of self-doubt about the matter, even though he recognized that much of the violence against them was devil's work on the part of the princes who carried it out. "If we are to preach God's word, we must preach the word that declares his wrath, as well as that which declares mercy. We must preach of hell as well as heaven, and help extend God's word and judgment and work over both the righteous and the wicked, so that the wicked may be punished and the good protected."[50] Many years later, at his table in the converted monastery where he established his home, Luther pointed to his lack of remorse about these events as an example of faith: "I, Martin Luther, slew all the peasants in the uprising, for I ordered that they be put to death; all their blood is on my neck. But I refer it all to our Lord God, who commanded me to speak as I did."[51] Thus Luther presents himself as a man who, by discovery of the truth, has overcome all moral doubt, all inclination to judge himself, all diabolical distrust of God, and all anxiety about his faith. Having accepted the bondage of depravity, he was beyond reproach.

---

[47] *The Freedom of a Christian, LW,* 31:353.

[48] *Against the Robbing and Murdering Hordes of Peasants,* trans. Charles M. Jacobs and rev. Robert C. Schultz, *LW,* 46:51–52.

[49] *Against the Robbing and Murdering Hordes of Peasants,* 50.

[50] *An Open Letter on the Harsh Book Against the Peasants,* trans. Charles M. Jacobs and rev. Robert C. Schultz, *LW,* 46:66.

[51] *Table Talk, LW,* 54:180.

No one who addresses the subject of Luther's teaching can avoid taking his psychology into account, if only because he made his personal experience central to the value and proof of his doctrine. Everywhere, even in his hymns, Luther speaks with the same voice of conviction, the same voice for which God is a "mighty fortress" against the "old, evil enemy," and which draws strength and even comfort from admitting that "I, Martin Luther, slew all the peasants." In the records of his conversation, we can see that the venerable Luther became an exemplary being whose heroic process of discovery was to be constantly retraced. His sense of self-justification in every aspect of life was a source of strength to his cause and a rebuke to his enemies. Luther had already vanquished his own greatest enemy, the devil in his conscience, and while the struggle could never cease in mortal days, Luther's certainty of the outcome was the chief trophy of his victory. It was a struggle constantly to be renewed in the life of Luther and his protestant descendants.

Even Luther's sympathetic interpreters concede that the case can be made for a diagnosis of "Paranoia reformatorica."[52] It is important to acknowledge, though, as we consider what it meant for Martin Luther to become one of the master psyches of modernity, that in many aspects of his cause Luther had the better side of the argument. I have already noted that his claim to theological orthodoxy has considerable weight. The value of his critique of the existing church is still more undeniable, and the simpler form of piety that he offered answered in many ways to the needs of his contemporaries. His attack upon confession as an unnecessarily intrusive and perfectionistic regimen, imposed by celibate priests upon the laity, gave relief to many, and the sense of the dignity of married life in the modern era is due in part to Luther's teaching. (Luther gave to marriage a mixed blessing: though his view of it was actually lower than that of Catholic thinkers,[53] it was higher relative to other ways of life, just as the body was now higher in relation to the soul.) It is impossible, furthermore, for modern sentiments entirely to regret the spectacle of Luther's old age, when he set up his entertainments in the former monastery he had transformed into a family dwelling. It was only one of the ways in which Luther's example incited the imagination of Rabelais. Luther began the demolition of the monastic kingdom of perfection and gave title to the secular realm, the only one worthy in his view of the fallen human being. We cannot imagine life without these developments.

Nevertheless, Luther's bitter denial of agency and his one-sided attack on the human fitness for ideals established a formidable example of suspicion, a structure of habits and relations that was also to be decisive for the culture that came after. Luther's model of thinking preserves the religious discrepancy between actual and ideal while seeing the ideal as in principle inaccessible and therefore a trap for the unwary. It establishes an exorbitant divide

[52] Oberman, *Luther,* 314.
[53] Delumeau, *Le peché et la peur,* 35.

between appearance and reality, making what is apparent no longer merely the imperfect reflection or accidental feature of what is hidden but rather its opposite. The apparent world becomes a mask of innocence hiding a diabolical deception. The Lutheran stance is one of heroic confidence in looking behind the surface to see the hidden truth. It makes a passionate source of polemical strength out of the belief that everything has already been determined and fixed, so that agency itself is next to an illusion.[54] It sees all of life nevertheless as a struggle against an all-powerful enemy whose hand is everywhere. All of these paranoid habits of thought were being given a new legitimacy and centrality. Finally, and perhaps most importantly, Luther's model polarizes not only the ontological division between the actual and ideal, and the epistemological division between the hidden and revealed, but it sets people, too, in absolute categories. There are no more good or evil acts, only people saved or damned, and therefore friends or enemies.

I have been citing Cervantes' portrayal of the paranoid Quixote—medieval and Catholic in its conception, though not to be written until some generations after Luther's death—as a point of reference for understanding the cultural significance of Luther's psychology. We see the two characters manifesting the same structural distortions within the same model, but in the first case the motive of the author was detached laughter toward an image of self-glorifying madness, in the second case it was deadly serious self-justification. It may seem odd to put a fictional character and real person on the same footing. My intention, of course, has not been to judge individuals but to show how these two images of paranoia look in different intellectual and cultural contexts. But could the analysis of paranoia not be extended to Cervantes himself since, as I have noted, he too was making a hostile interpretive gesture, neither toward enchanters nor toward aristocratic culture but toward the vulgar authors of the books of chivalry? Does not this motive, pursued to such extraordinary lengths, suggest a similar demonizing obsession, and could it not have similar infectious consequences? The answer, it seems to me, is that Cervantes' target is not a group of people but a culturally limited practice that could be renounced by those who make their living according to it or, less charitably, suppressed by authorities who should know better. There was a choice involved, just as Quixote himself shows a certain motive power of choice in the construction and defense of his delusion. For Luther, by contrast, the hated idea and the people who defend it cannot come apart. They are inseparably and equally to be damned, and his rejection of them both is total. There is no sign of the humorous and humane complicity with his subject that Cervantes himself displays in the final stages of his work. Not only are choice and responsibility illusory but the sense of

---

[54] As Kolakowski notes, the energizing effects of "fatalistic theology" can also be observed in early Islam and in Bolshevism as well as in the period of the Reformation. *God Owes Us Nothing,* 35–36.

responsibility is the surest sign of damnation and the myth of choice the most dangerous instrument of temptation. Cervantes directs a limited scorn and laughter at a narrowly delimited part of his world, whereas Luther directs an absolute and total scorn toward himself and all of the things and people that surround him, making it the very key to his exemplary self-justification and condemning those who do not share it.

5

The Terrors of Reform

Luther hoped to alleviate the distress of conscience that arose from the Catholic doctrine of works. Having rejected both the sacrament of penance and its moral and theological grounds, he sought to give to each believer a new confidence to stand justified before God, with intermediate authorities now blessedly removed. Anxious self-examination and the rite of confession were hence to be replaced by Luther's hard-won resignation and tranquility. From this time forward it was to be understood that no one on earth could call to judgment those whom God had already judged and delivered: "we are all priests of equal standing."[1] It was up to the individual to exercise judgment independently and, indeed, to resist excessive concern with the irrevocable judgment God had already made. "You will receive as much as you believe you receive," Luther told his followers.[2] When he turns his attention away from the relentless pulverizing of his adversaries to the care of his flock, a genuine note of consolation enters Luther's writing, a hopeful simplicity and a reliance on the beneficial effects of the will-to-believe. This emphasis upon the power of positive thinking about God's mercy could allow William James to classify Luther's teaching, without absurdity, under "the religion of healthy-mindedness."[3] Luther himself insists upon his concern to instruct and comfort. "I can testify," he writes, "that although my shell may be hard,

---

[1] *To the Christian Nobility,* vol. 44 of *Luther's Works,* American edition (St. Louis: Concordia Publishing House; Philadelphia: Fortress Press, 1955–86), 129.

[2] Quoted in Heiko A. Oberman, *Luther: Man between God and the Devil,* trans. Eileen Walliser-Schwarzbart (New Haven: Yale University Press, 1989), 240.

[3] William James, *The Varieties of Religious Experience: A Study in Human Nature* (New York: Modern Library, 1902), 126 27.

still my kernel is soft and sweet."[4] The moments of tenderness in the great hymns bear him out.

But if, for Luther and his followers, there was salvation in surrender and supreme consolation in the yielding of all power, autonomy, freedom, and responsibility to God, we have also seen that, even in Luther's own case, to live out one's personal destiny as the naked battleground of good and evil could become a new source of torment. It was not easy to relinquish autonomy and worth while retaining hope. In the Reformed faith,[5] as it was shaped by Zwingli, Calvin, and many others, the spiritual dangers of despair were greatly enhanced. This form of Protestantism was to leave the deepest impression upon modern culture. The absolute alterity of God and the unknowability of election were at the center of Calvin's message. Where Luther taught that the soul simply could not find the way to salvation without the all-determining assistance of God's grace, Calvin added predestinatory force to the choice of evil. Damnation, too, had been positively elected by divine Providence before the beginning of time, and souls had been created with eternal torment as the only possible outcome of their existence.

With the doctrine of "double predestination," a new kind of being was brought into the cosmos, a being designed precisely to be damned for the glory of God: "Behold! Since the disposition of all things is in God's hands, since the decision of salvation or of death rests in his power, he so ordains by his plan and will that among men some are born of certain death from the womb, who glorify his name by their own destruction."[6] Luther in his darkest moments could think of God as a kind of enemy, but it was always necessarily a mistake either for him or for his followers to do so, it being imperative that each of us trust and have faith. In the world of Calvin, however, there are souls for whom God genuinely is an enemy, souls for whom there is no hope of a conversion because God does not permit them either to believe or to trust him as they should. John Bunyan, in *The Pilgrim's Progress*, shows us the reprobate condition—a man shivering in an iron cage, whom no power on earth can release. "God hath denied me repentance; his word gives me no encouragement to believe; yea, himself hath shut me up in this iron cage: nor can all the men in the world let me out. O eternity! eternity! How shall I grapple with the misery that I must meet with in eternity?"[7]

---

[4] *Against Latomus*, LW, 32:142.

[5] The term *Reformed* has replaced *Calvinist* among scholars as a label for the branches of Reformation that diverged from Luther and Zwingli, since later generations of Protestants saw themselves as sharing their faith with Calvin rather than deriving it particularly from him. For a recent account of the social development of the Reformed faith, see Philip Benedict, *Christ's Churches Purely Reformed: A Social History Of Calvinism* (New Haven: Yale University Press, 2002).

[6] Jean Calvin, *Institutes of the Christian Religion*, ed. John T. McNeill, trans. Ford Lewis Battles, vols. 20–21 of *The Library of Christian Classics* (Philadelphia: Westminster, 1960), 21: 954.

[7] John Bunyan, *The Pilgrim's Progress*, ed. Roger Sharrock (New York: Penguin, 1965), 67.

Here is vividly figured the besetting danger of the Reformed mind-set: intellectual clarity mortified by spiritual impotence.

Now faith, of course, based upon God's revealed Word, prompts followers of Calvin to believe that God has chosen them to be saved, and to believe this in spite of the fact that all men and women deserve eternal punishment. The believer is one of a favored few whom God mercifully preserves; the rest of mankind he leaves to fester in its corruption. The principle of choice remains unfathomed. Calvin describes the process with clinical aplomb: "though all of us are by nature suffering from the same disease, only those whom it pleases the Lord to touch with his healing hand will get well. The others, whom he, in his righteous judgment, passes over, waste away in their own rottenness until they are consumed."[8] This would be comforting among the ranks of the saved except that in this world one's true spiritual identity remains unknown, there being no truly reliable sign to separate elect from damned, no sign of election that could not turn out to be a snare for the unredeemed. Calvin was the first major theologian habitually to differentiate God's corollary actions upon saved and reprobate souls.[9]

The need for the saints to distinguish signs of their salvation has been appreciated, of course, since the time of Max Weber, as an important and distinctive element in Calvinist culture. What has not been sufficiently emphasized, however, is the significance of the very real experience of reprobation for the Reformed soul. Calvin's doctrine sets out a cultural scheme of damnation, a "prescribed paranoia," as John Stachniewski calls it (18), a paranoia that makes the damnation of individual souls part of the unfathomable and unquestionable plan of the creation, with God as the all-powerful enemy who has designed to carry it out. For those who have the ill fortune to identify themselves as damned, the sense of persecution by an all-powerful agency cannot be dismissed as a personal, psychological distortion; it is rather an intellectually and socially determined role. "Religious despair," Stachniewski puts it, was in these circumstances "a rational response to unchallengeable tenets" (60).

Many suffered mightily from this despair, and found their experience reflected in the story of Francisco Spira, the Reformed Italian lawyer whose sense of reprobation led him to suicide after years of suffering (37–39). Robert Burton's *Anatomy of Melancholy* contains a vivid account of the torments of the self-convicted reprobate: "Many of them," Burton writes, "in their extremity think they hear and see visions, outcries, confer with devils, that they are tormented, possessed, and in hell-fire, already damned, quite forsaken of God, they have no sense or feeling of mercy or grace, hope of salvation, their sentence of condemnation is already past and not to be revoked, the devil will certainly have them."[10] Added to this sense of damna-

---

[8] Calvin, *Institutes*, 2:320.

[9] John Stachniewski, *The Persecutory Imagination: English Puritanism and the Literature of Religious Despair* (Oxford: Clarendon Press, 1991), 19.

[10] Robert Burton, *The Anatomy of Melancholy*, pt. 3, ed. Holbrook Jackson (New York: Vintage, 1977), 406. All of this chapter's quotations from the *Anatomy* are from this section.

tion, diabolic torment, and exclusion from light was, as Burton says, God's "heavy wrath." In this state of extremity the sufferers "are possessed, and through impatience they roar and howl, curse, blaspheme, deny God, call His power in question, abjure religion, and are still ready to offer violence unto themselves, by hanging, drowning, etc.; never any miserable wretch from the beginning of the world was in such a woeful case" (424).

It was, of course, far from Calvin's intention to inflict misery. He believed, like Luther, that his doctrine would be a tonic to those who were saved. He even exhibits tendentious solicitude for the spiritual misfortunes of those still suffering under Catholic perfectionism, especially those "most cruelly torn by this butchery" of Catholic confession and by the "anxieties" and "tortures" that "flayed helpless souls" taught to rely upon their own powers to keep God's law.[11] The trouble with Calvin's method of consolation, though, especially as it was to be developed by some of his English and American followers, was that although the saved and the damned were bent on entirely different paths, with every step in the one path being necessary to salvation, and every step in the other an inevitable movement toward hell, the two paths were remarkably similar. Both were marked by phases of hope and despair, though the hope of the reprobate was false and transient while the hope of the elect soul, no matter how often it failed, was true. It was therefore impossible to tell for certain whether one's faith was temporary and a product of self-deception or whether it was genuinely from God.[12] William Perkins, Calvin's most important English interpreter, even devised a chart showing that for each stage in the elected soul's progress toward salvation there was a counterfeit stage on the way to hell.[13]

The tendency to produce excesses of despair was a sore point of Reformed culture and a liability in the struggle with Rome. Pulpit oratory could lead to suicide, and in 1628 King Charles forbade the preaching of sermons on the most troubling doctrines (27). Burton took the view that, more than the obsessive contemplation of hell or the menacing passages in scripture, it was the preaching of "thundering ministers" that led to the most extreme desperation, when the "diseased souls" of the clergy infected the flock with their own melancholy about the signs of salvation and other "scrupulous points" about which they "intempestively rail" (399–400). The Catholic ministry was by ceremony and sacrament, the Protestant by oration, and, while the hell-fire of Protestant rhetoric has become a cliché, it is still shocking to recall the terms in which ministers from John Knox up to the time of Jonathan Edwards were willing to address their congregations. Pulpit orators like Edwards could communicate a sense of the nakedness and precariousness of sinners before God's wrath that is truly agonizing. Preaching in 1741, Edwards did not hesitate to tell his listeners that God was "a great deal more

[11] Calvin, *Institutes* 3:642.
[12] *Institutes* 3:10 and 12.
[13] Stachniewski, *Persecutory Imagination,* 164–65.

angry . . . with many that are now in this congregation . . . than he is with many of those that are now in the flames of hell," and that if none of them have died in their sleep that very night and awakened in hell, there is only God to thank.[14] Listening to Edwards, we are once again in the presence of those evil spirits who hovered about Burton's melancholy sufferers a hundred and twenty years earlier. "The devils watch them; they are ever by them, at their right hand; they stand waiting for them, like greedy hungry lions that see their prey. . . . The old serpent is gaping for them; hell opens its mouth wide to receive them."[15] What is most important, and the climax of Edwards's scene, is God's irresistible anger and complete lack of sympathy for those who do not repent in this life (even though their failure to repent is not their own doing but God's):

> O sinner! Consider the fearful danger you are in: it is a great furnace of wrath, a wide and bottomless pit, full of the fire of wrath, that you are held over in the hand of that God, whose wrath is provoked and incensed as much against you, as against many of the damned in hell: you hang by a slender thread, with the flames of divine wrath flashing about it, and ready every moment to singe it, and burn it asunder; and you have no interest in any Mediator, and nothing to lay hold of to save yourself, nothing to keep off the flames of wrath, nothing of your own, nothing that you ever have done, nothing that you can do, to induce God to spare you one moment. (318)

It would be impossible more vividly to illustrate the negative and frightening aspect of the powerlessness, utter heteronomy, rejection of mediation, and cosmic solitude that brought such comfort to Luther and Calvin.[16]

As Burton suggested, the torments envisioned in the pulpit were successfully communicated from preachers to their congregations. Edwards's listeners were seized with "an awful conviction of their sin and danger" as he spoke, and he had to silence their weeping in order to be heard.[17] A prominent suicide subsequently dampened the revival he had so painstakingly effected. John Bunyan's autobiography provides what is perhaps the most searing portrait of imagined reprobation. The spiritual serenity that marked

[14] Jonathan Edwards, "Sinners in the Hands of an Angry God," in *The Works of President Edwards in Four Volumes* (New York: Leavitt and Allen, 1855), 314.

[15] Edwards, "Sinners," 314–15.

[16] Frightening rhetoric on the theme of damnation was not, of course, anything like a Protestant monopoly, as Jean Delumeau has shown in *Le peché et la peur: la culpabilisation en Occident, XIIIe–XVIIIe siècles* (Paris: Fayard, 1983). The third chapter of James Joyce's *Portrait of the Artist as a Young Man* provides a late but striking example of the Catholic evocation of hell. It is not the intensity of Reformed rhetoric that is crucial but the hopelessness of changing God's will.

[17] Benjamin Trumbull, *A complete History of Connecticut, Civil and Ecclesiastical, from the emigration of its first planters, from England, in the year 1630, to the year 1764; and to the close of the Indian Wars,* 2 vols. (New Haven: Maltby, Goldsmith, 1818), 2:145.

his public mission was attained only after long struggle with the sense of damnation, including moments of the most intense and total exclusion from the good of creation, moments in which, he tells us, "methought I saw as if the sun that shineth in the heavens did grudge to give light, and as if the very stones in the street, and tiles upon the houses, did bend themselves against me; methought that they all combined together to banish me out of the world; I was abhorred of them, and unfit to dwell among them, or be partaker of their benefits, because I had sinned against the Saviour."[18]

Like any Christian work of spiritual confession, *Grace Abounding* is partly a self-authorizing fiction, partly an imitation of previous confessions in the line of Augustine. The narration of the great struggle serves to establish the preacher's credentials.[19] In the case of Bunyan, though, the subjective authenticity of the narrative is impossible altogether to deny, and especially that peculiarly painful dimension in which it differs from its great model. For while the struggle of Augustine's soul toward God is marked with many vacillations, there is nonetheless a clear teleological movement that governs the whole. The creature is drawn to a deeper and deeper recognition of its nature, gratefully discerning the hand of God at work in every moment of the past to bring him home to truth. It is an intellectual as well as a spiritual journey, and finds part of its reward in the great philosophical expositions of time and of memory that bring the work to a close. Bunyan's experience, by contrast, is one of radical oscillation between a conviction of salvation that he can scarcely manage to keep in mind and an overwhelming sense of sin that abolishes all but itself. At each reverse, Bunyan is back where he started, utterly excluded from light. The narrative ends with a list of seven abominations that remain with him still, tendencies of mind, beginning with unbelief, that recapitulate much of what has terrified him in the past. "I have wondered much at this one thing," he writes in his conclusion, "that though God doth visit my soul with never so blessed a discovery of himself, yet I have found again, that such hours have attended me afterwards, that I have been in my spirit so filled with darkness, that I could not so much as once conceive what that God and that comfort was with which I have been refreshed" (101–2).

The consoling purpose of Bunyan's narrative was to show that no amount of backsliding and vacillation on the part of the will could set one beyond the power of God's deliverance. Problems of the will were central to Reformed anxiety. The Catholic soul, endowed however imperfectly with the license of choice, could strive to set aside temptation and align itself with good. And when it failed it had the future: it was never too late for sin to be forgiven. Burton could not see how despair could overcome the papist, with such "easy rates and dispensations for all offences," such "comfortable remission" available to all (403–4). For the Reformed, however, no such self-

---

[18] John Bunyan, *Grace Abounding*, ed. G. B. Harrison (New York: Dutton, 1976), 58–59.
[19] Stachniewski, *Persecutory Imagination*, 44–46.

division was possible. Purity of heart, to recall Kierkegaard's formula, was to will one thing, but in this case it was a thing that cannot properly be willed, a belief and a feeling more than an action. The Reformed soul had to make itself a passive receptacle of God's influence, a theater of observation for his will, and any refractory impulse, no matter how small, could signify a radical departure from the creator. Reformed faith had to be far more perfect than Catholic works. One might not in truth be responsible for one's faith, but one was going to be treated in eternity as if one were.

This complex of ideas led to an obsession with self-observation and self-control that taxed the limits of mental discipline and prompted bizarre impulses of rebellion. Bunyan was tormented by the fear that he might betray Christ.

> Sometime it would run in my thoughts, not so little as a hundred times together, Sell him, sell him, sell him; against which I may say, for whole hours together, I have been forced to stand as continually leaning and forcing my spirit against it, lest haply, before I were aware, some wicked thought might arise in my heart that might consent thereto; and sometimes also the tempter would make me believe I had consented to it, then should I be as tortured upon a rack for whole days together. . . .
>
> But to be brief, one morning, as I did lie in my bed, I was, as at other times, most fiercely assaulted with this temptation, to sell and part with Christ; the wicked suggestion still running in my mind, Sell him, sell him, sell him, sell him, sell him, as fast as a man could speak; against which also, in my mind, as at other times, I answered, No, no, not for thousands, thousands, thousands, at least twenty times together. But at last, after much striving, even until I was almost out of breath, I felt this thought pass through my heart, Let him go, if he will! And I thought also, that I felt my heart freely consent thereto. Oh, the diligence of Satan! Oh, the desperateness of man's heart! (43–44)

Passages such as this strongly suggest a mind verging upon the extremes of melancholy and disease, but if so, it is a disease both meaningful and exemplary, a disease that merited inspired retelling for the instruction and comfort of others. In fact, it is the very extremity of Bunyan's case that makes it significant.

In cases like Bunyan's, when the soul finds itself at the limit of self-possession, internally divided and wracked by stray impulses against the rigors of perfection, we might expect scripture to be a comforting resource, as it was for those who could fix their hopes on the assurances granted to the saved. But for those like Bunyan who were uncertain of their spiritual gifts, the fate of the damned pressed home with extraordinary force, and these doubts and fears came armed with the weapons of scripture, showing "It is a fearful thing to fall into the hands of the living God."[20] Not only did such

[20] Heb. 10:31, quoted in *Grace Abounding,* 52–53.

passages strike terror into Bunyan's heart, as they had done more than a century earlier in the heart of the monk Luther; they also became for him "most fearful and terrible presences" by which, in his times of torment, he was "greatly affrighted." When God had comforted him, however, he "found their visage changed; for they looked not so grimly on me as before I thought they did" (69–70). The Bible itself, therefore, harbored for Bunyan a great host of persecuting presences. Even more disturbing, the passages of hope and despair became so closely integrated with his moods, or "frames of spirit," as he calls them, that he began to associate them not only with the thoughts they contained but also with the feelings they evoked in him, so that they actually became like living inhabitants of his psyche. Morbidly obsessed with the dismal implications of the story of Esau, who sold his birthright, Bunyan conceives the hope of cure by means of a curious inner alchemy of texts.

> And I remember one day, as I was in diverse frames of spirit, and considering that these frames were still according to the nature of the several scriptures that came in upon my mind; if this of grace, then was I quiet; but if that of Esau, then tormented; Lord, thought I, if both these scriptures would meet in my heart at once, I wonder which of them would get the better of me. So methought I had a longing mind that they might come both together upon me; yea, I desired of God they might. (66)

This is surely a remarkable passage. The passivity of the will, the sense of being controlled even by the words of others, has become nearly absolute, the one hope for the sufferer being that the right words will prevail in that obscure conflict within the heart. The destiny of the soul is being decided elsewhere in the remote being of an unfathomable God or in the turbidity of inner depths. We can see why the externalism of the allegorical form of *Pilgrim's Progress* held such appeal for Bunyan and for his audience. However full of snares might be the way to the Heavenly City, however difficult, at times, to tell the agents of good from ill, Pilgrim himself stands forth as a discrete and integral self setting a united front toward the dangers of the spiritual world. He witnesses vocations for salvation and damnation and sees all comfortingly glossed with applications of God's word. There is no ambiguity or inner distance, a great comfort for souls so tempestuously driven by the terrors of the Word, and with so few defenses of their own.[21]

Luther and his descendants altered the scale at which the human character stands in spiritual space. If the romantic rebel or existential hero of later

---

[21] It is possible, however, to see the narrative form of *Pilgrim's Progress* not as a relief from Reformed self-suspicion but an intensification of it deploying the metaphor of the journey itself as a temptation. See Stanley E. Fish, *Self-Consuming Artifacts: The Experience of Seventeenth-Century Literature* (Berkeley: University of California Press, 1972), 224–64.

imagination could raise a fist toward an empty sky, it was partly because Luther had obliterated the terrestrial landmarks and left the mortal agent contending with God alone. The process was one of elevation and expansion but also of degradation; it produced a heightening of spiritual intensity and a baleful loss of control. And because the God that emerged was a God of simple power, a figure of unfathomable will, so the being created in his image became unfathomable even to itself. The same expansion of distance into which the hidden God made his withdrawal also opened the inner dimension of the psychological—two reciprocal vanishing points at an absolute remove.

The Renaissance stage shows the fruits of this transformation. We need not ascribe to the works in which they appear a strictly Reformed theology to see in the most impressive figures of the English drama a fatal sense of grandeur and an irresistible corruption that mark their affinity with Reformation thought. Hamlet, Macbeth, Faustus, de Bosola, Beatrice Joanna, and Antony (in *Antony and Cleopatra*), to name just a few, all find themselves struggling at once with inner and outer forces. They battle as much for self-possession as for power in the world, their fates "hid midst things corruptible," to recall Middleton's phrase, their resistance to temptation fruitless, merely intellectual, and their renunciations and repentance quite impotent. The case is even clearer with the heroines and heroes of the Jansenist Racine. Inner compulsion has become the new force of destiny that enables the resurgence of tragedy in this age. The spectacle is one of treacherous depravity, yet a depravity that permits its bearers surprisingly to remain within the reach of human identification. These destinies transfix and mesmerize an audience which, out of training and experience, can readily believe in the spectacle of souls caught in the grip of impulses irremediably beyond their control.[22]

I have been emphasizing the negative aspects of Protestant psychology, the aspects that make paranoia at home—the recognition of control from outside, the neat division of the world into good and evil, the focus upon signs of hidden operations, the replacement of the apparent by the true reality, the grandiosity of the justified and the validation to be derived from the hostility of the Enemy. There was, of course, another side, a side that emphasized the sanctification of God's chosen, the joys and comforts of the spirit, and even the earthly foretaste of heavenly bliss. A fair account of the broader range of Protestant spirituality must take into account not only the violence

---

[22] As Stachniewski has it, "the villain-hero, structurally soliciting sympathy while morally reprobated, is . . . a product, as much as anything else, of a new category of human identity to which Calvinist discourse, in concert with the conditions that provided its opening, gave birth" (342–43). See "*Dr. Faustus* and Puritan Culture," chap. 7 of *The Persecutory Imagination;* "Calvinist Psychology in *Macbeth*," *Shakespeare Studies* 20 (1988): 169–84; and "Calvinist Psychology in Middleton's Tragedies," in *Three Jacobean Revenge Tragedies: The Revenger's Tragedy, Women Beware Women, The Changeling: A Casebook,* ed. R. V. Holdsworth (Basingstoke: Macmillan Education, 1990), 226–47.

of Luther, Donne, and Edwards but also the grave tenderness of George Herbert, the wide sympathies of Milton, and the mystical innocence of Traherne. It is also potentially misleading to exaggerate the degree of difference between the Catholic and Protestant elements of Christianity. Even if the first, enthusiastic generations of Reform had achieved the almost complete rejection of Catholic culture that they envisioned—which they did not—they were still building upon the same Christian basis as the culture they rejected, and much of their effort was spent in rebuilding the existing structure from materials that had been only partially altered. Nevertheless, on the issue of agency the change of emphasis was indeed a radical one. The renunciation of agency and its enforcement and the negation of human value had become the new, active modes of self-assertion, and, as we will see, this new paradigm of action was gradually extended to other spheres of cultural activity.

6

The Science of Suspicion

The tenuousness of self-possession that afflicted the Reformed soul was implicit in Luther's original attack upon confession. Confession could not work in the Lutheran account because it implied both a power and a knowledge that the soul could not actually possess, sin not being as transparent as the Catholics made it seem, but rather hidden in a dark place, beyond self-knowledge. This was why it was so difficult to establish the character of any one person's relation to God. The fate of the Christian community, though, and God's true church, seemed more palpably accessible to knowledge, since God had reformed his church for the benefit of the saved. This apparent certainty, however, was a source of greater difficulties to post-Reformation culture than the inner ambiguities of salvation, for the scope and membership of the true Christian community proved by no means easy to fix.

The Reformation began with a radical and total exclusion, directed not only against the decadent establishment of the present but embracing hundreds, even a thousand years of past hypocrisy and corruption. This grand exclusion brought with it a new conception of history. Medieval historical writing had been a comparatively minor adjunct to theology. Its function, as Anthony Kemp suggests, was to cope with the elapse of centuries, while establishing the essential continuity of the church back to the time of Christ.[1] Luther and his followers, having brought historical consciousness to the center of Christian concern, transformed its character. History became a parade of innovation, falsity, delusion, rupture, disintegration, and fall. The goal of Christians living in this historical nightmare must therefore be to awaken from it, free themselves from corrupt institutions and false idols, and return

---

[1] Anthony Kemp, chap. 1 in *The Estrangement of the Past: A Study in the Origins of Historical Consciousness* (New York: Oxford University Press, 1991).

to God. The search for the inner alignment with truth was indissoluble from the mission to establish a community of true believers who could throw off the temptations of Babylon in order to seek God's peace.

Such was the founding Protestant gesture. As Kemp succinctly puts it, "The elegance of the scheme is that it justifies revolution while denying innovation" (87). Its drawback, though, was that it made every innovation into a revolution. Time was now swollen with error, the ages of the past pregnant with nothing but error, and to depart from the stasis of orthodoxy by any novel gesture, any false step forward, was immediately to plunge all the way backwards to the original abyss. Thus, rather than setting up a counterpoint of stability against Catholic decadence, what Luther unleashed was a torrent of schismatic innovation. The rhetoric of purity and decadence proved infinitely adaptable, and the purity of one sect easily, almost inevitably, became the contamination of the next.

Luther thus replaced the static history of the church with a dynamic one. When we turn, therefore, from the question of personal salvation to the historical realm, we must alter to some degree our account of agency in the Protestant mode. Whereas the Reformers denied the efficacy of works and thus deprived the church of the grounds of its own claim to power, they did endow that church with a new kind of power, to be the agent of historical change, even if this change was in itself necessarily corrupt, a devolution. Such change needed constantly to be resisted, and so now it was the Protestant's turn to deny history while combating innovation wherever it was to be found. The sectarian conflict that ensued resulted in almost two hundred years of invective and bloodshed, first between Catholic and Protestant but quickly descending among the sects of reformers themselves; this pattern of schism and violence was to exert a decisive influence upon the character of modern culture. Each schism expanded the burden of history that the next had to leave behind. The progress of time became an ever-mounting indictment of the human character. With regard to salvation, men and women were impotent, but with regard to damnation and corruption, they showed themselves demonically gifted.

The drama of salvation was displaced, therefore, to the battleground of history, with a new kind of agency on earth, a kind that was efficacious primarily in doing ill. Preoccupied with the need to oppose this agency of evil and protect the Christian community, embattled souls turned with great relief from their conscientious bouts with Satan to the outer struggle with his worldly deputies. The intensity of Protestant inwardness lent itself immediately to the vigor of Protestant aggression, and it is this intensity of suspicious scrutiny in all directions that is characteristic. Just as behind one's own conscious motives there might well be secret sin, so behind the apparently good intentions of others, Satan's hand must certainly be in force. Negative theology gave birth to negative history.

It was particularly among the Reformed that the socially transformative aspects of Protestant culture were expressed. "The saints," writes Michael

Walzer, "saw themselves as divine *instruments* and theirs was the politics of wreckers, architects, and builders—hard at work upon the political world. They refused to recognize any inherent or natural resistance to their labors. They treated every obstacle as another example of the devil's resourcefulness and they summoned all their energy, imagination, and craft to overcome it."[2] The saints of the revolutionary period took it upon themselves to bring discipline not only to their own behavior but to society as well: their revolutionary form of religion "trained them to think of the struggle with Satan and his allies as an extension and duplicate of their internal spiritual conflicts, and also as a difficult and continuous war, requiring methodical, organized activity, military exercise, and discipline" (290). The saints of Reform in Walzer's account brought system and rule to the war against Satan, and thought of their existence fundamentally as the life-long pursuit of a world-historical struggle with the devil (290–92). Along with the humiliation of the agent that we have seen as the center of Luther's vision, then, there came a new heroism—the heroism of the instrument, suppressing its own unruly urges in order to fight in the service of a higher cause and in resistance to a greater enemy. And where Luther saw God's sanction behind the established authorities by the mere virtue of their existence, the revolutionary advocates of Reform saw God's sanction behind the impulse to rebellion by the mere virtue of its existence. There was no check, then, upon rebellion in the service of God. This heroic vision was confirmed in struggle. It began with the celebration of exile, persecution, and martyrdom, recapitulated with great artistry, for instance, in Foxe's *Book of Martyrs*. It was to culminate several decades later in regicide and civil war.

To Francis Bacon and to others of his generation, it was evident that, as he put it, sects in religion were the greatest of the "vicissitudes of things"— "For those orbs rule in men's minds most."[3] It was Bacon's mission, however, to turn men's minds away from these ruinous distractions, the "overweening and turbulent humours of these times,"[4] and redirect them toward their proper goal on earth, which was the improvement of human life and the increase of human power. By bringing "reform" to the sphere of natural knowledge, Bacon extended into the history of philosophical thought the Reformation critique of Catholic idealism as self-intoxicated fantasy and interested fiction. Taking "all knowledge" as a "province" under his protection and surveying it with ostentatious care,[5] he found there a "universal madness,"[6] a system of delusions so extensive and so long established as to have

---

[2] Michael Walzer, *The Revolution of the Saints: A Study in the Origins of Radical Politics* (Cambridge: Harvard University Press, 1965), 3.

[3] "Of Vicissitudes of Things," in *Francis Bacon: A Critical Edition of the Major Works*, ed. Brian Vickers (New York: Oxford, 1996), 452.

[4] "An Advertisement Touching the Controversies of the Church of England," in *Bacon: A Critical Edition*, 2.

[5] "Letter to Lord Burghley," in *Bacon: A Critical Edition*, 20.

[6] "The Masculine Birth of Time, or, The Great Instauration of the Dominion of Man over

become orthodox. Bacon's approach, therefore, had to be radical, nothing less than to "try the whole thing anew upon a better plan, and to commence a total reconstruction of sciences, arts, and all human knowledge, raised upon the proper foundations."[7]

In the *Advancement of Learning,* Bacon catalogues with unforgettable vividness the primary constituents of the orthodox system of delusions as it had come down to his own day: the "fantastical learning" of the alchemists, magicians, and astrologers, which unites "imposture and credulity"; the "delicate learning" of the humanist rhetoricians, of which Bacon gives a superb if misleading historical account centering upon the influence of the Reformation; and, most trenchantly, the "contentious learning" of the "schoolmen," who, with their "vermiculate questions" breeding one out of the other, "their wits being shut up in the cells of a few authors (chiefly Aristotle their dictator) as their persons are shut up in the cells of monasteries and colleges; and knowing little history, either of nature or time, did out of no great quantity of matter, and infinite agitation of wit, spin out unto us those laborious . . . cobwebs of learning, admirable in the fineness of thread and work, but of no substance or profit."[8] With this satiric portrait of scholasticism, Bacon gives new and pointed direction to what was already a long polemical tradition.

Bacon's critique is not limited to particular errors but extends to the natural capacity for knowledge itself. Suspicion, therefore, becomes his crucial resource. "Let every student of nature take this as a rule—that whatever his mind seizes and dwells upon with peculiar satisfaction is to be held in suspicion."[9] This rule conveys the essence of the Baconian attitude, a fundamental mistrust of our intellectual instrument. Defenders of the capacity for human knowledge had long asserted a natural fitness between the objects to be known and the mind that knows them. This fitness stems from the nature of the human being, which is to be the master of the natural world or even the fulfillment of its telos as a knowable order. Bacon, however, moves to the other extreme, seeing in the mind a natural unfitness for knowledge, evidence of inborn "Idols of the Tribe." The mind, he warns, "mixes up its own nature with the nature of things" and prefers its own "anticipations" to reality.[10] This tendency has sustained the system of delusions that Bacon finds in place from the time of Aristotle, through that of the scholastics, up to his own day. "Anticipations," appealing to the will as they do, can become "a

---

the Universe," in *The Philosophy of Francis Bacon: An Essay on Its Development from 1603 to 1609 with New Translations of Fundamental Texts,* trans. Benjamin Farrington (Liverpool: Liverpool University Press, 1964), 62.

[7] *The Great Instauration,* in *The Works of Francis Bacon,* ed. James Spedding et al. (Boston: Taggard & Thompson, 1863), 18.

[8] *Bacon: A Critical Edition,* 140.

[9] *The New Organon,* in *Works,* ed. Spedding, 8:86.

[10] *The Great Instauration,* in *Works,* 8:45.

ground sufficiently firm for consent,"[11] and men would rather agree with each other on the basis of a mutually pleasing fantasy than surrender their wishes to the reality of the world before them.

Bacon's critique highlights the weakness of human inquirers. They prefer the affirmative to the negative, the hopeful to the actual. They believe what strikes them with sudden force in preference to the results of patient investigation. Making use of the senses, they give too much credit to what is in front of them; making use of the intellect, they respect no limit of speculation, being unable to restrain themselves from following the chain of imaginary causes. The mischances of private experience and individual temperament, "Idols of the Cave," augment the confusion. Those who have been steeped in one mode of inquiry apply its tincture to the others. One mind hungers for resemblance, another for difference. All of these general and particular vagaries combine to create the great philosophical systems, the "Idols of the Theatre," which, like "stories invented for the stage," are "more compact and elegant, and more as one would wish them to be, than true stories out of history" (90). Finally, this world of wish-fulfillment is supported by the tyranny of words, "The Idols of the Marketplace." With a natural adherence to established concepts and habits of thinking, words keep the orthodox delusions solidly in place.

The convergence between the Reformation critique and Bacon's will be evident, as well as Bacon's debt to the humanists, whose excessive absorption in rhetoric he condemns. The center of his insight is a moral one, that human nature is imbued with a "natural though corrupt love of the lie itself." This love of the lie gives its energy to the very life of the mind: "A mixture of a lie doth ever add pleasure. Doth any man doubt, that if there were taken out of men's minds vain opinions, flattering hopes, false valuations, imaginations as one would, and the like, but it would leave the minds of a number of men poor shrunken things, full of melancholy and indisposition, and unpleasing to themselves?"[12]

It is easy to recognize in Bacon's conception an anticipation of Freud's distinction between the "pleasure principle" and the "principle of reality."[13] Both are inverted versions of Plato's intellectual Eros. In Plato's conception, Eros is always a dangerous force, for the soul in this world finds itself perpetually surrounded by unworthy objects of attraction. The remedy is the conversion of the soul, its turning away from false objects of love toward the true one. In the Christian version, of course, this true object is God. Bacon is novel in his suggestion that, for the true knowledge to be obtained, the in-

---

[11] *The New Organon*, in *Works*, 8:73.

[12] "Of Truth," in *Bacon: A Critical Edition*, 341.

[13] The key element is that, with the "pleasure principle," as with the Baconian philosophy "as one would," the delight of the fantasy itself is what sustains its interest, rather than any relation to the external world.

tellectual Eros itself must actually be overcome; rather than being redirected toward its proper object, its influence must be resisted or suppressed.

> The human understanding is no dry light, but receives an infusion from the will and affections; whence proceed sciences which may be called "sciences as one would." For what a man had rather were true he more readily believes. Therefore he rejects difficult things from impatience of research; sober things, because they narrow hope; the deeper things of nature, from superstition; the light of experience, from arrogance and pride, lest his mind should seem to be occupied with things mean and transitory; things not commonly believed, out of deference to the opinion of the vulgar. Numberless in short are the ways, and sometimes imperceptible, in which the affections colour and infect the understanding.[14]

It is evident from this passage that the failure to reach true knowledge is not simply an intellectual failure but also a moral and, ultimately, a spiritual one. Those who prefer to see the world the way they wish it to be rather than the way it is are setting their own intellectual creations above the works of God. The punishment that follows is proportionate to the crime, for by failing to give our attention to God's true creation, we lose our power to control it, so that "our dominion over creatures is a second time forfeited."[15]

"Nature to be commanded must be obeyed"—this is Bacon's central maxim.[16] Given the portrait of human nature that he has drawn, we can expect it will be supremely difficult for human beings to follow. To succeed in the project of inquiry one must separate oneself from all influence of tradition, all concern with the thoughts of others, all self-concern, and all natural inclination, in order to devote oneself entirely to the facts themselves. These facts constitute a natural world framed not in attunement with the human mind but, as Bacon puts it, like a labyrinth, full of "deceitful resemblances" and "ambiguities of way."[17] Much of the time Bacon professes a strategic humility about his own power to overcome such difficulties. "I am wont for my own part to regard this work as a child of time rather than of wit," he writes in the "Epistle Dedicatory" to the *New Organon,* "the only wonder being that the first notion of the thing, and such great suspicions concerning matters long established, should have come into any man's mind" (23). In this official vein of humility, Bacon's "great suspicions" come upon him almost unawares. There is more than a little grandeur, though, in the way he portrays the task of inquiry, guided by "the everlasting love of truth."

---

[14] *New Organon,* in *Works,* 8:82.
[15] "Description of a Natural and Experimental History Such As may Serve for the Foundation of a True Philosophy," in *Works,* 9:370–71.
[16] *New Organon,* in *Works,* 8:68.
[17] *Great Instauration,* in *Works,* 8:32.

For my own part at least, in obedience to the everlasting love of truth, I have committed myself to the uncertainties and difficulties and solitudes of the ways, and relying on the divine assistance have upheld my mind both against the shocks and embattled ranks of opinion, and against my own private and inward hesitations and scruples, and against the fogs and clouds of nature, and the phantoms flitting about on every side; in the hope of providing at last for the present and future generations guidance more faithful and secure. Wherein if I have made any progress, the way has been opened to me by no other means than the true and legitimate humiliation of the human spirit. For all those who before me have applied themselves to the invention of arts have but cast a glance or two upon facts and examples and experience, and straightway proceeded, as if invention were nothing more than an exercise of thought, to invoke their own spirits to give them oracles. (33–34)

The "true and legitimate humiliation of the human spirit" is the secret of Bacon's heroism and his knowledge. For him, just as for Luther, only when one relinquishes all claim to the value of one's own creative force can one hope to put oneself into the proper relation with God's will. One is delivered, therefore, by means of submission, from the "Idols" and "oracles" that bedevil the human character, and one can set oneself on the side of the true God. As in the service of all masters, pride leads to humiliation, humility to favor.

Bacon's God does not demand, like Luther's, an assent to the majesty of a paradoxical will or to an incomprehensible justice.[18] The strangeness now is all on the side of the human imagination, with its bizarre proliferation of schemes, the "mimic and fabulous worlds" of the philosophers, whereas, in the eyes of a natural philosophy properly established, God's creation is nothing other than what simply exists; those who want to know it "must go to facts themselves for everything."[19] It was no small part of Bacon's achievement to have adapted the religious rhetoric of humility to the defense of natural inquiry. Science in the Baconian manner becomes not simply acceptable to religion but a part of it, a gift, in fact, of the spirit, and Bacon himself is a "true priest of the sense."[20] Like Luther, he has made a virtue of exemplary self-suppression: "I interpose everywhere admonitions and scruples and cautions, with a religious care to eject, repress, and, as it were, exorcise every kind of phantasm" (50). It is a mark of Bacon's success that scientists continue to employ the rhetoric of self-discipline and humility even in conflicts with religion itself.

[18] Bacon's own religious outlook was, however, very much of the Reformed type, as shown by his personal "Confession of Faith." *Bacon: A Critical Edition*, 107–12.

[19] *Great Instauration, Works*, 8:46.

[20] *Great Instauration, Works*, 8:44. The fulfillment of Bacon's priestly purpose "is as the strewing and decoration of the bridal chamber of the Mind and the Universe, the Divine Goodness assisting." *Great Instauration, Works*, 8:46.

Many later analysts of modernity would see damage to human nature in the methods and findings of modern science. While it strengthened our control over the physical world, science threatened to destroy the mind's belief in its own creations. It is a mark of the peculiar historical ambivalence of Nietzsche and Freud that both of them advocated science as a worldview and as a model of human inquiry while believing at the same time that it could lead to nihilism or paranoia. Bacon does not suffer from this ambivalence. In his account, the results of inquiry exact no subsequent renunciations, only give benefits, and we cannot imagine him uttering Donne's lament about the destruction of the medieval world picture—"'Tis all in pieces, all coherence gone." Rather, for Bacon it is the renunciation that comes first. The findings of Baconian natural philosophy are the fruits of renunciation, the first fruits of philosophic discipline. Bacon's urge to destroy the human past has no bounds because he is God's servant in the endeavor. He is throwing off the bondage of impotence imposed by the false lights of others and taking possession of his unfallen humanity.

Bacon was aware of the difficulty of convincing his contemporaries that all past authorities should be treated with suspicion—their intellectual schemes not just imperfect but worthless, their influence "the dazzle of an alien and intrusive beam."[21] He could not offer discoveries of his own to prove his case; the arsenal at his command consisted almost entirely of satire, utopian projection, innovations of method, and critique. Bacon's rhetorical accomplishment looks even more astonishing when we remember that he himself did not recognize, as some of his contemporaries were able to do, the value of what seem to us to be the decisive scientific achievements of the age—the discoveries of Copernicus, Kepler, and Galileo. It was rather to practical innovations he could point as evidence of the benefits of science. His favorite examples were printing, gunpowder, and the compass.[22] In the early sketches for his program we see him experimenting with the problem of how to couch his "sweeping rejection of opinions and authorities" (117) in a way that would not itself seem like a fantasy. Here Bacon is not yet the suave and generally self-effacing expositor of the published works, but a self-consciously profound revolutionary, lecturing, sometimes in fictive guise, to unripe ephebes. Mere satire against the ancients, he admits, will not suffice for his purpose, "the metal of these errors" being "too firmly set to yield to satire" (103). Nor will it be possible simply to "drop all arts and subterfuges" and launch into a description of the "legitimate method" of natural philosophy itself, "when all the approaches and entrances to men's minds are beset and blocked by the most obscure idols—idols deeply implanted and, as it were, burned in." "Frenzied men," he warns in another

---

[21] "The Refutation of Philosophies" ("Redargutio Philosophiarum," 1608), in Farrington, *Philosophy of Francis Bacon,* 107. Parenthetical references in this and the next five paragraphs are from this text.

[22] *New Organon,* in *Works,* 8:162.

place, "are exacerbated by violent opposition but may be beguiled by art."[23] Furthermore, the art he seeks cannot be the art of dialectic, not only for the reason that he is dealing with "frenzied men" who cannot bear to be opposed but because there is not enough intellectual ground in common between the old philosophy and the new to make dialectic possible. "The difficulty is that the usual rules of argument do not apply since we are not agreed on first principles," Bacon's mouthpiece tells his fictive audience in the *Refutation of Philosophies.* "Even the hope of a basis of discussion is precluded, since I cast doubt on the forms of proof now in use and mean to attack them. In the present mental climate, I cannot safely entrust the truth to you. Your understandings must be prepared before they can be instructed; your minds need healing before they can be exercised" (108–9). The claim would remain an important element in the mature statement of Bacon's program in the *Novum Organum,* where he asserts about his opponents that "since we agree neither upon principles nor upon demonstrations there is no place for argument."[24] There is simply no way, then, for those who think in the old ways to do justice to Bacon's mode of procedure. In this manner he can reject the authority of the past as representing the jurisdiction of a "tribunal which is itself on trial" (8:75).

In making the assertion that true science as he describes it and the sciences of the past are of completely different kinds and can never be brought before the same tribunal, Bacon might seem to be anticipating Thomas Kuhn's notion of science as an activity carried out within "paradigms" whose languages and practices are "incommensurable" and whose practitioners are "living in different worlds." There is a family resemblance between Bacon's "tribunals" and Kuhn's "paradigms," but the relation between the two of them is not one of anticipation. Rather, the sense created by Bacon that there was a deep and total rupture between the classical and the modern traditions of science is part of what made Kuhn's theory seem at first so persuasive and attractive, especially to intellectuals in disciplines outside the philosophy of science. The Baconian sense of rupture reiterated by Kuhn is part of the mythology of the modern, though by putting the methods of modern science on the same footing as the self-enclosed and self-justifying "paradigms" of classical science, Kuhn was practicing a self-inclusive irony unknown to Bacon, the fruit, as we shall see, of later seventeenth-century developments.[25]

If Bacon cannot expect justice from the tribunals of the past, which he condemns, neither does he feel bound to give them any more than a rough justice of his own. The form that this justice takes is of great importance for

[23] "The Masculine Birth of Time," in *Philosophy of Francis Bacon,* 62.

[24] *New Organon, Works,* 8:89.

[25] See Thomas S. Kuhn, *The Structure of Scientific Revolutions,* 2nd ed., enlarged (Chicago: University of Chicago Press, 1970). For a critique focusing upon Kuhn's exaggerated sense of rupture, see Larry Laudan, *Science and Values: The Aims of Science and Their Role in Scientific Debate, Pittsburgh Series in Philosophy and History of Science,* vol. 11 (Berkeley: University of California Press, 1984), 67–102.

our subject. Bacon's solution is to begin the discrediting of his opponents not through an attack on the substance of their thought but through the discernment of discouraging "signs." This was the process by which he believed he could shake the hold of the authorities on the minds of his contemporaries.[26] As the lecturer in the *Refutation* puts it,

> I must not attempt a direct, abrupt encounter with things themselves, for they need to be approached by opening up and levelling a special path on account of the inveterate prejudices and obsessions of our minds. To ignore this would be to betray myself. Therefore I must devise an approach in keeping with my purpose. First I shall adduce certain "signs" which will put us in a position to pass judgment on philosophies. Then, with a view to undermining their authority, I shall point out, within the philosophies themselves, certain monstrous errors and intellectual absurdities. (103)

It was not lost upon Bacon that such a procedure, not to "discuss the essence of things but try to draw some tentative conclusions from external 'signs,'" is characteristic of the very naïveté and vulgarity of thought he is attempting to combat. In this case, however, he is willing to embrace the irony: "Let us assume the character of simple folk. . . . In this at least we shall be acting like common men." Looking for the first "sign," he asks, about these Greeks who have dominated the intellectual life of two millennia, "But what sort of people were they? I mean to go in for no abuse. I shall neither repeat nor imitate what others have said. I am content simply to remark that that nation was always precipitate mentally and professorial by habit—two characteristics inimical to wisdom and truth" (109).

Having established the national character of the first philosophers, Bacon looks for a second "sign" to the "character of the age in which philosophy was born and launched on its career."

> It took its rise . . . in an age that bordered on fables, was poor in historical knowledge, was little informed or enlightened by travel and knowledge of the earth, lacked both the respect for antiquity and the wealth of our modern times, and was deficient in dignity and precedent. We are free indeed, to believe that there were divine heroes in ancient times with wisdom loftier than the common condition of mankind. But it must be conceded that our age, even making no claims for the labours of great minds and the fruit of their mediations, enjoys in comparison with the past the experience of some two thousand years of history and the knowledge of two-thirds of the surface of the globe. (109)

---

[26] See Paulo Rossi, chap. 2 in *Francis Bacon: From Magic to Science* (Chicago: University of Chicago Press, 1968).

It is especially the limitation of Greek experience that is crucial for Bacon—"within what narrow confines the great intellects of those ages moved, or were shut in." Their travels were "mere suburban excursions," whereas since then "new worlds have come to light" (110).

Finally, Bacon turns to the consideration of the philosophers as individuals, and here he launches one of his earliest attacks on the figure who was to be his favorite target, Aristotle, the breeder of a "mental epidemic that sweeps like the plague through mankind."[27] It was Aristotle above all who had bewildered the wits of humankind by instilling in them a habit of logic that drew them away from the things they knew rather than toward them. In Aristotle, as in Aristotle's master, Alexander, Bacon finds an extreme egotism and contentiousness. He never tires of comparing him with the Ottoman Turks who strangled all their brothers upon access to the throne.[28] As the portrait of Aristotle develops from work to work, the Greek philosopher begins to sound more than a little like Bacon himself, proceeding "in such a spirit of difference and contradiction towards all antiquity; undertaking not only to frame new words of science at pleasure, but to confound and extinguish all ancient wisdom; insomuch as he never nameth or mentioneth an ancient author or opinion, but to confute and reprove; wherein for glory, and drawing followers and disciples, he took the right course."[29] It is hard to fathom how Bacon thought he could escape his resemblance to this unflattering portrayal of his opponent until we recall his constant protestations of humility, his disclaimers of comparison with the ancients, theirs being a course completely different from his, and his assertion that his method depended not upon great individual wits, in which he concedes superiority to the ancients, but only upon a constant, mechanical application of method.

By the time the speaker in the *Refutation of Philosophies* has finished reading the "signs" of ancient times and comparing them with his own, he is ready for a grand peroration: "Shake off the chains which oppress you," he tells his listeners, "and be masters of yourselves." This could be the voice of Luther, exhorting freedom from the demonic powers of Rome, but Luther would not have gone on to make Bacon's bold claim for the merits of his followers and their age.

Second only to your own merit, surely nothing can give you greater courage than reflection on the enterprise, good fortune, and great exploits of our own age. Not for nothing have we opposed our modern "There is more beyond" to the "Thus far and no further" of antiquity. The thunderbolt is inimitable, said the ancients. In defiance of them we

---

[27] "The Refutation of Philosophies," in *Philosophy of Francis Bacon*, 114.

[28] See "Thoughts and Conclusions," in *Philosophy of Francis Bacon*, 84, for an early example of this favorite Baconian jibe.

[29] *The Advancement of Learning*, in Vickers, *Bacon: A Critical Edition*, 193–94. Bacon tries to avoid the coining of new terms, preferring the more politic method of giving new meanings to the old ones.

have proclaimed it imitable, and that not wildly but like sober men, on the evidence of our new engines. Nay, we have succeeded in imitating the heaven, whose property it is to encircle the earth; for this we have done by our voyages. It would disgrace us, now that the wide spaces of the material globe, the lands and seas, have been broached and explored, if the limits of the intellectual globe should be set by the narrow discoveries of the ancients.[30]

In this passage the true protagonist of Bacon's adventure emerges—not mere men but the age. Just as it was the ages and circumstances of the past, combined with the foibles of human nature, that prevented inquirers of the past from making contact with Nature in itself, so this new age of discoveries and wonders makes possible a new science with new ends. These include not the mere contemplation of Nature but its transformation, and with it a transformation of life itself. What Bacon envisioned was not a mere advance in knowledge, but a thoroughgoing triumph over the disabilities of human nature, an almost complete reversal of the Fall.[31]

The list of scientific ambitions given at the end of *The New Atlantis* still captures the modern dream of science, including "The prolongation of life. / The restitution of youth in some degree. / The retardation of age. / The curing of diseases counted incurable. / The mitigation of pain. . . . / Making of new species. . . . / Instruments of destruction, as of war and poison."[32] Escaping from the oppression of the past would bring an extraordinary access of power. Without the Baconian method, were "all the wits of all the ages" gathered together and all the resources of humankind hereafter dedicated to science, no result would come of it, while, with the proper compilation of "natural and experimental history," "the investigation of nature, and the sciences" would be "the work of a few years."[33]

With the aid of this utopian vision, Bacon's calculated reading of "signs" achieved an astonishing success. Previous critics of the intellect such as the Pyrrhonists had catalogued its deficiencies, often, as we have seen, to end in skepticism and resignation. Bacon saw his likeness with these authors but could not bear the passivity of their conclusions.[34] The discounting of the intellect seemed to him one of the greatest symptoms of intellectual vanity and one of the greatest obstacles to progress. Where Bacon departs from previous inquirers is that he seeks not reasons to doubt but causes of error. He wishes not merely to observe our susceptibility to error but to overcome it.

[30] "The Refutation of Philosophies," *Philosophy of Francis Bacon*, 131. The "thunderbolt" is gunpowder, which comprised, as we have noted, along with the printing press and the compass, one of Bacon's three chief examples of the fertility of modern invention.

[31] *New Organon, Works*, 8:350.

[32] *The New Atlantis*, in *Bacon: A Critical Edition*, 488–89.

[33] "Description of a Natural and Experimental History Such As may Serve for the Foundation of a True Philosophy," in *Works* 8:354–55.

[34] *New Organon, Works*, 8:75–76.

At the same time, error becomes yet another object to be explained, another part of Nature to be traced by "signs" to its sources in racial, historical, and personal characteristics. This is why it is so important for Bacon to establish that the new philosophy and the old cannot be brought onto the same intellectual plane—the one, he hopes, will demonstrate its fitness in reason, while the other will be connected to reality only as a thing that itself requires explaining.

Bacon mapped out a vast territory of error, geographically and historically situated, and new principles by which it could be intellectually mastered. These are the principles, now familiar to us, of sociological and psychological reduction. At the same time he asserted a new method of thinking that he hoped would save modernity from this "dictatorship"[35] of delusion and slavish imitation, a method that would level all inquirers and liberate them from the private distortions of the mind. As for his theory of induction, which is his primary claim to scientific recognition, the most remarkable thing about it is that it is far closer in spirit to the method of Aristotle and to that of Aristotle's medieval continuators, Robert Grosseteste and Roger Bacon, than it is to the procedures of modern science. Bacon simply did not know the work of his theoretical precursors very well. Within the inductive tradition he was not an important contributor.[36]

Bacon's strongest claim to influence upon the practice of science has to do with his emphasis upon experiment; here he does stand as an inaugurator of the empirical strain in post-seventeenth-century inquiry. But this inauguration was something of a mixed blessing, for Bacon's mistrust of mathematics and deductive reasoning made him suspicious of the very science that was being transformed with brilliant results during his lifetime. The speculative daring of Copernicus, Kepler, Galileo, and Newton, their neo-Pythagorean mathematical formalism and willingness to rely upon an intuitive sense of harmony and fitness, were just the sorts of thing Bacon was most eager to suppress. He adhered to the geocentric cosmology all his life, and this area of science was of far less interest to him than the practical arts. Thomas Kuhn speculates that it was on account of this Baconian suspicion of mathematics and deduction that England produced no major mathematicians for more than a hundred years after Newton: it was not until the nineteenth century that the empirical, and largely amateur, approach to science dominant in England became fully integrated with the professionally organized mathematical disciplines flourishing on the continent.[37]

Since the nineteenth century, Bacon's legacy as a thinker has been a sub-

[35] *Great Instauration, Works*, 8:29.

[36] See E. J. Dijkterhuis, *The Mechanization of the World Picture*, trans. C. Dikshoorn (Oxford: Clarendon, 1961), 396–401, and Antonio Pérez-Ramos, "Bacon's legacy," in *The Cambridge Companion to Bacon*, ed. Marrku Peltonen (New York: Cambridge University Press, 1996), 311–34.

[37] Thomas Kuhn, *The Essential Tension: Selected Studies in Scientific Tradition and Change* (Chicago: University of Chicago Press, 1977), 58.

ject of dispute. For some he is the liberator of the modern intellect and prophet of the Enlightenment vision of scientific utopia;[38] for others he is the theoretician of power, of science as a manipulative instrument that eventually takes hold of human beings and makes them its creatures.[39] It seems impossible to deny that Bacon envisioned with marvelous clarity the practice of science as a collaborative endeavor focused upon the increase of human power and the practical amelioration of the human condition. It was an astonishing leap of the imagination to have grasped from within the confines of his historical position the magnitude of the advances that would be possible if such a collaborative discipline could be established. The vision of a utopian science based upon experiments gave direction and impetus to the scientific movement, and Bacon became one of the patron saints of the Enlightenment, the first of the great precursors cited, for instance, as "Ennemi des systèmes" in d'Alembert's "Preliminary Discourse" to the *Encyclopedia*.[40]

Bacon's critique of the intellect and its idols, furthermore, is an extraordinarily perceptive and valuable one, however little it may have to do with the conduct of science. It leant a critical dimension to modern thinking that was not available to the earlier tradition and opened a new terrain of inquiry—the study of human subjectivity. There is, though, a besetting danger to this mode in that it can easily foster a habit of avoiding genuine confrontation with one's intellectual opponents. Instead of engaging with the arguments put forth by others, one can reduce them to wish-fulfillments either social or personal, to what later theoreticians would label "ideology" or "narcissism."[41] Armed with such weapons, one can consign those with whom one disagrees to the domain of incoherence and error, looking behind the manifest content of their discourse to find hidden motives and causes, and setting them on entirely different grounds from the ones upon which one's own arguments are thought to stand. In this way, rational discussion is supplanted by suspicion. Bacon counsels harmony rather than competition among inquirers, and the lesson is an important one; while he is giving it, however, he wields his own critique of error in a supremely polemical spirit. Recognizing that a doctrine, to be accepted by the majority of human beings, often needs powers of attraction other than its truth, he glamorizes his method with the valor of submission and elevates the very form of his activity in contrast with the delusory constructions of the past. He inaugurates, thereby, along with his vision of science, the notion that modern intellectual culture will be of a completely different kind from that of the ancient and medieval past.

---

[38] For Bacon's contribution to the modern sense of progress, see J. B. Bury, *The Idea of Progress: An Inquiry into Its Origin and Growth* (New York: Dover, 1960), 50–63.

[39] See for instance the opening pages of Max Horkheimer and Theodor Adorno, *Dialectic of Enlightenment* (New York: Continuum, 1986), 3–7.

[40] *Encyclopédie, ou Dictionnaire raisonné des sciences, des arts et des métiers (articles choicis)*, ed. Alain Pons (Paris: Flammarion, 1986), 1:137.

[41] I have discussed the connection between Bacon and Freud in *Freud's Paranoid Quest: Psychoanalysis and Modern Suspicion* (New York: New York University Press, 1996), 69–77.

The sense of historical time thus becomes in the hands of Bacon a new and powerful weapon. In the mature version of his program, Bacon is careful to point out that "affectations of novelty and antiquity are the humors of the partisan rather than judgments; and truth is to be sought for not in the felicity of any age, which is an unstable thing, but in the light of Nature and experience, which is eternal."[42] But while he understood the dangers of partisanship, Bacon did as much as anyone to introduce the partisanship of the modern into intellectual life and to suggest the form that modern intellectual partisanship would take—validating its claims to discipline in suspicious contrast with the unruly regime of metaphysics, setting itself up as the only alternative to madness and fantasy, equating objectivity with the suppression of human interest, but still taking pride in its place at the center of a new order of expansion, world exploration, and practical progress. With Bacon we witness the arrival not of modernity itself but of the rhetoric and mythology of the modern—that late-arriving vantage point of culture that establishes its distance from and superiority to the past by seeing through all that has come before. Demanding the sacrifice of false, metaphysical satisfactions, it frees itself from the dominion of tradition and achieves a discipline promising both truth and utopia, a discipline that will actually overcome the defects of human nature itself.[43]

If suspicion of a special and unprecedented kind forms an essential part of the Baconian program, it may seem, nevertheless, that this suspicion, linked as it was with Bacon's hope to overcome the effects of the Fall, was not incompatible with an extraordinary sense of agency, a utopian program truly revolutionary and original, and one that promised to benefit the broadest sector of humanity. Indeed, Bacon insisted more than any utopian thinker before him that his transforming vision could be rapidly and unproblematically achieved if only the proper measures were put in place. It would be impossible to imagine a more aggressively activist stance than his, or one that could do more to extend the sense of human possibility—even to make of his fellow creatures "a blessed race" of "Heroes or Supermen."[44] But there

---

[42] *New Organon, Works,* 8:85.

[43] In drawing the contrast between modern and premodern thinking, Bacon did hit upon one difference that was eventually to be crucial—the banishing of final causes from the realm of the explanatory. It would be a long time, however, before the direct participation of God would be removed from natural explanation. Newton could not do without it, and not until the triumph of Darwin did the origins of the natural order become satisfactorily explicable without theological means. In every other domain Bacon misdrew or overdrew the distinction between premodern science and the science that was to arrive under his banner.

[44] This is from one of Bacon's early unpublished writings, where his enthusiasm carries him even further than in his later programmatic work. Here he promises his readers to "unite [them] with things themselves in a chaste, holy, and legal wedlock; and from this association you will secure an increase beyond all the hopes and prayers of ordinary marriages, to wit, a blessed race of Heroes or Supermen who will overcome the immeasurable helplessness and poverty of the human race, which cause it more destruction than all giants, monsters, or tyrants, and will make you peaceful, happy, prosperous, and secure." "The Masculine Birth of Time," in *Philosophy of Francis Bacon,* 72. I have slightly altered the translation.

is more than one reservation to be made. First, as we have seen, inquiry as Bacon understood it worked by self-suppression; it was by eliminating the natural contribution of the mind that truth could be achieved. Second, for all of Bacon's jibes against monasticism, the institutional implementation of his science was to be cloistered and hierarchical. As we can see from the arrangements of *The New Atlantis,* the knowledge of the inductive method and its results was to be kept among a few representatives of the state. Bacon's utopia is an exquisitely ceremonious and pompous one. Finally, the science that Bacon was hoping to establish was to be fundamentally an instrument of state policy, useful in managing the realm and in the extension of empire.[45] Citizens would participate in it largely as uninformed gatherers of information and passive beneficiaries. Such an inspiration came naturally to a man who spent a good deal of his career coordinating networks of spies, interrogating citizens suspected of rebellion, and attempting to reform the laws of the realm so as to increase the power of the crown.

It was this new agent, the absolutist state, that Bacon invested with the power to transform the world in order to create innumerable successors to the printing press, which had freed men's minds from Catholicism; the compass, which had brought the conquest of the New World; and gunpowder, which had destroyed a good deal of the old. Just as the doctrine of agency espoused by the Roman church served to rationalize its intermediary function between God and humanity, and just as Luther's denial of agency was an attempt to strip this function away, so Bacon's new science supported a new and powerful agent—natural philosophy in the service of the imperial, absolutist state.

The Architecture of Fortune

Bacon's emphasis upon sacrifice for the good of crown and kingdom is one of the constants of his writing. While he applies a suspicious deflation to virtually all the honored benefactors of humankind, he subscribes nevertheless to a typical idealism about public service, emphasizing the valor of serving king and people through the enhancement of human power. In a sense the emphasis upon public service accords well with the renunciatory element of his thinking about natural inquiry. Bacon elevates the public good at the expense of private intellectual satisfactions, such as the habit of contemplation affirmed by the ancients; he even invokes Christianity, with its validation of action and its fruits, against Aristotle's emphasis upon the good of knowl-

---

[45] The relation of Bacon's legal and political thinking to the form of his natural philosophy has been shown by Julian Martin in *Francis Bacon, the State, and the Reform of Natural Philosophy* (New York: Cambridge University Press, 1992). On politics and science in Bacon, see Julie Robin Solomon, *Objectivity in the Making: Francis Bacon and the Politics of Inquiry* (Baltimore: Johns Hopkins University Press, 1998).

edge for its own sake.[46] The maxim "Knowledge is power" is a direct re-buke to the traditional aims of philosophy.

But the ultimate renunciation of private satisfaction would hardly be con-sistent with Bacon's concern for the practical improvement of the human lot. His scruples, therefore, about the private satisfactions of the intellect do not apply to the seeking of an individual's fortune. This, rather, he finds to be part of another valuable sphere of knowledge, "Civil Knowledge," which he also brings under the organized scrutiny of science. It covers the conduct of practical affairs and is distinguished from moral knowledge in that it requires not a true excellence of character but "only an external goodness" (265), that which is necessary, in other words, for political effectiveness. Bacon con-siders civil knowledge to be another of those areas of inquiry that were too unglamorous for his precursors, with their "inborn pride." Turning aside from his exposition to address the king, he humbly volunteers to sacrifice all the dignity of the scientist and the philosopher in order to become "a com-mon labourer, a hodcarrier" in the royal service.[47] With this self-exculpa-tory gesture, Bacon once again leaves the kingdom of Ought for the kingdom of Is, the true kingdom of action.

In the *Advancement of Learning,* his survey of the state of all areas of in-quiry, Bacon sets the pursuit of individual, private good as a part of civil knowledge under the heading *"faber fortunae, sive ambitu vitae"* (*"The Architect of Fortune, or The Conduct of Life"*). In constructing the archi-tecture of fortune, Bacon for once accedes to the wisdom of a great but un-expected authority, Machiavelli. Bacon is rare among seventeenth-century philosophers even for mentioning Machiavelli in a work published under his own signature.[48] Bacon credits Machiavelli for having achieved in the sphere of politics the same escape from idealizing delusions, philosophy "as one would," that he had accomplished in the realm of natural inquiry. Bacon will further Machiavelli's initiative by taking the coldly pragmatic logic Machia-velli intended primarily for the guidance of princes and extending it into the sphere of private conduct.[49] "We are much beholden," he observes,

> to Machiavel and others, who write what men do and not what they ought to do. For it is not possible to join serpentine wisdom with the columbine innocency, except men know exactly all the conditions of the serpent; his baseness and going upon his belly, his volubility and lu-bricity, his envy and sting, and the rest; that is, all forms and natures of evil. For without this virtue lieth open and unfenced. (254)

[46] *Advancement of Learning, Bacon: A Critical Edition,* 246–47.

[47] This is how Bacon approaches moral knowledge in the *De Augmentis Scientiarum,* the ex-panded Latin version of *The Advancement of Learning,* in *Works,* 9:191–94.

[48] Robert K. Faulkner, *Francis Bacon and the Project of Progress* (Boston: Rowman & Lit-tlefield, 1993), 59–60. Faulkner credits an assertion by Richard Kennington that no living sev-enteenth-century philosopher "so much as mentioned Machiavelli" under his own signature. I know of no counter-examples.

[49] Napoleone Orsini, *Bacone e Machiavelli* (Genova: Emiliano delgi Orfini, 1936), 78–90.

Bacon's descriptions of evil and cunning, with all of their expansiveness and subtlety, display an unmistakable pride in the mastery of "serpentine wisdom." But the need to be familiar with the "conditions of the serpent" does not mean that Bacon endorses what he calls the "evil arts" of deception and malice (284). The knowledge of evil is to be a self-protective resource. What Bacon takes for granted, however, is that the individual agent finds himself surrounded by others who are utterly devoted to their own gains, that these gains come largely at the expense of others, that alliances or friendships between individuals are based upon them, genuine friendship being rare without mutual interest, and that the most important requirement in any man's success is his ability sufficiently to disguise his own motives and ends while penetrating the façades put up by others.

The natural result of these convictions is a powerful emphasis upon knowledge as a basis of action and its foundation in a vigilant suspicion. Just as natural philosophy depends upon finding out the secret parts of creation, so self-advancement depends upon finding out the secret parts of the human heart, which can sometimes be observed upon the countenance, but only in its "private and subtile workings": "We will begin therefore with this precept, according to the ancient opinion, that the sinews of wisdom are slowness of belief and distrust; that more trust be given to countenances and deeds than to words; and in words, rather to sudden passages and surprised words, than to set and purposed words" (274). What follows is a shrewd assessment of all the ways in which men's motives can be discerned. Bacon finds no indignity in this pursuit, no limit to the legitimate gathering of information about others. He does not scruple to recommend to every reader habits of information-gathering that he no doubt acquired in the professional roles of lawyer and inquisitor. "As for the knowing of men which is at second hand from reports," he advises, "men's weaknesses and faults are best known from their enemies, their virtues and abilities from their friends, their customs and times from their servants, their conceits and opinions from their familiar friends with whom they discourse most. . . . But the soundest disclosing and expounding of men is by their natures and ends; wherein the weakest sort of men are best interpreted by their natures, and the wisest by their ends" (275). The searching out of signs that reveals the hidden motives of the ancient philosophers will do with rival courtiers as well.

Having turned this all-searching scrutiny upon the behavior of others, it is not surprising that Bacon recommends with equal emphasis the control of one's own behavior. "All rising to great place," he says splendidly, "is by a winding stair."[50] The man who would succeed in obtaining fortune in the world must make a canny assessment of his own powers and of how they sort with the times and the profession in which he finds himself. He must learn to control his emotions and expressions so as not to give access to his enemies. He cannot take it for granted that his virtues will gain the credit

---

[50] "Of Great Place," in *Bacon: A Critical Edition*, 361.

they deserve; he must color all of his behavior so that his merits will be apparent and his faults disguised, mitigated, or excused. He must master what Bacon calls the "arts of ostentation."[51] The man who aspires to fortune must remain attentive at all times, "reducing" himself to "this watchful and serene habit, as to make account and purpose, in every conference and action, as well to observe as to act" (276). The wisest practitioner will not enslave himself to any one scheme or object, but will imitate the economy of Nature:

> Another precept of this knowledge is to imitate nature which doth nothing in vain; which surely a man may do, if he do well interlace his business, and bend not his mind too much upon that which he principally intendeth. For a man ought in every particular action so to carry the motions of his mind, and so to have one thing under another, as if he cannot have that he seeketh in the best degree, yet to have it in a second, or so in a third; and if he can have no part of that which he purposed, yet to turn the use of it to somewhat else; and if he cannot make anything of it for the present, yet to make it as a seed of somewhat in time to come; and if he can contrive no effect or substance from it, yet to win some good opinion by it, or the like; so that he should exact an account of himself, of every action to reap somewhat, and not to stand amazed and confused if he fail of that he chiefly meant; for nothing is more impolitic than to mind actions wholly one by one; for he that doth so leeseth infinite occasions which intervene, and are many times more proper and propitious for somewhat that he shall need afterwards, than for that which he urgeth for the present. (283)

It is important to note that Bacon carefully marks the dangers that may spring from his advice. Knowledge can lead to "light and rash intermeddling" (276) and often it is wise to stifle one's curiosity about the evil intentions of others in order to avoid becoming preoccupied with them. Cunning, secrecy, and dissimulation are the resorts of the weak and those who lack judgment about when to show themselves. Those who indulge in secrecy make their own ends obscure to those who would assist them. Lying and deception are to be frowned upon not because they are indecent but because they are ultimately not the best policy and because their habitual employment renders them less effective when they are truly necessary. "The best composition and temperament," he concludes in his essay on "Simulation and Dissimulation," "is to have openness in fame and opinion; secrecy in habit; dissimulation in seasonable use; and a power to feign, if there be no remedy" (351).

This strain of wisdom envisions a degree of calculation and self-control quite beyond ordinary human capacities, one that, if achievable, would foster a kind of social existence that could barely be called human. Bacon's

---

[51] "Of Vain-Glory," in *Bacon: A Critical Edition*, 444.

moral vision seems to emanate at a point no less distant from the mask he stands behind as from those he faces. There is, in fact, a renunciation here too, a sacrifice of one's natural impulses, as harsh as any religious demand, and Bacon himself observes that "it is as hard and severe a thing to be a true politique, as to be truly moral."[52] Yet the urgency and precision of his advice suggest that its neglect would be unacceptably hazardous.

The boldness and finish with which Bacon expresses his political intelligence enhances its alienating effect. Though he complains that the existing tradition of moral philosophy confined itself to those matters in which men could "glorify themselves for the point of their wit, or the power of their eloquence,"[53] his own moral writing by no means disclaims either of these effects. Its manner, though, is one of eerie detachment, presenting morally unvarnished wisdom in a rhetoric deliberately compact and agile, without reluctance or excuse. "If you would work any man," he tells us, "you must either know his nature and fashions, and so lead him; or his ends, and so persuade him; or his weaknesses and disadvantages, and so awe him; or those that have interest in him, and so govern him. In dealing with cunning persons, we must ever consider their ends, to interpret their speeches; and it is good to say little to them, and that which they least look for."[54] There can be no doubt in reading such passages that Bacon identifies fully with the perspective he conveys, and that he considers it a point of pride to convey it with force. It is from this point of view and this one only that the dealings between men in the real world can be understood. Anything else is as much of an "intellectualist" fiction as the idols of the philosophers, a "columbine innocency" that leaves us prey to the serpent. The renunciation, self-control, and suspicion that are the grounds of success in natural philosophy must also in Bacon's view be ruthlessly applied to everyday life.

I have suggested that, in developing the scientific rhetoric of suspicion, Bacon was extending the reach of Reformation polemical critique, and that the ostentatious humility of his stance was a natural resource of Protestant self-justification. This exemplary humility by no means prevented him from making grandiose claims for the value of his discoveries and for science itself. Such grandiosity was no doubt part of Bacon's character, but we cannot at the same time forget that he was acting as a courtier soliciting royal patronage as a means of advancing the cause of science. Such patronage would not be forthcoming unless the courtier-scientist could promise results extraordinary enough to enhance the royal name. Bacon failed in this regard during his lifetime, while the remarkable success of Galileo as a courtier prior to the debacle of his later career rested no doubt in part on his ability to dazzle and

---

[52] *Advancement of Learning*, in *Bacon: A Critical Edition*, 272. The editor, Vickers, glosses *politique* as a "shrewd and expedient man" (664).

[53] *De Augmentis Scientiarum*, in *Works*, 9:193.

[54] "Of Negotiating," *Essays*, in *Bacon: A Critical Edition*, 436. Vickers glosses *work* as "influence, manipulate" (771).

reap glory for his clients; to the coat of arms of the Medici he was able to contribute four newly discovered moons of Jupiter.[55]

And if the grandeur of Bacon's program derives in part from the requirements of his intended role at court, his suspicion about the motives of previous inquirers also resonates deeply with the courtly milieu, in which everything depended upon personal favor and the ability to discern the true interests and allegiances both of one's allies and one's enemies. The treachery of court is a commonplace of European culture and a theme of English literature going back at least to the time of Skelton. Castiglione makes it clear that court civility is an art of deception and the management of impressions. The tendency of courtly social dynamics to incite suspicion, fear, and resentment conditioned the outlook of many of the figures discussed in this book. It is clear from reading Bacon's private papers and from his public conduct that he self-consciously practiced the Machiavellian code he preached.[56] What is remarkable, however, is not so much the sharpness of his practice as the openness with which he acknowledges that such conduct is a normal aspect of life. Many counselors warn of the evil that others will do to us; Bacon evenhandedly integrates this serpentine wisdom into his science. Suspicion has become the keynote of wisdom both in politics and in science. It is only by suspicion that we can save ourselves from the false idealism of the past and the clever façades put up by the men and women around us.[57]

[55] Mario Biagioli, *Galileo, Courtier: The Practice of Science in the Culture of Absolutism* (Chicago: University of Chicago Press, 1993), 45–47 and passim.

[56] See especially Bacon's private memoranda in the *Commentarius Solutus*, in *Works*, 11.40–95. The assessment of Bacon's character has become an industry. For a condensed but canny appraisal, see Perez Zagorin, *Francis Bacon* (Princeton: Princeton University Press, 1998), 3–24.

[57] Some historians have suggested that people in early modern Europe were typically cold, detached, suspicious, and indeed paranoid. Lacy Baldwin Smith takes the treacherous atmosphere of the Elizabethan court as typical of English life, and for Lawrence Stone the men and women of the ancien régime all resemble Bacon in temperament, the softer sentiments of modern humanity having emerged only with the rise of the middle class late in the century. As critics have pointed out, this view overlooks many kinds of evidence, including the imaginative literature of the period. See Smith, *Treason in Tudor England: Politics and Paranoia* (Princeton: Princeton University Press, 1986), esp. 40–58; Stone, *The Family, Sex, and Marriage in England, 1500–1800* (New York: Harper & Row, 1977); and Alan MacFarlane's review of Stone's work in *History and Theory* 18.1 (Feb. 1979): 103–26.

7

The Demons of Descartes and Hobbes

The philosophical regime of René Descartes, as presented both in the *Discourse on Method* (1637) and the *Meditations* (1641), begins with a now-familiar gesture, the rejection of the influence of all past intellectual activity; however, it is formulated in a way still more radical than we have seen. Everything that can be doubted must be doubted—all preconceived opinion, all evidence of the senses, all the accumulated prejudice of childhood and the life of the body. The "simple reasoning" of a single "man of good sense" starting from the beginning, Descartes asserts, has a better chance to succeed than a work to which many have put their hands.[1] In his rejection of the scholastic tradition, Descartes is a follower of Bacon, but, as recent scholarship has emphasized, he was also repeating an essential gesture of philosophical negation that belongs to the Socratic and Platonic-Augustinian modes.[2] Like his modern and Platonic precursors, Descartes introduces his critique of thought not to end in skepticism but to arrive at truth. But whereas Bacon employs critical instruments, such as the Idols, simply in order to clear away his opponents, Descartes introduces doubt as an indispensable moment in the progress of his thought. He expresses this thought not simply as a group of axioms and conclusions that can be abstractly mastered but as a personal discipline with a set of phases that others will have to retrace and internalize if they are to free themselves from common sense and blind tradition as well as radical doubt. In the *Discourse,* Descartes provides a "picture" of his own intellectual life's course, a personal "history" or

---

[1] *The Philosophical Writings of Descartes,* 3 vols., trans. John Cottingham et al. (Cambridge: Cambridge University Press, 1985–91), 1:117.

[2] See especially Stephen Menn, *Descartes and Augustine* (Cambridge: Cambridge University Press, 1998).

"fable" as a model for imitation (1:112). He describes a childhood nourished upon error, an education in sterile letters and philosophy and the barbarous moral teachings of the ancients. The sad fruits of this education bring him to a solitary decision never to accept anything as true if it can possibly be doubted. After nine years spent reading in the book of himself and in the "great book of the world" (1:115), "trying to be a spectator rather than an actor in all the comedies that are played out there" (1:125), the philosopher finally arrives at certain crucial metaphysical arguments that alleviate his doubt. Four years later, in the *Meditations,* Descartes presents a more muscular version of the regime of doubt and the philosophical resources that allow one to escape from it, not in autobiographical form but as a discipline modeled on Ignatius de Loyola's *Exercises.*[3] The reader who meditates along with Descartes will pass through the stages of absolute negation to a new-found grasp of the certainty of consciousness and the existence of God. The last of the meditations even achieves a return to the security of a reestablished physical world. In fact, the world-dissolving meditation does much to benefit Cartesian natural philosophy, which depends upon freeing the mind from an Aristotelian world-picture that, in the view of Descartes, remains naïvely shackled to the evidence of the senses. Daniel Garber describes the *Meditations* as a "Trojan Horse that Descartes is trying to send behind the lines of Aristotelian science."[4] Once it has been taken in, the self-evidence of the world of the senses will never be the same, and the Cartesian mind will eventually find itself set over against a world of body as reliably calculable as its thought is clear and distinct.

In devising his phase of radical doubt, Descartes relies partly upon the repertoire of skeptical arguments that were transmitted from the Pyrrhonist tradition by Sextus Empiricus and elaborated at the end of the sixteenth century by Montaigne, Charron, and others.[5] He does, however, introduce a novel element, and one that is most important for our study. It arises as a way of coping with human credulity, the irrepressibly naïve confidence in human nature that makes us want to believe our opinions about the world around us to be based upon certain knowledge, when they are, in reality, at best "highly probable." However much we recognize how the senses can deceive us or how dreams make vivid their illusions, we cannot easily sustain the suspension of belief that is necessary for the Cartesian enterprise. As a remedy, Descartes imagines the drastic state that would prevail if God himself should prove to be a deceiver, so that all the world before us were noth-

---

[3] See L. Aryeh Kosman's discussion of the meditation form in "The Naive Narrator: Meditation in Descartes' *Meditations,*" in *Essays on Descartes' "Meditations,"* ed. Amélie Oksenberg Rorty (Berkeley: University of California Press, 1986), 21–44.

[4] Daniel Garber, *Descartes Embodied: Reading Cartesian Philosophy through Cartesian Science* (Cambridge: Cambridge University Press, 2001), 223.

[5] See the opening chapters of Richard H. Popkin, *The History of Scepticism: From Savonarola to Bayle* (New York: Oxford University Press, 2003) and also chapters nine and ten on Descartes himself.

ing but an illusion. This scenario, however, proves untenable, for deception would not be compatible with our idea of God's nature. Faced with this obstacle to his thought experiment, Descartes finds it necessary to deceive himself in an original way.

> In view of this [our tendency to lapse into merely "highly probable opinions"], I think it will be a good plan to turn my will in completely the opposite direction and deceive myself, by pretending for a time that these former opinions are utterly false and imaginary. I shall do this until the weight of preconceived opinion is counter-balanced and the distorting influence of habit no longer prevents my judgment from perceiving things correctly. . . . I will suppose therefore that not God, who is supremely good and the source of truth, but rather some malicious demon of the utmost power and cunning has employed all his energies in order to deceive me. I shall think that the sky, the air, the earth, colors, shapes, sounds and all external things are merely the delusions of dreams which he has devised to ensnare my judgment. I shall consider myself as not having hands or eyes, or flesh, or blood or senses, but as falsely believing that I have all these things. I shall stubbornly and firmly persist in this meditation; and, even if it is not in my power to know any truth, I shall at least do what is in my power, that is, resolutely guard against assenting to any falsehoods, so that the deceiver, however powerful and cunning he may be, will be unable to impose on me in the slightest degree. But this is an arduous undertaking. (2:15)

The argument that follows is perhaps the most famous in the history of philosophy. Even when the meditator Descartes finds himself in the grasp of "some supremely powerful and, if it is permissible to say so, malicious deceiver, who is deliberately trying to trick [him] in every way he can" so that the most radical withholding of belief is the only resource available, there remains one thing that cannot be taken away—"thought; this alone is inseparable from me. I am, I exist—that is certain. But for how long? For as long as I am thinking. . . . I am, then, in the strict sense only a thing that thinks; that is, I am a mind, or intelligence, or intellect, or reason—words whose meaning I have been ignorant of until now. But for all that I am a thing which is real and which truly exists" (2:18).

It requires no stretch of interpretation to describe the hypothesis of the malicious demon as a paranoid fantasy. Although Descartes proposes it in order to represent an epistemic state of ungrounded perception and knowledge, it is not simply a piece of shorthand for a set of arguments. We are meant to meditate upon it as if the situation were real, to internalize it as an instrument of mental discipline, just as religious believers of the period dwelt in their minds upon the scene of the crucifixion. The scenario of the demon also helps us place Descartes as a member of the same culture and era that produced Don Quixote and his malicious enchanters, and it has even been suggested that Quixote's delusion might have inspired Descartes' thought experiment.[6] In the *Discourse on Method,* Descartes refers indirectly to Quixote in order to characterize the learned mind deluded by tradition, a state that extends in the philosopher's view not just to the books of chivalry but to the history of thought in general (1:113). In the course of the *Meditations,* however, "first philosophy" manages to deploy our potential for the most extreme version of Quixotic bedevilment to rescue us from the condition of absolute irony besetting knights-errant. By the end of the last meditation, the "exaggerated doubts" that have troubled the thinker during the days of the meditation can be "dismissed as laughable" (2:61).[7]

Descartes was familiar with scholastic proponents of the idea that leads him to the demon hypothesis in the *Meditations,* the idea that God himself could be a deceiver.[8] It is impossible, however, to read this seventeenth-century text without connecting the notion of an all-powerful deceiver to the God of Luther and Calvin.[9] Some of Descartes' contemporary readers indeed took the demon to be a blasphemous portrayal of God himself.[10] Now Descartes is exemplary among Catholic thinkers for his insistence that God's power is absolute and that all truths, even mathematical ones, are true by virtue of God's will, a faculty that in God is inextricable from intellect;[11] this distinguishes him from some late scholastics and contemporary Augustinians, who defended the older notion that God wills the truth because it is independently valid.[12] But even though Descartes' God does in some equivocal sense have the power to deceive us, truth being his own creation, for him to do so, Descartes believes, would be to contradict the fact of his goodness. By appealing to a *malicious* omnipotent being, however, Descartes conjures up for his reader a figure as frightening and unaccountable as Calvin's God seen from the viewpoint of a sinner in doubt of his faith.

This paranoid predicament, however, yields to Descartes' ingenuity. The

[6] Steven Nadler, "Descartes's Demon and the Madness of Don Quixote," *Journal of the History of Ideas* 58, no. 1 (1997): 41–55.

[7] That Descartes personally experienced the achievement of knowledge as an escape from demonic presence is suggested by the first of the three famous dreams of 10 November 1619, recorded in his now lost *Olympica* notebook, which he interprets as a struggle with "an evil spirit." As in the *Meditations,* however, the confrontation with the demonic turns out to be a step on the way to enlightenment, leading Descartes to the vision of a book in which all the sciences are combined. See the section from Adrien Baillet's *La Vie de M. Des-Cartes* (1691), in *Œuvres de Descartes,* ed. Charles Adam and Paul Tannery, 2nd ed. (Paris: J. Vrin, 1974–1989), 10:180–88.

[8] Descartes cites Gabriel Biel and Gregory of Rimini in the reply to the second set of objections to the *Meditations,* 2:90.

[9] Michael H. Keefer, "The Dreamer's Path: Descartes and the Sixteenth Century," *Renaissance Quarterly* 49, no. 1 (1996):65–68.

[10] See Descartes' angry letter to Princess Elizabeth, 10 May, 1647, 3:317.

[11] See the relevant passages in Descartes' three letters to Mersenne from April and May of 1630, 3:23–26.

[12] Stephen Gaukroger, *Descartes: An Intellectual Biography* (Oxford: Oxford University Press, 1995), 202–10.

mere existence of a thought, even if it be a thought enslaved to deception, clearly and distinctly implies the existence of a thinker, the one who is being deceived. And once the thinker exists, even in this deceived condition, it is clear and distinct in the mind of Descartes that this being must be aware of its imperfections, implicit in the very doubts that have permitted him to be sure that he exists. Such an awareness of privation requires the notion of a being that is without these imperfections; there must exist, therefore, a being greater than himself to give rise to this idea in the thinker's mind:

> And indeed it is no surprise that God, in creating me, should have placed this idea in me to be, as it were, the mark of the craftsman stamped on his work—not that the mark need be anything distinct from the work itself. But the mere fact that God created me is a very strong basis for believing that I am somehow made in his image and likeness, and that I perceive that likeness, which includes the idea of God, by the same faculty which enables me to perceive myself. That is, when I turn my mind's eye upon myself, I understand that I am a thing which is incomplete and dependent on another and which aspires without limit to ever greater and better things; but I also understand at the same time that he on whom I depend has within him all those greater things, not just indefinitely and potentially but actually and infinitely, and hence that he is God. The whole force of the argument lies in this: I recognize that it would be impossible for me to exist with the kind of nature I have—that is, having within me the idea of God—were it not the case that God really existed. By "God" I mean the very being the idea of whom is within me, that is, the possessor of all the perfections which I cannot grasp, but can somehow reach in my thought, who is subject to no defects whatsoever. It is clear enough from this that he cannot be a deceiver, since it is manifest by the natural light that all fraud and deception depend on some defect. (2:35)

The economy of Descartes' argument is startling. From the existence of a doubt he has proved the doubter; from the existence of the same doubt he has proved the doubter's imperfection; and from the relation implied by this idea of imperfection he has proved the existence of a perfect being. The notion of a Fall or original imperfection in human nature, which had traditionally provided an indispensable ontological resource for explaining how it is possible that an ideal creator could coexist with a fallen world, becomes in Descartes' argument epistemically primary, leading to the necessary existence of that creator. So if we take up the paranoid notion that an all-powerful evil demon is exercising complete control of our faculties of knowledge, we are led by an inevitable course of argument to the existence of a benevolent God who guarantees that we are not fundamentally deceived. Descartes can then proceed to reinstate our knowledge of the physical world, all this being possible once the problem of knowledge has been subtly conflated with the problem of evil.

Descartes' philosophy, therefore, seems to have been devised as a deliberate antidote to what we have been describing as the alienation of agency at the root of modernity. His method of doubt, as Bernard Williams puts it, turns out to be a kind of "pre-emptive scepticism, which serves the aim of answering sceptical doubts by taking them as far as they can be taken and coming out on the other side."[13] Although it begins with Baconian contempt for the entire tradition of inquiry, it ends with a reestablishment of the most traditional theology, and upon new grounds, with proofs, he says, "of such a kind that I think they leave no room for the possibility that the human mind will ever discover better ones" (2:4).[14] Further, though in its course it conjures up a spectacle of frightening heteronomy like what we witness in the pages of Calvin and Cervantes, this too comprises but a stage in the dialectic of reason, and one that is directly to be overcome.

It is not only in the domain of knowledge, furthermore, that Descartes establishes with renewed vigor the autonomy and integrity of the self. He finds the scope of his experience of freedom to be even broader than the certainty grounded in the *cogito* argument: "It is only the will, or freedom of choice, which I experience to be so great within me that the idea of any greater faculty is beyond my grasp; so much so that it is above all in virtue of the will that I understand myself to bear in some way the image and likeness of God" (2:40). If human action goes awry, it is only because we use our freedom of action in ways that do not respect the limits of our knowledge (2:40–41).

Descartes' ethical teaching emphasizes the value of human autonomy. In *The Passions of the Soul* (1649) he writes that "I see only one thing in us which could give us good reason for esteeming ourselves, namely, the exercise of our free will and the control we have over our volitions. For we can reasonably be praised or blamed only for actions that depend upon this free will. It renders us in a certain way like God by making us masters of ourselves, provided we do not lose the rights it gives through timidity." The grounding of esteem in the "the exercise of our free will" is one of the two components of the central Cartesian virtue of "la vraie générosité," the other of which is a person's feeling of "a firm and constant resolution to use it well—that is, never to lack the will to undertake and carry out whatever he judges to be the best. To do that is to pursue virtue in a perfect manner" (1:384). Thus Descartes' program reinstates an authentic moral idealism as well as a vision of epistemic security that marks him as an opponent of the self-alienating and self-renouncing trends I have been describing so far.

---

[13] Bernard Williams, *Descartes: The Project of Pure Enquiry* (New York: Penguin, 1978), 62.

[14] I have slightly altered the translation of this passage. Cf. René Descartes, *Meditationes de Prima Philosophia,* ed. George Heffernan (Notre Dame: University of Notre Dame Press, 1990), 64.

The account I have been giving of Descartes' philosophy, with its emphasis upon God's underwriting of our knowledge and upon the freedom and mastery of the will, seems to introduce a problem for our argument, in that the author of the *Meditations* is commonly recognized as the great originating figure of modern philosophy. His inaugural gesture, it is generally believed, was developed with great originality and force in the writings of Spinoza, Leibniz, Locke, Kant, Hegel, Fichte, Husserl, and others in the central line of modern philosophical development. These figures typically preserve not only the Cartesian centrality of consciousness but also the emphasis upon human autonomy and freedom, even if it is often freedom of a sort compatible with determinism of one kind or another. Descartes' model of consciousness has proven so seductive and influential for subsequent thought that materialistically-oriented philosophers of the mid- and late twentieth century have labored mightily to grasp the precise nature of the Cartesian enchantment and how it might be dispelled.[15] Within the discipline of philosophy, Descartes has proven far more difficult to shake off than his demon. If, therefore, Descartes and his followers largely reinstate the autonomy of human agency and the grounded self-certainty of consciousness in philosophy, does this not drastically qualify the argument I have been making about the alienation of agency and the deep resonance of paranoia in modern thought?

Descartes' assertion of freedom and autonomy does serve as a counterweight to the alienation of agency in modernity, one that was to maintain its force through the transition from religious to secular culture. We do not find in his writing the Baconian theme of submission in the realm of thought; still less is there a Lutheran humbling of the will.[16] The Cartesian self comes into being by a kind of withdrawal, the erecting of an interior fortress, but this fortress does permit the security, the certainty, that Descartes sought. Although the modern emphasis upon the centrality of the self is often attributed to the influence of Protestant piety, it is unlikely that any Protestant thinker could have affirmed the integrity of the inner dimension—not merely as a theater for God's workings but as the locus of human will and thought—with the force brought to it by Descartes, some of whose readers detected in him a revival of the Pelagian heresy.[17] The Cartesian affirmation of con-

---

[15] See, for example, the influential discussion in Richard Rorty, *Philosophy and the Mirror of Nature* (Princeton: Princeton University Press, 1979), 17–69.

[16] In works of popular Cartesianism, however, such as Fontenelle's *Conversation on the Plurality of Worlds* (1686), the conservative political implications of the idea of a natural order are clearly drawn. Margaret C. Jacob, *Scientific Culture and the Making of the Industrial West* (New York: Oxford University Press, 1997), 48–49.

[17] This anxiety appears, for instance, in Descartes's Jansenist defender Antoine Arnauld. See Steven Nadler, "Occasionalism and the Question of Arnauld's Cartesianism," in *Descartes and His Contemporaries: Meditations, Objections, and Replies,* ed. Roger Ariew and Marjorie Grene (Chicago: University of Chicago Press, 1995), 129. See also Descartes' letter to Mersenne, March 1642, 3:211.

sciousness, his "invention of the mind" as Richard Rorty calls it, was to prove important for future developments, but Descartes' manner of escaping from self-alienation has two essential drawbacks. The first is that, having achieved a radical separation of consciousness and the material world, and having banished Aristotelian substances, Platonic forms, final causes, and other metaphysical junctures of intellect and matter, Descartes did not succeed in articulating a coherent relation between consciousness and material being. His dualism remains, therefore, a conundrum. His account of soul and body remains an ungainly contraption, and his free and autonomous realm of thought finds itself with only an instrumental or manipulative relation to the world in which it is embedded. Spinoza's apportionment of the material and the mental to different aspects of a single reality, and Kant's division into different domains of reason—the kingdoms of freedom and necessity—merely displace or redescribe Descartes' problem rather than solve it. Materialist and mentalist forms of explanation remain rivals to the present day, and the dominance of modern science fosters the reduction of agency to material causes.[18]

The second limitation of Descartes' thinking is perhaps even more crucial for our subject: the philosophy of consciousness has not proven a rich source of ethical insight. Its assertion of the mastery and freedom of the will tends to remain formal and abstract, on a metaphysical rather than an ethical plane of discussion. It offers, thus, a decidedly thin version of selfhood, as attenuated and ascetic as a mathematical point.[19] The criticism applies even to Kant, perhaps the most significant ethical thinker in this tradition. While the materialist vein of modern thinking has a native satiric force, a potently ironizing moralism that has proven corrosive in its effect against idealistic notions of agency, the idealist legacy has tended either toward either Cartesian-Kantian otherworldliness or, in its later versions, toward the aggressive subjectivism exemplified by Nietzsche. This later mode produces, needless to say, its own alienation. Descartes' interior fortress was to offer, therefore, only a temporary and fragile respite for the embattled self.

If the philosophy of consciousness has not tended to produce rich results in the domains of ethics, we cannot attribute the thinness of Descartes' ethical thought and the nonexistence of politics in his writing entirely to the intellectual limitations of his method, since natural philosophy was Descartes' primary concern. Like Bacon, he believed that the form of inquiry he inaugurated would allow human beings to achieve an unprecedented control of

[18] The fact that Descartes' enthusiastically affirms the freedom of the will does not mean, of course, that he succeeded in solving the problem of free will, particularly with regard to the conflicts between divine omnipotence and human responsibility. See Vere Chappell's exposition in *The Cambridge History of Seventeenth-Century Philosophy*, ed. Daniel Garber and Michael Ayers (Cambridge: Cambridge University Press, 1998), 2:1206–12.

[19] See Charles Taylor's discussion of what he calls Locke's "punctual self" and its Cartesian preparation in *Sources of the Self: The Making of the Modern Identity* (Cambridge: Harvard University Press, 1989), chapters 8 and 9.

the physical world, to "make ourselves," as he puts it, "lords and masters of Nature," including the part of Nature that was of most concern to him, the human body.[20] On the brink of publishing the culmination of his investigations into Nature, Descartes was deterred by the condemnation of Galileo (1633) because his own system, like Galileo's, clearly implied the truth of the Copernican model. And so he diverted his energies away from the investigation of Nature toward the legitimation of that activity, aspiring to set himself in place of the scholastics as the supreme philosophical interpreter of the Catholic religion.[21] Descartes' dualism of soul and body thus enabled a second, social and professional dualism and wedding of unlike things—theology and natural philosophy, or Catholicism and mechanism. That was enough of a practical agenda for any philosophy.

The character of Descartes combined supreme boldness and grandiosity in the realm of thought with the utmost caution in practical affairs. His ambition to improve human existence was no less extraordinary than Bacon's. In the title of the *Discourse on Method* he advertises "the Plan of a universal Science which is capable of raising our nature to its highest degree of perfection" (1:109). He frequently proclaimed the originality and the conclusiveness of his methods and results, and was much given to wrangling about priority. In the midst of one controversy, he insisted that "If we survey all the past ages in which earlier philosophies flourished and make a list of all the problems solved by these philosophies, they will be found to be both fewer and less important than the problems solved by means of my own philosophy."[22] And though he shrewdly invited criticism of his work, publishing a set of seven replies along with his *Meditations,* Descartes regarded his critics with contempt. A recent biographer describes his behavior as "characterized by moodiness, misanthropy, and at times what can only be described as paranoia."[23] The philosopher of autonomous intellect shunned society and patronage till the very end of his life. He spent most of it in self-imposed exile, moving from place to place in search of the privacy that was conducive to his work, living a life, he said, "as solitary and withdrawn as if I were in the most remote desert" (1:126).[24] His correspondence reveals a mind in constant and pressing anxiety about the repercussions of publication, a philosopher struggling to defend both his originality and his orthodoxy on all occasions.

It is not surprising, then, to see Descartes disclaiming the "meddlesome

---

[20] *Discourse on Method,* 1:142–43. In a late letter to the Marquess of Newcastle of October, 1645, Descartes asserts that "The preservation of health has always been the principal end of my studies," 3:275.

[21] The condemnation of Galileo did not initiate Descartes' interest in metaphysics. See Menn's account of his meeting with Cardinal Bérulle and his turn to metaphysical issues after 1628. *Descartes and Augustine,* 45–53.

[22] *Letter to Father Dinet,* 2:391.

[23] Gaukroger, *Descartes,* 18.

[24] The rest of the quotations in this paragraph are from the *Discourse on Method.*

and restless" character of a reformer (1:118), and insisting that the meta-physically guaranteed freedom he had endorsed in theory should be em-ployed in the realm of practice with the utmost caution and in a way that deliberately conforms with existing authority. The first maxim of his "pro-visional" ethical code, the code that we should adopt in the light of our un-certain knowledge, is "to obey the laws and customs of my country, holding constantly to the religion in which by God's grace I had been instructed from my childhood, and governing myself in all other matters according to the most moderate and least extreme opinions—the opinions commonly ac-cepted in practice by the most sensible of those with whom I should have to live" (1:122).[25] Here, in the sphere of practice, Cartesian interrogation finds its limit. While the initial difficulties of metaphysical knowledge have been overcome and the knowing subject of the *Meditations* has been restored to the keeping of a beneficent deity, with the study of Nature newly legitimized and grounded, Descartes refrains from attempting to extend this new philo-sophical light to the investigation of social existence.

The Rule of Leviathan

With Thomas Hobbes it was a different matter. His major work, *Leviathan,* "occasioned by the disorders of the present time" as he says in the last para-graph (*L* 728), is nothing less than a full-scale attempt to apply the assump-tions of natural philosophy to politics.[26] Hobbes offers a new analysis of the origins of political authority that will serve as a guide for the practice of gov-ernance and, even more crucially, for the reshaping of political culture. It has been a subject of dispute as to whether the doctrine of *Leviathan* constitutes a genuine expression of the method of natural philosophy as Hobbes de-scribed it or whether his political thought stands on its own.[27] There can be

[25] The rest of Descartes' *da provisio* code is faithful to his concern with self-mastery. The sec-ond maxim is "to be as firm and decisive in my actions as I could, and to follow even the most doubtful opinions, once I had adopted them, with no less constancy than if they had been quite certain"; the third, "to master myself rather than fortune, and change my desires rather than the order of the world"; the fourth, to "devote my whole life to cultivating my reason and ad-vancing as far as I could in the knowledge of the truth, following the method I had prescribed for myself," 1:123–24.

[26] Unless stated otherwise, I shall be quoting the works of Hobbes from the following edi-tions: *The Elements of Law Natural and Politic,* ed. J. C. A. Gaskin (Oxford: Oxford Univer-sity Press, 1994), referred to as *E* in the text; *Leviathan,* ed. C. B. Macpherson (Baltimore: Pelican Classics, 1968), referred to as *L* in the text; *Man and Citizen* (*De Homine* and *De Cive*), ed., Bernard Gert (Indianapolis: Hackett, 1991), referred to as *C* in the text; *Behemoth, or, The Long Parliament,* ed. Ferdinand Tönnies (1889; Chicago: University of Chicago Press, 1990), referred to as *B* in the text.

[27] The difficulty of Hobbes' philosophy, its richness in contradictions, has generated a wealth of competing interpretations, particularly in recent years. The scope of this volume does not permit me to engage closely with the debates surrounding Hobbes's philosophy. My own view is that its contradictions stem inevitably from the task that he set himself, which was to ac-

little doubt, however, that the force and originality of Hobbes' political philosophy depends crucially upon the intellectual constraints that also govern his scientific outlook—materialism, nominalism, empiricism, and determinism. Like the greatest of his predecessors, Hobbes draws a portrait of essential human nature, then derives from it the scheme of political life. He had seen human nature revealed in the sequence of upheavals that marked his career, especially the English Civil War and the Fronde. To the witness of these events, the terms "state of nature" and "Civil War" acquired a single meaning. In Hobbes's philosophy the dissension and destruction triggered by Luther's rebellion and the conditions that fostered it became the raw data for a new and influential account of human nature.

Hobbes's analysis begins with the individual, a procedure that follows from his nominalism and materialist reductionism. Human beings are no longer to be described as political animals finding their essential fulfillment in the order of society, as Aristotle taught; rather, for Hobbes they are positively hostile to each other. "The dispositions of men," he says, "are naturally such, that except they are restrained through fear of some coercive power, every man will distrust and dread each other" (C, 99). Given that the threat we see in others is a real one, human beings having powers so equal as to make all vulnerable to all, the state of nature is naturally a violent one (L, 183). We can see the truth of this, Hobbes observes, in the constant precautions that we take against strangers and in the mutual distrust of states (C, 99). It is not that every man is necessarily wicked, but that the threat that some may be wicked requires the fear of all.[28]

This leads Hobbes to the important conclusion that, since in the state of nature there is no other force to protect us but our own, each of us has the right to all of the power he can possibly acquire (L, 189–90). The state of nature being a state of war, the right of nature is nothing other than the right of war. This right is subject to no limit; it includes even the right to appropriate the persons of others. The vision of a war of all against all led to Hobbes' memorable description of the "incommodities" of the state of nature: "no commodious Building; . . . no Knowledge of the face of the Earth; no account of Time; no Arts; no Letters; no Society; and which is worst of all, continuall feare, and danger of violent death; And the life of man, solitary, poore, nasty, brutish, and short" (L, 186).

The observation of ordinary life does show us, of course, that we are, in fact, social beings; we seek society, however, according to Hobbes, neither

---

commodate the following groups of intellectually awkward bedfellows: (1) a very consistent materialism, a frequently reiterated empiricist skepticism, and a minimal or latitudinarian religious orthodoxy; (2) political absolutism and a version of popular sovereignty; (3) nominalism and at times even relativism and a doctrine of the laws of Nature or right reason.

[28] "We need not ascribe this wickedness to nature, for selfishness is not wicked in children but only in adults who have not been properly educated. Wicked men are grown-up children." C, 100.

naturally nor for its own sake, but only for "honour or profit" (C, 111). His description of men in company is revealing.

> How, by what advice, men do meet, will be best known by observing those things which they do when they are met. For if they meet for traffic, it is plain every man regards not his fellow, but his business; if to discharge some office, a certain friendship is begotten, which hath more of jealousy in it than true love, and whence factions sometimes may arise, but good will never; if for pleasure and recreation of mind, every man is wont to please himself most with those things which stir up laughter, when he may, according to the nature of that which is ridiculous, by comparison of another man's defects and infirmities, pass the more current in his own opinion. And although this be sometimes innocent and without offence, yet it is manifest they are not so much delighted with the society, as their own vain glory. But for the most part, in these kind of meetings we wound the absent; their whole life, sayings, actions are examined, judged, condemned. Nay, it is very rare but some present receive a fling as soon as they part; so as his reason was not ill, who was wont always at parting to go out last. And these are indeed the true delights of society. . . . All society therefore is either for gain, or for glory; that is, not so much for love of our fellows, as for the love of ourselves. (C, 111–12)[29]

Hobbes's private experience speaks in this passage, the experience of a scholar and courtier spending a long life in bachelor attendance upon the great, an honored tutor and advisor but still a kind of servant, and therefore always vulnerable to the words of others. In such an atmosphere, one's standing and reputation are always a matter of contention, and Hobbes is acutely aware that honor is a quantity of which there is never enough to go around. The emphasis upon the consequences of human self-love is crucial to Hobbesian moralism. Pride is one of his constant themes, along with "vain-glory," which goes beyond mere practical self-seeking and constitutes an incessant need to indulge in the overestimation of our powers. "Vain-glory," Hobbes tells us, "which consisteth in the feigning or supposing of abilities in our selves, which we know are not, is most incident to young men, and nourished by the Histories, or Fictions of Gallant Persons" (L, 125).[30]

This is the Quixotic temptation, and Hobbes must have had Cervantes in mind. He goes on quite matter-of-factly to say that it is "corrected often times by Age, and Employment," but the term remains a constant resource

---

[29] I have made a slight adjustment to the translation of this passage. See *De Cive: Latin Version*, ed. Howard Warrender, in *The Clarendon Edition of the Philosophical Works of Thomas Hobbes*, vol. 2 (Oxford: Clarendon, 1983), 90–91.

[30] See the discussions of glory and vain glory in *Elements of Law*, 50–51.

in his thinking, no less pressing a tendency of human nature than the self-infatuation of Bacon's "intellectualists." In a society that dwelt upon reputation as an ultimate value and still fostered comparisons of honor based upon, as Hobbes elsewhere puts it, beauty, riches, strength, victory, "et à avoir tué son homme" (E, 49), the negotiation of glory, vain-glory, and laughter, or "sudden glory" (L, 125), both in one's own behavior and in that of others, constituted a daily hazard. It is here that Hobbes finds the fault-line in the groundwork of social existence. Our constant need for comparisons with others forms the root cause of our aggressiveness and hence the violence of the state of nature:

> If now to this natural proclivity of men, to hurt each other, which they derive from their passions, but chiefly from a vain esteem of themselves, you add, the right of all to all, wherewith one by right invades, the other by right resists, and whence arise perpetual jealousies and suspicions on all hands, and how hard a thing it is to provide against an enemy invading us with an intention to oppress and ruin, though he come with a small number, and no great provision; it cannot be denied but that the natural state of men, before they entered into society, was a mere war, and that not simply, but a war of all men against all men. (C, 117–18)

The logic of the analysis is clear. There is a fundamental irrationality in human behavior, a Quixotic love of self-flattering falsity that makes us competitive, mistrustful, and violent; but, once this analysis has been posited, our mistrust of each other and our willingness to use violence against each other both become rational. In the state of nature, the willingness to use violence is justified given what we know of each other, and the only moral distinctions left to be made will be between those who use violence in proportion with their own interests and those who indulge in it for its own sake. The honor and glory that men seek in each others' company share in part the Quixotic character of vain-glory, but they are also signs of that basic power that all must gather to themselves as much as they can in a world of small security and unlimited threat.

In Hobbes's earlier writings (*Elements of Law*, 1642), this conception of the human condition is encapsulated in his way of defining the basic term "power." By its very nature, the need for power sets men at odds with one another, for power is a relative distinction, one man's power having meaning only in contention with that of others. Thus, "because the power of one man resisteth and hindereth the effects of the power of another: power simply is no more, but the excess of the power of one above that of another" (48). The war of all against all, then, is fundamental to human experience, since the good lies primarily in our superiority to others. One can feel respect, in that case, only toward those who exceed one in power. "The acknowledgment of power is called HONOUR; and to honour a man (inwardly in the mind) is to conceive or acknowledge, that that man hath the odds or excess of power above him that contendeth or compareth himself" (*EL*, 48). By the time of *Leviathan* (1651), Hobbes has muted this formula: "The POWER *of a Man,* (to take it Universally) is his present means, to obtain some future apparent Good" (*L*, 150). Now it seems as if power, taken "Universally," can be a value subsistent in itself, an absolute distinction: power is not necessarily power over others but merely the power to secure what one takes to be good for oneself, whether it involves disadvantage to others or not. In this "universal" perspective, power includes all of the natural and social advantages that can bring a person any sort of benefit.

But Hobbes quickly introduces another crucial distinction that cannot be universalized because it depends intrinsically upon the thinking of others—the notion of "value." Far more than power, value is an unstable quality. Men differ crucially from each other, and "the same man, in divers times, differs from himself" (*L*, 216). Value and power are closely bound up with each other because so much of one's power depends upon how others assess it. "The *Value,* or WORTH of a man," Hobbes writes, "is as of all other things, his Price; that is to say, so much as would be given for the use of his Power: and therefore is not absolute; but a thing dependant on the need and judgement of another" (*L*, 151–52). Value is crucially dependent upon particular circumstances; the values of peace, for instance, are not the values of war. Such circumstances are generally beyond control of the agent in question, with the result that "not the seller, but the buyer determines the Price" (*L*, 152). While the honor that men pay to one another is a sign of their opinion of each other's power, a power good in itself, that power is inextricably related to the social context in which it is situated. As long as men are in the state of nature, then, they will never rationally be able to accept a limit upon their access to power, nor will they be able to assess their power except in relative terms.

The nature of power and the relativity of value with regard to one's own honor and power set men against each other by the very terms of their existence, yet at this point we have only begun to grasp the magnitude of the problem at the root of social existence. It is not only the value, "price," honor, and power of persons that is treacherously unfixed; the value of all other objects of desire is equally unsettled and therefore a subject of contention, as Hobbes asserts in two famous sentences of *Leviathan:*

> But whatsoever is the object of any mans Appetite or Desire; that is it, which he for his part calleth *Good:* And the object of his Hate, and Aversion, *Evill:* And of his Contempt, *Vile,* and *Inconsiderable.* For these words of Good, Evill, and Contemptible, are ever used with relation to the person that useth them: There being nothing simply and absolutely so; nor any common Rule of Good and Evill, to be taken from the nature of the objects themselves. (*L*, 120)

If Hobbes is correct, the terms we use to articulate human motivation are undermined as unreliable, essentially private. It is not only that we cannot agree on who should have a right to what commodities—riches, honor, pride—but the very terms of pleasure and reward are constantly and by their nature subject to contest. It is like playing a game in which the stakes are mortal but the rules constantly change at the whim of the players. Where Bacon was impressed by the way men and women through the ages had achieved a remarkable degree of consensus based upon what he considered to be self-generated fictions, Hobbes presents social life as a shadowy forum where solipsisms do not meet but cross.

Given the privacy of value as Hobbes envisions it, one might hope to establish an ultimate good in one's own possession and cling to it in self-positing bliss. Human nature, however, makes even this impossible. Not only is the *summum bonum* upon which, as the ancients imagined, all human aspirations ultimately converge, a mere fiction; the notion of an end that could be final even for an individual also contradicts human nature. The essence of human desire is an endless movement that can never rest in simple satisfaction. "Felicity," states Hobbes, "is a continuall progresse of the desire, from one object to another; the attaining of the former, being still but the way to the latter" (*L*, 160). The need to secure "the way of . . . future desire" absolutely excludes the possibility of rest,

> So that in the first place, I put for a generall inclination of all mankind, a perpetuall and restlesse desire of Power after power, that ceaseth onely in Death. And the cause of this, is not alwayes that a man hopes for a more intensive delight, than he has already attained to; or that he cannot be content with a moderate power: but because he cannot assure the power and means to live well, which he hath at present, without the acquisition of more. (*L*, 161)

Not only, then, is the human being fundamentally competitive, self-oriented, violent, deceptive, and self-deceptive; and not only are the conditions of existence and terms of value that govern his behavior so inherently unstable and relative that the need to enhance our power can never let us rest: now we can see that the nature of desire itself makes it impossible for us to be satisfied with our present state of power, howsoever great it may be.

We are, therefore, by nature seekers constantly after more, and the dilemma of the state of nature for this reason looks utterly insoluble. There is, however, according to Hobbes, a saving resource, a single, vital insight that is accessible to universal human reason and so can form the basis of a solution to the problem of Nature—the insight that the state of war is absolutely and universally an evil, and that peace, even for the mighty, is always preferable to it. When we see that men differ not only from each other but "the same man, in divers times, differs from himself" in the judgment of good and evil, "whence arise Disputes, Controversies, and at last War," it cannot but be evident that, whatever their situation, all men should agree on one thing, "that Peace is Good, and therefore also the way, or means of Peace" (L 216). This is the one fact about which there can be no rational dispute, and henceforth it must constitute the one sound basis for civil society. It gives rise to what Hobbes calls the "fundamental law of nature": "to seek peace and follow it," and, while this law does not contradict the right of nature to use all things as means for self-defense, it leads directly to the all-important second law in which we renounce the remainder of our basic right:

> That a man be willing, when others are so too, as farre-forth, as for Peace, and defence of himselfe he shall think it necessary, to lay down this right to all things; and be contented with so much liberty against other men, as he would allow other men against himselfe. (L, 190)

Whereas up to this point Hobbes has been charting all the sources of our self-delusion, all of the frailties that keep us in hostile confrontation with each other, here he finds the intellect unexpectedly adequate to its object. It is capable of understanding the dreadful consequences of its own limits and the difficulty of overcoming them. One who has grasped these factors will be willing to accept peace almost at any price, and to do so will be the core of rationality. We will still protect ourselves, of course, under extreme circumstances; the right of self-preservation in the face of death can never be alienated or impugned. But we will no longer assert our general right to self-defensive domination, our will-to-power, for the sake of security. We enter into a renunciatory covenant for the sake of peace. In the process, we achieve a startling act of creation. A new political entity springs into being by means of which the citizens, formerly divided against each other, "reduce all their Wills, by plurality of voices, unto one will": "This is more than Consent, or Concord; it is a reall Unitie of them all, in one and the same Person, made by Covenant of every man with every man." This "reall Unitie" is the Common-wealth itself, "that great LEVIATHAN, or rather (to speake more reverently) . . . that *Mortall God*, to which wee owe under the *Immortall God*, our peace and defence" (277). Divisions of power are overcome when they merge into the form of a single divinity.

At this point, having engineered the departure from the state of nature, or Civil War, Hobbes has established the kingdom of reason and morality. He is able to educe nineteen natural laws in which all of the traditional virtues are endorsed, along with some essential legal principles. The wise man, for example, will be just, sociable, grateful, forgiving, without pride, and without vengefulness; judges will treat witnesses equally and will not take bribes; life will now proceed on a rational, natural basis. If any man should find this system of laws too elaborate to operate as a universal code, Hobbes finds that it has already been "contracted into one easie sum, intelligible, even to the meanest capacity; and that is, *"Do not that to another, which thou wouldest not have done to thy selfe"* (L, 214). Natural law and virtue, the

teachings of the golden rule, prove to be the same, and the distinction between prudence and virtue is accordingly erased. The golden rule in Hobbes's
negative version is the sum of the "Rules of Reason" that the individual observes in order to gain the maximum advantage from the social covenant.
The citizen who understands the value of peace embraces it on practical
grounds and he will adopt all of the other virtues for the same reason. Such
are the arts of kindness. Pursued in the right way, they will sustain the thin
veneer of civility that keeps our natural violence from erupting. They are
also, coincidentally or providentially, the best way to prepare for the afterlife.

It is evident that in the "Common-wealth," as Hobbes calls the artificial
creature brought into being by this covenant, we have overcome the relativism
and the epistemic discord that accompany the state of nature, or Civil War. Insofar as men fail to agree because of the problems of knowledge, the judgment
of the state will become the criterion by which disagreements can be settled.
And insofar as their disagreements arise because the meanings of terms such
as good and evil are relative to those who use them, they will be settled by the
"person" representing the sovereign, "whom, men disagreeing shall by consent set up, and make his sentence the Rule thereof" (L, 121). Now the laws
of nature become the laws of the state; they provide a robust set of ethical
norms grounded in objective reality. And though they have been derived from
considerations of prudence, they are given the true status of laws, i.e. commands, by divine sanction (L, 217). They are "Immutable and Eternall. . . .
For it can never be that Warre shall preserve life, and Peace destroy it" (L,
215). Natural law can never be brought into doubt. At this point Hobbes
sounds like a supreme rationalist and optimist about our human powers.

It quickly becomes clear, however, that although he believes that the truth
of natural law is available to all, and condensable into a simple, universally
applicable and traditionally sanctioned formula, this does not mean that
Hobbes thinks human beings actually have the rationality to follow such a
law and live with each other guided by its light. The founding recognition of
the necessity of peace and the need for renouncing the right of nature is a
flash that illuminates all but cannot be sustained. Mere self-interest does not
provide a true enough light for peace, nor can there arise a moral community based upon respect for others, for our most typical expression of the
need for approval is not social virtue but vainglory, and any kind of glory is
a commodity fundamentally limited and therefore a source of competition.
It is fear, rather, that gives the stimulus to reason: "the original of all great
and lasting societies consisted not in the mutual good will men had towards
each other, but in the mutual fear they had of each other" (C, 112–13).
Hobbes is still speaking in this passage of the state of nature; but the insight
he articulates, that fear, not honor, is the great adhesive, is a crucial one for
understanding his notion of the Common-wealth. This is clear in his central
discussion of the formation of the state, which, with all the "Power and
Strength" of the citizenry concentrated into one body, will "by terror
thereof" be "inabled to forme the wills of them all" to publicly useful pur-

poses (*L*, 227). The need for "terror" is the psychological underpinning for Hobbes's most distinctive and perhaps notorious conclusion—that for the state of nature to be overcome, all power must be concentrated in the hands of the sovereign, making it single, simple, and absolute. Even in a regime in which we have renounced our natural rights and accepted the rule of natural law, there must be an absolute power that can preserve the element of fear at the basis of the state.

The logic upon which Hobbes's doctrine is based is a devastating one. Except with regard to the fundamental law, human beings are incapable of political agreement, and therefore difference is always fatal. Wherever there is a division of power among them there will also be a division of thought and will, and so a tendency toward violence. Peace, therefore, requires a single power with a single will: "seeing right reason is not existent, the reason of some man, or men, must supply the place thereof" (*EL*, 181). Because individuals have little capacity to coalesce on the basis of intellect or will, it is fear, the recognition of power, that becomes the joining principle. Its dictates have the status of law not only because they are prudent apart from the sovereign's influence, but because that power makes it prudent to obey them. In a sense, the power of the state must be absolute in order to guarantee the absolute validity of natural law. This is not to say, of course, that sovereignty must inhere in a single person: it can be invested in an aristocratic body or in a popular assembly (*L*, 230–51). But whatever form sovereignty takes, its power admits of no limit.

Hobbes does understand the origins of sovereignty to inhere in an original act of renunciation by the people, a covenant through which the sovereign is authorized. The sovereign does the people's will by proxy, and the state is in this sense an extension of that will (*L*, 228). Once the people have ceded their power to the state, however, their renunciation is final (*L*, 229). There can be no reclaiming it. Furthermore, though the sovereign stands to the people in the relation of agent to authorizing power, the covenant that creates the state does not include the sovereign (*L*, 230). Leviathan remains, strange to say, in the state of Civil War with regard to its subjects. It is not bound by civil statute nor can it be forced to conform with natural law (*L*, 313). The sovereign retains the right of nature to take any means necessary for its self-preservation. It is also important to understand that the acquisition of sovereignty does not necessarily depend upon a specific authorizing act on the part of the people. It is power itself that creates sovereignty: "the name of Tyranny," Hobbes warns, "signifieth nothing more, nor lesse, than the name of Sovereignty" (*L*, 722). Those who understand the fundamental natural law mandating peace will transfer their political obligation to any agent who possesses the power to rule and protect them (*L*, 721). The law of nature demands that they do so. The war of all against all ends, therefore, not so much with a covenant as with a victory of one against all. Unlike Descartes, Hobbes had conjured up a demon, a Leviathan, not to escape from it but to submit to it utterly and without recourse.

The Burden of History

It is essential to the Hobbesian system that no one can rationally be in doubt about the benefits of peace. At the same time Hobbes more than recognizes that peace is hardly the uniform condition of mankind. It is not that men do not appreciate peace but that they do not know how to achieve it. The causes both of war and of peace have till the present moment remained obscure. But in spite of this chronic poverty in the realm of theory, Hobbes recognizes that peaceful government has been a frequent accomplishment. In comparison with the chaos of post-Reformation Europe, antiquity looks to him like a "golden age" when authority was respected and obedience maintained innocent of all questions about the right to rule.

> For before such questions began to be moved, princes did not sue for, but already exercised the supreme power. They kept their empire entire, not by arguments, but by punishing the wicked and protecting the good. Likewise subjects did not measure what was just by the sayings and judgments of private men, but by the laws of the realm; nor were they kept in peace by disputations, but by power and authority. Yea, they reverenced the supreme power, whether residing in one man or in a council, as a certain visible divinity. Therefore they little used, as in our days, to join themselves with ambitious and hellish spirits, to the utter ruin of their state. For they could not entertain so strange a fancy, as not to desire the preservation of that by which they were preserved. In truth, the simplicity of those times was not yet capable of so learned a piece of folly. Wherefore it was peace and a golden age. (C 99)

The violent events of Hobbes's lifetime, viewed in the dim reflection of this "golden age," called out, then, for a special explanation and, indeed, a philosophical cure. The attempt to administer this cure forms the great burden of *Leviathan*. There is no doubting its importance. We have seen that the inherent selfishness of the human perspective is a great obstacle to peace because it makes us unfit for society. Once society has been established, however, civil order faces another formidable threat. This threat derives supremely from our capacity for ideals, and especially religious ideals.[31] In Hobbes's lifetime it was not the quest for worldly power but religious controversy that "Set folks together by the ears."[32] Hobbes's solution was that in the Christian Common-wealth, as he calls it, religious authority too must belong to the sovereign, whose orthodox teachings demand at least the ex-

---

[31] On this sometimes neglected aspect of Hobbes's thinking, see S. A. Lloyd, *Ideals as Interests in Hobbes's "Leviathan": The Power of Mind over Matter* (Cambridge: Cambridge University Press, 1992); and also Paul D. Cooke, *Hobbes and Christianity: Reassessing the Bible in "Leviathan"* (Lanham, Md.: Rowman & Littlefield, 1996).

[32] Samuel Butler, *Hudibras,* ed. John Wilders (New York: Oxford University Press, 1967), 1.1.4.

ternal conformity of all (*L*, 426).[33] To defend this solution it was necessary for Hobbes to rule out all human access to sources of knowledge or authority that could lead one to contradict the religious teachings of the state.

There are two prongs to Hobbes's attack. One is epistemological and attempts to draw narrow limits to what one can know in the sphere of religion; the other is critical and attempts to expose the systems of error that have led to religious conflict in the past. In the process of accomplishing the first Hobbes largely evacuates the sphere of religious knowledge; in the course of the second he rewrites the history of religious belief in the language of psychopathology.

The political problem of religion arises when men believe that their religious convictions set them in conflict with the state. Hobbes's strategy is to obliterate the grounds upon which such conflict can occur. Here his empiricism comes powerfully into play. Disagreements about the nature of God, for instance, become otiose when we recognize that all knowledge comes to us through the senses and that God is not an object of sense. This being the case, we do not actually have an idea of God.[34] The words of praise we address to him, according to Hobbes, are meant only to show "how much we admire him" and not "to declare what he is" (*L*, 403). They are a means to recognize his power without specifying his attributes.

While the empiricist premise is primarily directed against reasoning about God, it also calls into question the possibility of immediate spiritual illumination. Hobbes's materialism counts even more strongly against such a notion. It guides his interpretation of the Bible, where he cannot even find the notion of spirit as it was traditionally conceived. On the basis of a searching investigation, Hobbes legislates that "the proper signification of *Spirit* in common speech, is either a subtile, fluid, and invisible Body, or a Ghost, or other Idol or Phantasme of the Imagination" (429). God, the angels, and the human spirit are bodies. However odd this may seem coming from a man who was ostensibly an Anglican philosopher, Hobbes defends his position with enormous erudition and seriousness, arguing with equal dexterity on the philosophical and on the scriptural fronts just as he does in his controversy with Bishop Bramhall about the compatibility of determinism with the freedom of the will. We also see him attempting to cope with the unorthodox implications of his position and making some compensatory theological innovations of his own. Modern readers who take Hobbes as a serious religious thinker point out the similarities between some of his positions and those of Milton,[35] and an important strain of scholarship, starting

---

[33] Thus Hobbes's definition of a Church: "*A company of men professing Christian Religion, united in the person of one Sovereign; at whose command they ought to assemble, and without whose authority they ought not to assemble*" (*L*, 498).

[34] The boldest expression of this conclusion occurs in Hobbes's Objections to Descartes' *Meditations*. See *The Philosophical Writings of Descartes*, trans. John Cottingham, Robert Stoothoff, and Dugald Murdoch (Cambridge: Cambridge University Press, 1984), 2:127.

[35] Nathaniel H. Henry, "Milton and Hobbes: Mortalism and the Intermediate State," *Stud-*

with A. E. Taylor, has sought to ground Hobbes's doctrine of natural law in the sanction of divine command.[36] Hobbes's contemporaries did not read him in that spirit,[37] but it is hard to doubt, given the enormous development of these themes in *Leviathan,* that he was making a genuine attempt to convince his religious readers that neither scripture nor the best efforts of political philosophy can license resistance to the power of the state.

Hobbes's most important and characteristic argument in favor of the renunciation of religious conscience is that, unless we have direct evidence of God's will through a special and private revelation, we are always relying upon some other authority to make scripture into law. The law can only speak to us through interpretation (*L,* 322). It is always a question, then, of which or whose authority we are to take as decisive. In a commonwealth this can be no serious question at all. Authority belongs to the state (*L,* 426). Leviathan is the person in whom authority is vested and there is no appeal, for Hobbes, to any authority other than the authority of persons. The emphasis on the personal at the basis of politics is the very marrow of his thought. One of many egregious errors he finds in Aristotle's *Politics* is the belief that "in a wel ordered Common-wealth, not Men should govern, but the Laws. What man, that has his naturall Senses, though he can neither write nor read, does not find himself governed by them he fears, and beleeves can kill or hurt him when he obeyeth not? Or that beleeves the Law can hurt; that is, Words, and Paper, without the Hands, and Swords of men?" (*L,* 699). Hobbes's skepticism about the power of laws made out of mere "Words, and Paper" applies to the laws of reason and conscience as well. Everything in the realm of right and good depends ultimately upon the will, and therefore the power, of the interpreter. Unless we are willing to remain in the state of nature, in cases of conflict we must bow to "that *Mortall God,*" the sovereign (*L,* 227). Only the sovereign is in a position to enforce his decisions peacefully.

It is important to emphasize that the likening of the sovereign to an "*Immortal God*" is not merely rhetorical. Both God and sovereign rely for their authority upon precisely the same basis, which is power alone. As we have seen, though the state is an artificial creation derived by covenant, a single person who managed to acquire absolute power would have an equal right to obedience with a sovereign body erected by popular consent. Divine and human rulers each rule by the terror of superior force. "The Right of Nature, whereby God reigneth over men, and punisheth those that break his Lawes, is to be derived, not from his Creating them . . . but from his *Irre-*

---

ies in Philology 48 (1952), 241–44, cited and discussed in Willis B. Glover, "God and Thomas Hobbes," in *Hobbes Studies,* ed. K. C. Brown (Oxford: Basil Blackwell, 1965), 167.

[36] The most important of these is Howard Warrender, *The Political Philosophy of Hobbes, His Theory of Obligation* (Oxford: Clarendon Press, 1957).

[37] See Quentin Skinner, "The Context of Hobbes's Theory of Political Obligation," in *Hobbes and Rousseau: A Collection of Critical Essays,* ed. Maurice Cranston and Richard S. Peters (Garden City, N.Y.: Anchor Books, 1972), 136–142.

sistible Power," just as it would be according to the right of nature among men "if there had been any man of Power Irresistible. . . . To those therefore whose Power is irresistible," Hobbes continues, "the dominion of all men adhaereth naturally by their excellence of Power; and consequently it is from that Power, that the Kingdome over men, and the Right of afflicting men at his pleasure, belongeth Naturally to God Almighty; not as Creator, and Gracious; but as Omnipotent" (*L,* 397).

God's treatment of Job in the work from which Hobbes drew the titles of two of his books, *Leviathan* and *Behemoth,* exemplifies this very point. The case of Job, he explains, "is decided by God himselfe, not by arguments derived from *Job's* Sinne, but his own Power" (*L,* 398). Power is the ultimate term here, and God's power is the ultimate example of it. We are back in the archaic cosmos, Semitic and Greek, where gods and human beings strive with each other in the same dimension. It could not be more clear, then, when God's dealings with Job become the paradigmatic example for the ground of obligation in power, that the notion of power Hobbes has in mind is not adequately conveyed by the definition "present means, to obtain some future apparent Good." God's power needs no end or good beyond itself and can have none. It includes his right to punish Job merely as a sign of his power, without Job having done anything to deserve it (*L,* 398). The power of Leviathan is to be made in the image of this.

In *Leviathan* Hobbes provides his readers with substantial and serious considerations as to why they should surrender the rights of conscience, whatever the prompting of their inner light may be. His fervent wish is to bring the heroic age of religion to an end. This epistemic venture, to fix the limits of religious knowledge, has its beginnings in Hobbes's early writings.[38] In *Leviathan* a second instrument, of satire and critique, makes its appearance.[39] Hobbes deploys extraordinary fertility and wit in developing a satiric history of thought in which he unmasks the sources of all past contention. Much of the substance of religious thinking comes, in Hobbes's mind, from the misunderstanding of the senses and from overwrought imagination, which brings men living in fear to take the reality of the mind for truth.

> By which means it hath come to passe, that from the innumerable variety of Fancy, men have created in the world innumerable sorts of Gods. And this Feare of things invisible, is the naturall Seed of that, which every one in himself calleth Religion; and in them that worship, or feare that Power otherwise than they do, Superstition.
>
> And this seed of Religion, having been observed by many; some of those that have observed it, have been enclined thereby to nourish,

---

[38] E.g., chapter eleven of *The Elements of Law* on "What Imaginations and Passions Men Have, At the Names of Things Supernatural."

[39] For a detailed discussion of Hobbes's use of satiric rhetoric, see Quentin Skinner, *Reason and Rhetoric in the Philosophy of Hobbes* (New York: Cambridge University Press, 1996).

dresse, and forme it into Lawes; and to adde to it of their own invention, any opinion of the causes of future events, by which they thought
they should best be able to govern others, and make unto themselves
the greatest use of the Powers. (*L,* 168)

This is by no means a novel insight when applied to paganism, the "religion
of the gentiles," but what is striking is how Hobbes is able to integrate this
insight with his empiricist psychology, allowing him to treat both pagan and
Christian errors with the same mordant irony. The common elements will always be fear and the need for some agency that we can hold responsible for
the way things are.

This perpetuall feare, alwayes accompanying mankind in the ignorance
of causes, as it were in the Dark, must needs have for object something.
And therefore when there is nothing to be seen, there is nothing to accuse, either of their good, or evill fortune, but some *Power,* or Agent
Invisible: In which sense perhaps it was, that some of the old Poets said,
that the Gods were at first created by humane Feare: which spoken of
the Gods, (that is to say, of the many Gods of the Gentiles) is very true.
(*L,* 169–70)

Our need to fill the gap in responsibility, to displace our own responsibility
onto forces unknown, becomes for Hobbes one of the besetting human
weaknesses. It is what makes us so very susceptible to manipulation by all
of those charlatans and madmen who are willing to invent new agencies out
of their own heads. That fear should be the basis of religion lends new irony
to Hobbes's argument that fear is the preeminent social adhesive and the one
that provides the basis of the state. To invent a Leviathan, then, is to bring
into being a real and universal, though man-made, object of fear, with the
purpose of replacing the phantasmal man-made objects of fear brought into
existence by private individuals to serve their own interests.

Religion is thus for Hobbes at its very basis a creature of darkness and
abuse. Its capacity for both of these was taken to its extreme in Catholicism.
Hobbes, like almost everyone else in seventeenth-century England, took the
Catholic Church to be a contraption of shameless superstition and vain philosophy, exemplifying every religious perversion at its worst. He invokes its
horrors with devastating effect very much in the Reformation manner. In a
sardonic extended metaphor, he likens the "whole Hierarchy or Kingdom of
Darkness" of the Catholics to the kingdom of the fairies, with its ghostly language and its universal king. "The *Ecclesiastiques* are *Spirituall* men, and
Ghostly fathers. The Fairies are *Spirits* and *Ghosts. Fairies* and *Ghosts* in-
habit Darknesse, Solitudes, and Graves. The *Ecclesiastiques* walke in Obscurity of Doctrine, in Monasteries, Churches, and Churchyards" (*L,* 713).
This is no doubt a facile exercise, but behind it lies a serious point, that the
likeness between the kingdom of the faeries and the kingdom of the pope be-

trays their common origin in the fantasies of the human mind. Hobbes's treatment of the history of philosophy, which he associates closely with the Catholic tradition, is hardly less charitable.[40] In fact, his dismissal of the whole of past speculation is no less absolute than Bacon's, and all of its offenses culminate in the absurdity of the scholastics, whose fatuous profundities served as a screen for the practices of a corrupt religion. In this direction Hobbes's contempt is total. Where even Bacon found among these authors evidence of "great wits" suffering unnatural confinements, Hobbes takes them for "the most egregious blockheads in the world, so obscure and senseless are their writings" (B, 41).[41] His more typical charge goes even further—that they are actually insane. Having quoted what he takes to be an incomprehensible passage by the late scholastic philosopher Suárez (1548–1617), Hobbes puts the question as baldly as possible: "When men write whole volumes of such stuffe, are they not Mad, or intend to make others so?" (L, 147).

The critique of the Catholics and the scholastics was, at the time of Hobbes's writing, already proverbial. It is surprising, however, in the course of the same text, to see the satiric vein applied to the Protestant mode of inspiration with equal vigor. Burton, of course, had discovered melancholy in the excesses of both; but while they evoke in him a certain therapeutic irony, his treatment leaves the norms of religious experience unimpugned. Hobbes, however, undermines the value both of Catholic intellectualism and of Protestant inner light. Of the two modes, the Protestant appears the more virulent and dangerous, the more evidently leading to madness. Hobbes treats the notion that human beings can receive knowledge by inspiration with a smirking but matter-of-fact reduction to the physical.

On the signification of the word *Spirit*, dependeth that of the word IN-SPIRATION; which must either be taken properly; and then it is nothing but the blowing into a man some thin and subtile aire, or wind, in such manner as a man filleth a bladder with his breath; or if Spirits be not corporeall, but have their existence only in the fancy, it is nothing but the blowing in of a Phantasme; which is improper to say, and impossible; for Phantasmes are not, but only seem to be somewhat. (L, 440)

Hobbes goes on to say that when the words "spirit" or "imagination" appear in the Scriptures, therefore, they are to be treated metaphorically, since to take them literally would be to imagine a human being as a bladder with air blowing in and out. Hobbes's Protestant readers are left with the choice either of admitting the nonexistence of spirit or of accepting the notion that their spiritual afflatus is a literal gust of wind. It was a superb image to set

---

[40] In *Behemoth*, Hobbes observes that philosophy was the weapon of a deadly elite even in the time of the Druids, leading in the hands of their priests to the deaths of kings. B, 90–96.

[41] He is writing here of Peter Lombard and Duns Scotus.

against an age swarming with idealistic enthusiasm and inflated by pulpit oratory.

The thought of Reformed preaching always evokes in Hobbes a complex and agitated irony. "In the use of the spiritual calling of divines," he writes,

> there is danger sometimes to be feared, from want of skill, such as is reported of unskilful conjurers, that mistaking the rites and ceremonious points of their art, call up such spirits, as they cannot at their pleasure allay again; by whom storms are raised, that overthrow buildings, and are the cause of miserable wrecks at sea. Unskilful divines do oftentimes the like; for when they call unseasonably for *zeal,* there appears a spirit of *cruelty;* and by the like error, instead of *truth,* they raise *discord;* instead of *wisdom, fraud;* instead of *reformation, tumult;* and *controversy,* instead of *religion.*[42]

The ironic formula of the brilliant final sentence permits a degree of innocence by which "*zeal*" is misdirected into "*cruelty,*" "*truth*" into "*discord,*" and so on. In fact, Hobbes believes that the preachers' "*zeal*" is nothing but a front for their "*cruelty,*" their "*wisdom*" nothing but a form of "*fraud*" in men who have set themselves up as rivals to the king's authority. The demons they unleash in their parishioners are of the very same kind as the demons they harbor within.

Hobbes has been at pains to deflate any biblical or historical credit to the notion of demonic inspiration, which he casts now as madness. This madness must do the work that Satan accomplished for Luther, to inflate his enemies with their insane enthusiasm. Such men are not possessed by a spirit but by an *opinion,* whose impact, when communicated to a multitude, is as great as any plague of demons. Here Hobbes brilliantly evokes the swelling effects of a multiplied insanity:

> Though the effect of folly, in them that are possessed of an opinion of being inspired, be not visible alwayes in one man, by any very extravagant action, that proceedeth from such Passion; yet when many of them conspire together, the Rage of the whole multitude is visible enough. For what argument of Madnesse can there be greater, than to clamour, strike, and throw stones at our best friends? Yet this is somewhat lesse than such a multitude will do. For they will clamour, fight against, and destroy those, by whom all their life-time before, they have been protected, and secured from injury. And if this be Madnesse in the multitude, it is that same in every particular man. For as in the middest of the sea, though a man perceive no sound of that part of the water

---

[42] "The Answer of Mr. Hobbes to Sir William Davenant's 'Preface before *Gondibert,*'" *English Works of Thomas Hobbes,* ed. Sir William Molesworth (London: John Bohn, 1840), 4:448.

next him; yet he is well assured, that part contributes as much, to the Roaring of the Sea, as any other part, of the same quantity: so also, though wee perceive no great unquietnesse, in one, or two men; yet we may be well assured, that their singular Passions, are parts of the Seditious roaring of a troubled Nation. And if there were nothing else that bewrayed their madnesse; yet that very arrogating such inspiration to themselves, is argument enough. (*L* 140–41)

Just as the philosopher's arrant verbiage betrays the taint of his mind, so the enthusiast's opinion, properly amplified to the scale of national sedition, shows his delusion. Once again, as with Luther and Bacon, we see from the perspective of Hobbes the hazards and perversions that come with the refusal properly to renounce one's political, intellectual, and spiritual authority to those to whom they properly belong. What was for Luther a conspiracy of demons became for Hobbes a conspiracy of madmen. The vocabulary has been secularized but the psychology of suspicion and the rhetorical structure that supports it remain the same.[43]

Madness and the abuse of intellect thus become for Hobbes the key to the understanding of the entirety of past thinking. But the sources of madness are not innocent. The history of religious struggle is a sequence of interests warring against each other in their attempt to impose their will upon the multitude. Madness and conspiracy are therefore closely allied, a fact most evident in *Behemoth,* Hobbes's analysis of the English Civil War. In that work Hobbes shows how a wide range of factors—the mystifications of the universities and rebellion preached from the pulpit to an ignorant people, along with a vision of aristocratic republican government transmitted from ancient times and the eagerness of the merchants of London to ape the freedom of their Dutch counterparts—all contributed to the destruction of royal power. False teachers were the fatal influence, not so much for what they taught the people to believe but for whom they taught them to trust: "For the power of the mighty hath no foundation but in the opinion and belief of the people" (*B* 16).

Few of Hobbes's intellectual descendants have been willing to claim him as a precursor, yet his influence is great and his importance for our subject immeasurable. He was born into a world that was hierarchical and authoritarian to the core, governed by a small elite that sanctioned its rule with invocations of divine will. Social and political arrangements were thought to have the providential blessing of God. In theory—and it is the power of theory that is our subject here—the dimensions of the social and the political

[43] The deployment of the term *enthusiasm* was to have a long development. J. G. A. Pocock calls it "The Antiself of Enlightenment." "Enthusiasm: The Antiself of Enlightenment," in *Enthusiasm and Enlightenment in Europe, 1650–1850,* ed. Lawrence E. Klein and Anthony J. La Volpa (San Marino, California: Huntington Library, 1998), 7–28. See also Michael Heyd, *"Be Sober and Reasonable": The Critique of Enthusiasm in the Seventeenth and Early Eighteenth Centuries* (New York: Brill, 1995).

were not autonomous realms of practice but organically linked in the broader fabric of being. Their hierarchical forms mirrored the order of the cosmos, of Nature, and even of the human body, which was the microcosmic image of those greater orders. In the seventeenth century the notion of a hereditary right of kings was added to this arsenal of social adhesives. Further, the rhetoric of loyalty and fealty that sustained the monarchy found its resonance in a world of dense local obligations and personal connections. The tissue of the medieval social fabric had long been frayed but it was still the crucial fact of life. It bound king and people in relations that depended upon a rhetoric of confidence, trust, paternal sanction, and obedience, envisioning an ideal social unity, as the poet Nicholas Breton put it early in the century, "one law, one love, and one life, one voice, one heart, and one people."[44]

Until the time of Hobbes, then, it was still not by any means customary to view the dimension of the social in hostile terms or to conceive the interests of the individual in a meaningful way apart from it. To separate one's interests from those of the king and his loyal subjects was to yield to depravity. Complaints about the social order, when they were made at all, were typically conjoined with the blaming of treasonous private individuals. Conspiracy-hunting was an important mode of political activity, an inexhaustible resource for diverting responsibility away from the monarchy. The private person who came athwart the social order was always to blame.[45]

Hobbes's response to the breakdown of this order was to move to the opposite theoretical extreme. In the state of nature it is always the individual who is right. There is nothing he cannot do to protect himself and secure his future. Toward others he exists in a relation of competition and power, power being the ultimate and only real basis of social relations. Human beings, therefore, are entitled to as much freedom as they can command. Others exist for them primarily as resources for their use or limits to their power. Mutual suspicion, therefore, is fully licensed. And given Hobbes's view of human nature, it is fully justified.

The anthropological outlook here is essentially Calvin's. Hobbes shares Calvin's denial that men have freedom in their actions other than to follow the will as it is given to them by God—God, that is, considered by the philosopher as the prime efficient cause. (Freedom for Hobbes is nothing more than the absence of external constraint upon our action.) Like Calvin, Hobbes sees men as undone by their pride. They fail to recognize the limits of their knowledge and power with regard to God and, more to the point for Hobbes, with regard to their fellow men. This is why they need Leviathan,

---

[44] Nicholas Breton, *A Murmurer* (1607), in *The Works in Verse and Prose of Nicholas Breton*, ed. Alexander B. Grosart (Edinburgh: T. & A. Constable, 1879), 12, quoted in Lacy Baldwin Smith, *Treason in Tudor England: Politics and Paranoia* (Princeton: Princeton University Press, 1986), 134.

[45] Baldwin Smith, *Treason,* 138.

who is, as he reminds us, the "king of the proud" (*L,* 362). As with Luther and Calvin, then, Hobbes's remedy for the illusion of freedom of choice is renunciation and submission to a higher power, a Leviathan that will save human beings from themselves and from each other. And, as with Calvin, this higher being remains an agent fundamentally other.

Hobbes's superb adaptation of the story of Job endows the sovereign state with the privilege and majesty of an unquestionable God. At the same time, the majesty of divinity is transferred to the state in a way that leaves its original possessor in eclipse. Hobbes's God is a perpetual rhetorical presence here, but the religious rhetoric and the exhaustive scriptural exegeses work primarily as a concession to the theological constraints operating upon the discourse of the time. Religion is a limit upon Hobbes's thought and not, except as a social fact, a motive for it. I do not presume to know whether Hobbes accepted that limit willingly or not. However, it is into the hands of Leviathan, the state, that he was willing to entrust the guidance of our salvation—both in this world and in the next.

It is hardly necessary to observe that the premodern image of organic social unity was an inspiring fiction which happily suppressed those aspects of existence that did not fit its idealizing mode. Still, we may note one of its advantages. It permitted social relations to be grasped as a unity. It could imagine an articulation of parts into a whole; it could recognize the existence of individuals and set them in relation to each other in a way that was not always or necessarily that of hostility. It even thought of rhetoric as an instrument of political and social cohesion rather than a mode of deception. The Hobbesian model, on the other hand, is entirely atomic. The unity of the social is the unity of naturally repellant particles forced into relation with each other through fear of an individual more powerful than themselves. It sees not unity *of* but unity *against*. As his adversary Bishop Bramhall complained, Hobbes "taketh pride in removing all ancient landmarks, between prince and subject, father and child, husband and wife, master and servant, man and man."[46] Hobbes does believe, of course, in the benevolence of the sovereign's role; he recommends that the sovereign should act for the benefit of all its citizens and that it should interfere with their lives as little as possible. He is a liberal, then, in the modern sense.[47] The basis for this liberal recommendation, however, is a natural law to which the sovereign cannot be held.

---

[46] Quoted in Skinner, "The Context of Hobbes's Theory of Political Obligation," in *Hobbes and Rousseau,* 139.

[47] In his early work, Hobbes also draws a limit to the public interest, one that leaves the inner realm of conscience undisturbed. "No human law," he writes, "is intended to oblige the conscience of a man, but the actions only." This leads him as far as to say that not even the apostles chosen by Christ "did . . . themselves pretend dominion over men's consciences, conserning the faith they preached, but only persuasion and instruction." *EL,* 142. The claim to bind consciences, then, becomes perhaps one more of those claims of power that masquerade as religion, whereas Leviathan will not need to penetrate to the interior of the soul. Here we find a small latitude of personal judgment, protected until it gives rise to action.

The relation between the individual and the state in Hobbes is a relation between less and more powerful individuals whose interests are only accidentally in harmony, if they come to be so at all.

It is instructive to consider some of the correspondences between the intellectual movement traced in *Leviathan* and that of Descartes' *Meditations*. Descartes, in order to escape the history of error, begins for the sake of argument in a condition of absolute solipsism and, to grasp the full dimension of that solipsism, posits an all-powerful, malevolent other who holds him almost entirely in thrall. By means of the *cogito* argument, however, and the conclusions he is able to draw from it, he manages to alter the character of that other from evil to good. Thus having validated the natural light by which he reasons, Descartes can go about the business of inquiry. Were we to confine our view of Hobbes solely to epistemological issues, we would be able to trace a similar movement. In order to escape the history of error and the solipsism of the senses, Hobbes posits a new form of intellectual discourse beginning with the rigorous definition of terms in order to obtain a result as deductively certain as that of geometry. There is no need of a demon here nor of a God. A kind of natural light is shed through the self-positing clarity of words. It is only when we come to political discourse that an all-powerful other is required. As with Descartes, this God gives to the discourses of law and value their substance. Leviathan determines the nature of good and evil. But unlike Descartes' God, he does so first for his own benefit. This God, therefore, remains an other in the full sense.

It is important to remember, of course, that for Descartes, as for Luther, there was no ultimate basis of judgment beyond the will of God. Good and evil, true and false were made so by that will. But it remained, nevertheless, the will of the creator, and it is just this source of right that Hobbes denies. God and His Leviathan rule by power alone, not by any special role in the creation. The products of the sovereign will are like the truth only in being single and absolute. It is their power, not their grounding in reality nor the goodness of their nature, that sustains them in place.

Power is the basic term in the Hobbesian vocabulary. History is the history of power working against power. Suspicion, therefore, is always justified. To escape from this situation, Hobbes's system demands a single individual in possession of all power and therefore subject to the will of no other. But human power is by its nature limited and vulnerable. It remains so even in the form of Leviathan, which is why renunciation and control remain essential. *Leviathan* is a great intellectual scheme for the renunciation and suppression of great intellectual schemes. Its end is the silencing of all other voices but those of the sovereign. Leviathan can survive only by controlling its citizens so that they will accept their subordination with good will, recognizing that such a subordination is better than chaos and old night.

Hobbes is one of the style-setters of paranoid modernity. He developed the satiric critique of the Catholic and Protestant modes in the language of science and in the process secularized the religious rhetoric of suspicion. Even more than Bacon, he licensed the novelty of his method by means of this suspicious critique. His ironic empiricism and satirically reductive materialism were to become central instruments in the arsenal of the modern, perennially available for deployment against idealistic opponents whenever they might emerge. The persistent connection in modern opinion between materialism and a dark view of human nature is also rooted in Hobbes. It would be richly developed up to the time of Freud and beyond. The connection between nominalist, individualist thinking and contractualism in a secular political context was also to have a long legacy. For our purposes, though, what is most crucial is Hobbes's insistence upon the absolute renunciation of sovereignty by the individual to the state. His citizen faces the power of the Common-wealth as an absolute and unaccountable other, a rule unto itself. All who will not accede to this situation must be self-seeking conspirators of the most deadly sort.

Hobbes is the first political philosopher to make control the primary issue of concern, and it is to this end that he deploys the intellectual means at hand. Against the illusion that the intellect and the senses are in possession of a politically divisive truth he employs the critique of method. To the fictions invented by selfishness and vanity he opposes the strictures of natural law once we have recognized the necessity of peace. To the delusions of religious and philosophical authority he opposes a clinico-historical analysis of controversy. One can come away from *Leviathan* with the impression that one has been given the program for an intellectual regime that will use political philosophy to sustain obedience to the state. This is, however, a misimpression. Hobbes thought of political philosophy not as an instrument of governance but a means of discovering the instrument. His primary hope was that his arguments would convince the sovereign (*L*, 408). The policy he endorsed was not the teaching of Hobbesian philosophy but the implementing of it. Men were to be controlled not by reading Hobbes but by being bombarded with his conclusions and sheltered from all other modes of thought. The universities, the pulpits, the mercantile community, the authors of books were all to be rigorously schooled in obedience. "Common People," Hobbes warns, "know nothing of right or wrong by their own meditation; they must be taught the grounds of their duty, and the reasons why calamities ever follow disobedience to their sovereign" (*B*, 144).

Hobbes understood ideas to be the main instruments of control, to be constantly repeated and impressed upon the minds of men and women in order to keep them in proper terror both of the state of Civil War and of the being who protects them from it. But one cannot rely, of course, entirely upon ideas, for that would be to miss the point of *Leviathan*. Weapons are also indispensable. In the brief *Prose Life* he composed sometime during his later years, Hobbes, writing in the third person, describes the purpose that drove the author of *Leviathan*: "In that work he described the right of kings in both spiritual and temporal terms, using both reason and the authority of sacred scripture. This was done so that it might be made clear to all that it was impossible to establish peace in the Christian world unless that doctrine was accepted, and unless a military force of considerable magnitude could compel cities and states to maintain that concord" (*E*, 248) Since terror is the chief principle of rule, we who have understood political philosophy will know that the more considerable the magnitude the better.

Part 3

UNMASKINGS

8

Pascal and Power

The model of agency whose development we have been following began with the rejection of a prior model of agency within a specifically theological context. Luther's immediate object was the rejection of the Catholic model of agency, and he adopted another model of agency that depended for its appeal upon the promise of escaping from the first. The renunciation of agency became therefore a most vehement and dynamic form of agency. Exemplary submission to authority rather than to reason, and to scripture rather than to the order of creation, became the typical gestures of a broad cultural style. It was not that the terms of the Catholic model had been altogether discarded but that they had been rearranged and revalued. The reconciliation of the Ideal and the Actual that was thinkable in terms of the earlier model now came to look like an illusion. Ethical ideals were no longer a task set by God. They were potential snares of the devil, and the human capacity to live up, however intermittently, to God's ethical commandments was not evidence of goodness but entirely a sign of God's unaccountable grace. The idealistic notion of responsibility had become a vehicle of the will of others, means by which others could presume to come between believers and God. The domain of the other, therefore, had increased remarkably and in a sense now included God himself. The challenge of faith was to accept the radical discrepancy between our human ideas of justice and goodness and God's unaccountable will.

The subsequent history of Protestantism was in large measure a gradual mitigation of the extremity of this vision, the conversion of God himself from an unsearchable Leviathan to a covenant-making potentate and finally to a constitutional monarch. But in Bacon and Hobbes we see the Reformation model of renunciation acquiring a renewed virulence as it turns back upon itself. In their writings, there is still the call to a complete mistrust of our-

selves and of our fellow creatures. There is still the vision of life as the setting of power against power, the evocation of a hidden reality behind the surface of events, and the call to surrender all of our authority to a single,
privileged other. Now, however, the specific object of rejection to which this
rhetoric applies is the theological dimension itself. Both Bacon and Hobbes
aim to set aside the entire history of theological controversy in order to
achieve practical gains. While each of them accepts the bonds of religious
duty, both take aim against the inner certainty that motivated the Protestant
model. As a result, that model itself now threatens to fall into the degraded
realm of the other. Finally, in both writers a new kind of explanation comes
to the fore, a reductionism that depends upon the discovery of madness as
the common basis of the intellectual culture of the past. It is no longer sin
but self-aggrandizing madness that links the disturbers of the present peace
with the history of folly. From the viewpoint of Hobbes, Quixote's condition
can no longer be thought of as a private aberration. Rather, it becomes the
explanatory principle that unlocks most of human behavior, and each of us
must recognize his or her reflection in the Quixotizing mirror that Hobbes
provides. The grandiosity and suspicion of the paranoid are slowly becoming the norm of human expectation.

In part 4, we will see the eventual overthrow of the Reformation model
of agency that was turned to secular use by Bacon and Hobbes. Here we will
examine three influential adaptations of this model, by Pascal, La Rochefoucauld, and Swift, each revealing the model's potential for creative, idiosyn-
cratic development.

Although Pascal's *Pensées* were published after the third edition of the
Maxims of the Duc de La Rochefoucauld, they were in fact written prior to
it, so there is little question of influence between the two works. It is impossible to imagine men of more different courses. While La Rochefoucauld
lived among royalty and had a hand in the destiny of the state, Pascal's search
for distinction moved entirely in the world of intellect. He was raised and
educated at home by an intellectually ambitious father who did everything
to nourish the boy's precocious talents in natural philosophy and mathematics. His success was hindered only by constitutional weaknesses, and
some of his feeling of the absurdity of man's physical existence and the te-
diousness and irony of worldly life must have derived from the fact that, for
most of his own life, Pascal's body was to him a kind of enemy. The contrast
between the expansiveness of the intelligence and the limitation of the body
was greater in his case than others because his intellect was more capacious
than almost anyone's and his physique more radically limited. At the same
time Pascal's ambivalence toward worldly achievement must have been fueled by the strange drama in which his father, in a remarkable reversal of
events, was rescued from his fugitive existence as an opponent of exploitative state policies to become an instrument of state cruelty toward the peo-

ple of Rouen.[1] In spite of the ironies and vicissitudes of his life, however, Pascal's renunciation of the world was slow, difficult, and finally, perhaps, incomplete. He long resisted his brilliant sister Jacqueline's vocation for the convent, before an experience of mystical illumination—"Fire," as he called it—confirmed his turn against the world. Pascal's brilliant defense of Jansenism in the anonymous *Provincial Letters* gave him the chance to use his intellectual brilliance in opposition to worldly power, and he pursued the struggle against the Jesuits and the government that supported them with a zeal and boldness that alarmed even those he set out to defend.

For more than a hundred years after his death, the name of Hobbes ranked next to Machiavelli's in infamy, while Pascal, by contrast, has often been regarded as a saint or a genius even by the enemies of Christianity. Yet the political thinking of the two men is strikingly similar. Here, for instance, is one of Pascal's thought-experiments, on the origin of society.

> The bonds that attach the respect of men one to another are in general bonds of necessity; for it is necessary that there be differences in rank, all men wanting to dominate and not all being able to do so, only a few.
>
> Let us, then, imagine we see these bonds beginning to form. It is certain that men will fight each other until the stronger group oppresses the weaker, and finally becomes dominant. But once this is determined, then the masters who do not want the war to continue arrange it so that power will be transmitted as they please. Some give it over to the choice of the people, others to the order of birth, etc.
>
> And it is here that imagination begins to play its role. Until now pure power had done it. Now power is maintained in a certain group by means of imagination—in France the nobility, in Switzerland the commoners, etc.
>
> These bonds that attach the respect of men to such and such an individual are therefore the bonds of imagination.[2]

The first of these paragraphs asserts that all men are similar in wanting to rule each other; the second observes that some actually do rule. The rulers establish the means to sustain and transmit their power to their heirs, evok-

---

[1] The reversal was brought about by the heroic efforts of Jacqueline Pascal. This undoubtedly important episode is susceptible to opposing interpretations. Jacques Attali takes it as confirming Pascal's distrust of worldly justice; for Jean Mesnard it inspired in Pascal a horror of popular movements and inspired his doctrine of submission to authority. Jacques Attali, *Pascal ou le génie français* (Paris: Fayard, 2000), 54–61 and 67–68; and Jean Mesnard, *Pascal: L'Homme et l'œuvre* (Paris: Boivin, 1951), 26.

[2] Louis Lafuma, *Pascal: oeuvres complètes* (Paris: Éditions du Seuil, 1963), 828. I have identified the *Pensées* by their numbers in the text according to the order established by Lafuma. The translations are my own, but I have benefited from the versions by A. J. Krailsheimer (New York: Penguin, 1966; revised 1995) and W. F. Trotter (New York: Dutton, 1958).

ing well-known sources of legitimacy. So far Hobbes and Pascal are in agreement, and Hobbes may be considered one of those among the ruling group who work at establishing the rules of peaceful succession. The next paragraph brings a surprise, however, coming to it with Hobbes in mind, because imagination, which for Hobbes is one of the great disturbers of the peace, becomes in Pascal's deeper scrutiny the soundest guarantor of peace. Pascal does not see imagination primarily as a tool by which subversive characters can excite the multitude but rather as an instrument of power that will always be most effective in the hands of those who rule. Imagination keeps us in thrall to the order of the world. The respect we give to the individuals who rule, and to all who enjoy the benefits of worldly "greatness," rests upon nothing more substantial than the "bonds of imagination."

The recognition that imagination is the great jailer of society does not make Pascal into a political revolutionary. No less than Hobbes does he espouse a careful adherence to the arbitrary arrangements of the world, not only because this is the one pragmatic response to our human situation but also because it is God's wish. It is also what our decrepit nature dictates in the wake of the Fall. But once we recognize that imagination, embodied in the social order, is all that keeps us where we are in the world of power, we will be much more in need of God's help to accept this fact than we were when we thought the order of the world to be just. Only the most detached irony or the most saintly humility can make this injustice bearable. Another hazard is that the pride of *seeing through* the parade of worldly appearances may outweigh the humiliating character of the revelation itself. Exaltation and humiliation, *grandeur et misère,* are the two poles between which Pascal is always attempting to balance, both in his political thought and in his view of existence as a whole. For Pascal, to live as a human being after the Fall is constantly to live out the truth of our divided nature, of being both intellect and body.

"Our intelligence," Pascal tells us, "holds the same rank in the order of intellect as our body occupies in the expanse of Nature" (199). It is in describing the expanse of Nature that Pascal succeeds in portraying the state of the intellect. No one has ever expressed better than he the precarious position of human being and human reason in the universe as modern science was beginning to understand it. In what is perhaps the most famous of the *Pensées,* he evokes the infinite degree to which the vastness of physical space exceeds our power of conception, then directs his intelligence to the human scale and beneath it to the "infinity of universes" contained within the world of the atom, each containing further infinities, so that man "is now a colossus, a world, or rather an all in relation to the nothingness we cannot reach," a thought that makes him feel afraid of himself, hanging between "the two abysses of infinity and nothingness."

For what, finally, is man in the natural world? A nothing in comparison with the infinite, an all in comparison with the nothing, a mean between nothing and everything, infinitely removed from comprehending the extremes; for him the end of things and their principles are impregnably hidden in an impenetrable secret. . . .

What will he do, then, if not fix his attention upon some phenomena of the middle scale of things in an eternal despair of knowing either their principle or their end. All things have come from nothing and are borne into infinity. Who will follow these marvelous processes? The author of these marvels understands them. None other can do so. (199)

Pascal's meditations are even more impressive than the great sermons of Donne, Bossuet, and Edwards. Their import is the humbling of the intellect in submission to God, but at the same time they measure human reason by a high ambition and constitute in themselves a formidable display of intellect. While their intention is to chasten readers on account of their inability to conceive the nothing and the infinite, the beginnings and the ends of life, and to frighten them just as Pascal is frightened by the vertiginous immensities of scale, there is also a superb exhilaration in the imaginative evoking of what is beyond the intellect to conceive. Pascal shows the mind stretching farther and farther into the terrain of the unknown, enlarging its perspective to a dizzying height, and establishing the vastness of what is still inconceivable in comparison with the extent of the intellectual territory it has already crossed. By this means he seems to take hold of the infinite through that very inconceivability which defines our sense of it. The effect is sublime just as Kant was to describe it, evoking the presence of the unrepresentable at the limit of representation. Pascal's meditation upon infinity points in two directions, toward the instability and incomprehensibility of our place in Nature, which makes us humble, and toward the power of intellect, which makes us able to see that we should be humble. "Thus all of our dignity consists in thought" (200), he says, setting the paradox of the human being, a creature both wretched in the knowledge of its limits yet mysteriously standing above Nature because it knows them. "In space," he writes, "the universe encompasses and swallows me up like an atom; in thought, I encompass the world." There is an evident satisfaction for the natural philosopher beholding the world that towers above and engulfs him (113).

In passages such as these Pascal sounds very much like a Stoic philosopher. Epictetus, for instance, in one of his *Discourses,* asks, "Do you know how small a part you are in comparison with the universe? That is, as regards the body. But as regards rationality you are not inferior to the gods nor smaller. For rationality's size is not assessed by its length or by its height but by its judgments."[3] For Pascal, the comparison with divinity would of course be presumptuous, but he does ascribe greatness to the human being in respect of intellect. The human intellect, weighed against the insentience of Na-

---

[3] Epictetus, *Discourses,* 1.12.24, quoted and translated in A. A. Long, *Epictetus: A Stoic and Socratic Guide to Life* (Oxford: Clarendon Press, 2002), 155.

ture, possesses a genuine excellence. "The greatness of man is in knowing himself to be miserable. A tree does not know itself to be miserable. It is, then, to be miserable to know oneself to be miserable; but it is also to be great to know that one is miserable" (114). Our miseries, by Pascal's logic, prove the greatness of what we have lost. They are the "miseries of a great lord. Miseries of a dispossessed king" (116).

Pascal's portrayal of the duality of human nature is his way of showing, empirically as it were, the truth of the Fall, which he takes to be the only conceivable explanation for the existence of a being at once so sublimely exalted and so wretchedly debased. It is an untranscendable insight: even having recognized the *grandeur* that our knowledge confers upon us, we are incapable of taking possession of it. Our fallen nature holds us back from greatness, while our greatness keeps us from being able to submit to our fallen nature without unhappiness and fear. To believe in the freedom and autonomy of the will advocated by Stoics and Jesuits would be to surrender to pride; to leave the intellect in the complacent self-confusion and conformity with the world advocated by the ancient skeptics and Montaigne would be to yield to despair and emptiness.[4] And so we dwell in a middle state, awaiting God's grace, which is of another order altogether. With the human being whose spiritual condition he aspires to illuminate, Pascal adopts the following procedure:

> If he exalts himself I humble him.
> If he humbles himself I exalt him.
> And I always contradict him.
> Until he comprehends
> That he is an incomprehensible monster.
>
> (130)

What Pascal is aiming at, sketched imperfectly in the *Pensées,* is a kind of Christian dialectic, an exemplary process of self-interrogation that would produce an *epoché,* a self-withholding from the world in preparation for surrender to God.[5] We can see this in a remark he makes to his spiritual confessor, that those Christian souls who were too humble and abased might be helped by reading Epictetus, and those who were too proud could be helped by reading Montaigne, for both of these teachers hold a partial truth that Christian wisdom completes.[6] If it is a mistake, according to Pascal, to overestimate our powers, our freedom to know or to act without the grace of God, it is just as much of a mistake to yield to complete skepticism and despair of our human powers. It is vanity to complain that we cannot support

---

[4] See *L'Entretien avec M. de Saci,* in *Œuvres,* 292–97.

[5] Jean Mesnard, *Les Pensées de Pascal* (Paris: Société d'enseignement supérieur, 1976), 173–76.

[6] *L'Entretien,* in *Œuvres,* 297.

all of our beliefs by reason because reason needs first principles, and first principles cannot be proven any more than our most primitive assumptions about the world around us can be proven. This is the import of his famous maxim, "The heart has its reasons that reason does not know" (423). *Coeur* for a seventeenth-century reader suggests the immediacy not only of feeling but of intuition or sudden insight, "the most intimate thought, the most secret disposition of the soul."[7] For Pascal, it is intuition, not deductive reason, that knows God (424). Nature keeps us from doubting what we would perish to ignore, and absolute skepticism refutes itself. Under the heading "Instinct, reason" Pascal writes that

> We have an incapacity for proof insurmountable by all dogmatism.
> We have an idea of truth invincible to all skepticism. (406)

This is our human condition, unable to verify what we must believe, unable to rest without verification. Pascal would have us move back and forth within the limited space of intellect until its paradoxes are exhausted and God's grace will enter.

Among the Christian thinkers of the last several centuries, Pascal has had perhaps the greatest influence upon secular intellectuals. This is due in part to what we may call his genius and to his achievements as a scientist and mathematician, but even more to his dialogue with philosophy and his willingness, even after his "conversion," to address his arguments to those who are not committed Christians. Pascal's dialectic of the Fall is addressed to the unimproved human reason. His description of the human condition does not assume the existence of God but seeks to move toward it. One can accept the description without accepting the theistic conclusion Pascal draws from it. This was perhaps what suggested to him the need for the famous argument of the wager, the point of which is that, in this game with infinite stakes, "neutrality is impossible—we have already embarked" (418). Believing in God is a wager because his existence cannot be proven; like other facts of the heart, it can be known but not deduced from principles. Reason, however, can understand the rationality of the wager by recognizing its own limitations.

Pascal's description of the fallenness of man is a properly Augustinian one in its inspiration; it expresses an absolute distrust of our human will, the self destroyed by the Fall. It is "unjust in itself since it makes itself the center of everything. It is a danger to others since it would enslave them; for each self is the enemy and would like to be the tyrant over all others" (597). Pascal is distinctive, however, and important for our subject, not so much for his emphasis upon the corruption of the flesh, upon passion and violence, nor upon our imperfect love of God as creator and redeemer—all elements central to

---

[7] See the entry for *coeur* in Gaston Cayrou, *Dictionnaire du français classique: la langue du XVIIe siècle.*

the Augustinian and medieval tradition—but for his concentration upon and searching exploration of what we might call the sins of truth, our deep incapacity to be honest about what we are. Whereas one comes away from Augustine's *Confessions* with a sense of the long struggle of flesh and heart with God and the deep providential care of God to bring the soul, through all its windings, back to truth, with Pascal we are left primarily with an intellectual irony toward our human pretenses and a heightened consciousness of the world as masquerade.

For Pascal, our inability to be honest with others derives immediately from our inability to be honest with ourselves, which in turn derives from our basic *amour-propre*. It is not so much that we blame our faults on others, in Quixotic fashion, but rather that we learn to suppress the very consciousness of our imperfections. Our self-knowledge becomes a kind of curse from which we must escape.

> The nature of *amour-propre* and of this human self is to love only itself and consider only itself. But what will it do? It cannot prevent the object that it loves from being full of faults and misery; it wants to be great, and sees itself small; it wants to be happy, and it sees itself miserable; it wants to be perfect, and it sees itself full of imperfections; it wants to be the object of the love and esteem of men, and it sees that its faults merit only their aversion and contempt. This predicament in which it finds itself produces in it the most unjust and criminal passion that can be imagined; for it conceives a mortal hatred against that truth which rebukes it and which convinces it of its faults. (978)

This is the essential basis for Pascal's understanding of human behavior. Our *amour-propre,* which is here identical with our "human self," our *moi,* makes us at bottom enemies of truth. Our nature is "mere disguise, falsehood, and hypocrisy." Afraid to see that we are nothing, we prefer "a perpetual illusion." Society is a great conspiracy to cover up our littleness. We do not tell the truth to ourselves because our self-love prevents it, and we do not tell the truth to others because our self-interest prevents it. The more successful we become, the less we are inclined to be honest with those upon whom our interests depend. "The society of men is founded upon this mutual deceit; and few friendships would endure if each knew what his friend said of him in his absence, although he then spoke in sincerity and without passion" (978).

The collaboration of human beings in covering up the "nothingness of our being" accounts for the character of society as a whole. Discontented in ourselves, we live "a fictive life in the imaginations of others" (806). We prefer apparent virtues to real ones. This is why the order of society rests upon arbitrary distinctions generated by a "faculty of imagination" that "dispenses reputation, awards respect and veneration to persons, works, laws, and the great" (44). Pascal does not leave this as a general observation; it becomes the empirical key to the world around him. Every order, every profession is sustained by gilded props and trinkets.

> Our magistrates knew this mystery well. Their red robes, the ermine in which they wrap themselves up like furry cats, the courts in which they render judgment, the fleurs-de-lis, all this august ornament was quite necessary; if the physicians did not have their gowns and their mules, if the learned doctors did not have their square caps and their robes four times too big, they would never have duped the world, which cannot resist such an authentic display. If the magistrates had true justice, and if the physicians had the true art of healing, they would have no occasion for square caps. The majesty of these sciences would of itself be admirable enough; but having only imaginary sciences, it is necessary for them to take up these vain instruments, which strike the imagination that they must engage, and through which, in fact, they inspire respect. (44)

In this brilliant series of *tableaux,* we see the Augustinian suspicion of the world combined for the first time with a powerful sociological irony. This irony is deepened by Pascal's conviction that it is not only the trappings of our social roles that are imaginary but the goals and rewards that drive them too. They are less valuable to us than the diversion they provide from the reality we fear. That is why we "prefer the hunt to the capture," and why struggle, distraction, motion of any kind are more attractive than a rest which leaves us alone with ourselves. All of our unhappiness, he famously remarks, comes from not being able to sit quietly alone in our rooms. Kings are among the most deluded of beings because there is no one who will tell them the truth, but they are also among the most fortunate because they never have to be alone. They are surrounded by people whose only business is to keep them from thinking of themselves. Such is the wretchedness of our natural condition that we will do anything to escape from what we are (136).

Because we are enemies of truth and in flight from it, our nature is also strangely malleable. For man, "There is nothing he cannot make natural. There is nothing natural he cannot lose" (630). In a different context, this might sound hopeful. For a being capable of reason, the possibility of transforming its nature in conformity with reason would promise freedom. But again, Pascal is no optimist or Stoic. The malleability of our nature is the sign not of our capacity for reason but of our enslavement to the imagination.

> This arrogant power, the enemy of reason, who likes to control and dominate it in order to show how thoroughly it can do so in all things, has established in man a second nature. It has its happy and unhappy men, its healthy and unhealthy, its rich and poor. It brings men to believe, to doubt, to deny reason. It suspends the senses and it sharpens

them. It has its fools and its wise. And nothing annoys us more than to see that it fills its guests with a satisfaction altogether more full and complete than reason does. Those who imagine themselves to be clever are far more pleased with themselves than the prudent could ever reasonably be. They look upon others with a dominating air, they hold their own in argument with boldness and confidence—others with fear and self-mistrust—and that gaiety of countenance often gives them the advantage in the opinion of the listeners, so that the imaginary wise enjoy the favor of judges of the same nature. Imagination cannot make fools wise, but it makes them happy, in comparison with reason, which can only make its friends miserable; one covers with glory, the other with shame. (44)

Passages like this one seem to set Pascal in the detached position of the satirist, observing in a spirit of irony the Quixotic pageant of folly. He insists, however, "I do not speak of fools, I speak of the wisest, and it is among them that imagination has the greatest power. Reason protests in vain; it cannot set a price on things" (44). There can be no community of the wise united on the grounds of reason, no position of solidarity where the enemies of truth can join together in laughter, for each of them has too much to lose. The pretense of reason itself is a kind of folly: "Men are so necessarily mad that not to be mad would only be another turn of madness" (412). The power of imagination makes our human flexibility frightening. It does not mean that we can be improved but that, in our natural madness, there is no limit to our degradation—nothing to keep us from lapsing completely into the depravity of our illusions or from falling under the sway of the illusions of others and accepting them as a second nature.

The recognition that reason cannot "set a price on things" or see them in their actual value casts a special light on Pascal's portrait of society as a conspiracy against truth, for the truth we fear is not one that could actually sustain us were we able to grasp it. It is essentially negative, the unmasking of pretenses to worth. It cannot be a basis for life. Posed against the infinite we are nothing, and such a nothing cannot assume any other dignity than that knowledge. It is from this insight that Pascal's withering treatment of political authority and worldly justice derives. While Augustinian Protestants tended to deny value to things of this world, they tended nonetheless to emphasize respect for worldly authority. Pascal, on the other hand, looks at worldly authority with special mistrust. Unable to make justice powerful, he says, we have made power just (103). Justice is as arbitrary as custom, of which it is a species, and as variable. It alters according to the coordinates of the material world. "Three degrees of latitude reverse all jurisprudence; a meridian decides the truth. . . . Theft, incest, the murder of children and of fathers have all had their place among virtuous actions" (60). Those who have been born to high places should look upon themselves as if having been put there out of mistaken identity: they should occupy their positions as "kings of concupiscence" while always retaining a "double consciousness" ("une double pensée"), one that includes the awareness that the great are kept in place not by any natural superiority, only by power or chance. The order of society is dictated by a system of worldly illusions. The powerful have imagination on their side.[8]

Since for Pascal we have no access to justice, we should follow the laws simply because they are the laws, and for no other reason, there being "neither any true or just ones to introduce. . . . We know nothing of these" (525). Pascal makes this point, however, in a very different spirit from Hobbes. He does not lose sight of the irony of establishing order based upon the absence of reason. After his death, his Jansenist collaborator Pierre Nicole neatly condensed and explicated a number of the *Pensées* to create this précis of Pascal's attitude toward power:

> The most unreasonable things in the world become the most reasonable because of the unruliness of men. What is less reasonable than to choose the first son of a queen to rule a state? We do not choose as captain of a ship the passenger who is of the best family. This law would be ridiculous and unjust, but because men are so themselves and always will be so, it becomes reasonable and just, for whom will men choose? The most virtuous and able? We come at once to blows, each claiming to be the most virtuous and able. Let us then attach this quality to something incontestable. This is the eldest son of the king. That is clear; there is no dispute. Reason can do no better, for civil war is the greatest of evils.[9]

The double use of *reason* here points toward the central distinction in Pascal's thought, between pre- and post-lapsarian human being. Reason in the first sense is capable of revealing the absence of reason at the basis of the social order, but a second and more chastened reason bids us to accept what we do not have the power to improve. The reason we have left to us is best applied against itself.

Pascal himself did not always sustain this degree of intellectual humility and irony, especially when he was led to compare the rationality of which his own mind was capable with the irrationality of the world around him. In his letter to the Queen of Sweden he asserts that the realm of the intellect is a "second empire" as worthy of respect as the one in which she ruled by virtue of her birth.[10] And in the "Three Discourses on the Condition of Aris-

---

[8] This is from the "Trois discours sur la condition des grands," three brief but powerful edifying speeches apparently delivered to the son of the Duc de Luynes and recorded by Pierre Nicole. See *Œuvres,* 368 and 366.

[9] *Pensées,* 977. Nicole includes here numbers 30 and 94 joined with other themes expressed in the *Pensées.*

[10] Pascal pays Christina the compliment that she is the long-awaited ruler who is a queen in both. Letter to Queen Christina of Sweden, June 1652. *Œuvres,* 280.

tocracy," he makes a strong distinction between worldly and natural aristocracy ("des grandeurs d'établissement et des grandeurs naturelles"). One owes external signs of respect, the ceremonies of the world, only to the former on account of their position, while one owes internal respect only to the latter, on account of their natural abilities. As holder of the crown, a king can expect every sign of formal obeisance, but he cannot expect internal respect unless he also has some natural talent or goodness as a man—unless he happens to be a fine geometer or an *honnête homme*.[11] With this assertion of the aristocracy of intellect, Pascal was on the verge of freeing the *grandeur* of our nature from its *misère* and acquiescing to a set of values quite outside the Augustinian mode. The natural consequence would have been a rejection of the claims of the aristocratic class in favor of a regime of merit. But Pascal's deepening devotion to Christianity prevented him from becoming the defender of a secular intelligentsia. Allowing any group the claim to such virtue, or endowing any human distinction with such significance, would have been to overthrow the balanced terms of his dialectic. As Pascal grew older, even his idea of *worldly* excellence moved away from that of the *savant,* with his specialized expertise, to the *honnête homme,* the man of good sense and good conversation who could represent what is universal in the species.[12] Thus, he insists that to abandon the mean would be to abandon the greatness of the human (518). The portrait of humanity given in the *Pensées,* however, leaves little to value in an *honnêteté* which is nothing more than an attempt to disguise the infinitely contemptible and duplicitous self under a more amiable demeanor.

In insisting upon the centrality of *amour-propre* in the understanding of our human condition, Pascal struck a common note of the mid-seventeenth century.[13] He believed that he and his fellow Jansenists were holding to orthodoxy on the issue of human freedom against the overly optimistic teachings of the Jesuits. In the *Provincial Letters,* he portrays the alignment of the various Catholic parties against Arnauld and his supporters as a conspiracy of deception and a public relations trick based upon merely verbal formulas of agreement that served to mask the true intellectual commitments on all sides. But whereas Pascal is in line with the Protestant critics of Catholic optimism about grace and the efficacy of human action with regard to salvation, he does not adopt a similar revaluation of ordinary life. The notion of a divine calling in this world that was so enabling to Protestant culture could hardly be compatible with Pascal's view of society, which Paul Bénichou aptly characterizes as "Jansenist nihilism."[14] Jansenism centered around a monastic community for women, and it seems likely that had it been allowed to develop it would have offered such a course to men as well. The counter-

---

[11] *Œuvres,* 367.
[12] Letter to Pierre de Fermat of 10 August 1660. *Œuvres,* 282.
[13] Mesnard, *Pascal,* 130–77.
[14] Paul Bénichou, *Morales du grand siècle,* 2nd ed. (Paris: NRF, 1948), 128.

weight to its total suspicion of worldly existence was a renewal of monastic perfectionism.

After the death of Pascal, the Port-Royale experiment enjoyed a period of grace, making possible the appearance of the *Pensées* in a softened version (1670), before the Jansenist movement was suppressed for the remainder of the seventeenth century. Though it had a long afterlife in the history of French culture, it never achieved the institutional form that would have been the proper refuge for its suspicion of the world. This fact of history has not blunted but, rather, intensified the impact of Pascal's critique and has made him one of the great models of intellectual revolt. Like most Christian teachers, he points out the emptiness of the social world, but he exceeds almost all of his predecessors in the subtlety and clarity with which he analyzes the fallen and senseless manner of its operation. One is not asked to reject the world until one understands it, but having understood it and rejected it in one's heart, one must still be able to resign oneself to its follies and to give it the qualified concession of allegiance that it demands. Such a feat, Pascal knows, can only be attained by a special class of people, "the able," with their "hidden reasons," or by "perfect Christians," who honor those who have place in the world "by another and higher light" (90).

For those who do not have these convictions and their attendant virtues, the Pascalian perspective leaves one with an exhilarating form of suspicion and a penetrating nostalgia for the majesty of our prelapsarian state, inhabiting a world of self-deluded knights-errant, yet waiting to reclaim one's own sense of greatness. Because the dialectic of *grandeur* and *misère* is so much more gripping and accessible than the paradoxical notion of grace that would relieve it, intellectual alienation threatens to become a self-sufficient state of mind. "Shall I believe that I am nothing?" Pascal asks himself in one of the *Pensées*. "Shall I believe that I am God?" (2). Both of these thoughts, and the grandiose and suspicious aspects of self that go with them, were accessible to him, and he pursued them to their extremes. To surrender to either would be madness, and together they make a proper paranoia. It was Pascal's commitment to the doctrine of the Fall and his belief in the grace of God that allowed him to hold these two insights in balance. Such belief and such grace were not matters of reasoning and could come only to a chosen few, among whom he no doubt counted himself, though only after a long struggle. It is not surprising that Pascal's conviction and the experience of grace that sustained it have proven far more local and fragile than the poles of the dialectic itself.

9

The Art of Polite Disguise

Unlike Pascal, La Rochefoucauld was born to worldly greatness and spent the years of his prime attempting to secure the signs of his position, first by courtly means and, when those failed, by conspiracy and revolt. Among the non-amorous objects that motivated his participation in the Fronde in tandem with his mistress, the Duchess de Longueville, were the *droit de tabouret,* which would have allowed his wife to sit down in the presence of the queen, and the *droit du Louvre,* which would have allowed him to drive his carriage through the front gates of the royal palace.[1] Bitter disappointments and betrayals were the fruit of his quest, along with three grievous wounds, the last of which—from a bullet in the eye—put an end to his career as a soldier. It was a life of pure imagination just in the terms in which Pascal describes that condition, a life hungering for the trappings of power. In the forced leisure of his retirement he produced its anatomy, first in the form of *Memoirs* and then the *Maxims.* Whereas in the *Pensées* we have in fragmentary form the efforts of a broad and capacious intellect brought to bear upon fundamental questions of existence in the widest context, in the *Maxims* we have the product of a much more limited mind reflecting upon a broader, more tumultuous experience and seeking to distill it into elegant formulas. Each of the *Maxims* is an atom to Pascal's universe, yet they have a cumulative weight of alienated insight almost as formidable as the *Pensées.*

The root assumption of the *Maxims* appears in the small essay on *amour-propre* that stood at the head of the first edition but was purged from later ones, probably because of its insufficiently lapidary form. There La Rochefoucauld offers his definition of *amour-propre*—"love of oneself, and of all

[1] For an absorbing account of La Rochefoucauld's career, see Morris Bishop, *The Life and Adventures of La Rochefoucauld* (Ithaca: Cornell University Press, 1951).

things for oneself"—and states the crucial fact that "it makes men idolaters of themselves, and makes them tyrants over others if fortune gives them the means to do it."[2] This formula takes the implications of the definition in two directions: toward ourselves we are in a fundamental position of weakness, that of idolaters, worshippers of a false image; toward others we aspire to a position of strength, a tyrannical domination that will use whatever means come to hand. A true self, which could find small gratification in the tribute of such idolatry, plays little role here. What is important is the idol of the self which we love and to which we are enslaved. And yet this idol has great powers and is like a god, a hidden god whose actions can never be fathomed by the mortals whose service it compels: "No one can sound the depths nor pierce the shadows of its abysses. There it is hidden from the most penetrating eyes; it makes a thousand undetectable movements to and fro" (*MS* 1). What is perhaps still more unsettling, however, is that this deity, so clandestine and so delicate in its movements, is also the dupe and prisoner of its own maneuvers. It labors under cover and fails to recognize its own productions. "There where it is often invisible to itself, it conceives, nourishes, and raises, without knowing it, a large number of affections and hatreds, some of such monstrosity that, when they see the light of day, it does not know them, or cannot bring itself to recognize them" (*MS* 1).

If, however, our *amour-propre* blinds us to the true meaning and nature of our inner machinations, it nevertheless gives us a penetrating view of what is taking place around us. Like the eye, La Rochefoucauld tells us, it sees all but itself. "Where the violence of its wishes summons all of its attention, it sees, it feels, it understands, it suspects, it penetrates, it divines everything, so that one is tempted to believe that each of its passions has a special magic of its own." And yet, for all the magical penetration of its vision, *amour-propre* is constantly changing its goals. It is not only that it seeks our interests, but more importantly, it determines them, and in the most unaccountable manner. It alters with the flux of circumstance and contradicts itself incessantly. "It is imperious and deferential, sincere and feigning, merciful and cruel, timid and audacious." Beyond the changes that come from without, it produces "an infinity" of changes from within.

> It is inconstant out of inconstancy, out of insouciance, out of love, out of the desire for novelty, out of lassitude, or out of disgust; it is capricious, and one sees it sometimes working with the greatest urgency, and with incredible labor, to obtain things which are no advantage to it, which are even harmful, but which it pursues because it wants them. It is bizarre, and often puts all of its effort into the most frivolous em-

---

[2] This is the first of the *Maximes Supprimés* in La Rochefoucauld, *Maximes,* ed. Jacques Truchet (Paris: Garnier Frères, 1967). All translations from the *Maximes* are based on this edition. I identify them in the text by number according to the 1678 edition, as Truchet gives it, with a prefix of *MS* for the *Maximes Supprimés* and *MP* for the *Maximes Posthumes.*

ployments; it can take all of its pleasure in the most insipid of them and maintain all of its pride in the most contemptible. (*MS* 1)

The bizarre and whimsical element of *amour-propre* is one of La Rochefoucauld's great discoveries. Self-indulgence may even assume the form of the most painful austerities. It is protean, and when it destroys itself in one place, it reappears in another. It remains unfixable and unknowable except as an image of change. "Thus the portrait of *amour-propre*, the entire life of which is only a great and protracted agitation; the sea is a palpable image of it, and *amour-propre* finds in the flux and reflux of its never-ceasing waves a faithful expression of the turbulent sequence of its thoughts, and of its eternal movements." In passages like this, La Rochefoucauld seems to have opened up a new and vast inner territory of the mind, a vista that surpasses the scale of the human, subjecting it to tides and rhythms in relation to which its conscious life is nothing more than a fragile surface. We think of Pascal and the terrifying spaces he discovered within the recesses of infinity: La Rochefoucauld's depths are moral and psychological rather than physical, but they are no less terrifying for that.[3]

It is sobering to discover that *amour-propre* is our quintessential motive and that, as La Rochefoucauld puts it in the epigraph to the second edition of the *Maxims*, "Most often our virtues are only vices in disguise." The result is to imagine a world in which seeming is the greater part of being, and in which no one is what he or she seems. It is important, however, not to forget the qualification "most often," for La Rochefoucauld is not a philosophical egoist. He does not deny the existence of the virtues, only their rarity and essential elusiveness. Still, there is no mitigating the darkness of his vision. "In the adversities of our best friends," he alleges, infamously, "we always find something that does not displease us" (*MS* 18). The reaction to this hard saying was strong enough to warrant its removal after the first edition. La Rochefoucauld does not say whether the thing which does not displease us is some subsidiary interest that we cannot refrain from noting even while we share our friends' suffering or whether there is something in their adversities themselves that appeals to us. That is the beauty of the maxim's brevity as a form—and a considerable part of its force. A systematic philosopher would have been obliged to explain himself, whereas La Rochefoucauld's "compressed style"[4] permits him to articulate only those glimpses of human nature that highlight what we normally conceal, leaving the connections for readers to make. Few of our terms of praise survive his scrutiny.

What appears to be generosity is often only a disguised ambition that disdains small interests in order to make its way to greater ones.

---

[3] Jean Starobinski, "La Rochefoucauld et les morales substitutives," *Nouvelle Revue Française* (juillet–aôut, 1966): 19.

[4] "Style serré" is La Chappelle-Bessé's phrase in the *Discours* that preceded the *Maxims* in the first edition. *Maximes,* 279.

Our repentance is not so much a regret for the harm that we have done as a fear of what may happen to us on account of it.

The love of justice in most men is only the fear of suffering injustice.

We often do good in order to be able to do evil without being punished.

The gratitude of most men is only a secret desire to receive greater benefits.[5]

It has often been observed that the *Maxims* first appeared within a year of Molière's *Tartuffe*,[6] and certainly La Rochefoucauld exposes great deal of Tartuffian hypocrisy and duplicity. Even love comes in for its share: "In love deception almost always goes farther than mistrust" (335). In general, one can never be suspicious enough, and those occasions that apparently offer the least opportunity for suspicion come to demand it the most, for "we would often be ashamed of our most shining deeds if the world saw all the motives that produced them" (409). Yet the general tendency of the *Maxims* is not the exposure of simple dishonesty or brazen hypocrisy like Tartuffe's. What they disclose is the multidirectional complexity of our motives, a quality that makes individuals so much more difficult to understand than human nature in general (436).

What we take for virtues is often no more than a collection of diverse actions and diverse interests, which fortune or our ingenuity knows how to arrange, and it is not always out of valor and chastity that men are valiant and women chaste. (1)

Unlike most of the sentences I have quoted above, this one has a vertiginous effect. Moral consciousness and moral language seem to move in unaccustomed directions, and the suppressed dissertation on *amour-propre* is given a demonstration in action. It is not simply that what appear to be virtues are only vices in masquerade but that the unity and fixity of character that are supposed to be the basis both of virtue and vice are called into question. Those moral qualities that we naïvely and confidently ascribe to character seem no longer to be single or simple enough either to be praised or blamed. Instead they are broken down into the variety of actions from which they were originally inferred and paired with the variety of interests and impulses that it is normally the part of virtue to disclaim: "The virtues lose themselves in interest the way rivers disappear into the sea" (171). The note to the reader that stands at the head of the second edition informs us that "by the word *Interest* is not always meant interest in profit, but more often an interest in

---

[5] The maxims gathered here are numbers 246, 180, 78, 121, and 298.
[6] W. G. Moore, *La Rochefoucauld: His Mind and Art* (Oxford: Clarendon, 1969), 31.

honor or fame."[7] This clarification removes the narrowly materialistic con-
notations of *interest* but also absorbs fame and honor into its murky, self-
centered sphere. What is most striking, though, in the first maxim is not the
discovery of interest within virtue so much as the revelation of the fragility
and superficiality of the moral perspective itself. The virtues are an *assemblage*, a "collection" of unlike elements that have to be "arranged" because
the appearance they present is not at all a natural one. The fact that they contain actions that would conventionally pass as virtuous does not lighten the
picture, for this appearance is obviously what needs arranging. The fact that
it is mere "ingenuity" which "knows how" to achieve this arrangement—is
armed, that is to say, with a practiced mode of artifice—emphasizes the im-
provisational quality of our moral posture, while the fact that the same result can be achieved accidentally, by fortune, underlines the tenuousness of
the performance, of the situations that permit it, and of the impression that
it makes. Just as the inner depth of *amour-propre* can be glimpsed only beneath a transitory surface, so we arrange our virtues as a transitory surface
to the outer world. Whereas the Christian moralist often finds behind the
pose of virtue a firm commitment to passion and self-interest, La Rochefoucauld finds not so much self-conscious corruption, or even vice properly understood, as a weakness for falsehood operating in those fugitive zones of
consciousness between what we know intermittently somewhere in our
hearts, what we are willing to admit plainly to ourselves, and what we can
acknowledge in front of others. The indulgence of disguise is only in part deliberate, and its effects are not entirely in our control. "We are so accustomed
to disguising ourselves to others that we finally disguise ourselves to ourselves" (119). Our imaginary virtues become real to us when others believe
in them while, at the same time, "We easily forget our faults when they are
known only to us" (196). Instead of being proud because we are good, we
are good in order to be proud: "Virtue would not go so far if vanity did not
keep it company" (200).

Important consequences flow from the confluence of vice and virtue. If
the virtues need the assistance of their opposites in order to be sustained,
then the vices are not altogether to be regretted.

> The vices enter into the composition of the virtues the way poisons en-
> ter into the composition of medicine. Wisdom gathers and tempers
> them, and uses them against the ills of life. (182)

This strangely beautiful maxim stood at the head of an early manuscript of
the *Maxims* and of the pirated Dutch edition that preceded La Rochefoucauld's authorized edition by two years. Like maxim 1, which I have quoted
above, it bespeaks a surprising *assemblage* but one that is composed of
something more than appearances. It invests "wisdom" with considerable

---

[7] *Maximes*, 5.

strength. This does not mean, however, that La Rochefoucauld is willing to ascribe the most genuine merit to actions in which our vices and weaknesses play a significant part. While he recognizes a "vast" middle-ground between "perfect courage and complete cowardice" (215), for instance, he continues to hold up the idea of perfect courage, as his superb definition makes clear. "Perfect courage is to do without witnesses what one would be capable of doing in front of the whole world" (55). Clearly for La Rochefoucauld and men of his class, the failure of nerve in front of others is hardly to be admitted as a possibility, while the failure to hold ourselves up to the public image of our virtues is a constant temptation.

La Rochefoucauld, then, is both an ironist and a moralist, one who views society as a great masquerade of vice and morality as largely a disguise, but still holds out the possibility of genuine virtue even though there are times when he seems content to sit back and enjoy the comic spectacle the world puts before us. We imagine our moral conduct to be a brave negotiation between detached virtue and clear-sighted self-interest, when in fact, according to La Rochefoucauld, we are rarely capable of either. Weakness and inattentiveness are more common, and more dangerous, than energetic vice. Our susceptibility to boredom and to indolence are two of our most harmful qualities (172, MS 54). And however much we may pretend to disapprove of the vices, determined vice has the mark of command that we admire, for "There are heroes in evil as in good" (185). Success makes virtues out of our vices and victories out of our crimes (MS 68). What we want most is to be admired. To the extent that the world admires goodness, we want to be good, and to the extent that it admires strength, we want to be strong, but because we are mediocre in force, most of our performances stop at the point where the world will be satisfied with us. (215, 219).

Strength, la force, is La Rochefoucauld's most important term.[8] It demarcates the limits of the moral realm: "No one merits being praised for goodness if he does not have the strength to be wicked: all other goodness is most often only indolence or a weakness of the will" (237). Pity is a feeling of which La Rochefoucauld himself claims to have little, and he would like to have none at all.[9] "Weakness," he says, "is the only defect that cannot be corrected" (130). Lack of strength makes up not only a good deal of vice but a good deal of virtue, too, an insight that dictates some of La Rochefoucauld's most pungent sentences: "We make promises according to our hopes and keep them according to our fears" (38); "When vices desert us, we flatter ourselves with the belief that it is we who have deserted them" (192); or, better still: "Old men love to give good advice in order to console themselves for no longer being in condition to give bad examples" (93). After reading

---

[8] We do not have to agree with W. G. Moore that La Rochefoucauld's perspective is "more biological than ethical" with regard to amour-propre to see that for him human beings are "more weak than vicious." Moore, La Rochefoucauld, 40–41.

[9] See his portrait of himself in Maximes, 256–57.

the *Maxims,* it is hard to believe in the truthfulness of moral self-restraint, which comes to look very much like La Fontainian sour grapes: "Moderation has been made a virtue in order to limit the ambition of great men, and to console the mediocre for their lack of fortune and their lack of merit" (308). It is not hard to see why Nietzsche admired the *Maxims.*[10]

There is a certain degree of heroic exuberance in La Rochefoucauld's emphasis upon the power of strength to compel our admiration. In the light of it, our very claim to admire the Christian virtues comes into doubt. It is important to recognize, however, that for La Rochefoucauld *la force* does not simply name a trait of character but is in large part a biological characteristic. It belongs to some men by nature more than to others, to the young much more than to the old, and determines as much of our mental as our physical virtue: "Strength and weakness of mind are badly named; they are in effect only the good or bad health of the organs of the body" (44). Perseverance, for instance, a virtue of which La Rochefoucauld was sometimes found lacking, is largely a matter of personal taste or sentiment, not worthy of praise or blame (177), and moderation is either a matter of pride or of temperament (18, 17). In general, says La Rochefoucauld, "It seems that nature has prescribed to each man from his birth both the limits of his virtues and of his vices" (189).

It is noticeable that the emphasis on biological determinism diminishes to some degree with succeeding editions of the *Maxims.* La Rochefoucauld removed from the first edition the bluntest invocation of humor psychology: "All of the passions are nothing other than the differing degrees of hot and cold in the blood" (*MS* 2). Even without this change in emphasis, however, it would be a mistake to take La Rochefoucauld for a strong biological determinist. "The humors of the body," he says, "have a normal and regular course, which moves and which turns our will imperceptibly; they circulate together and one after the other exercise a secret power within us, so that they have a considerable part in all of our actions without our being able to recognize it" (297).[11] This "considerable part" is not, therefore, the only part, however considerable it may be.[12]

---

[10] See, for instance, number 35 of *Human, All Too Human,* trans. Marion Faber with Stephen Lehmann (Lincoln: University of Nebraska Press, 1984).

[11] In the first edition, where it is number 48, this maxim begins by contrasting the obvious effects of the "extraordinary movements of our humors and temperaments, such as the violence of anger" with their more "normal and regular movements," which have their "secret control." *Maximes,* 294.

[12] Some of La Rochefoucauld's most able critics have given in to the temptation to see him as more of a materialist than he is or to make *amour-propre* too much like an anticipation of Freud's unconscious. Jean Starobinski, for instance, claims that for La Rochefoucauld passion usurps the soul like a parasite, making man into a puppet. Starobinski, 17. See also Paul Bénichou, "L'Intention des Maximes," in *L'Écrivain et ses travaux* (Paris: José Corti, 1967), 3–37; and, most extreme, Tzvetan Todorov, "La Comédie humaine selon La Rochefoucauld," *Poétique* (fevrier 1983): 41. But cf. E. D. James, "Skepticism and Positive Values in La Roche-

La Rochefoucauld's treatment of the "secret power" of humor within the body is importantly connected with the theme of fortune. "Fortune and the caprices of our humor," he says, "rule the world" (435). Humor and fortune are the two powers whose responsibility we deny when we take credit for our actions. They are the two great sources of instability, one internal and one external, that our *amour-propre*, with its need to appear autonomous and strong, is constantly and simultaneously attempting to manage (*MS* 1).[13] And remarkably enough, "the caprices of our humor are even more bizarre than those of fortune" (45). We are more unpredictable to ourselves than the diverse collection of events which do not depend on us at all. When we stand back and consider the constant changefulness of the external world, and the even more unstable inner processes that determine how we react to those changes and put a value on them, then add to this the feebleness and feck-lessness of that compromising power, *amour-propre*, caught between inner and outer spheres and posing as the master of all, the tenuousness of human agency comes fully into view.

La Rochefoucauld has not abolished the domain of virtue, then, but he has narrowed it almost to a point, and the careful reader of the *Maxims* will now be in a position to judge to a nicety the small degree to which we are responsible for our standing in the world and, at the same time, the equally small degree to which the world does justice to our worth. Perhaps the surest tribute others can give to our virtues is the way they resent them, for "The ill that we do does not attract as much persecution and hatred toward us as our good qualities" (29). This is undoubtedly one of the reasons why "It takes greater virtues to sustain good fortune than bad" (25). We actually please others more often by our bad qualities than by our good ones (90). Doing good to others is a perilous adventure, for benefactors can be hated as well as loved (14, 238). The only reliable means of pleasing others, it seems, is a superficial one—to have the kind of manner that tends to please them—and this seems to be a gift of Nature. "Each of the sentiments has a tone of voice, gestures, and expressions proper to it, and how they corre-spond—well or ill, agreeably or disagreeably—is what makes people please or displease others" (255). The noblest character, then, can find himself trapped in an instrument of self-presentation that does not allow him to do justice to his strengths. Whereas moralists of all ages have concentrated pri-marily on what their readers can control, La Rochefoucauld has an eye for what we largely cannot help.

It is remarkable that, after having exposed in the *Maxims* the oceanic depths of our duplicity, one of La Rochefoucauld's chief pieces of advice in

---

foucauld," *French Studies: A Quarterly Review* 23, no. 2(1969): 349–61; and Jean Lafond, *La Rochefoucauld: augustinisme et littérature*, 2nd ed. (Paris: Klincksieck, 1983), 35–43 and 99–106.

[13] *Maximes*, 135.

the *Réflexions diverses* is to preserve the unaffected naturalness of manner that always enables children to please.[14] But that, of course, is only another deception, and the author of the *Maxims* does not conceal the costs. "Nothing so much prevents us from being natural as the desire to appear so" (431). For La Rochefoucauld, all of society is composed of masks facing each other (256). The greatest fortune is to have the natural strength to put on a mask that reflects one's best opinion of oneself.

> There is a kind of elevation that does not depend upon fortune: it is a certain manner that distinguishes us and seems to destine us for great things: it is a value that we imperceptibly give ourselves; it is by this quality that we usurp the deference that belongs to other men, and that sets us above them more often than birth, honors, and even merit. (399)

Clearly La Rochefoucauld admires, even envies, this power of taking by means of appearances what others deserve by right, since without the command of appearances none of us can secure the benefit of what we possesses in truth. Again the theme of force is the crucial one: the value that we set upon ourselves is what allows us to command the respect of others.

It is obvious that the Rochefoucauldian gaze, however politely it can be disguised, must be a threatening one, for there is no demonstration of virtue that it is likely to accept as final unless it is the virtue of strength. Yet we cannot forget that there are times when he genuinely seems to be dividing vice from virtue, with a hopeful sense of the latter. It is hard to think, for instance, that he is speaking only of manners when he says that "False *honnêtes gens* are those who disguise their faults to others and to themselves. True *honnêtes gens* are those who know them perfectly and confess them."[15] Shortly afterwards we read that "It is to be truly an *honnête homme* to want to be continuously exposed to the view of *honnêtes gens*" (206). If there are any such people, then we are entitled to imagine for them a meeting ground where the *honnêtes* can expose themselves fearlessly in the society of the self-knowing. At other times, however, La Rochefoucauld seems to be introducing a rigor of judgment into the precincts of the virtues that threatens to dissolve them altogether, as when he claims that "Fidelity in love is a perpetual infidelity, which makes our heart attach itself successively to all the qualities of the person that we love, sometimes giving preference to one, and sometimes to another, so that this fidelity is only infidelity arrested and confined to the same object" (175). It is not enough, it seems, to be faithful to

---

[14] "There is a manner that suits the figure and the talents of each person; one always loses out when one departs from it in order to take on another. We should try to know what is natural to us, not to leave it, and to perfect it as much as possible." "De l'Air et des manières," *Réflexions diverses,* no. 3; in *Maximes,* 188–89.

[15] See no. 202. In earlier editions the *honnêtes gens* were even more candid, perfectly knowing and confessing "the corruption of their hearts." First edition (1665), number 214, in *Maximes,* 330.

the same object of love in order to be counted honest; we must also love in the exactly the same way. Here La Rochefoucauld seems to be exerting unusual ingenuity to undermine the integrity of love, which, along with the virtues of women, is one his most frequent objects of attack. Friendship fares only a little better. "We cannot love anything except according to our own inclinations, and we are only following our taste and our pleasure when we prefer our friends to ourselves; nevertheless, it is by this preference alone that friendship can be true and perfect" (81). Here there is at least a hopeful ambiguity: we are not being told that friendship does or does not exist, only that if it does, the fact that our self-love participates in it makes it truer and more complete than it would be if it were entirely selfless. The rigorism that brings irony to the love experience here begins to cede to a tenuous rehabilitation of at least one of the passions.

Scholars have not found it easy to agree about the true meaning and purpose of La Rochefoucauld's work. The *Maxims* have been seen variously as providing an amoral ethic of intensity "for want of a better," a rigorous morality "in spite of everything," the "autopsy of a dying class," or, along with the *Réflexions diverses,* a prescient handbook for the "profane art of living."[16] Some of the difficulty lies in the aristocratic nonchalance and refusal of explanation that make for the pleasure of the *Maxims,*[17] some in the chaste abstraction and generality of La Rochefoucauld's language,[18] and some in the penumbra of defensive operations that accompanied its original publication. The work has a complicated history.[19] It grew out of a pastime among the author and his friends Madame de Sablé and Jacques Esprit, the taking up of "lovely precepts in a corner by the fire," as La Rochefoucauld put it in one of his letters.[20] The pirated edition brought out in Holland may have spurred publication of the first edition of 1665, not signed by La Rochefoucauld but introduced by his brief "Advice to the Reader" and furnished with an anonymous *Discours* by another friend, the lawyer Henri de la Chappelle-Bessé. Both of these prefatory documents make the point that, however shocking might be the *Maxims'* portrayal of the falsity of human virtues, their view of human nature was in line with that of the Fathers of the Church, so to attack them was to call into question the sacred authori-

---

[16] Starobinski, 27; Lafond, *La Rochefoucauld,* 106; Moore, 3; and Bénichou, "L'Intention des *Maximes,*" 29.

[17] See Pierre Campion, *Lectures de La Rochefoucauld* (Rennes: Presses universitaires de Rennes, 1998), 120, on the aristocratic qualities of the *Maxims.*

[18] In the *Discours* that stood at the head of the 1665 edition, La Chappelle Bessé mentions their obscurity as one of the complaints that had been leveled at the *Maxims,* presumably based upon their circulation in manuscript. *Maximes,* 278. On the drawbacks of seventeenth-century French for the making of fine psychological distinctions, see the interesting comments of Odette de Morgues in *Two French Moralists: La Rochefoucauld and La Bruyère* (New York: Cambridge University Press, 1978), 8–13.

[19] See H.-A. Grubbs's classic article, "La Genèse des «Maximes» de La Rochefoucauld," in *Revue d'Histoire de la Littérature de la France* 40 (1933): 2–37.

[20] Letter to Jacques Esprit in 1662. *Maximes,* 544.

ties. The "Advice to the Reader" also takes up the argumentative ploy, later adopted by Sigmund Freud, whose way of thinking is thoroughly in tune with that of La Rochefoucauld, that the ingenuity and heat that critics had invested in attacking the *Maxims* was proof of their truth, "the sort of truths to which human pride cannot accommodate itself."[21] La Rochefoucauld goes on to offer the puckish advice that the reader should imagine that the work pertains to everyone but himself, which will allow him to accept the truth in it and "give pleasure to the human heart."[22]

The *Maxims,* then, came into the world bearing the mask of pious instruction in an apparently unnecessary attempt to forestall religiously motivated complaints. La Chappelle-Bessé's *Discourse* and most of the "Advice to the Reader" disappeared in the second edition, which also shows a pruning of the sparse flourishes of religion in the *Maxims* themselves.[23] La Rochefoucauld continued to sharpen, add to, and rearrange the *Maxims* through four later editions, but however much his view of the human character may be compatible with that of Augustine, or indeed of Pascal, Rochefoucauldian moralism leads neither to the renunciation of this world nor to a rededication of the self to God, but only to a cold, ironic, and suspicious wisdom.

A second, somewhat more helpful clue to the purpose of the *Maxims* is provided by its frontispiece, which shows a gloomy-faced bust of Seneca, the Stoic philosopher, being gleefully mocked by a cherub, Love of Truth, who has just removed the philosopher's smiling mask. La Rochefoucauld's outlook could indeed hardly be more opposed to that of Stoicism, with its insistence upon the attainability of virtue, its belief in universal reason and order, and its optimism about the goodness of the world. Self-possession is the Stoic credo, and La Rochefoucauld mocks self-possession of every kind. One of the earliest maxims is an unmasking of constancy, a chief Stoic virtue, which La Rochefoucauld sees as the mere suppression of our natural agitation (20). The last and longest of the *Maxims* is a rebuke to the notion that any philosophy could give us tranquility in the face of death (504). It is entirely reasonable, then, to take see the *Maxims* as part of the reaction against the revival of Stoicism that began at the end of the previous century.[24]

To see La Rochefoucauld, however, primarily as an opponent of Seneca is to make him into more of a philosopher than he intends to be, and to make the *Maxims* much narrower in scope than they really are.[25] Were they pri-

---

[21] *Maximes,* 267.

[22] La Rochefoucauld's phrase is "font encore grâce au coeur humain." *Maximes,* 268.

[23] The Augustinian note remained in evidence twelve years later, however, in Jacques Esprit's treatise, *La Fausseté des vertus humaines,* 1678.

[24] Lafond, *La Rochefoucauld,* 59–66. Pascal Quinard sees both La Rochefoucauld and Jacques Esprit as embodying an "antisénéquisme total." See the "Traité de l'Esprit" at the head of his edition of *La Fausseté des vertus humaines* (Paris: Aubier, 1996), 40–41.

[25] The most extensive example is Louis Hippeau, *Essai sur la morale de La Rochefoucauld* (Paris: A.-G. Nizet, 1948), especially 75–96.

marily an unmasking of Stoic pretensions, it is unlikely they would have outlived the interest of the object they were meant to expose. The targeting of
Stoicism in the frontispiece may be another sign of La Rochefoucauld's concern, in the launching of the first edition of the *Maxims,* to hew as close as
possible to Christian orthodoxy. The unmasking of Seneca, in that case, is
itself a mask. During this same period, La Rochefoucauld gave to Père
Thomas Esprit, who helped him with the publication of the *Maxims,* an interesting explanation of what he meant when he used the inclusive "we"
whose ruses are his constant target. "When I say we, I mean the man who
believes he owes to himself alone whatever he has of good, as did the great
men of antiquity. . . . I believe there was pride, injustice and a thousand other
ingredients in the magnanimity and liberality of Alexander and many others."[26] Now this explanation is clearly a screen, for the "we" of the *Maxims* is surely not confined to any group holding a single opinion, Stoic or
otherwise; "we" is rather that universal group of people who cannot help
behaving in certain ways, whatever their opinions may be. To deprive the
work of this level of generality would be to remove its candor and its force.
The *Maxims* are not about opinion but about behavior, not about what we
think but about what we do in *spite* of what we think.

Nevertheless, the Stoic doctrine is a symptom of a wider human tendency
that La Rochefoucauld is very much concerned to expose. The Stoics' insistence upon autonomy, freedom, and self-control makes an epitome of our irrepressible tendency to exaggerate not only the quality of our motives but
also the deliberateness and simplicity of our behavior, to make our actions
look purer, stronger, more clear-sighted, and above all more deliberate than
they are. It is a tendency that is magnified not only in Stoic philosophy but
in the aristocratic ethos from which Stoicism emerged.

Obviously the aristocratic virtues come in for rough treatment in the *Maxims,* along with the general pose of strength and independence that human
beings like to assume in the eyes of the world. Paul Bénichou, in one of the
most brilliant discussions of La Rochefoucauld, understands the work as
part of a determined opposition to high aristocratic literature, the insipid
sublimations of the romances such as *Astrée* so much in vogue during the
early seventeenth century, and the orgies of self-sacrificial grandeur on display in the dramas of Corneille. The "demolition of the hero," as Bénichou
puts it, was a trend of the later century to which Pascal, Racine, La Fontaine,
and Molière all contributed. It coincided broadly with the destruction of the
power of the high aristocracy in France through the brilliant efforts of Riche-
lieu, Mazarin, and Louis XIV.[27]

It was not just the goodness of the heroic nature but its force that had
been so painfully discredited, and there is a sense in which much can be understood about the psychology of the *Maxims* by reading them as a post-

---

[26] Letter of 6 February 1664. *Maximes,* 578–79.
[27] Bénichou, *Morales du grand siècle,* 96–111.

mortem on the Fronde. That tendency toward vacillation and irresolution, a lack of fixity of purpose, which the Cardinal de Retz famously ascribed to La Rochefoucauld,[28] was the besetting weakness of the Frondeurs as a group. In the *Maxims* it defines the character of *amour-propre* itself, with its endlessly shifting motives, multiplicity of purpose, and earnest pursuit of triviality—all of those elements of our nature that keep the great moment from being seized. To be preoccupied with such moments and with how they were lost is a symptom of the old soldier in defeat. La Rochefoucauld knew that character does not depend entirely upon us, that we need fortune to provide the stage for our heroism (380), but in his case, fortune had provided many opportunities and he had let himself be bettered by men like de Retz who made more judicious use of chance. When we read, in the *Réflexions diverses*, of the infinitely flexible manager of *amour-propre* and in the *Maxims* of the man of ability who can turn anything to his advantage (59), we think not of La Rochefoucauld but of his enemies, and especially Mazarin. Many of the truths of the *Maxims* are the truths of defeat.

We have seen that La Rochefoucauld contributed to the seventeen-century vogue of the *honnête homme*. The term is conveniently ambidextrous: it can indicate moral probity of a certain rigor but also social graces of a very superficial kind. As La Rochefoucauld has it, "The true *honnête homme* is one who does not pride himself upon anything.[29] This distinguishes him from the great-souled men of earlier centuries, who were obliged to insist upon their worth. Corneille's heroes are hardly *honnête* in this sense. Their goodness and their greatness are identical, and modesty for them would be injustice. The rash frankness of Molière's *Misanthrope* is a vestige of this older heroic sensibility, where competition for admiration must always be taken in earnest, and where the confined atmosphere of the court does not allow sufficient scope for aristocratic freedom.[30] La Rochefoucauldian wisdom is just the opposite of this rude courage. In the *Réflexions diverses*, not published during his lifetime, La Rochefoucauld counsels his readers to do everything to avoid arousing the resentment of those with whom they come into company.

> Everyone wants to find his pleasure and his advantages at the expense of others; we always prefer ourselves to those among whom we intend to live, and we almost always make them feel this preference; this is what troubles and destroys our relations with others. It is at least necessary to hide this desire of preference, since it is too natural in us for

[28] Cardinal de Retz, *Mémoires,* ed. Maurice Allem and Edith Thomas (Paris: Gallimard, 1956), 155.

[29] See no. 203. As the editor comments, "This celebrated definition is perfectly in accordance with the ideas of the chevalier Méré, who passed for the grand theoretician of *honnêteté*: 'It is desirable, in order to be agreeable at all times, to excel in everything that is fitting to *honnêtes gens,* without, nevertheless, taking pride in anything'" *Maximes,* 51–52, n. 4.

[30] Bénichou, *Morales,* 214–16.

us to be able to thwart it; we must give pleasure to ourselves and to others, manage their *amour-propre,* and never wound it.[31]

This is true *honnêteté.* When it comes to human nature in general we can be honest, but when it comes to dealing with our friends we must remember that they are human and it may not be tactful to show that we can see into the folds of their hearts.[32] Thus we find La Rochefoucauld, the inquisitor of hypocrisy, flattering his friends in those letters in which he submits his scathing maxims for their approval, playing upon their irrepressible vanity for the satisfaction of his own.

The *honnête homme* represents an important modification of the aristocratic character, a further step in a long "civilizing process," inculcating artificiality and self-control, that goes back to the time of Castiglione.[33] The *honnête homme* has learned to "manage" the *amour-propre* of others, as La Rochefoucauld recommends, by curbing his own[34] in order to avoid the hazards both of ordinary selfishness and Corneillian "noble pride."[35] He does not insist upon his virtues, his rank, or even his special accomplishments, but there is no doubt he would still like these to be recognized. For all the sweetness of his manners, he wants his *tabouret.* The *Maxims* expose many of the ruses he employs to get it. He praises others in the hopes that they will praise him. He refuses praise in order to be praised twice. He is more willing to admit some weakness and faults than others: he will complain, for instance, of his memory but never of his intelligence. And there are some vices of which he tends to be proud. His *amour-propre* is still there, but it has become guilty, subtle, indirect, subterranean, and, therefore, ready to be unmasked. This new delicacy of the *honnête homme* was La Rochefoucauld's fascination. Each of the maxims is a kind of inverted compliment to the ruses of *honnêteté,* using wit to cover up the exciting intimacy of all transactions that expose our secret wishes.

The "we," then, exposed by the *Maxims* is not the Stoic who believes that he himself is the source of "whatever he has of good," but the man of self-deluded self-idolatry who knows—though only partially, furtively, and intermittently—that his responsibility for what he has of good is largely a contrivance of "fortune or [his] ingenuity," but who knows just as well that responsibility is a fiction he cannot do without. Not only is society made up

[31] From "De la Société," *Réflexions diverses* 2, *Maximes,* 185–86.

[32] *Maximes,* 188.

[33] See Norbert Elias, *The Civilizing Process: Sociogenetic and Psychogenetic Investigations,* trans. Edmund Jephcott, ed. Eric Dunning, Johan Goudsblom, and Stephen Mennell, corrected edition (Malden, Mass.: Blackwell Publishers, 2000).

[34] This is a contemporary definition of *honnêteté* attributed to Saint-Évremond and to Damien Mitton: "It is this management of Happiness for ourselves and for others that we should call *Honnêteté,* which is only, properly speaking, *Amour-propre* well-managed." See Lafond, *La Rochefoucauld,* 54, and n. 150.

[35] Pierre Corneille, *Le Cid* (Paris: Librairie Marcel Didier, 1946), line 93.

of contrived façades facing each other, but without them men would be unable to live with each other, leading unavoidably to the conclusion that we can only learn to manage them (256; 87). There is a hint of aristocratic protest at this state of affairs: the stronger we are the less we have need for, and patience for, disguise. But we are not very strong. The true *honnête homme* is capable of real sincerity, but few, if any, are strong enough to be *honnête*, and their *honnêteté* comes not of itself but is a sign of strength and pride in its possession.

The writing of the *Maxims* must be recognized as an impressive act of intellectual fortitude. Behind the "we" who conceals there is the "I" who has been willing to tip his mask far enough for others to get a glimpse. Many readers have had the same reaction as Madame de Lafayette writing to Madame de Sablé: "Ha, Madame! what corruption he must have in his mind and in his heart to imagine all that!"[36] But La Rochefoucauld does not call on God to forgive him, nor does he propose a new moral or amoral code of behavior. What he does is to hold up the self-idolatrous behavior of others in the light of their own idealistic postures, adding to their hypocrisy and subterfuge his own complicity, and harvesting the credit of both these revelations. And though his insights can be called instructive, the space of responsibility is so attenuated here, there is so little room for hope or anger, admiration or blame, that we are left primarily with the uneasy joys of unmasking and the risky sensation of disillusioned intimacy.

In previous chapters we have seen suspicion in the service of God, of science, and of political authority. La Rochefoucauld strikes a new note: suspicion for the pleasure of the spectacle and the risk of the performance— suspicion as a social activity and an art in its own right. He is one of essential purveyors of psychological depth, as Nietzsche held him to be, and though the scholars who emphasize what he shares with the Augustinian tradition cannot be faulted, the spirit of his inquiry is a far different one from Augustine's or Nietzsche's. In a maxim that he never published, La Rochefoucauld offers us his version of the Fall:

> God, in order to punish man for original sin, allowed him to make for himself a god out of his own *amour-propre* in order to be tormented by it in all the actions of his life. (*MP* 22)

If this had been meant as a contribution to theology, it would be possible to read it in a perfectly orthodox way. What interests the author here, though, is not the Augustinian explanation but the irony: whereas in Augustine's account the first human beings surrendered their right to paradise for the pleasure of indulging their *amour-propre,* for La Rochefoucauld the need to indulge the tyrant *amour-propre* was not only the cause of the Fall but its punishment as well. In the torment of our fallen nature, therefore, there is a

---

[36] Letter to Madame de Sablé, 1663. *Maximes,* 577.

perfect economy and irony, a kind of justice that goes beyond religion and in a sense replaces it. And whereas Nietzsche would advise us to free ourselves from a myth of moral responsibility that is our own creation, La Rochefoucauld has a better idea of our strength—which is to say, our weakness. Recognizing that none of us can free ourselves from that service to the love of self which is the essence of our morality, La Rochefoucauld invites us rather to admire the wit, the subtlety, and the beauty with which we have devised our own predicament.

10

Swift and the Satiric Absolute

I have tried to show how the temptation to paranoia was contained within the medieval model of human agency, and how that model was later transformed toward an enthusiastic negation of agency, the second development being an immediate intellectual and social response to the first. The dynamic of schism, rupture, and violence that arrived with the second, Reformation model eventually brought about a general change in the terms of cultural debate. It is here that we step into the waters of Lethe from which we will emerge, after a long progress, into modernity. The stages of the journey have often been retraced, either to lament the outcome or to secure it. The creature that stumbled into the modern light has some recognizable features of Protestant individualism: reliance upon private judgment, the rejection of priests, and a form of economic rationality that Max Weber equated with Calvinist self-scrutiny. These features of the earlier model are transmogrified in the later one. The tendency of modern culture that is of special interest to this study, though, is one that the inventors of the modern borrowed directly from the religious culture they hoped to derail—the habit of suspicion.

Protestant culture in all of its forms invested heavily in difference. It began by asserting its difference from Catholicism, and each new establishment of Protestant orthodoxy drew the lines more sharply and radically among the Protestant sects themselves. The Protestant denial of agency, and especially the agency of the clergy, proved empowering to schismatic teachers and secular opponents of Catholic power. At the point, however, when the socially disruptive effect of Protestant contentiousness became as visible and threatening as the corruptions of Catholic authority had been—and this is a fair description, it seems to me, of what occurred for many observers of the English Civil War—the Protestant rhetoric of difference became unexpectedly vulnerable. For analysts of the revolution such as Hobbes, and for

Restoration wits like Samuel Butler, Catholic and Protestant could come to seem no more worth distinguishing than rival forms of mania, one given to "worshipp[ing] stocks and stones," to recall Milton's phrase, but the other following an "Inner Light" so much a vagabond that, as Butler jeered, it could never be out of its way.[1] The long-established critique of Catholic ritual as magic and superstition was joined with the critique of Protestant enthusiasm, the two now conflated as opposite forms of degraded imagination. The point is most memorably asserted in the satire of the Big and Little Endians in *Gulliver's Travels*. This satiric tendency, Blanford Parker has shown, became a general mode of culture in the years after 1660—the reign of Augustan "general satire."[2] Its peculiar irony is intimately connected with the origins of the novel as traced by Michael McKeon,[3] and its eventual achievement of a literary mode of skepticism comparable to and historically connected with the philosophy of empiricism.[4]

In its initial and most pointed phase, beginning with Hobbes, general satire has a distinctly Augustinian flavor; it enforces a mordant contempt for human nature, a characteristic preserved in mature examples such as Swift. Its mode of expression is, as Parker observes, a "material monism."[5] This monism is the orphaned lower half of Augustine's dualism. It presents a degraded world of physical appetites and objects not only to mark the absence of the intellectual, the spiritual, and the ideal but as a rebuke to our affinity for such fictions. Luther and Calvin denied that the human intellect could guide us to salvation and that human works could be a way to it. They did not impugn the fitness of the intellect for common affairs or the study of Nature. The Reformed faith that throve in England and its American colonies had in fact largely reabsorbed the heritage of medieval scholasticism and its very grand sense of intellectual possibility;[6] radical Protestantism, particularly during the Interregnum, was more than friendly to Bacon's program of natural philosophy. Reform may have been in some broad sense anti-humanistic, but it was by no means anti-intellectual. The Augustan image of humanity, by contrast, is distinguished by sheer buffoonery. The laceration of intellect is total and the evisceration of agency nearly complete. The vision that emerges from these works is of a creature often demonically ener-

---

[1] Samuel Butler, *Hudibras,* ed. John Wilders (New York: Oxford University Press, 1967), 1.1.495–98.

[2] Blanford Parker, chap. 1 in *The Triumph of Augustan Poetics: English Literary Culture from Butler to Johnson* (Cambridge: Cambridge University Press, 1998).

[3] For McKeon, "status inconsistency" causes the bitter irony and skepticism of the Augustans. See *Origins of the English Novel, 1600–1740* (Baltimore: Johns Hopkins University Press, 1987), esp. pt. 1..

[4] For Hume's view of the sickness of the English Revolution and its connection with the disease of philosophy, see Donald W. Livingston, *Philosophical Melancholy and Delirium: Hume's Pathologizing of Philosophy* (Chicago: University of Chicago Press, 1998), esp. 225–36.

[5] Parker, *Triumph,* 34.

[6] Perry Miller, *The New England Mind: The Seventeenth Century* (Cambridge: Harvard University Press, 1954).

getic but whose energy reveals not a capacity for action but a brutal enslavement to folly and to need.

It is therefore, as Parker observes, a serious distortion to depict the Augustan period as a last expression of Renaissance humanism (7, 11–13). Still
less was Augustan irony the spontaneous product of a world grown newly
modern, that is to say, envisioned according to the novel lights of modern
science. The antithesis between science and religion that seems so inevitable
to us is the backward projection of a later age. What gave the post-Restora-
tion period its distinctive intellectual atmosphere was the determination on
the part of many, including the government, to complete the Hobbesian project of suppressing every source of religious dissent either by blunting or ex-
punging the authority of faith, reason, inspiration, and tradition. As Parker
puts it, "the spirit of the age of Locke and Shaftesbury, and the succeeding
one of Pope and Walpole, was not the inevitable result of the *Zeitgeist* of that
century—an unconscious growth of empiricism and latitude—but in part a
neatly crafted program founded upon the useful art of forgetting for the
maintenance of public order" (3). The Augustan agenda was pursued with
determined violence and single-mindedness of spirit. Whereas Hobbes had
erected an impressive scheme of definitions and deductions to buttress his
program of repression, to the still more cynical spirits of the next generation
even this degree of ambition appeared Quixotic. The intellectual grandeur
of Hobbes's system, its radical character, and its ostentatious aura of innovation mark its unacknowledged kinship with the products of the Interregnum, the breeding ground of Levellers, Seekers, Shakers, Muggletonians,
Fifth Monarchy men, Ranters, Quakers, and other prophets and projectors
whose radicalism would become anathema to succeeding generations.[7]

In *Hudibras,* Butler's sprawling burlesque of Interregnum innovation,
Quixote and Sancho are reborn,[8] but the object of their infatuation, and of
Butler's mirth, is no longer the culturally marginal set of literary habits
mocked by Cervantes; in their place religion itself now serves as the incitement to ridicule and folly. It hardly matters whether that religion be the erudite hypocrisy of Hudibras or the untutored effusions of his squire. The long
set of controversies between Catholic and Protestant, Anglican and Dissenter, have been reduced to absurdity. Their adherents are divided between
hypocrisy and ignorance, their conflict no more noble or meaningful than a
great carnival of bear-baiting, to recall one of the central scenes of Butler's
poem. Butler's genius for physicalizing reduction and the collapsing of distinctions was to provide a repertoire of satiric instruments without which
Dryden, Swift, Pope and their successors can hardly be imagined.[9]

---

[7] The classic account is Christopher Hill, *The World Turned Upside Down: Radical Political Ideas During the English Revolution* (Baltimore, Md.: Penguin, 1975; rptd. with changes from the Maurice Temple Smith edition, 1972).

[8] Ronald Paulson, *Don Quixote in England: The Aesthetics of Laughter* (Baltimore: Johns Hopkins University Press, 1998), 9.

[9] Parker, *Triumph,* 53–60.

The narrative of *Hudibras* invites the reader to adopt a relaxed observer's curious enjoyment of the spectacle of religious vanity and folly in every possible form. The description of Hudibras's religion is one of Butler's most successful and telling passages:

> For his *Religion* it was fit
> To match his Learning and his Wit:
> 'Twas *Presbyterian* true blew,
> For he was of that stubborn Crew
> Of Errant Saints, whom all men grant
> To be the true Church *Militant:*
> Such as do build their Faith upon
> The holy text of *Pike* and *Gun;*
> Decide all Controversies by
> Infallible *Artillery;*
> And prove their Doctrine Orthodox
> By Apostolick Blows and Knocks;
> Call Fire and Sword and Desolation,
> A *godly-thorough-Reformation,*
> Which always must be carry'd on,
> And still be doing, never done:
> As if Religion were intended
> For nothing else but to be mended.
> A Sect, whose chief Devotion lies
> In odde perverse Antipathies;
> In falling out with that or this,
> And finding somewhat still amiss:
> More peevish, cross, and spleenatick
> Then Dog distract, or Monky sick:
> That with more care keep holy-day
> The wrong, then others the right way:
> Compound for Sins, they are inclin'd to,
> By damning those they have no mind to;
> Still so perverse and opposite,
> As if they worshipp'd God for spight.
> The self-same thing they will abhor
> One way, and long another for.
> Free-will they one way disavow;
> Another, nothing else allow.
> All Piety consists therein
> In them, in other men all Sin.
> Rather then faile, they will defie
> That which they love most tenderly,
> Quarrel with *minc'd Pies,* and disparage
> Their best and dearest friend, *Plum-porredge;*

Fat *Pig* and *Goose* it self oppose,
And blaspheme *Custard* through the nose.
(1:1.187–231)

It is difficult to exaggerate the importance of the change in attitude toward religion embodied in writing such as this. Butler goes much farther even than Hobbes in the portrayal of religious excess, and in a form much more popular and widely disseminated, one that would come to represent, through succeeding refinements, a norm of feeling and of taste. Until this moment, Christianity, however vicious and glaring its corruptions, could still lay claim to a strong presumptive connection with virtue, just as atheism, when it existed, was self-evidently a shield for vice. In Butler's treatment, religion itself has begun to look like a form of vice; it is, as the quoted passage suggests, the expression of perverse whimsicality, false intellect, animal cunning, restless violence, hypocrisy, and gross creaturely self-indulgence. The last two of these features are brilliantly combined in the final sally, "And blaspheme *Custard* through the nose," which glances with caustic mirth at the Dissenters' high-pitched mode of trumpeting the Gospel. Butler's humor is as broad as possible without being the least bit good-natured.

It is not that Butler is showing how poorly the Dissenters live up to their ideals; rather, the ideals themselves are coming into question. His thrust against the "Errant Saints" of the "Church *Militant*" could find its mark against any religiously inspired heroism or, in fact, against sectarian idealism per se. All saints are in danger of appearing Quixotic and "Errant," either losing themselves in senseless intellectual distinctions or making them an excuse for the gross imperatives of the body. The connection of what are normally thought of as the highest aspects of human nature with animal impulses, with "Dog distract or Monkey sick," is a constant feature of Butler's imagination. It looks forward to Rochester's "Satyr against Reason and Mankind," where the comparison of human with animal will be to the brutes' advantage. Taking in view Butler's great vision of the chaos of his age, it would be hard to think of a more graphic counterpart to Pierre Bayle's notorious suggestion that a society of atheists would be more inclined to peace and virtue than a society of believers.[10] In fact, Butler understood the Restoration precisely as a natural transition from one of these modes to the other, from religious imposture to atheistic apathy, for, as he wrote in his Notebooks, "the Licentiousness of the present Age owes its originall to nothing so much as the Counterfeit Piety of the last."[11] When the "civil fury" of doctrinal controversy had been quenched forever, the underlying appetites could finally express themselves without need for disguise.

---

[10] See the ninth letter of Pierre Bayle, *Pensées diverses sur la comète*, ed. A. Prat (1911), reissued with notes by Pierre Rétat (Paris: Société des Textes François Modernes, 1994).

[11] Samuel Butler, *Prose Observations*, ed. Hugh De Quehen (Oxford: Clarendon Press, 1979), 54.

Royalist and Anglican readers, including Charles II himself, relished Butler's pulverizing scorn of papist and presbyter without understanding the
deeper import of his teaching for all hierarchy and religion, including their
own.[12] In fact, the text of *Hudibras* mentions neither God, King, nor State,
perhaps because, as Earl Miner speculates, Butler simply had no interest in
them.[13] The poem, he says, "gives allegiance to little outside itself" (158).
Modern readers can look to the author's long-unpublished notebooks and
Characters to discover what nourished Butler's spirit in the midst of the wastes
his intellect had made. What they will find is one or two endorsements of a
faculty of reason that grasps the order of things in the world (65), an assertion
of the plausibility of the afterlife (211), and an expression of belief that the Order of Nature is a copy of the divine wisdom (66–67). These opinions are el-
egantly stated but seem far from the center of Butler's concern. The notebooks
also show that, like all educated men of his era, Butler's mind was well-fur-
nished with biblical lore suitable for moralizing explication as the occasion required. This does not mean that he believed in Revelation, for the Bible, he
asserts, is merely a book written by men (114, 189); nor does it mean that he
thinks we have knowledge of God except "as he is a Creator" (274). Butler,
then, is a kind of proto-Deist. He lacks, however, even the insipid theistic enthusiasm of Voltaire. The bent of his intellect was toward neither the vertical
nor the abstract, but fastened instead upon his fellow creatures. With a gaze
cold and patient, he was driven to pursue the logic of every human folly and
deceit to whatever length the investigation required. Lacking any inclination
toward idealism, he never tired of exposing the falsity of others' ideals, nor did
he scruple to chronicle the narrowest windings of the human will.

The volume of Butler's *Characters*, published in 1759, constitutes one of
the great monuments of spleen. In assembling its more than one hundred and
fifty entries, the author proves his excellence in the taxonomy of foible, mis-
demeanor, and fault. Consecutive in the table of contents we find "A Pedant,
A Hunter, A Humorist, A Leader of a Faction, A Debauched Man, The Seditious Man, An Affected Man, A Medicine-taker, The Rude Man, The Miser,
A Rabble, A Shopkeeper, A Quaker, A Swearer, The Luxurious, An Un-
grateful Man, A Knight of the Post, An Undeserving Favourite, A Cuckold,
A Malicious Man, A Squire of Dames, A Knave, An Anabaptist, A Vintner,
An Hypocrite" and so on and on.[14] Each and every one of them has his or
her own insidious game, yet in spite of this apparently rich array, Butler's human bestiary can hardly be described as varied. There is a single theme—the
besotted contrivances of the human heart as subjected to witty vivisection
by an indefatigable savant.

---

[12] Parker, *Triumph*, 30.

[13] Earl Miner, *The Restoration Mode from Milton to Dryden* (Princeton: Princeton University Press, 1974), 175.

[14] Samuel Butler, *Characters*, ed. Charles W. Daves (Cleveland: Press of Case Western Reserve University, 1970). I have modernized some of Butler's spelling.

Butler's project of unmasking aims at empirical completeness. The value he sets upon intellect is that it helps one to avoid both credulity and inhibition: "A man gaines nothing by being wise (which he may not as well obtaine without it) but only that he is less liable to cheates, and troubled with fewer unnecessary Scruples, than Fooles usually are."[15] Wisdom of the more positive kind actually does harm to one's fortune, for it puts one too far out of harmony with the "general temper" of the species.

> The reason why Fooles and knaves thrive better in the world then wiser and honester men, is because they are nearer to the Generall Temper of mankind, which is nothing but a Mixture of Cheat and Folly, which those that understand and meane better cannot comply with, but entertaine themselves with another kinde of Fooles Paradise of what should be, not what is: while those that know no better take Naturally to it, and get the Start of them. (11)

This passage presents us with the heart of the Augustan point of view, which counsels a complete renunciation of the "Fooles Paradise of what should be" in favor of the satiric pageant of the real. The satirist's vision of knaves and fools becomes the only variety of knowledge worth having. It is valued for its practical import only as the means of unmasking idealistic pretense, ideals being a façade either for "Folly" or "Cheat." The philosopher, according to Butler, is a bearded ignoramus and the mathematician no better.[16] The natural philosopher is a self-deluded nincompoop less observant than his footboys.[17] As for classical learning, for all the "Paines and industry and time" such attainments require, they "commonly prove no better bargain than he makes who breaks his teeth to crack a nut that has nothing but a maggot in it."[18] In Butler's imagination, every nut contains the treasure of a maggot.

Insofar as Butler can be said to have a religious doctrine, it is one of social conformity. "Men ought to do in Religion as they do in war," he counsels.

> When a Man of Honor is over-power'd, and must of Necessity render himself up a Prisoner, Such are always wont to indeavor to do it to some Person of Command and Quality, and not to a mean Scoundrell: So since all men are oblig'd to be of some Church; it is a more honorable (if there were nothing else in it) to be of that which has some Reputation, then such a one as is contemptible, and justly despised by all the best of men. (37)

[15] Butler, *Prose Observations*, 12.
[16] Butler, *Characters*, 94–95 and 119.
[17] See "The Elephant in the Moon," Butler's brilliant satire of the Royal Society, in Samuel Butler, *Satires and Miscellaneous Poetry and Prose,* ed. René Lamar (Cambridge: Cambridge University Press, 1928), 3–16.
[18] Butler, *Prose Observations*, 257.

This calculating endorsement of bland conformity sounds odd coming from Butler only because, having read his papers, it is difficult to think of him finding more honor in one church than another, or any honor in a church at all. He is as scathing on the subject of the clergy as Milton. "Clergymen," he says, "are like Scavengers that pollute and Defile their own Soules and Consciences in clensing those of other men" (200); they are pure self-seekers who "would have all men love Religion enough to serve their own Interests, and no more" (195). The clergy seem to be perfectly attuned with the spirit of "Cheat and Folly" and the "Generall Temper of mankind," except of course when they run in the fanatic vein, not surrendering with honor to the establishment but flaunting their own tyrannical instrument, the conscience. Where the Book of Ecclesiastes had counseled "Fear God, and keep his commandments: for this is the whole duty of man," conscience in Butler's day has become a license to oppress. "There is no wickednesse in the world," he says, "that It will not make Its Duty. Nor any inhumanity so horrible that It will not render the whole duty of man."[19] What had been the seat of moral judgment is now the great font of hypocrisy and an ultimate source of terror.

Butler takes religious excess as the touchstone of every kind of folly. The only equal object of his contempt is the fanatic's chief instrument, "the Rabble." Butler's class animus is the natural reflex of a court pensioner, but it fits seamlessly with his suspicious and satiric point of view. It is interesting to compare his attitude toward politics with that of Hobbes, whose philosophy Butler dismantles as an ungainly system of paradoxes. "The Hobbists will undertake to prevent Civil wars by proving that Mankind was borne to nothing else, To reduce men to Subjection and obedience, by maintaining that Nature made them all equal, Secure the Rights of Princes, by asserting that whosoever can get their Power from them has right enough to it, and persuade them and their Subjects to observe imaginary Contracts, by affirming that they are invalid as soon as made" (227). Hobbes' reasoning strikes Butler as facile, but one cannot avoid the impression that the philosopher's first mistake must have been that of resorting to reason at all. For Butler, however, "the chiefest Art of Government is to convert the Ignorance, Folly, and Madness of Mankinde (so much as may be) to their own good, which can never be done, by telling them Truth and Reason, or using any direct means; but by little Tricks and Divices (as they cure Madmen) that worke upon their Hopes and Fears to which their Ignorance naturally inclines them" (112–13). This is the philosophy of the imaginary carrot to go with the real stick. Where Hobbes's sovereign is an honest knave among knaves, Butler's is a trickster-therapist among fools. His view of life offers only two positions, the gull or the cheat. This is not merely the implication of Butler's writing but its central emphasis and the great burden of its empirical substance.

[19] Butler, *Prose Observations*, 302. Cf. Ecclesiastes 12:13. *The Whole Duty of Man* (1674) was the title of a work of piety attributed to Richard Allestree.

Swift and Madness

In Hobbes and Butler we witness the emergence of a general irony, an om-
nivorous habit of satire at once intellectually revolutionary and socially repressive. The very idea of taking a stand upon ultimate matters as they had
formerly been conceived was rendered not only dangerous but absurd. The
result was to be a permanent change in the tone and character of English culture. But though *Leviathan* and *Hudibras* are the two great originating gestures of Augustanism, it is to Swift that we must look for its profound literary
expression. If it is wise to be skeptical of the frequently admired poise and
balance of high Augustan writing, and especially that of Pope, there is a con-
vulsiveness in Swift's early prose that cannot be mistaken either for poise or
balance. It not only betrays Swift's peculiarly agitated and violent temperament but also marks him as a generation closer to the great political and ideological struggles of the later Restoration. The irony of *A Tale of a Tub,*
written near the end of the seventeenth century and published early in the
next, is of a swirling, disorienting, and unstable kind, a moral and intellectual vacuum into which rush all the confused elements of post-Reformation
controversy and modern learning. The allegorical tale of the three brothers
at the center of the work sets the moderation of the Anglican Church between the exorbitant corruption of the Catholics (Peter) and the mad severity of the Dissenters (Jack); the vehicle, however, is a knockabout farce,
which begins with the representative of Anglicanism (Martin) joining his
brothers as they break into society.

> They Writ, and Raillyed, and Rhymed, and Sung, and Said, and said
> Nothing; They Drank, and Fought, and Whor'd, and Slept, and Swore,
> and took Snuff: They went to new Plays on the first Night, and got
> Claps: They bilkt Hackney-Coachmen, ran in Debt with Shop-keepers,
> and lay with their Wives: They kill'd Bayliffs, kick'd Fidlers down
> Stairs, eat at *Locket*'s, loytered at *Will*'s. . . . Above all, they constantly
> attended those Committees of Senators who are silent in the *House,*
> and loud in the *Coffee-House,* where they nightly adjourn to chew the
> Cud of Politicks, and are encompass'd with a Ring of Disciples, who
> lye in wait to catch up their Droppings. The three Brothers had ac-
> quired forty other Qualifications of the like Stamp, too tedious to
> recount, and by consequence, were justly reckoned the most accom-
> plish'd Persons in the Town.[20]

This is how Swift portrays the pre-Reformation unity of the church. The allegorical subject, with all its historical weight and consequence, is repre-

---

[20] *A Tale of a Tub: Written for the Universal Improvement of Mankind* (1710), in *The Prose
Works of Jonathan Swift,* ed. Herbert Davis (Oxford: Blackwell, 1939), 1:45.

sented by a vehicle so mean, trivial, and irrelevant that the discrepancy between subject and vehicle can barely be measured and is no longer the point.
Rather, the vehicle simply replaces the thing it was ostensibly designed to
convey. It is not that Swift is asking his readers to accept the tale of the three
brothers as an authentic portrait of Reformation controversy, but rather that
the intellectual substance of religious struggle itself is simply not real or important enough to hold his attention. The author's fancy strays toward other,
more immediate objects of satiric malice, the debauched and free-thinking
court and coffee-house milieus of own his day.

Distraction, of course, is symptomatic of the *Tale*. Its most insistent satiric
thrust is directed against what Swift sees as the false pretenses of modern
scholarship: thus the farrago of appendages—servile and pointless dedica-
tions, wandering digressions, facile, all-encompassing systems of explanation, and vain lore of every sort. This state of distraction, however, is the
natural form of expression for a consciousness in which serious intellectual
distinctions have been levelled, and levelled so absolutely that the controversies of the last century have become no more meaningful than a trend in
fashion. It goes without saying that moral distinctions must be equally tenuous for a narrator who does not visibly distinguish between killing bailiffs,
kicking fiddlers downstairs, and eating in a tavern. Just as the grotesquery
of Butler's burlesque expresses a contempt too violent and absolute to be
controlled in genuine wit, so Swift's impatience with the intellectual poverty
of religious controversy is too intense to permit anything other than the mortification of intellectual, historical, and moral differences. Swift's contemporary readers were justified to complain that his way of contending with
abuses in religion was likely to bring religion itself into disrepute. William
Wotton, one of the victims of the *Tale*, speaks with considerable justice when
he complains that "In one Word, God and Religion, Truth and Moral Honesty, Learning and Industry are made a May-Game, and the most serious
Things in the World are described as so many several Scenes in *A Tale of a
Tub*."[21]

Swift does, of course, take on enemies that might have polished his sectarian credentials. Hobbes, for example, is one of the visible targets of *A Tale
of a Tub*. Swift's relation to Hobbes, though, as to all of his targets, is a highly
ambiguous one. While he was undoubtedly hostile to Hobbes's political absolutism, his materialism, and his system-building ambitions,[22] Swift's imagination absorbed, nevertheless, the Hobbesian critique of enthusiasm, and in
the *Tale* he deploys it with genius, especially in the two great digressions,
chapters eight and nine. The established method for ridiculing the perfec-

---

[21] *A Defense of the Reflections upon Ancient and Modern Leaning, In Answer to the Objections of Sir W. Temple, and Others. With Observations upon The Tale of a Tub* (1705), in *A
Tale of a Tub*, ed. A. C. Guthkelch and D. Nicol Smith (Oxford: Clarendon, 1920).

[22] "THE SENTIMENTS OF A *Church-of-England* MAN, With Respect to RELIGION *and* GOV-
ERNMENT" (1708), *Prose Works* 2:15.

tionistic zeal of the Dissenters had been to denounce it as hypocrisy.[23] The hypocritical Puritan is a figure older than Shakespeare's Malvolio, and religious hypocrisy was still the central target of Butler's humor. It was difficult, however, to sustain the argument that so many years of bloodletting and chaos had been set in motion primarily to sustain false pretenses. The wit of Butler's "Apostolick Blows and Knocks" does not penetrate quite to the depth of its object. In the *Tale*, Swift follows Hobbes in assimilating religious enthusiasm to madness, a more absolute and complete derangement of the mind than Burton's melancholy, and he develops Hobbes's etymological reduction of spirit to wind with nauseating vividness. The narrator devotes section 8 to "the Learned *Aeolists*," a sect founded by the Calvin figure of the *Tale*.[24] The Aeolists take *Wind* to be the principle from which "this whole Universe was at first produced, and into which it must at last resolve" (95). They "affirm," therefore, "the Gift of BELCHING to be the noblest Act of a Rational Creature" and they employ a wide array of techniques for inducing it. Furnished with a syllogism to prove that "*Learning is nothing but Wind*,"

> the philosophers among them, did in their Schools, deliver to their Pupils, all their Doctrines and Opinions by *Eructation*, wherein they had acquired a wonderful Eloquence, and of incredible variety. But the great Characteristick, by which their chief Sages were best distinguished, was a certain Position of Countenance, which gave undoubted Intelligence to what Degree or Proportion, the Spirit agitated the inward Mass. For, after certain Gripings, the *Wind* and Vapours issuing forth; having first by their Turbulence and Convulsions within, caused an Earthquake in Man's little World; distorted the Mouth, bloated the Cheeks, and gave the Eyes a terrible kind of *Relievo* [elevation]. At which Junctures, all their *Belches* were received for Sacred, the Sourer the better, and swallowed with infinite Consolation by their meager Devotees. (1:97)

The tone of this passage is crucial to its effect, and it is therefore important to acknowledge the doubleness of Swift's procedure in dealing with the objects of his abuse. The reduction of radical enthusiasm to displaced physical energies is trenchant and apropos insofar as it applies to its proper object, but it is put forth by the narrator with a straight-faced and literal-minded credulity that seems unaware of the satiric motive. Thus the irony moves in at least two directions, the narrator participating unself-consciously in the folly he describes and making a parade of the self-glorifying

---

[23] Philip Harth, *Swift and Anglican Rationalism: The Religious Background of "A Tale of a Tub"* (Chicago: University of Chicago Press, 1961), 70–71.

[24] He is also meant to remind us of Huguenots, Anabaptists, and John Knox, "Knocking Jack of the North." 1:88–89. See Swift's notes on page 88.

nonsense that Swift regards as modern erudition. The multi-directional aspect of Swift's irony has more than one function. The use of a comically naïve persona, a persona unaware of the extremity of its procedures, allows Swift to take the violence of the satiric image to an almost unprecedented level. There is something Dantesque in the result; Swift's way of condemning the religiously motivated behavior that he opposes is not to reason against it, nor merely to hold it up in the light of the behavior it produces, but to express it as a revolting distortion of the human form. But whereas Dante justifies his physicalized judgments as expressions of divine love and wisdom, the "somma sapienza e'l primo amore" emblazoned on the gates of the Inferno, Swift's come to the reader through the persona of a madman. This allows him to convey the comic vision of low church afflatus in a physically reductive vocabulary without becoming responsible for the intellectual assumptions that vocabulary implies. In fact, the intellectual distortions of the narrator's mind are precisely equal to the physical contortions of the bodies he describes. Each of them is a rebuke to the other: one would have to be as mad as the narrator of the *Tale* not to see the absurdity in the Aeolists' doctrines and to describe their behavior with open-minded neutrality.

There is another source for Swift's Aeolists. In *Enthusiasmus Triumphatus*, first issued in 1656 and enlarged in 1662, the Cambridge Platonist Henry More sets forward the thesis that

> the *Spirit* . . . that wings the *Enthusiast* in such a wonderful manner, is nothing else but that *Flatulency* which is the Melancholy complexion, and rises out of the Hypochondriacal humour upon some occasional heat. . . . Which fume mounting into the Head, being first actuated and spirited and somewhat refined by the warmth of the Heart, fills the Mind with variety of *Imaginations*, and so quickens and inlarges *Invention,* that it makes the *Enthusiast* to admiration *fluent* and *eloquent,* he being as it were drunk with new wine drawn from that Cellar of his own that lies in the lowest region of his Body, though he be not aware of it, but takes it to be pure *Nectar,* and those waters of life that spring from above.[25]

In More's account, religious enthusiasm takes its place among the other intellectual aberrations that arise from melancholy distortions of the imagination—dreams, drunkenness, lychanthropia, prophetic megalomania, Paracelsian alchemy and magic. He repeatedly emphasizes that a person can be deluded in one set of ideas yet be within his right mind in others; this is the key to understanding the false inspiration of the enthusiast. Philip Harth, in a classic study, assimilates Swift's treatment of enthusiasm to More's "Anglican rationalism," seeing both of them as engaged in a limited attack upon

[25] Henry More, *Enthusiasmus Triumphatus* (1662; Los Angeles: Augustan Reprint Society, 1966), 12.

the abuses of reason while preserving the proper use of reason itself. There are enough endorsements of reason in Swift's writings to make this interpretation a plausible one, but Harth does not pay enough attention to Swift's tone, which makes as much comedy out of the style of analysis More was practicing as it does out of the thing to be analyzed. Insofar as the narrator of the *Tale* has a unity of consciousness at all, that consciousness itself is hovering on the brink of insanity. More's treatment of the varieties of enthusiasm tends to mitigate the blame of characters who are in the grip of an imagination that they cannot control, whereas Swift's reduction of the operations of the spirit to mechanical means is at once a nihilating expression of contempt and a symptom of enthusiasm in a different vein.

There are further respects in which the comparison between Swift and More is an illuminating one, for while More is ingenious in extending the category of enthusiastic melancholy, he is careful to draw its limit. The existence of false inspiration does not discredit the existence of genuinely "enravished Souls" like Plato and Plotinus.

> To such Enthusiasm as this, which is but a triumph of the Soul of man inebriated, as it were, with the delicious sense of the divine life, that blessed Root and Originall of all holy wisdom and virtue, I must declare my self as much a friend, as I am to the vulgar fanatical Enthusiasm a professed enemy. And eternall shame stop his mouth that will dare to deny but that the fervent love of God and of the pulchritude of virtue, will afford the spirit of man more joy and triumph than ever was tasted by any lustfull pleasure, which the pen of unclean wits do highly magnify both in Verse and Prose. (45)

These words are unimaginable coming from the pen of Swift. His temperament was incompatible with even the most benign enthusiasm, or indeed with anything "fervent" other than the "savage indignation" professed in his epitaph. There is no mention of the love of God in any of his published sermons, and while he recommends that we love our neighbor as ourselves, he interprets this to mean that we should help our neighbor when it is convenient and entails no loss to ourselves.[26] In another sermon, looking back upon the idealism of the early Christians, he attributes the virtuous solidarity of those days to the advantage of being surrounded by enemies.[27] Swift's Christianity is of a resolutely unenthusiastic sort, seeming to live more or less entirely upon the resources of suspicion, disapproval, and rejection.

Both More and Swift were attempting a daring maneuver. Having placed certain kinds of religious thinking and behavior in the category of delusion, More may be suspected of having opened the door to a wholesale pathologizing of Christianity, and Swift, as we have seen, writing behind the screen

---

[26] "Doing Good: A Sermon" (1724), *Prose Works* 9:232.
[27] "*On* BROTHERLY LOVE" (1717), *Prose Works* 9:171.

of anonymity, evoked this complaint from his readers. In general, the willingness to deploy wit and ridicule on the most serious subjects was a signature of the time, and authors like Swift, Mandeville, and Shaftesbury, whatever their explicit intentions, were frequently regarded as lowering the tone of the age to the detriment of religion and manners.[28] In the defensive "Apology" to the second edition of A Tale of a Tub (1710), Swift defends his work as an attack upon abuses in religion, not upon religion itself (1:1–3). He appeals to the parodic tendency of the narrative, asserting that "there generally runs an Irony through the Thread of the whole work, which Men of Taste will observe and distinguish" (4). This irony, it is implied, mitigates the violence of his treatment of religious themes. The trouble with this defense is that the irony directed toward the narrator of the Tale does not genuinely undermine the force of its satiric representations. What it undermines is the moral stance of the narrator, which is subject to its own distinct set of ironies. The derisory portrayal of enthusiasm as Aeolism is for Swift a just and inevitable one, and the narrator's bizarre insouciance does not change that. The narrator himself is little more than a collection of verbal and intellectual habits, an epiphenomenal excrescence of print culture[29] and a figure too "plural," too much a contrivance of the narrative moment, to be a character in the novelistic sense.[30] Neither the narrator of the Tale nor any single author his work might be thought to parody has the weight or substance to absorb the destructive energies invested in the text.

It has been remarked that, although Swift is considered a "supreme ironist," he is rarely ironic in the modern sense.[31] Swift rarely says what he does not mean; it is, rather, the naïvely inhuman way in which the truths are put that creates the effect of irony. Henry More, we have seen, was careful to admit that for a person to be in the grip of enthusiasm on one subject did not necessarily mean that he would be unreasonable on others, and he was careful to limit the degree to which enthusiasm can be confined to the devalued realm of melancholy. More is evidently concerned to preserve the dignity of the human image. Swift, by contrast, speaking in the enthusiastic tones of his mannequin-narrator, is eager to extend the domain and force of madness so as to cover all extraordinary behavior, however much it is ostensibly to be admired.

> For, if we take a Survey of the greatest Actions that have been performed in the World, under the Influence of Single Men; which are The

---

[28] See John Redwood, Reason, Ridicule, and Religion: The Age of Enlightenment in England 1660–1750 (Cambridge: Harvard University Press, 1976), 39.

[29] Hugh Kenner, Flaubert, Joyce, and Beckett: The Stoic Comedians (Boston: Beacon, 1962), 37–44.

[30] See Denis Donoghue, Swift: A Critical Introduction (Cambridge: Cambridge University Press, 1969), 8–19, and Claude Rawson, Gulliver and the Gentle Reader (Boston: Routledge, 1973), 27–28.

[31] Donoghue, Swift, 23.

> *Establishment of New Empires by Conquest: The Advance and Prog-*
> *ress of New Schemes in Philosophy; and the contriving, as well as the*
> *propagating of New Religions:* We shall find the Authors of them all,
> to have been Persons, whose natural Reason hath admitted great Rev-
> olutions from their Dyet, their Education, the Prevalency of some cer-
> tain Temper, together with the particular Influence of Air and Climate.
> (1:102)

At first glance the narrator of this passage might seem to be using irony when
he refers to the "the greatest Actions that have been performed in the World,
under the Influence of Single Men," but this is not the case; he is simply unaware that consigning this behavior to the realm of physical causes is incompatible with the image of humanity implicit in the very notion of
greatness. As the analysis proceeds, the sense of moral discrepancy becomes
much more extreme, with Swift's narrator taking care to anticipate the
reader's unwillingness to believe that greatness could arise from such dis-
crepant sources.

> For the *upper Region* of Man, is furnished like the *middle Region* of
> the Air; The Materials are formed from Causes of the widest Differ-
> ence, yet produce at last the same Substance and Effect. Mists arise
> from the Earth, Steams from Dunghils, Exhalations from the Sea, and
> Smoak from Fire; yet all Clouds are the same in Composition, as well
> as Consequences: and the Fumes issuing from a Jakes, will furnish as
> comely and useful a Vapor, as Incense from an Altar. (102)

By the time we get to the final leveling of "comely and useful Vapors," it becomes impossible to take this passage as anything but biting satire. Yet,
though the narrator's insensitivity is extreme, the analysis retains its force,
enacting a physicalist reductionism of the most universal and absolute kind.
With its emphasis upon the identity of the material substrate underlying the
variety of physical causes, we are reminded of Lucretius, who is named later
in the "Digression" as one of the great mad "Introducers of new Schemes in
Philosophy," though he was among Swift's lifelong favorite authors. Even if
Swift would not have endorsed such a philosophy—or any philosophy—in
a systematic way, it furnished him with a powerful representation of the limits of human agency and a vital satiric means for the undermining of human
dignity. It is imaginatively irresistible to him.[32] And if the scatology of Swift's
reduction reminds us of Luther's colloquy with the devil, there is also a key

[32] The psychology of the humors, which Swift's narrator manipulates with such abandon,
was centuries old, and the term *humor* itself testifies to a long connection with satiric thinking.
The traditional psychology was beginning to be transformed by a more nerve-oriented physi-
ology in the seventeenth century. See Roy Porter, *Mind-Forg'd Manacles: A History of Madness
in England from the Restoration to the Regency* (Cambridge: Harvard University Press, 1987),
47–48.

difference: while Luther includes himself in the degraded world of the body, Swift is uncannily absent.

Swift invented a mode of writing by means of which one form of absurdity could be used to mock another, in a way that frees the author not only from having to commit himself to either doctrine but also from having to take them seriously enough to confront them, as it were, face to face. In setting one absurdity against another, Swift does not have to take up any stance of his own—not even the stance of the mocker. He has set in motion a machinery of reduction and a mannequin to work the levers. The concealment of his own agency corresponds with the destruction of the agency of his targets. Let us follow the mannequin-narrator another step further as he provides an example to support his thesis that madness is the source of all great accomplishments. "A certain Great Prince raised a mighty Army," he tells us, putting the whole world in "trembling Expectation" and "profound Conjectures" about his intentions.

> Some believed he had laid a Scheme for universal Monarchy: Others, after much Insight, determined the Matter to be a Project for pulling down the *Pope,* and setting up the *Reformed* Religion, which had once been his own. Some, again, of a deeper Sagacity, sent him in *Asia* to subdue the *Turk,* and recover *Palestine.* In the midst of all these Projects and Preparations; a certain *State-Surgeon,* gathering the Nature of the Disease by these Symptoms, attempted the Cure, at one Blow performed the Operation, broke the Bag, and out flew the *Vapor;* nor did any thing want to render it a complete Remedy, only, that the Prince unfortunately happened to Die in the Performance. Now, is the Reader exceeding curious to learn, from whence this *Vapor* took its Rise, which had so long set the Nations at a Gaze? What secret Wheel, what hidden Spring could put into Motion so wonderful an Engine? It was afterwards discovered, that the Movement of this whole Machine had been directed by an absent *Female,* whose Eyes had raised a Protuberancy, and before Emission, she was removed into an Enemy's Country. What should an unhappy Prince do in such ticklish Circumstances as these? . . .
>
> Having to no purpose used all peaceable Endeavours, the collected part of the *Semen,* raised and enflamed, became adust, converted to Choler, turned head upon the spinal Duct, and ascended to the Brain. The very same Principle that influences a *Bully* to break the Windows of a Whore, who has jilted him, naturally stirs up a Great Prince to raise mighty Armies, and dream of nothing but Sieges, Battles, and Victories. (1:103–4)

This passage is justly famous. Beginning with the pompous air of social comedy, it achieves an ostentatiously powerful rhetorical build-up, which it then releases, derisively mimicking the deflationary effect with which the physician breaks "the Bag" and lets the vapors fly. Then, with a series of rhetorical questions once again soliciting the reader's curiosity about the "Secret Wheel" that "could put into Motion so wonderful an Engine," a brilliant battery of shocking technical terms emerges to convey the workings of the "Hidden Spring"—"Protuberancy," "Emission," "*Semen,* raised and inflamed, become adust" (burnt) and "spinal Duct." The result is an ineffaceable description of the process set into operation by an "absent *Female,*" showing how all the great and heroic motives of the world are reduced to one. We do not have to assume that Swift shares the mechanistic intellectual vocabulary employed by the narrator here in order to see that he thoroughly endorses the equivalence the narrator has drawn between the "Great Prince" and the "Bully." As a moral and psychological argument the case is air-tight, and if the terms display an insensitivity that is also disturbing, their reductive tendency is no less than fitting in the description of such debased examples. The dehumanizing rhetorical effects in this passage such as the clinical employment of the word *female,* which is one of Swift's signatures, can be found throughout his writing, including the poetry, which also offers plentiful evidence that Swift was revolted by the facts of sexuality and the feminine physique. He prefers a vocabulary that permits the greatest possible detachment from ordinary human feelings. Readers who came of age in the twentieth century may feel an impulse to apply a Freudian model, or even to see Swift as anticipating Freud in the recognition of the hidden courses of sex, but in fact Swift was one of the sources for Freud's satiric method. Freud perfected the deployment of reductive, mechanistic psychology for satiric purposes and went a long way toward making the satiric perspective invented by Cervantes and Swift into a normative one.[33]

Now let us examine the words in which the narrator of the work sums up his findings.

Having therefore so narrowly past thro' this intricate Difficulty, the Reader will, I am sure, agree with me in the Conclusion; that if the *Moderns* mean by *Madness,* only a Disturbance or Transposition of the Brain, by Force of certain *Vapours* issuing up from the lower Faculties; Then has this *Madness* been the Parent of all those mighty Revolutions, that have happened in *Empire,* in *Philosophy,* and in *Religion.* For, the Brain, in its natural Position and State of Serenity, disposeth its Owner to pass his Life in the common Forms, without any Thought of subduing Multitudes to his own *Power,* his *Reasons* or his *Vision;* and the more he shapes his Understanding by the Pattern of Human Learning, the less he is inclined to form Parties after his particular Notion; because that instructs him in his private Infirmities, as well as in the stubborn Ignorance of the People. But when a man's Fancy gets *astride* on

---

[33] John Farrell, chap. 5 in *Freud's Paranoid Quest: Psychoanalysis and Modern Suspicion* (New York: New York University Press, 1996).

his Reason, when Imagination is at Cuffs with the Senses, and common Understanding, as well as common Sense, is Kick out of Doors; the first Proselyte he makes, is Himself, and when that is once compass'd, the Difficulty is not so great in bringing over others; A strong Delusion always operating from *without,* as vigorously as from *within.* (1:107–8)

The doctrine of this passage is clear—that the world is divided between two types of men (and it is indeed the male that Swift has in mind here): first there is the sane man, who passes his life "in the common forms" and "shapes his Understanding" as much as possible "by the Pattern of Human Learning," and then there is the madman who, driven by the urge to subdue "Multitudes to his own *Power,* his *Reasons* or his *Vision*" and inclined to prefer his own "particular Notions" to the "common forms" that guide the rest of mankind, becomes intoxicated with his own fancies and gathers "Parties" around him, there being "a peculiar *String* in the Harmony of the Human Understanding," as the narrator has explained, whereby intellects, "by a secret, necessary Sympathy," will resonate to the "same Tuning" (1:106). This passage from the "Digression on Madness" has long been recognized as crucial, for it is the only one that offers us even a glimpse of the normal. Phrases such as "the common forms" and "the Pattern of Human Learning" ("Human Learning" meaning *humane letters*) are strikingly free of the glamour of modernist enthusiasm. They are of a rather different sympathetic tuning. Yet in the larger perspective, what is breathtaking is the extent of the domain that Swift imaginatively concedes to megalomania. It embraces Dissenting in religion, the ethos of trade and the military adventures it fosters, martial heroism more or less per se, natural science, and most philosophy from ancient times to the present. It may be that Swift would have exempted Plato and Aristotle from the stigma of innovation; in his *Advice to a Young Gentleman, Lately enter'd into Holy Orders* (9:73) he warns against facile attacks upon pagan philosophy; but his treatment of philosophy in *Gulliver's Travels* is not encouraging. We have seen Bacon and Hobbes consigning their philosophical predecessors to the realm of delusion. Swift was as eager as they were to bring an end to the history of enthusiasm, both in the forms of religion and of speculative thought. His aim was not, however, like theirs, to restore thought to its proper methods but to suppress its ambitions almost entirely. What we are left with, then, is the sense that any attempt to distinguish oneself from others is a reflex cognate with insanity and likely to stimulate the springing up of all-disruptive "Parties."

The phrase "Life in the common forms" has often been cited as representing the unstated value that underlies Swiftian satire—a broad endorsement of the social, religious, and intellectual status quo and one which puts the onus of insanity upon anyone who cannot accept the self-evident authority of the present establishment. Such an endorsement does not require a self-searching affirmation of tradition, only a willingness to submit to it. Were we able, by a careful equilibration of the multi-directional ironies of the *Tale,* to extract this as its central doctrine, our grasp upon it would indeed be fortified by the record of Swift's later opinions. Throughout his career he remained in most respects a figure of massive social conservatism. It would be a mistake, however, to claim that this is what *A Tale of a Tub* was saying for its contemporary audience, or that it was primarily what Swift himself meant to convey by the work, for, based solely upon the text, one could as easily make the argument that the narrator's contrast between the workings of the "Brain in its natural Position and State of Serenity" and the brain distract has the primary effect of emphasizing the rather unsettling fragility and contingency of these two conditions. More than that, the idea that the brain in its "natural Position" would typically enjoy anything like a "State of Serenity" smacks of un-Swiftian credulity.

The dominant impression left by the *Tale* is not of resignation but the ferocious energy with which it wields the reductive genius of Hobbesian materialism and the expanded and desacralized notion of madness offered by Burton, Hobbes, and More against the all the recognized forms of human ambition. The great discovery of the narrator of the *Tale* is that the mind is entirely at the mercy of the body and that, once assailed by a "Protuberancy" or displaced from its "natural Position," it leads one irresistibly to megalomaniacal adventures, either in the realms of war, sex, politics, or speculation. When we look into history, then, what we see is nothing less than a series of lunatics imposing their private fantasies upon public reality by the force of imagination, aided by the tendency of their own visions to resonate with the errant fantasies of others. Here again Butler was a forerunner of Swiftian whimsy, though Swift could not have read the sentence of the *Characters* in which Butler observes that "among madmen the most mad govern all the rest, and recognize a natural Obedience from their Inferiors" (98). The conception of history as a parade of what we now might call paranoid fantasies in action was deployed by Bacon and Hobbes as a rationale for the reform of thought, but for Swift, as for Butler, it was a rationale for the humiliation of thought and the constraint of social and religious energies. The method by which it operates is not to be taken seriously in itself; to succumb to it would be to enter the intellectually degraded world of the sycophantic projector-narrator, a poor hack who spins out his own fantasies to earn a meager living according to the arbitrary fashions and humors of the time. Of these fashions the *Tale* is self-admittedly an excrescence. What we are left with, though, at the end of the *Tale,* is that, while the narrator's point of view leads one to madness and is a form of it, as a way of explaining human behavior it is *as good as true.* It might just as well be true given the intellectual, spiritual, and political chaos Swift sees as the recent past.

The vision of life put forward in the *Tale* is not an easy one to accept for all but the most determinedly repressive of temperaments. "Life in the common forms" offers only the most fragile peace and serenity, while all of the more compelling motives of human existence have been debased, and the human agent in general subjected to a frightening heteronomy. It was not to be expected, however, that the narrator who has fostered this tale with such enthusiasm, opening up the depths and "Secret Springs" of human consciousness with such uninhibited analytical display, would be likely to remain satisfied with a dispiriting conclusion of this kind. Returning to a Baconian topos with an un-Baconian, and un-Swiftian, toleration for fancy, "what mighty Advantages," he sighs, "Fiction has over Truth; and the Reason is just at our Elbow; because Imagination can build nobler Scenes, and produce more wonderful Revolutions than Fortune or Nature will be at Expense to furnish" (108). This surge of nostalgia for the pleasures of imagination on the part of the narrator suddenly gives way to a notorious outburst of violence:

In the Proportion that Credulity is a more peaceful Possession of the Mind, than Curiosity, so far preferable is that Wisdom, which converses about the Surface, to that pretended Philosophy which enters into the Depth of Things, and then comes gravely back with Informations and Discoveries, that in the inside they are good for nothing. The two Senses, to which all Objects first address themselves, are the Sight and the Touch; These never examine farther than the Colour, the Shape, the Size, and whatever other Qualities dwell, or are drawn by Art with Tools for cutting, and opening, and mangling, and piercing, offering to demonstrate, that they are not of the same consistence quite thro'. Now, I take all this to be the last Degree of perverting Nature; one of whose Eternal Laws it is, to put her best Furniture forward. And therefore, in order to save the Charges of all such expensive Anatomy for the Time to come; I do here think fit to inform the Reader, that in such Conclusions as these, Reason is certainly in the Right; and that in most Corporeal Beings, which have fallen under my Cognizance, the *Outside* hath been infinitely preferable to the *In*: Whereof I have been farther convinced from some late Experiments. Last Week I saw a Woman *flay'd,* and you will hardly believe, how much it altered her Person for the worse. Yesterday I ordered the Carcass of a *Beau* to be stripped in my Presence; when we were all amazed to find so many unsuspected Faults under one Suit of Cloths: Then I laid open his *Brain,* his *Heart,* and his *Spleen;* But, I plainly perceived at every Operation, that the farther we proceeded, we found the Defects increase upon us in Number and Bulk: from all which, I just formed this Conclusion to my self; That whatever Philosopher or Projector can find out an Art to sodder and patch up the Flaws and Imperfections of Nature, will deserve much better of Mankind, and teach us a more useful Science, than that so much in present Esteem, of widening and exposing them (like him who held *Anatomy* to be the ultimate End of *Physick*.) And he, whose Fortunes and Dispositions have placed him in a convenient Station to enjoy the Fruits of this noble Art; He that can with *Epicurus* content his Ideas with the *Films* and *Images* that fly off upon his Senses from the *Super-*

ficies of Things; Such a Man truly wise, creams off Nature, leaving the Sower and the Dregs, for Philosophy and Reason to lap up. This is the sublime and refined Point of Felicity, called, *the Possession of being well deceived;* The Serene Peaceful State of being a Fool among Knaves. (109–10)

It is on account of his ability to engage in outbursts such as this that so many readers of Swift have been tempted to pronounce him a madman. As we have seen, there is not enough psychological depth or consistency in the narrator to make such an outburst into a morally intelligible symptom belonging to a character, so that its deranged logic and violence might be safely contextualized within the larger framework of the narrative. And although the narrator of the *Tale* may be no less besotted with words and texts than Don Quixote, this passage does not have intertextual moorings of a kind that would justify its peculiar intensity. Swift is impugning the insouciance of the modernist, and Denis Donoghue is no doubt partly correct to say that his satiric target is the brutality of the experimental spirit (8), a fact that betokens some irony, since Swift is himself one of the greatest examples of the experimental spirit he mocks. Swift attains strange liberation in the face of the madness around him by observing it from a distance, entering into it sportively and giving it play, allowing his readers to be amused, tempted, and infuriated by it, without taking up the responsibility of articulating anything else to which it might be opposed. Such absolute freedom of wit must, by the same token, be an absolute subjection to wit, for a world that is suited only to the demands of mockery leaves one with precisely the choices that Swift's narrator has outlined here, to be either Fool or Knave, that is, to live upon the vain pleasures of the surface or to engage in a brutal anatomy leaving nothing of value beneath.

The violence that seems excessive in Swift's writing is not only a reflex of his frustration at not finding before him a world morally adequate to his criticism, but also one that can only be mocked for taking its knavish self-knowledge so lightly. The "woman flay'd" is the only alternative to the false glamour of enthusiasm that Swift's narrator can imagine, and this recognition sends him fleeing back to the pleasures of delusion, while Swift, having seen the flayed carcass of human dignity, cannot go blithely back to his folly. Rather he finds himself emboldened in the spirit of heroic irony, confirmed by his ability to accept the dismal truth of the human situation while mocking the absurdity, effrontery, and callousness of those who persist in their illusions even after they have been exposed.

11

A Flight from Humanity

Swift's satiric animus toward both the philosophies of matter and spirit reflects his participation in the philosophical struggles of the age, but, as one of his most perceptive critics, Robert Martin Adams, has observed, Swift's position represents a peculiar refusal of the terms with which that struggle was fought. "While Locke was rendering Christianity reasonable in terms of a mechanical philosophy and while Berkeley was quietly gathering the spiritual principle into a defiant solipsism, Swift, instead of trying to reconcile the alternatives of spirit and matter or to choose between them, made it his concern to repudiate them both. He figures, then, as a man utterly deprived of those usual philosophical supports and props of belief with which the average man surrounds himself."[1] Swift's preference for the most retrenched and negative imaginable view of the intellect derives both from the peculiar severity and self-suspicion of his nature and from his extreme sensitivity to the political resonances of the epistemological debate: the need of those in power to portray the capacities of the intellect and spirit in such a carefully restricted way as to preserve the public peace without, in the same gesture, undermining the value of these faculties altogether. The problem of containment remained a constant of Swift's thinking, and especially in the sphere of religion. While he deplored, for instance, Hobbes's willingness to locate the sovereignty in the executive power rather than *only* in the legislative, Swift was no less willing than Hobbes to cede to the sovereign power the right to establish religion. Freedom of conscience in his vocabulary means the freedom to be silent in one's unorthodox opinions or doubts. In his anonymous programmatic pamphlet, "The Sentiments of a Church-of-England Man With

[1] Robert Martin Adams, *Strains of Discord* (Ithaca: Cornell University Press, 1958), 156–57.

Respect to Religion and Government," he rules out principled innovations in religion on the grounds that "any great Separation from the established Worship, although to a new one that is more pure and perfect, may be an Occasion of endangering the publick Peace; because, it will compose a Body always in Reserve, prepared to follow any discontented Heads, upon the plausible Pretexts of advancing *true Religion,* and opposing Error, Superstition, or Idolatry. For this Reason, *Plato* lays it down as a Maxim, that *Men ought to worship the Gods, according to the Laws of the City*" (2:11). Swift never forgets this "Body always in Reserve" and capable of "endangering the publick Peace." In his sermon on "Brotherly Love," he warns his Dublin flock about "the Weakness and Folly of too many among you, of the lower Sort, who are made the Tools and Instruments of your Betters, to work their Designs, wherein you have no Concern."[2] With such conspiracies afoot, the people should rely neither upon their own powers of reason nor upon the advice of those who stand to benefit from misleading them, but only upon the counsels of their true teachers, which is to say, the Anglican clergy such as Swift himself.

It cannot be said, of course, that Swift absolutely discourages reason as applied to religious matters, but his attitude is primarily one of distrust. "*Reason* itself," he tells his parishioners, "is true and just, but the *Reason* of every particular Man is weak and wavering, perpetually swayed and turned by his Interests, his Passions, and his Vices."[3] In giving counsel about preaching to a "Young Gentleman, Lately enter'd into Holy Orders," he discourages the exploration of "Mysteries" (9:77) and the resort to any of those meaningless words that have confounded the "science" of divinity—"*Omniscience, Omnipresence, Ubiquity, Attribute, Beatific Vision,* with a thousand others so frequent in Pulpits" (9:66). Swift's contempt for the entire history of theology shows how thinly his sense of tradition is clad.

The key fact to be recognized, however, regarding Swift's anti-intellectualism is that, given his position as an Anglican clergyman in Ireland, the appeal to reason in religion could be of little use. There was no profit in trying to convert the Dissenters; for the Established Church, they were beyond the pale of discourse,[4] their madness certified by their official exclusion from the franchise. It was in the interests of the Anglican clergy to fortify the pale rather than to break it down, and theology threatened to be one of its solvents. Orthodoxy and establishment, and not debate, had to furnish the primary resources of self-justification for a national church originally founded upon a political divorce and, after 1688, severed from its dynastic underpinnings.[5] Both intellectually and historically, the Anglican position had be-

---

[2] "*On* BROTHERLY LOVE" (1717), *Prose Works* 9:172.

[3] "On the Trinity," in *Three Sermons* (published 1744), *Prose Works* 9:166.

[4] Harth, *Swift and Anglican Rationalism: The Religious Background of "A Tale of a Tub"* (Chicago: University of Chicago Press, 1961), 70.

[5] For a trenchant account, see Warren Montag, chap. 1 in *The Unthinkable Swift: The Spontaneous Philosophy of a Church-of-England Man* (London: Verso, 1994).

come an empty fortress. The strange belatedness of the concerns of the *Tale of a Tub*—in so many ways Swift is a Butler forty years after the fact—not only reveals the fascination with which his agitated mind dwelt upon the violent events of the regicide and rebellion, but also the degree to which the Anglican position still depended for rhetorical comfort and strength upon the rehearsing of this primal crime.

Ritual retellings of the rebellion and its aftermath enforced the repression of Swift's adversaries and kept their sincerity from becoming a meaningful rebuke to his own cultivated reticence. The speaker of the *Argument against the Abolishing of Christianity*, Swift's satirical defense of the Sacramental Test that preserved the establishment of the Church of Ireland, begins by disclaiming the defense of anything more than a "nominal" Christianity and goes on to insist upon the need for religion to be an outlet for destructive energies that might otherwise be directed against the body politic.[6] This is almost as good as to admit that the primary benefit of the distinction between Anglican and Dissenter was to preserve the psychic economy of the state. The solidarity of the Anglican *via media* and, later, the Enlightenment itself, of which it was a major tributary, depended almost as a structural necessity upon the ritual renouncing of fanaticism and the denunciation of the past.

If the mere recognition of true Dissenters as rational beings was out of the question for Swift, it would have been equally out of the question for him to take up the defense of Christianity against the free-thinkers. While George Berkeley, Swift's friend and fellow Anglican divine, with all of his philosophical agility, could not keep himself from parodying the arguments of his free-thinking opponents, Swift could not even admit them as rational interlocutors.[7] For Swift, in fact, questions of belief do not really seem to be matters of intellect at all. Atheism is a symptom not of an unsound intellect but only a sham or a sign of low morals. Atheists cannot be reformed by arguments, he says superbly, because "*Reasoning* will never make a Man correct an ill Opinion, which by *Reasoning* he never acquired" (9:78). Better to ignore such dissolute characters than "to perplex the Minds of Well-Disposed People with Doubts, which probably would never otherwise have come into their Heads." This train of thought leads to a core conviction. Swift announces,

> I am of opinion, and dare be positive in it, that not one in a Hundred of those, who pretend to be *Free-Thinkers*, are really so in their Hearts. For there is one Observation that I never knew to fail, and I desire you

---

[6] *An Argument To prove, That the Abolishing of Christianity in England May, as Things now Stand, be attended with some Inconveniencies, and perhaps not produce those many good Effects proposed thereby* (1708), *Prose Works* 2:27.

[7] See J. S. Mill's trenchant comments on Berkeley's *Alciphron* in the *Fortnightly Review* (1871) 59, N. S., 519–20, rptd. in *Alciphron, or The Minute Philosopher in focus*, ed. David Berman (New York: Routledge, 1997), 175–76.

will examine it in the Course of your Life; that no Gentleman of a liberal Education, and regular in his Morals, did ever profess himself a
Free-Thinker. Where are these Kind of People to be found? Amongst
the worst Part of the Soldiery, made up of Pages, younger Brothers of
obscure Families, and others of desperate Fortunes; or else among idle
Town-Fops; and now and then a drunken 'Squire of the Country. (9:78)

Religion for Swift is the first refuge of a gentleman. It is not that a man of
taste will never have doubts but that he will never be so foolish as to speak
them.[8] Given the solidarity of gentlemanly reticence, free-thinking must be
limited to the same ranks of society that produce characters like the hack-
narrator of the *Tale;* their intellectual gymnastics are no less tasteless and
contrived, their intellectual depths no less of a façade.

It has often been pointed out that while Swift mocks the pleasures of the
surface extolled by the narrator of the *Tale,* he was himself mainly a pre-
server of surfaces.[9] It is not, however, for the pleasure of being well-deceived
that questions of external behavior must be tended to. Manners to Swift are
an affair of ultimate consequence, more important than institutions in the
rise and fall of states.[10] In his emphasis upon the priority of habit over doctrine, Swift is superficially Aristotelian but profoundly modern, almost be-
haviorist, in his outlook. It is the impoverishment of reason that leads to the
elevation of habit. External conformity preoccupies Swift in matters extending far beyond religion. His writings show an imperious eagerness to exert the minutest form of observation and regulation over, among other
things, the conduct of polite conversation, the use of the English language,
and the behavior of servants, prostitutes, and married ladies. Bentham's
panopticon surely would have appealed to him.

When Swift thinks of altering the religious climate of his time, it is to a
change of manners that he appeals. He was not, of course, by any means
alone in doing so; what is remarkable is the shallowness of his approach. In
the *Project for the Advancement of Religion and Reformation of Manners*
(1709), Swift proposes the restoration of religion by making it "as much as
possible, to be the Turn and Fashion of the Age" (2:59). Interest is the key
to improvements in religion: the greatest benefits will result once we have
succeeded in "making it every Man's Interest and Honour to cultivate Religion and Virtue; by rendering Vice a Disgrace, and the certain Ruin to Prefer-
ment or Pretensions" (2:47). Even hypocrisy is beneficial in this respect
(2:56–7). The *Project* was one of two works published during Swift's lifetime to which he was willing to affix his name, and it is both ironic and telling

---

[8] "I am not answerable to God for the doubts that arise in my own breast, since they are the
consequence of that reason which he hath planted in me, if I take care to conceal those doubts,
if I use my best endeavours to subdue them, and if they have no influence on the conduct of my
life." *Thoughts on Religion,* in *Prose Works,* 9:262.

[9] F. R. Leavis, *The Common Pursuit* (New York: Stewart, 1952), 85.

[10] "Sentiments," in *Prose Works,* 2:14–15.

that, among all of them, it is here alone that he comes out sounding like one of his own projectors. "For, as much as Faith and Morality are declined among us," he writes with a straight face, "I am altogether confident, they might, in a short Time, and with no very great Trouble, be raised to so high a Perfection, as Numbers are capable of receiving" (44).

The passages I have been citing in illustration of Swift's attitude toward thought were all written long after *A Tale of a Tub*. In a sense they clarify the distinction made in the *Tale* between original thinking and "Life in the common forms," which amounts to nothing other than the distinction between what is orthodox and what is not. The sphere of individual thought and conscience is to remain free but entirely private, so as not to disturb the state. It is also important to recognize, at the same time, that in the political sphere, where no deeper metaphysical issues were to be broached, and where, after the fall of the Tory ministry in 1714, he was in the position of an outsider rather than the member of a protected orthodoxy, Swift was more than willing to stake out fundamental intellectual positions and to act upon them. As a "Church-of-England Man" he had already endorsed the revolution principle, common, as he says, to most Whigs and Tories of the period, that monarchs who do not do justice to their subjects should be overthrown.[11] And in his performance as "the Drapier" Swift was willing to portray the struggles of the Irish nation against the English as a contest of "*Truth, Reason & Justice*" against "the *Love and Torrent* of Power."[12] In political and practical affairs Swift could stand up against the crown and parliament and all of their agents, and do so with such firmness and ingenuity as to make him one of the models of political resistance in the modern world. No lack of intellectual courage, or courage of any sort, stood behind the absolutism of his satiric stance. It was simply that the negation of agency and intellect had become for him the most natural, strategic, and effective means of self-assertion.

But if, as I have been arguing, the peculiarly unlocatable and unmeasured quality of Swift's satire, its irascible instability and excess, were in large part a response to the social and intellectual conditions under which he lived, they were also, obviously, the product of his peculiar temperament, with its surges of pride and barely governable violence. "When a true Genius appears in the World," he writes in one of the free-standing aphorisms that constitute his *Thoughts on Various Subjects* (1711), "you may know him by this infallible Sign; that the Dunces are all in Confederacy against him."[13] It is impossible not to hear a personal plea in this famous grandiose and persecuted sentence. Typically, it was not the Dissenters but the dunces closest to home who were most vexing to Swift. They could be found among fellow Tories and Angli-

---

[11] He does, however, believe in the absolute power of the sovereignty which resides in the legislature. See "Sentiments," *Prose Works*, 2:15.

[12] *The Drapier's Letters*, in *Prose Works*, 10:62–63.

[13] *Thoughts on Various Subjects*, in *Prose Works*, 1:242.

cans, at court, and even on the throne; one can see from *Gulliver's Travels* that a decade after his departure from London Swift was still smarting from his treatment by the late queen and her ladies-in-waiting. As he grew older, he depended more and more upon the esteem of his fellow Scriblerians, a melancholy society of the unappreciated and misunderstood. Samuel Johnson was correct in the observation that "From the letters that pass between [Swift] and Pope it might be inferred that they, with Arbuthnot and Gay, had engrossed all the understanding and virtue of mankind, that their merits filled the world; or that there was no hope of more."[14] Yet even in this anointed circle Swift's pride and egotistical hunger made him a difficult ally. The "Verses on the Death of Dr. Swift" (1731) show a man now connected to life largely through friendship yet suffering from La Rochefoucauldian suspicions of all about him, and unable to refrain from insisting on his own virtues—his freedom from petty interest and bitterness, from concern for wealth or ambition, virtues that not all of his friends would have recognized.[15]

We shall never know the original causes of the sense of injury that plagued and goaded Swift all of his life, though the early loss of his parents and his treatment in the house of his first patron, William Temple, seem to have had a formative effect. His animus was fueled by disappointment with the patronage of the Tories, while having to witness at the same time, as he wrote in *The Examiner,* how "a great Part of the Nation's Money got into the Hands of those, who by their Birth, Education, and Merit, could pretend no higher than to wear our Liveries."[16] What is certain is that through all of his years, along with an acutely vulnerable feelings of pride and disgust with the current state of the British nation, Swift held a serious grudge against life and many of its vital attractions. He could take pride in what is almost an anchorite's disgust for physical human being, and he apparently refused to propagate his species, defending such behavior on the basis of a degree of reason that God had denied to most of humankind.

> Although reason were intended by providence to govern our passions, yet it seems that, in two points of the greatest moment to the being and continuance of the world, God hath intended our passions to prevail over reason. The first is, the propagation of our species, since no wise man ever married from the dictates of reason. The other is, the love of

[14] Samuel Johnson, *Lives of the English Poets,* 3 vols., ed. George Birbeck Hill (Oxford: Clarendon Press, 1905), 3:61.

[15] "Had he but spar'd his Tongue and Pen/He might have rose like other Men:/But, Pow'r was never in his Thought,/And Wealth he valu'd not a Groat:/Ingratitude he often found,/And pity'd those who meant the Wound:/But, kept the Tenor of his Mind,/To merit well of human Kind:/Nor made a sacrifice of those/Who still were true, to please his foes" (lines 355–64). "Verses on the Death of Dr. Swift" (1731), *Swift: Poetical Works,* ed. Herbert Davis (New York: Oxford, 1967). All quotations of Swift's poetry are from this edition.

[16] Swift, *Examiner,* no. 14 (9 Nov. 1710), in *Prose Works,* 3:12.

life, which, from the dictates of reason, every man would despise, and wish it at an end, or that it never had a beginning. (9:263)

It is doubtful that this final paragraph of the *Thoughts on Religion* conforms with the spirit of Judeo-Christian teachings, of which "Be fruitful and multiply" is one of the oldest. Swift's disgust with particular human folly and madness stands out against the background of a more general loathing of human nature. This disgust, at least in theory, includes Swift himself, but it is clear that he consoles himself in his superior capacity for renunciation: what he loses in participation, he makes up in pride. Perhaps the genuine reform of humanity that he professed to seek, had it miraculously come about, would have demanded too great a sacrifice from Swift by depriving him of his license to mock.

A Conversion to Madness

In *A Tale of a Tub,* Swift expresses a vision of history as the competition of egotistical megalomaniacs driven by explosive and uncontrollable forces of the inner psyche, and he does so in the guise of a narrator whose naïveté is such that he cannot even recognize the obscenity of the spectacle or of his own complaisance in observing it. In *Gulliver's Travels,* Swift portrays the progress of a narrator from a comparable gullibility and moral obtuseness to an opposite state of paranoia and misanthropy so extreme that he can no longer tolerate creatures of his own kind. The *Travels,* of course, is not a Bildungsroman, and Gulliver never acquires the weight and consistency of a novelistic character; he remains alternately a mouthpiece and a butt of the author. The unity of the work depends upon achieving not so much a complete portrayal of the main character as a complete expression of Swift's satiric interests. What occurs, though, in book 4, is a sudden change of angle between character and author, when Swift turns finally from the spectacle of moral obliquity to that of moral mania. Gulliver is no less gullible than he was in the earlier books, but now he is gullible in a perfectionistic and suspicious, indeed paranoid way, and this poses for Swift the challenge of setting out the difference between an insane idealist's moralizing stance and his own.

Gulliver's Travels presents the reader with the bright surface of a world minutely and elaborately described, an invitation to the fantasies of children and to the credulously misguided like Gulliver himself. At times, especially in book 1, Swift's procedure verges upon allegory, but with a difference: allegory in the familiar sense seeks an ultimate rapprochement between surface and depth. They are mutually enhancing registers. The education of Dante in the course of the *Commedia* represents the typical progress of the soul, which, however permeated with blindness from the start, can nevertheless ultimately be reclaimed at the telos of the journey. Here, however, the details of the surface and Gulliver's empiricizing interpretations of them pro-

duce a world of falsity and a falsity of mind to go with it. Such depths as the
fable offers will undermine, destroy, and replace the surface, even if it is uncertain that they can survive on their own terrain without force of contrast.
The distance between tenor and vehicle signifies not levels of wisdom but stu-
pidity, and the surface is not an invitation to higher understanding but a
screen for wit and malice.

Swift's rage against the world stood in balance with his success in preserving a certain domain of imaginary, and indeed infantile, pleasures. He
oscillated between the official language of adulthood and the little language
he employed to communicate with the woman he called Stella. This is a quality that he shares with many authors, but in Swift it is developed to an exceptional degree, and he is by no means blind to the fact. The pervasiveness
of infantile feelings and behavior is perhaps the central theme of *Gulliver's
Travels*. It is easy to see that Gulliver in Lilliput in some sense represents Swift
the genius among the dunces: indeed, the conceit of tiny people on parade is
calculated to lift the spirits of any satirist. The wisdom of the Brobdingnagians, however, is belittling to Gulliver's sense of worth, a fact that serves as
a key to the psychological dimension of the allegory: in the presence of the
virtuous, the satirist, reduced to impotent egotism and vanity, becomes a tiny
pet, while in the presence of the vain he swells to a gargantuan stature of
moral strength. For the one whose virtue lies only in criticism, the spectacle
of vanity empowers while the spectacle of generosity deflates.

It is clear that for Swift the English are characteristically guilty of absurdly
overestimating their own importance and that English life has been struc-
tured for generations along self-aggrandizing lines of distinction such as
Protestant and Catholic, Whig and Tory, distinctions that are no more meaningful than Big- and Little-Endian or High heel and Low heel. Freud, who
attributed extraordinary wisdom to this book, could have found no better
application for the most valuable of his phrases, the "narcissism of small differences."[17] While Swift must be recognized as a bitter partisan both in politics and in religion, this did not keep him from recognizing that differences
of faction were illusory and that these illusions had had a degrading effect
upon the character of the English nation. In a sense, this was a way of standing with Brobdingnagian stature above the fray. Yet Swift was genuinely
frightened by the capacity of his contemporaries to divide so neatly and passionately into groups and factions, so that "every Man alive among us is en-
compassed with a Million of Enemies of his own Country, among which his
oldest Acquaintance and Friends, and Kindred themselves are often of the
Number: Neither can People of different Parties mix together without Constraint, Suspicion, and Jealousy, watching every Word they speak, for Fear
of giving Offence, or else falling into Rudenesses and Reproaches, and so
leaving themselves open to the Malice and Corruption of Informers, who

---

[17] Sigmund Freud, *Das Unbehagen in der Kultur*, in *Gesammelte Werke chronologische
geordnet* (London: Imago, 1948), 14:474.

were never more numerous or expert in their Trade."[18] Gulliver finds that it is his acts of generosity in Lilliput that earn him the animosity of the court; his honors bring him jealousy, he is surrounded by informers, and his unwillingness to commit atrocities leads to plots for his undoing. The royal decision to limit his punishment to blinding strikes him at the time as barbaric, though later experience shows its unusual mercy. The smallness and vanity of human nature manifests itself supremely for Swift in the obsession with invidious distinctions.

If Lilliput is a satirist's paradise, where the traveler stands superior over vain and petty multitudes, in Brobdingnag the situation is reversed. Gulliver is confronted with a race both more powerful and more reasonable than he, a race whose philosopher-king can look down upon him and all his kind and see them for what they are, "the most pernicious Race of little odious Vermin that Nature ever suffered to crawl upon the Surface of the Earth" (11:116). The observer now becomes the observed, and Gulliver's attempts to articulate how the political, social, and military practices of his own country are grounded in reason have the opposite effect of exposing their true insanity. Gulliver's is incapable of comprehending the horror his narrative evokes in his interlocutor, and when the Brobdingnagian king refuses the Englishman's offer to introduce gunpowder into the realm, Gulliver wonders over the effects of such a confined education. In Lilliput, Gulliver's Toryish principles made him unwilling ever to be an "Instrument of bringing a free and brave People into Slavery" (11:37); in Brobdingnag, he would be a willing slave to an absolute monarch.

If Gulliver's intellectual and moral nullity make him impervious to the king's opinion of him, he remains acutely attuned to the social discomforts of his plight, as brilliantly dramatized in the narrative by his inferior size. First he is the property of an ignorant farmer who uses him as a carnival attraction; then he becomes a pet at court, a complement to the queen's dwarf and the court monkey. Here Swift's own bitter experience as a client is undoubtedly at issue. If he delighted to play at big and little languages and big and little men, this was in part because his life had been one long negotiation about the proportions of his worth in relation to others.[19] Late in life he wrote of himself that "He never thought an Honour done him,/Because a Duke was proud to own him,"[20] but this was sensitivity speaking in its own defense.[21]

---

[18] "On BROTHERLY LOVE," *Prose Works* 9:176.

[19] The "little language" was, of course, Swift's manner of writing to Stella. With both of the women who were devoted to him, and with others as well, he liked to oscillate between the roles of the invasive and opprobrious schoolmaster and the all-controlling, verbally playful infant. See Carol Houlihan Flynn, *The Body in Swift and Defoe* (Cambridge: Cambridge University Press, 1990), 120–31.

[20] "Verses on the Death of Dr. Swift," lines 319–20.

[21] See, for instance, the exquisite exchange of feather-smoothing letters between Swift and Lord Carteret (9 and 20 June, and 9 July 1724) incited by Swift's pique at not being answered quickly enough. *The Correspondence of Jonathan Swift*, ed. Harold Williams (Oxford: Clarendon 1963), 3:13–14 and 3:16–17.

Gulliver's reaction to the Brobdingnagian king's laughter at him for his vile account of European affairs is to observe how impossible it is to be on a dignified footing with the great (11:108)—a home truth for Swift, even if out of place. He expected his talents and accomplishments to earn him an equality of regard with men above him in rank, but even when they did, he resented the generosity of their condescension. His own condescension to those he considered beneath him was adamant, and his contempt for their pretensions to worth could be scathing. When we see Gulliver the pet making a success at the court of giants with his acrobatic piano playing and his clever way of killing Brobdingnagian flies, it is not only human vanity that is aimed at but the game of aristocracy as well. Swift takes the comedy of court rivalry as far as it can go. The dog, the cat, the rat, the monkey, and the dwarf each present a threat not only to Gulliver's life but to his self-image, as if to show the animal level at which courtly competition really takes place. Yet Gulliver does not treat his miniaturized adventures with irony. On the contrary, he is always willing to go father in vanity than the situation demands. One of the emblematic scenes of the *Travels* shows him, just for the glory of it, attempting to leap over a Brobdingnagian pile of cow dung and plopping squarely in the middle of it (11:108). Few authors have shown such thorough self-knowledge with so little forgiveness.

If the land of the Brobdingnagians is a nightmare from the point of view of competitive status, and portrays status competition in a peculiarly hair-raising fashion, it also assaults the aesthetic integrity of the human image with an unsettling exploration of physical humanity grossly enlarged. In their moral character, the Brobdingnagians are unremarkable in a way that Swift finds admirable. We do not see among them the treacherous courtiers or the purveyors of vain ingenuity that infest books 1 and 3. The Brobdingnagian kingdom is a peaceful and simple land-based aristocracy. Its vices are the ordinary vices of humanity—the farmer's greed, the lubricious levity of the Maids of Honour (102–3). But in their physical dimensions, the Brobdingnagians are frighteningly hideous, and it was the master stroke of Swift's uncomfortable wit to invert the correlations between goodness and beauty, and evil and ugliness, that are standard in the heroic genres. The vain Lilliputians enjoy a miniaturized perfection, while to watch the Brobdingnagian Queen "craunch the Wing of a Lark" for dinner, "although it were nine Times as large as that of a full grown Turkey" (11:90), makes a perennial strike against the glamour of aristocracy and the simple appeal of human nature. The broad-spirited Rabelaisian humor of Gargantua's splendid appetite here becomes a jibe against dignity itself. It is particularly the loathsomeness of women's bodies that is emphasized, as when Gulliver finds himself being dandled humiliatingly upon the naked breasts of the Brobdingnagian Maids of Honor. And the sight of the cancerous breasts of the beggar woman completes the squeamish inventory of the social classes (11:96–97).

The scene with the Maids of Honor brings together many of Gulliver's, and possibly Swift's, anxieties: to be stripped of his clothing and his social rank and subjected to the spontaneous impulses of female human nature. These Maids of Honor may be the most attractive of their gender, but their scale has rendered them a horror, and made all human vanity seem the effect of the very partial and arbitrary perspective from which we see. Physical existence is entirely denuded of dignity and meaning, and it is no wonder that, from this perspective, one might eagerly retreat to the state of being well-deceived. David Hume, having made the physical world seem no more real or reliable a phenomenon than a dream in the eyes of philosophy, could thank Nature for not having given him the power to take his philosophy beyond the threshold of the study. Swift will not let his reader off so easily.[22] One we have seen through all glamorous appearances and all sources of human dignity, we have to go on living with them anyway.

In books 1 and 2, Swift has provided a working demonstration of the infantile vanity of human intelligence. Book 3 provides something of a breather before the harrowing dilemmas of book 4. In it, Gulliver returns to his role as a neutral observer. The aim of book 3 is to provide a kind of encyclopedia in which all of the forms of human ambition are definitively and categorically mocked. The search for knowledge is exposed as a charade, and the heroic episodes of history are undermined by revelations of accident and false report. The ambitions of science appear as absurd, not because technology is faulty in itself but because its attractions are grounded in vanity and delusion. Swift's projectors would rather fail miserably by the light of their own ingenuity than succeed by common sense. When technology does produce remarkable results, as in the case of the Flying Island, it is exploited for the purposes of political domination—an episode that glances toward Swift's resistance to the English exploitation of Ireland. As usual, political resistance is the exception to Swiftian cynicism. The "Sextumvirate" of "Destroyers of Tyrants and Usurpers, and the Restorers of Liberty to oppressed and injured Nations" (11:180) are the only human objects of admiration in the entire *Travels*. Brutus is the greatest man among the dead, and Thomas More, one of the first opponent of the split with Rome that produced the Anglican church, is there beside him. Swift's admiration for More, "the only Man of true Virtue that ever England produced," is a mark of the ironies attached to his Anglican career.[23]

The Justification of Misanthropy

Gulliver's role in the satire of the *Travels* has been changing from book to book and often from scene to scene. He becomes a neutral observer, a butt,

[22] David Hume, *A Treatise of Human Nature,* ed. L. A. Selby-Bigge, second edition revised and with notes by Peter Nidditch (Oxford: Clarendon, 1978), 263–74.

[23] I am spelling out the words written in the margins of Swift's copy of Lord Herbert of Cherbury's *Life and Raine of Henry VIII,* which also give abundant evidence of Swift's apoplectic dislike of the founder of the Anglican Church, "a Dog, a true King." *Prose Works,* 5:247.

or a morally adequate witness depending upon Swift's purpose. The insertion of book 3 has the effect of rehabilitating him to some degree in the eyes of his reader after the debasement of his image among the Brobdingnagians.[24] It turns out, however, that this rehabilitation is only the preparation for a new debasement, one that will take Gulliver in the opposite, Quixotic direction. In book 4, Gulliver's position and the position of mankind become the primary focus of the narrative, as Swift turns his scrutiny backward on his own satiric stance. Gulliver finds himself and his kind caught between two morally contrasting species each of which lives in harmony with its nature: on the one hand, a species of rational horses, and on the other, a race of brutish and unreasoning creatures who bear the form of the human. *Houyhnhnms* and *Yahoos*—the first seems to me to be the horse locution of *human,* the second its deformed inversion. Gulliver the chronic social climber, tormented by his resemblance to the Yahoos who claim their kinship to him by the most visceral means possible, seeks desperately to assimilate among the horses. What he undergoes is an authentic conversion, a surrendering of his past life and all that it represents, an attempt to become wholly new and rational. But instead of rationality, madness is the result.

Swift's attitude toward the Houyhnhnms is one of the great cruxes of modern criticism. While readers of the *Travels* had long seen the idealized race of horses as the vehicle of an unanswerable rebuke toward human nature, later interpreters, especially following the persuasive work of Kathleen Williams, have tended to soften the satiric thrust of the book by discounting the Houyhnhnm virtues.[25] For such readers, the Houyhnhnms' lack of passion makes them heartless. Their naïveté seems laughable, their eugenic system too coolly efficient, and their claim to be "the Perfection of Nature" both a manifestation of pride and a symptom of the kind of optimism Swift abhorred. All these judgments, however, seem to me wrongheaded. The Houyhnhnms' belief that they are the "Perfection of Nature" is a plausible factual observation of the world they know, and their notion that creatures like Gulliver would lack the physical equipment to survive, while short-sighted, is not implausible, for he lacks the adaptations that are enabling to the Yahoos. What is presented as remarkable about the Houyhnhnms, in any case, is not their intellectual acuity or their knowledge—they have less need of these than human beings do—but their wisdom and rationality, their ability to "cultivate Reason and be governed by it" (251). Their reason leads them to refer everything to Nature and accept its judgments in Stoic fashion, showing a confidence in their own natural goodness that would be absurd either for a human being or a Yahoo. In the Houyhnhnms, this trust in Nature is

[24] Howard Erskine-Hill, *Gulliver's Travels* (Cambridge: Cambridge University Press, 1993), 51.

[25] Kathleen Williams, *Jonathan Swift and the Age of Compromise* (Lawrence: University of Kansas Press, 1967), chapter seven. For a classic analysis of the debate, see James Clifford, "Gulliver's Fourth Voyage: Hard and Soft Schools of Interpretation," in *Quick Springs of Sense,* ed. Larry S. Champion (Athens: University of Georgia Press, 1974), 33–50.

indeed natural and therefore not ridiculous.[26] Gulliver tells us that they have no pride. They feel no rivalry with each other, other races are unknown to them, and the Yahoos are beneath comparison.

In colloquy with the Houyhnhnm master, then, Gulliver again finds himself and his civilization held up before a court of genuine rationality. But where Gulliver in the hands of the philosopher-giant is made to feel the comical disproportion of pride and power in human being, here Gulliver is faced not with irony but with the sheer incomprehension of a creature who truly cannot enter into the irrational assumptions that make human behavior to some degree predictable. At first, Gulliver attempts to preserve his dignity by maintaining the position that species in Europe and in the land of the Houyhnhnms stand toward each other in a simple relation of inversion—rational human beings making use of animal horses in Europe, rational horses making use of brute human beings among the Houyhnhnms. It is not long, however, before Gulliver has come to see the full incomprehensibility of human behavior everywhere, that it is based upon a distortion or, indeed, a perversion of rationality. Take, for example, the workings of the English law as Gulliver explains them to his master:

> I said there was a Society of Men among us, bred up from their Youth in the Art of proving by Words multiplied for the Purpose, that *White* is *Black*, and *Black* is *White*, according as they are paid. To this Society all the rest of the People are Slaves.
>
> For Example. If my Neighbour hath a mind to my *Cow*, he hires a Lawyer to prove that he ought to have my *Cow* from me. I must then hire another to defend my Right; it being against all Rules of *Law* that any Man should be allowed to speak for himself. Now in the Case, I who am the true Owner lie under two great Disadvantages. First, my Lawyer being practiced almost from his Cradle in defending Falsehood; is quite out of his Element when he would be an Advocate for Justice, which as an Office unnatural, he always attempts with great Awkwardness, if not with Ill-will. The second Disadvantage is, that my Lawyer must proceed with great Caution: Or else he will be reprimanded by the Judges, and abhorred by his Brethren, as one who would lessen the Practice of the Law. And therefore I have but two Methods to preserve my *Cow*. The first is, to gain over my Adversary's Lawyer with a double Fee; who will then betray his Client, by insinuating that he hath Justice on his Side. The second Way is for my Lawyer to make my Cause appear as unjust as he can; by allowing the *Cow* to belong to my Adversary; and this if it be skillfully done, will certainly bespeak the Favour of the Bench. (11:232–33)

---

[26] To "live in accordance with nature" (Epictetus, *Discourses* 1.26.1) is "the standard Stoic definition of the good life." A. A. Long, *Epictetus: A Stoic and Socratic Guide to Life* (Oxford: Clarendon Press, 2002), 188.

This is one of the wittiest speeches in Swift's work, yet neither Gulliver himself nor the Houyhnhnm master recognize its humor. The Houyhnhnm has no more need for a sense of humor than he has need of the law, there being no discrepancy in his experience between what should be and what is, and no errant behavior among his own kind either to mock or to regulate. And while, for Swift and his reader, the laughter that arises from this passage stems from a familiar recognition of human misdirection hyperbolically expressed, Gulliver offers it as brute fact. He has stepped beyond the framework of the human to take up the perspective of unadulterated reason, and he can only concur with the Houyhnhnm that what passes for reason among Europeans is only the sophistication of vice.

While Gulliver is attempting to assimilate among the Houyhnhnms by becoming as reasonable as they are, it is only his clothing—the façade of civility—that keeps him from being taken for an outright Yahoo. His need for clothing is a marker of the middle state he occupies between Houyhnhnm and Yahoo, a creature both fallen and proud, departed from Edenic perfection and ashamed of his animal nature. The Houyhnhnm master cannot understand Gulliver's need for clothing, or, as he puts it, "why Nature should teach us to conceal what Nature had given" (11:221). The field of his experience contains only Houyhnhnms, who have nothing to be ashamed of, and Yahoos, who do not know enough to be ashamed. Clothing, of course, represents for Swift the facile manipulations of the surface and the contrivances of social convention.[27] It is these contrivances of which Gulliver is constantly being stripped during his travels—first by the Lilliputian committee to search his pockets, then by the Maids of Honor in Brobdingnag, for purposes Gulliver cannot mention, and now among the Houyhnhnms, when his animal nature is finally exposed for what it is. When Gulliver's own clothing wears out he is forced to dress himself in animal skins, a habit that no longer partakes of the language of distinction with regard to other human beings but serves only to establish his difference from the animals who provide the materials. The soles of Gulliver's shoes are made of Yahoo skins, and here we may almost feel as if the logic of the story is taking Swift beyond what his intelligence was prepared explicitly to recognize—the inhumanity of his relentless contempt for the human body.

To Gulliver's distress, the more the Houyhnhnm master learns about Europeans, the more he is able to recognize the rudiments of all human vice in the primitive behavior of the Yahoos, a resemblance that confirms for the

---

[27] For the narrator of the *Tale*, clothing becomes a metaphor not only for our physical pretenses but for our metaphysical and moral ones as well: "To conclude from all, what is Man himself but a *Micro-Coat*, or rather a compleat Suit of Cloaths with all its Trimmings? As to his Body, there can be no dispute; but examine even the Acquirements of his Mind, you will find them all contribute in their Order towards furnishing out an exact Dress: To instance no more; Is not Religion a *Cloak*, Honesty a *Pair of Shoes*, worn out in the Dirt, Self-love a *Surtout*, Vanity a *Shirt* and Conscience a *Pair of Breeches*, which, tho' a Cover for Lewdness as well as Nastiness, is easily slipt down for the Service of both." *Prose Works*, 1:47.

Houyhnhnms the probable origin of the indigenous Yahoos in a pair of migrant human beings who spawned a degenerate race among them. This illumination, presented to the Houyhnhnm assembly, leads the master to propose the castrating of the Yahoos and subsequently a ruling by the assembly that the master must banish Gulliver as a particularly dangerous member of the breed. Ironically, it is the European castration of horses that suggests the solution to the Yahoo problem. Because the Yahoos are animals without reason, like European horses, there is no reason why this strategy should not be applied to them. Gulliver could not but agree, except that the same logic leads to his exile. He finds that "it might consist with Reason to have been less rigorous," the one complaint he ever utters about the Houyhnhnms (11:264).

The Houyhnhnm master is reluctant to part with Gulliver, but he has been "exhorted" by the assembly and it cannot be disobeyed. Swift believed in the absoluteness of sovereignty properly invested in the legislative power, whose dictates should have no appeal,[28] but that is not in question in here. The Houyhnhnm do not have the intellectual resources even to comprehend the distinction between individual opinion and reason. This is why they merely "exhort" (11:264). We can see from this case that their judgments may differ on the basis of differences in individual experience, but that among them the space for the distinction between public authority and private conscience simply does not exist. The choice of the word *exhort* has a quaint but not derisory ring to it, like *Saying the thing which is not* as an expression for lying.[29] Both show that irrationality cannot in the proper sense be understood even though its causes may be grasped.

Gulliver is now in a sorry state, banished from the peaceful domain of reason and forced to go back to a world of Yahoos. He has turned against all of those among whom he was born and is on the way to adopting the image of a horse:

> When I thought of my Family, my Friends, my Countrymen, or human Race in general, I considered them as they really were, *Yahoos* in Shape and Disposition, perhaps a little more civilized, and qualified with the Gift of Speech; but making no other Use of Reason, than to improve and multiply those Vices, whereof their Brethren in this Country had only the Share that Nature allotted them. When I happened to behold the Reflection of my own Form in a Lake or Fountain, I turned away my Face in Horror and detestation of my self; and could better endure the Sight of a common *Yahoo,* than of my own Person. By conversing with the *Houyhnhnms,* and looking upon them with Delight, I fell to

---

[28] "Sentiments," *Prose Works,* 2:16.

[29] I am not convinced by Paul Turner's suggestion that the non-coercive form of Houyhnhnm governance is a glance at the behavior of the Quakers. See his edition of *Gulliver's Travels* (New York: Oxford, 1998), note to page 265.

imitate their Gait and Gesture, which is now grown into a Habit; and my Friends often tell me in a blunt Way, that *I trot like a Horse;* which, however, I take for a great Compliment: Neither shall I disown, that in speaking I am apt to fall into the Voice and manner of the *Houyhnhnms,* and hear my self ridiculed on that Account without the least Mortification. (11:262–63)

At this point Gulliver is obviously mad. He can no longer endure his own image or that of his kind. His human identity has all but disappeared. And however admirable the reasonableness of the Houyhnhnms, nothing could be more ludicrous than for him to wish to become a horse. After all his Houyhnhnm education, he is still aping manners and saving appearances rather than being governed by Nature and reason. Even the human smell has become unbearable to him. On this account he finds the charity offered by Pedro de Mendez, the sea-captain responsible for his rescue, barely tolerable, and after years back in England, his wife and children still smell to him like Yahoos. He prefers the conversation of his horses to that of human beings and spends four hours in the stable with them every day. A peculiar idealism has stripped him of all the habits and customs that connected him with his fellow human beings and degraded him to the level of an animal. Gulliver cannot actually grasp this idealism. He cannot stand where it stands except to see what is excluded. It dispossesses him of his nature without offering him anything but disgust and the suspicion of others.

It is now possible to measure some of the distance that we have traversed the from the late Middle Ages to the age of the Augustans by recalling the ending of *Sir Gawain and the Green Knight,* in which the laughter that greets the hero has a healing and restorative force, one that preserves the worth of human life while accepting its inevitable fault. In the case of *Don Quixote,* while the knight's adventures have finally destroyed his will to live, they have not quite cut him off from the moral community of his fellow human beings. In *Gulliver's Travels,* however, while the myth of the Fall may still be in force as an intellectual structure, the human being no longer has the dignity even of a fallen creature who can see his fallenness, and there is no hint of redemption or reconciliation. The distance between ideal and actual, between rational and irrational or Houyhnhnm and Yahoo, can no longer be bridged. In fact, the ideal itself has now become a primary source of alienation. It provides a sense of distinction that is both undeniably valid and obviously untenable for human beings. Gulliver's banishment and his moral self-annihilation result from the application to human beings of a standard that they cannot satisfy on the basis of their own powers, nor, it seems, is there any higher power promising to redeem them. We are left with the great question, Is Gulliver guilty of an avoidable piece of Quixotism or is he an everyman whose fate we all must share if we do not want to be Yahoos?

It is undeniable that Swift shows an intellectual and temperamental kinship with the Augustinian tradition. Just as to Calvin, for instance, ideals of conduct primarily teach us that we cannot keep the law, so with Swift the dictates of reason primarily teach us that we cannot behave rationally. For Calvin, however, as for his predecessors, this recognition is an incitement to faith. Its proper outcome is surrender to God. For Swift it is surrender only to laughter and bitterness. The myth of the Fall seems to have survived its intended remedy. Confronted with human pride, Swift sees not a theological vice but a piece of effrontery insufferable to his own vanity. Gulliver is unquestionably speaking for the author when he rants on the last page of the *Travels,*

> My Reconcilement to the *Yahoo*-kind in general might not be so diffi-
> cult, if they would be content with those Vices and Follies only which
> Nature hath entitled them to. I am not in the least provoked at the Sight
> of a Lawyer, a Pick-pocket, a Colonel, a Fool, a Lord, a Gamester, a
> Politician, a Wordmonger, a Physician, an Evidence, a Suborner, an At-
> torney, a Traitor, or the like: This is all according to the due Course of
> Things: But, when I behold a Lump of Deformity, and Diseases both in
> Body and Mind, smitten with *Pride*, it immediately breaks all the Mea-
> sures of my Patience; neither shall I be ever able to comprehend how
> such an Animal and such a Vice could tally together. (11:280)

In Christian teaching, pride is a cardinal sin because it is an affront to God. Gulliver's renunciation of pride, however, envisions it in merely social terms, as nothing more than the inflation of our value in relation to other people— or rather, more to the point, as our resentment of others' inflation of their value relative to us, for, as La Rochefoucauld puts it, "If we had no pride of our own, we would not complain about the pride of others."[30] Swift paid tribute to La Rochefoucauld, "my Favorite because I found my whole character in him."[31]

The passage in which Gulliver lists the many social incommodities of which he is free in the land of the Houyhnhnms is extraordinarily revealing both about his paranoid state of mind and what it means for Swift. He has been describing the regime he has established among the Houyhnhnms, his "little Oeconomy" settled to his "Heart's Content," with its "Springes made of *Yahoos* Hairs," rabbit-skin clothing and shoes with soles of Yahoo-skin:

> I enjoyed perfect Health of Body, and Tranquility of Mind; I did not
> feel the Treachery or Inconstancy of a Friend, nor the Injuries of a se-
> cret or open Enemy. I had no Occasion of bribing, flattering or pimp-
> ing, to procure the Favour of any great Man, or of his Minion. I wanted
> no Fence against Fraud or Oppression: Here was neither Physician to
> destroy my Body, nor Lawyer to ruin my Fortune: No Informer to

---

[30] No. 34 in Jacques Truchet, *Maximes* (Paris: Garnier Frères, 1967).
[31] Letter to Alexander Pope of 26 November 1725, in *Correspondence*, 3:118.

Watch my Words and Actions, or forge Accusations against me for Hire: Here were no Gibers, Censurers, Backbiters, Pickpockets, Highwaymen, House-breakers, Attorneys, Bawds, Buffoons, Gamesters, Politicians, Wits, Spleneticks, tedious Talkers, Controvertists, Ravishers, Murderers, Robbers, Virtuoso's; no Leaders or Followers of Party and Faction; no Encouragers to Vice, by Seducement or Examples: No Dungeon, Axes, Gibbets, Whipping-posts, or Pillories; No cheating Shopkeepers or Mechanicks: No Pride, Vanity or Affectation: No Fops, Bullies, Drunkards, strolling Whores, or Poxes: No ranting, lewd, expensive Wives: No stupid, proud Pedants: No importunate, over-bearing, quarrelsome, noisy, roaring, empty, conceited, swearing Companions: No Scoundrels raised from the Dust upon the Merit of their Vices: or Nobility thrown into it on account of their Virtues: no Lords, Fidlers, Judges or Dancing-masters. (1:260–61)

Gulliver is so besotted with Houyhnhnm virtue that the possibility of human goodness is entirely lost to him. All he remembers is the varieties of human treachery, the temptations to corruption he will avoid in hiatus from human society, and the ill effects to his health caused by practitioners of medicine. However much we might share Gulliver's opinion of eighteenth-century medicine, the assumption that diseases are primarily the result of doctoring is one of the symptoms of his enthusiasm. Nevertheless, there is a trenchancy in the list of the ills of social life that begins this catalogue. It is as impressive in its way as Hobbes's description of the state of nature. But after the second colon of the second sentence ("for Hire:"), which introduces the Butlerian cast of rogues, from "Censurers, Backbiters," and "Pickpockets" to "Lords, Fidlers, Judges or Dancing-masters," there is a change of register. It is not plausible that Gulliver, mad as he is, would, at this point when he believes he has escaped from human society altogether, put "Dancing-masters," "Fidlers," and "Controvertists" on the same plane of relief as treacherous friends, injurious enemies, and other fundamental causes of the social misery he has experienced in his travels. In the second half of the list, Gulliver's complaint gives over to satiric ingenuity and spite, which is far more enraged by social posturing than by moral iniquity, and therefore delights in setting Ravishers and Murderers into the same list as "Wits," "Judges" (taking their corruption maliciously for granted), and worst of all, "Virtuoso's." From the perspective of a merely social indignation, all offenses are the same. This passage shows that even when Gulliver is maddened with misanthropy, he cannot be ostentatiously absolute enough to become the plausible vehicle of Swift's still broader malice. In moments like this one, the perspective of the moralist Swift cedes to a kind of ultimate animus, the relaxation of distinctions in an all-embracing imaginative and social contempt. Hungry for recognition but suspicious of the distinctions upon which it rests, its egotism can find outlet only in the leveling of all.

It is obvious, then, that *Gulliver's Travels* is not an inverted form of Christian apology, so that I cannot be accused of failing to take it seriously enough on religious grounds. Perhaps it might be objected that I am taking it too seriously, that I am forgetting it is a satire the purpose of which is to mock and to reform, not to redeem. This would be a valid objection if one could find a hint of reforming spirit in *Gulliver's Travels* or a fragment of human nature worth redeeming, but this is not easy to do, as contemporary readers were quick to complain. William Warburton, for instance, asks "Where is the sense of a general Satire, if the whole Species be degenerated? And where is the Justice of it, if it be not? The Punishment of Lunaticks is as wise as the one; and a general Execution as honest as the other."[32] Swift seems to mock the reforming value of satire itself when he makes Gulliver complain in the prefatory letter to the 1735 edition of the work, dated by Gulliver several months after the appearance of the first edition, that none of the thousand "Reformations" aimed at by the work had occurred (11:xxxiv–xxxv). This is a final sally against Gulliver's Houyhnhnm enthusiasm, but it also turns back upon the true author of the book, whose humorous efforts at reform have been as gratifyingly ineffective as he would have predicted.[33]

At the end of the day, then, Swift is able to stand apart from the mad condition of his character only because he recognizes that the human creature is simply incapable of meaningful change, whereas Gulliver does not. Swift's misanthropy, therefore, is more absolute and complete than Gulliver's. He knew, of course, that the charge of misanthropy could be lodged against him; the subject is broached at a number of places in the narrative. Gulliver's anxious revelations about his cleanliness in Lilliput are at once a transgression of manners on the part of Swift and a confession of the hazards of such transgressions; likewise, the story of dousing the fire in the queen's apartments is a comical self-justification for the violence of *A Tale of a Tub*, which had offended Queen Anne, and a kind of belated revenge for her unwillingness to reward him. Swift also takes up the issue directly in his correspondence, most notably in a famous letter to Pope in which he urges his friend, "when you think of the World give it one lash the more at my Request."

> I have ever hated all Nations professions and Communities and all my love is towards individuals; for instance, I hate the tribe of Lawyers, but I love Councilor such a one, Judge such a one, [and] so with Physicians (I will not Speak of my own Trade), Soldiers, English, Scotch, French, and the rest, but principally I hate and detest that animal called

---

[32] William Warburton, *A Critical and Philosophic Enquiry into the Causes of Prodigies and Miracles, as related by Historians. With An Essay towards restoring a Method and Purity in History* (1727), in *Swift: The Critical Heritage*, 71.

[33] McKeon argues that the unavailability of reform is built into the structure of Swift's audience, bifurcated between those not worth talking to and those who already know what Swift has to say. "Cultural Crisis and the Dialectical Method: Destabilizing Augustan Literature," in *The Profession of Eighteenth-Century Literature: Reflections on an Institution,* ed. Leopold Damrosch (Madison: University of Wisconsin Press, 1992), 56.

man, although I heartily love John, Peter, Thomas and so forth. This is the system upon which I have governed my self many years (but do not tell) and so I shall go on till I have done with them. I have Materials Towards a Treaties proving the falsity of that Definition *animal rationale;* and to show it should be only *rations capax.* Upon this great foundation of Misanthropy (though not Timon's manner) the whole building of my Travels is erected: And I never will have peace of mind till all honest men are of my Opinion.[34]

If the commandment to love one's enemies seems too rigorous to be a fair basis of judgment, it is no recommendation to a person's character that he can tolerate only his friends, especially given Swift's belief that the division of friends and enemies is likely to be based upon the most arbitrary distinctions. In another place Swift is proud to point out that his hatred of mankind was no reflex of old age, since he had been consistent in his misanthropic views from the time of his youth. Then, in a sudden change of direction, "I tell you after all that I do not hate Mankind," he says, "it is vous autres who hate them because you would have them reasonable Animals, and are Angry for being disappointed." Now it is the extremity of Swift's contempt that makes for tolerance. "I am no more angry with [Walpole] Then I was with the Kite that last week flew away with one of my Chickens and yet I was pleas'd when one of my Servants Shot him two days after."[35] For Swift, most human beings not only fail to be "reasonable Animals," they are not moral creatures at all. They are worthy neither of pity nor contempt. "Expect no more from Man than such an Animal is capable of," he writes to his friend Thomas Sheridan, "and you will every day find my Description of Yahoos more resembling. You should think and deal with every Man as a Villain, without calling him so, or flying from him, or valuing him less. This is an old true Lesson."[36] This chastened relaxation of standards, though, occurs hardly anywhere in Swift's published or unpublished writing. As one Yahoo writing to another, Swift was expecting a great deal, unless he was indulging in an exception.

Swift's last stroke of self-justification comes at the end of his brilliant late poem, "Verses on the Death of Dr. Swift," in which he inventories his own virtues and chronicles, sometimes as a means of flattery, his envy and resentment toward his many friends. Near the end of the poem (305–6), Swift's "Character impartial," drawn by a "quite indiff'rent" witness, concludes in this way:

> "Perhaps I may allow, the Dean
> Had too much Satyr in his Vein;

---

[34] Letter to Alexander Pope of 29 September 1725, in *Correspondence,* 3:103. I have added some punctuation to this very irregular passage.

[35] Letter to Alexander Pope of 26 November 1725, in *Correspondence,* 3:118.

[36] Letter to the Reverend Thomas Sheridan, 11 September 1725, in *Correspondence,* 3:94.

otal juncture. Part of his force lies in what he shares with Luther and Pascal, an ability to see and depict the divisions and paradoxes of human nature, the hopelessness of struggle within Christian ideals, the absurdity of human vanity and of the arbitrary and fanciful distinctions upon which it depends, and to pronounce a grand, suspicious judgment about it all. At the same time, he prefigures men like Nietzsche and Freud who would prove that the Lutheran model of suspicion had a strange power to outlive the roots from which it grew, and who would make the Augustinian image of mankind, separated from its religious grounds, an endlessly renewable source of attractively disturbing ironies and an apt vehicle for heroic mythologies of self.

Part 4

REGIMES OF NATURE

And seem'd determin'd not to starve it,
Because no Age could more deserve it.
Yet, Malice never was his Aim;
He lash'd the Vice, but spar'd the Name;
No Individual could resent,
Where Thousands equally were meant.
His Satyr points at no Defect,
But what all Mortals may correct;
For he abhorr'd that senseless Tribe
Who call it Humour when they gibe:
He spar'd a Hump, or crooked Nose,
Whose Owners set not up for Beaux.
True genuine Dulness mov'd his Pity,
Unless it offer'd to be witty.
Those, who their Ignorance confess'd,
He ne'er offended with a Jest;
But laugh'd to hear an Idiot quote
A Verse from Horace, learn'd by rote."
                                    (459–78)

This is a superb statement of the satirist's credo, but it is also a questionable
one, for, having begun his poem by explicitly endorsing the view of mankind
offered in La Rochefoucauld's *Maxims,* educing his own vanity and selfishness to confirm it, Swift will be hard pressed to defend the notion that human beings have a tendency to correct their defects. Moreover, it is not only
that Swift did not always live up to his principle to spare the name when he
lashed the vice, or spare the person when he spared the name. To spare only
"a Hump or crooked Nose/Whose Owners set not up for Beaux" is to make
no accommodation for human vanity, which, Swift knows, is an inextricable part of our nature. It is indeed to play the part of the misanthrope just as
Molière diagnosed it.

My intent here is not to indict Swift the man, whose talents and virtues
speak for themselves better than I, or he, ever could. The point I wish to make
is that what we find in Swift's defense of himself is not the Pascalian rationale for depicting the fallenness of man—that it is a sign of the truth of Christianity—but rather an implicit defense of satire and contempt as a worldview
and a way of life, the glory of telling the truth to debased creatures who will
not listen to it or, if they do, will not understand it, or, if they do that, will
not change on account of it. Perhaps the most bitter part of Swift's message
is that Gulliver does show the human capacity for change, in fact for total,
idealistic self-conversion, but this change is what leads him to the greatest
absurdity, leaving readers to be grateful for whatever intellectual and moral
sloth they can command. Both the rigidity and the malleability of humankind
are terrifying because neither can be based upon reason.

In the movement of history outlined by this study, Swift stands at a piv-

12

Invisible Agents

We have been following a two-hundred-year trend in which the prophets of modernity found in suspicion a dynamic form of self-assertion. Across the spectrum of human concerns, the note of the negative always rang true. But in the seventeenth century, the countervailing strains of a new optimism had already begun to sound. The English Revolution brought early manifestations of the liberal potential of Protestant culture to the surface.[1] Bacon's program of science and the model of unapologetic self-exploration provided by Montaigne exerted a gradual but powerful effect. Natural philosophers developed practices of trust and communal validation that could defuse the aristocratic ethos of honor and suspicion, which was not suited to the freedom of scientific discussion.[2] By the middle of the century, the force of Reformed religion was on the wane, and Newton's physics offered the basis for a modernizing not only of natural philosophy but of theology as well. We have seen that the philosophy of Descartes provided a hedge against suspicion and an influential if rather abstract rehabilitation of human agency and knowledge. It became the harbinger of an important renewal of the metaphysical tradition manifested in different forms in the writings of Spinoza, the Cambridge Platonists, and Leibniz, whose attempt to integrate his own version of Platonic metaphysics with the findings of natural philosophy would not bear its fullest results until the era of Hegel and Schelling. In works of the imagination, a newly experimental frame of mind is visible in the increasing interest in primitivism of various kinds and in the vogue of utopian fantasy and philosophical travels, from the time of Cyrano de Bergerac and

---

[1] Christopher Hill, *Milton and the English Revolution* (Boston: Faber, 1977), 268–78.
[2] See Steven Shapin, *A Social History of Truth: Civility and Science in Seventeenth-Century England* (Chicago: University of Chicago Press, 1994).

Fénelon's *Télémaque* to the *Persian Letters* and Diderot's *Supplément*. There is a secularizing tendency here, but its prominence is partly an effect of hindsight. One of the emblematic figures in the midst of these new directions is John Milton, whose Biblical fundamentalism does not make him any less potent an advocate of human freedom and responsibility, the sacredness of individual reason and conscience, or the value of flourishing in this world. If anything like paranoia can subsist in the universe of *Paradise Lost,* it is with Satan, not the human figures. Only for Satan and his demonic comrades is Providence an enemy to be outwitted, and their attempts at outwitting it have, like the flight of Oedipus, already been taken into account in the contrivance of their fate.[3] Satan's grandiosity, like Quixote's, depends upon a contemptible delusion regarded by the author with satiric detachment.[4] It is where Milton verges upon the medieval that he seems most modern, in his enhanced vision of human power.

Christian humanism, however, was not to provide the dominant model for the Enlightenment image of humanity.[5] The human passions would undergo an enhancement of value in the new century, but only with the exclusion of the higher capacities to which they had traditionally been contrasted. Human nature was now elevated at the expense of its capacity to strive for higher ideals and to fail in reaching them. Thus the contrast between reason and passion suffered persistent deflation along with the distinction between human nature as it is and human nature as it ought to be.[6] Reason could now serve as, in Hume's famous formula, the "slave of the passions"[7] rather than their master, a mere instrument of human ends rather than their arbiter and source. The great truism of the age was that reason and Nature are the same. Taken literally, this slogan would suggest that reason is barely necessary as long as we can depend upon the goodness of Nature. Its true import, however, is to relax the tension between these two long-opposing faculties, so that reason can speak with a voice of true wisdom about the sources of our happiness.[8] The role of enlightened reason is frequently to help us over-

[3] "If then his providence/Out of our evil seek to bring forth good/Our labour must be to pervert that end,/And out of good still to find means of evil,/Which oftimes may succeed, so as perhaps/Shall grieve him, if I fail not, and disturb/His inmost counsels from their destined aim" (1.162–68). John Milton, *Paradise Lost,* ed. Alastair Fowler, 2nd edition (New York: Longman, 1998).

[4] Ronald Paulson makes the connection in *Don Quixote in England: The Aesthetics of Laughter* (Baltimore: Johns Hopkins University Press, 1998), 43.

[5] This is perhaps a good place to say that, in speaking of the Enlightenment in the singular, I do not mean to ignore the diversity of culture in this period, only to indicate that the elements I am highlighting in this study were widely shared.

[6] See Albert O. Hirschman, *The Passions and the Interests: Political Arguments for Capitalism Before Its Triumph,* pt. 1 (Princeton: Princeton University Press, 1977).

[7] David Hume, *A Treatise of Human Nature,* ed. L. A. Selby-Bigge, second edition, revised by Peter H. Nidditch (Oxford: Clarendon, 1978), 415.

[8] As Jean Ehrard puts it, "The Moderns such as Fontenelle, Montesquieu and above all Marivaux do not deny the charms of *je ne sais quoi,* they try to analyze them. The 'rationalists' defend the rights of the irrational; even their skepticism moves in the direction of a new humanism;

come the scruples so long instilled by the misguided wisdom of tradition. Our search for happiness could even be thought to begin, as Voltaire's mistress Madame du Chastelet put it, with the conviction that "we have nothing else to do in this world than to furnish ourselves with agreeable sensations and feelings."[9]

The passions, of course, whenever they become philosophical, tend to speak boldly in favor of this attitude. Its defenders can be found in ancient sources, among the French libertines, on the Restoration stage, and in popular works such as the *Advice to His Son* (1656) by Hobbes's friend Francis Osborne. The locus classicus in this period is the poems of a model rake, the Earl of Rochester, whose "Satyr against Reason and Mankind" derides the fate of the philosopher whose "wisdom did his happiness destroy,/Aiming to know that world he should enjoy."[10] While there is a touch of ostentatious humility here, it is not of the idealistic kind. It leads the poet to "despise" the very notion of the spirit that originally grounded it, the "supernatural gift, that makes a mite/Think he's an image of the infinite" (76–77). For Rochester, a true and sober assessment of our capacities will bring the clear-sighted man to acknowledge his kinship with the beasts in order to make the most of his earthly pleasures.

> Thus, whilst against false reasoning I inveigh,
> I own right reason, which I would obey:
> That reason which distinguishes by sense
> And gives us rules of good and ill from thence,
> That bounds desires with a reforming will
> To keep 'em more in vigor, not to kill.
> Your reason hinders, mine helps to enjoy,
> Renewing appetites yours would destroy.
> My reason is my friend, yours is a cheat;
> Hunger calls out, my reason bids me eat;
> Perversely, yours your appetite does mock:
> This asks for food, that answers, "What's o'clock?"
> This plain distinction, sir, your doubt secures:
> 'Tis not true reason I despise, but yours.
>
> (99–111)

In addition to their frank hedonism, these couplets anticipate much of the Augustan attitude and style, but Rochester adds to Butler's caustic reduc-

---

their intention, often poorly understood, is not to subjugate human nature to reason but to use reason to defend the integrity of human nature." *L'Idée de nature en France à l'aube des lumières* (Paris: Flammarion, 1970), 171.

[9] Madame du Châtelet, *Discours sur le bonheur,* ed. Robert Mauzi (Paris: Société d'édition "Les Belles lettres," 1961), 4.

[10] David Vieth, ed., *The Complete Poems of John Wilmot, Earl of Rochester* (New Haven: Yale University Press, 1968), lines 33–34.

tionism an argumentative lucidity and fluency that would only be matched occasionally even by Swift.

The dissoluteness, obscenity, and social rebelliousness of Rochester were just what religious teachers had always pictured as the inevitable result of a decline in orthodox observance, but the Enlightened successors to the orthodox Christian rarely followed in that dissolute vein. After the Restoration period, the libertine would not again become a figure of significance until the time of Laclos, de Sade, and Byron. The morality of Nature indeed took the stage, but it was not Nature according to Augustine or Hobbes, with vicious proclivities on display, but the rather more benevolent Nature of Shaftesbury, Addison, Fielding, and Diderot. The natural man was a creature who could find his place in a harmonious cosmic order created by a Supreme Being and set in motion according to laws established by Newton. There was no need to resort to metaphysics to prove the existence of a Creator whose hand was ever more distinctly visible in his works, no need for disputes about biblical authority or the details of revelation for a creature whose reason was the servant of his nature, and little need to trouble about an afterlife that was beyond Nature. As Ernst Cassirer observed, the doctrine of original sin was the "common opponent" that united all sides of Enlightened thought.[11] And whereas for a thousand years no laughter could have done justice to the degradation of the unregenerate human soul, in the newer, brighter world of the eighteenth century, laughter at the expense of humankind could seem excessive and uncivilized, hearkening unpleasantly backward to the time of contempt.[12] The "rallying Humour," the Earl of Shaftesbury complained, "has passed from the Men of Pleasure to the Men of Business. Politicians have been infected with it: and the grave Affairs of State have been treated with an Air of *Irony* and *Banter*. The ablest Negotiators have been known the notablest *Buffoons*: the most celebrated Authors, the greatest Masters of *Burlesque*."[13] Shaftesbury turns his own agile irony back upon the mockers of mankind, accusing them of promulgating a "general Scepticism" in order to combat particular dogmas (1:95). The question he puts to Hobbes's egoism—"Whence is this Zeal in our behalf?"—is tellingly ironic, for it unmasks the hidden altruism of the author of *Leviathan;* while other selfish hypocrites speak only the best of human nature, this one is eager to unmask his wolfish nature, thus inadvertently revealing the hidden generosity of his purpose (1:92).

Pleasure, in this new dispensation, is no longer a thing to be disapproved,

[11] Ernst Cassirer, *Philosophy of the Enlightenment,* trans. Fritz C. A. Koelln and James P. Petegrove (Princeton: Princeton University Press, 1951), 141.

[12] It is in this period that the recuperation of Don Quixote begins. The knight-errant becomes a fixture of eighteenth-century imagination, but he is less and less the utterly degraded butt imagined by Butler in *Hudibras,* more and more the genially eccentric and antiquated idealist like Addison's Sir Roger de Coverley. Paulson, *Don Quixote in England,* 33–41.

[13] Anthony Ashley Cooper, Earl of Shaftesbury, *Characteristics of Men, Manners, Opinions, Times,* 3 vols. (Birmingham: J. Baskerville, 1732), 1:62.

neither the sublime pleasures of Beauty in Shaftesbury's Platonizing conception, nor the pleasures of the senses. Pleasure acquires a new seriousness, part of the long development out of Protestantism that Charles Taylor calls "the affirmation of ordinary life,"[14] and it now become far more self-conscious and forthright in its own defense. At the same time there occurs an interesting reversal of roles. Whereas Protestants tended to blame their enemies, either Catholics or other Protestants, for exaggerating human goodness and power, the Enlighteners blamed both Catholics and Protestants for undermining them. Michel Foucault was following directly in Rochester's vein when he coined his brilliant designation of the soul as "the prison of the body."[15] Whereas in Christian, and especially Neoplatonic, theology, it was the body—the seat of the accidental, the contingent, and the mortal—that kept the soul from its true home in God, for many figures of the Enlightenment it was the *idea* of the soul—a fictive intervention of contingent will—that kept the body from realizing its simple and natural heaven on earth.

With the turn to a more hopeful view of human life and Nature, it would seem that our story might be arriving at an impasse. Where was the potential for suspicion and paranoia when Luther's punishing father-God had been tamed to Newton's bland mechanic, and Hobbes's Leviathan to the beneficent umpire of the "pursuit of happiness" invoked by the American founders? The answer lies in the problems for agency inherent in the optimistic but anti-intellectual conception of Nature at the core of Enlightenment thought.[16] Nature, in this mode, is rarely a value-neutral term, though it often benefited from concealing the fact. It represents a state of actuality that is always and by definition what it should be—a unity of Actual and Ideal. That which is natural cannot fail to be good. Pope was being quite literal when he wrote that "Whatever IS, is RIGHT." Reason, which once held itself above Nature, henceforth came to be considered identical with it just in the way Rochester claimed, reason being preeminently the impulse to obey Nature. Abstract metaphysical reasoning, reasoning from first causes or ide-

---

[14] The title of pt. 3 of Charles Taylor, *Sources of the Self: The Making of the Modern Identity* (Cambridge: Harvard University Press, 1989).

[15] *Surveiller et punir: naissance de la prison* (Paris: Gallimard, 1975), 34.

[16] The description of Enlightenment naturalism and its still more revolutionary Romantic successor comprised one of the great tasks of twentieth-century scholarship. In addition to the comprehensive work by Ehrard cited above, see Basil Willey, *The Eighteenth-Century Background: Studies on the Idea of Nature in the Thought of the Period* (London: Chatto & Windus, 1941); Paul Hazard, *La Crise de conscience européene, 1680–1715* (Paris: Boivin, 1935); Lester G. Crocker, *An Age of Crisis; Man and World in Eighteenth-Century French Thought* (Baltimore: Johns Hopkins University Press, 1959) and *Nature and Culture; Ethical Thought in the French Enlightenment* (Baltimore: Johns Hopkins University Press, 1963); Perry Miller, *The New England Mind: From Colony to Province* (Cambridge: Harvard University Press, 1953) and *Nature's Nation* (Cambridge: Harvard University Press, 1967); M. H. Abrams, *Natural Supernaturalism: Tradition and Revolution in Romantic Literature* (New York: Norton, 1971); and Michel Foucault, *Les Mots et les choses: une archéologie des sciences humaines* (Paris: Gallimard, 1966).

alistic principles, violates Nature, and the demands it exacts are an abuse. The separation between Nature and the Ideal, or, more properly, the very notion of an Ideal above Nature, becomes from this point of view either an illusion or a manipulative tool of privilege seeking to discipline or exclude its victims. The space of agency and critique, of the region that lies between what should be and what is, has by definition been abolished.

If Luther, Hobbes, and La Rochefoucauld found it necessary to put a suspicious interpretation upon all appearances of goodness, the builders of natural systems found it equally necessary to explain away all appearances of ill. In either case, paranoia or anti-paranoia, a higher perspective had to be evoked to annul the apparent one, converting it in Quixotic fashion into its opposite. The problems of optimism, then, are in some ways the mirror image of the tendency to which it responded. Because optimism always looks facile next to pessimism, it is easy to miss the similarity of the two modes, just as readers of Voltaire's *Candide* frequently overlook the fact that Pangloss and Martin—and by implication Leibniz and Luther—are only mirror versions of the same mistake, both equally in need of therapeutic gardening.

The potential for suspicion within the Augustan mode appears clearly in a figure who stands against the new trend of optimism but does so in such a paradoxical way that he becomes part of it. Bernard Mandeville, a transplanted Dutchmen living in England, provided one of the most trenchant and persuasive versions of the position that all of our actions are governed by egoistical concern, and he seems to make this claim with the moral opprobrium of a Church father; yet when it comes to the practical, social effects of the egoistic tendency of our nature, Mandeville draws an unexpected moral—that egoism is not only pervasive but also necessary for the economic good of society. Vice, therefore, according to Mandeville's paradox, is the source of prosperity, not its undoing—hence his famous slogan, "Private Vices, Publick Benefits." Whatever effects it may have upon the fortunes of the individual, vice among a certain class of people is wholesome for society. This leads to a wry kind of moral embarrassment: we can neither renounce the fruits of vice nor do without them unless we want to revert to the poverty of the early Christians.

The moral extremity with which Mandeville sets this predicament calls his sincerity into question, especially in light of the fact that, while insisting on the reality of vice, he hardly seems to believe in the possibility of virtue. Public virtues are always private vices in disguise. Their social currency can only be explained with reference to the efforts of men in power to sustain the social order. Such efforts are fundamentally misguided: men in power, who did not understand that the true sources of their wealth lay in consumption, had introduced the competition for virtue as an instrument of social control. "This was the manner," Mandeville claims, "after which Savage Man was broke; from whence it is evident, that the first Rudiments of Morality, broached by skilful Politicians, to render Men useful to each other as well as tractable, were chiefly contrived that the Ambitious might reap the more

Benefit from, and govern vast Numbers of them with the greater Ease and Security."[17] Mandeville even goes so far as to deny a religious origin to virtue. Its function from the beginning was purely instrumental. "It is visible," he says, "that it was not any Heathen Religion or other Idolatrous Superstition, that first put Man upon crossing his Appetites and subduing his dearest Inclinations, but the skilful Management of wary Politicians; and the nearer we search into Human Nature, the more we shall be convinced, that the Moral Virtues are the Political Offspring which Flattery begot upon Pride" (1:51). The note of protectiveness toward the unspoiled nature of the savage is unmistakable, with the implication that civilization does not require we give up the joys of the primitive, as corrupt politicians would lead us to believe. The notion of the deceptive lawgiver is an ancient one, but Mandeville gives it a critical and suspicious turn that would not be fully recaptured until the time of Nietzsche. Later in the century Adam Smith, by making a distinction between vice and self-interest, was able to preserve some of the benefits of Mandeville's irony within a naturalistic analysis, suppressing the misguided interventions of the politician in favor of the workings of an "invisible hand"—the cumulative effect of the market.

Mandeville's analysis of society remains on the level of the social and the economic, which is to say, on a scale at which it was possible to imagine that the natural working of the whole could be perverted by the misplaced good intentions of the few. The central strain of Enlightenment optimism, however, was to achieve a scale that stood above such possibilities, a cosmic and metaphysical scale equal to the pessimism it displaced. It was Leibniz, of course, who provided the scaffolding. His defense of creation as the "best of all possible worlds," originally framed in response to Pierre Bayle, has produced a great deal of amusement in retrospect, yet his starting point was inevitable for an age that took the existence of the Creator for granted. Since a visibly imperfect world lies before us and since God created it as it is, he must have chosen it as the best out of all the logically consistent ones his omniscience could survey. If the world contains real evil in parts, which Leibniz did not dispute, this had to be necessary in order for the whole to be the best it could possibly be—in order for it to have, he went on to explain, the most perfection, the greatest harmony, order, beauty, variety, power, and economy of effects.[18] It was a line of thought that stretches back to Plato's *Timaeus*.[19] The essential point, to be tirelessly repeated, was that, for the world as a whole to be as good as it can be, and indeed for it to be, as Leibniz believed, not just relatively but absolutely good, did not mean that every part of it, or

[17] Bernard Mandeville, *The Fable of the Bees, or, Private Vices, Publick Benefits*, ed. F. B. Kaye (Oxford: Clarendon Press, 1957), 1:46–47.

[18] The notions are complexly interrelated. For an account of Leibniz's thought that starts with his theodicy, a term he invented, see Donald Rutherford, *Leibniz and the Rational Order of Nature* (Cambridge: Cambridge University Press, 1995), esp. pt. 1.

[19] The classic discussion is A. O. Lovejoy, *The Great Chain of Being: A Study in the History of an Idea* (Cambridge: Harvard University Press, 1936).

every person, had to be or even could be good (251). Human freedom pre-supposes license for doing ill, and Leibniz was enough of an orthodox Christian to believe in a heaven and hell to balance out the local evils and injustices in the humanly inhabited portion of the "best of all possible worlds" (132).

If God permits expressions of evil, those brought about by his creatures and those that stem from the nature of the creation, it is not, of course, because his power over the world can actually be thought of as limited; God could avert the evils we see before us if he were willing to intervene case by case. For him to do so, however, would impair the beauty and order of the whole, which must operate autonomously by general principles. Not to see this is not to appreciate the genuine intellectual perfection of creation. "Must God spoil his system, must there be less beauty, perfection and reason in the universe, because there are people who misuse reason?"[20] For God to diminish creation in that way would be for him to do less than justice to himself as a mind in contemplation of the created order, for "Nothing would be less rational than these perpetual miracles" (193). Leibniz's strange conclusion is that if the world did not have the faults that are so visible to us, it would be less beautiful, less satisfying as an object of divine regard, and implicitly as an object of human regard as well, since, made in God's image, we also participate in the contemplation of the whole. The Leibnizian spectator would rather see necessary evils occur in their proper place than admit an arbitrary good into creation.

Our ability to recognize the existence of evil, then, but to accept and love the creation nonetheless, is a sign of our participation in divine intellect, a sign of our higher nature, just as our capacity to do evil is a sign of our freedom. It also seems, however, that our sense of participation in divinity depends partly upon the limitations of our knowledge. God, in presenting man with intelligence and making him an image of divinity, centers him in the confined sphere or microcosm that corresponds with the reach of his intellect.

> [God] leaves him to himself, in a sense, in his small department. . . . He enters there only in an occult manner, for he supplies being, force, life, reason, without showing himself. It is there that free will plays its game: and God makes game (so to speak) of these little Gods that he has thought good to produce, as we make game of children who follow pursuits which we secretly encourage or hinder according as it pleases us. Thus man is there like a little god in his own world or *Microcosm,* which he governs after his own fashion: he sometimes performs wonders therein, and his art often imitates nature.[21]

---

[20] Gottfried W. Leibniz, *Theodicy: Essays on the Goodness of God, the Freedom of Man, and the Origin of Evil,* ed. Austin Farrer, trans. E. M. Huggard (Lasalle, IL: Open Court, 1995), 191.

[21] *Theodicy,* 215–16. I have slightly altered Huggard's rendering of this passage. Cf. *Die*

In this passage, the doings of "Earth's little god," to borrow a phrase from Goethe's heaven, are subject to an authentically Faustian irony. By describing free will as a game, Leibniz does not mean to suggest that the freedom of the human will is not real but that the conditions of its freedom and the conditions under which we exercise it are entirely matters of God's choice. God allows us a minor form of divinity in our capacity to understand good and evil, in our freedom, and in the self-divinizing light by which we exercise it. The limits of our knowledge, then, become a compensation for the limits of our power, and this forms part of the benevolence of the divine plan.

Where Luther and Pascal, then, like Scotus and Ockham before them, left the logic of God's cosmic arrangements largely mysterious from the point of view of man, Leibniz offers us a God of ontological compromises that can partially be understood. The "best of all possible worlds" does contain human evil and even original sin, and this is why it is not paradise, though the philosopher does "make bold to say that we shall find, upon unbiased scrutiny of the facts, that taking all in all human life is in general tolerable. And adding to this the motives of religion, we shall be content with the order God has set."[22] But for those who are not content with the order God has set and who are unable to put their human sense of justice so easily in abeyance while surveying the fabric of the cosmos, this claim of the necessity of evil and suffering can look very much like an ontological excuse. When Leibniz seeks to help his readers cope with the discrepancy between the apparent evil and real goodness of God's scheme, his mind shifts to analogies from mathematics— the way the numbers in a series or points of a line can look random until their equation has been grasped:

> The question of *physical evil*, that is, of the origin of sufferings, has difficulties in common with that of the origin of *metaphysical evil*, apparent irregularities of the universe. But one must believe that even sufferings and monstrosities are part of order; and it is well to bear in mind not only that it was better to admit these defects and these monstrosities than to violate general laws, as Father Malebranche sometimes argues, but also that these very monstrosities are in the rules, and are in conformity with general acts of [God's] will, though we be not capable of discerning this conformity. It is just as sometimes there are appearances of irregularity in mathematics which issue finally in a great order when one has gotten to the bottom of them.[23]

Neither analogies of this kind, though, nor the appeal to cosmic beauty, variety, lawfulness, and harmony, were likely to be helpful to those like

---

Philosophischen Schriften, 7 vols., ed. C. I. Gerhardt (1875–90; Hildesheim: Georg Olms, 1961–62), 6:197.

[22] *Theodicy,* 286. Huggard's rendering has again been slightly altered. Cf. Gerhardt, 6:271.

[23] *Theodicy,* 276–77.

Voltaire who were willing to confront the reality and extremity of human suffering:

> Tristes calculateurs des misères humaines,
> Ne me consolez point, vous aigrissez mes peines.
>
> . . . .
>
> Et vous composerez dans ce chaos fatal
> Des malheurs de chaque être un bonheur général![24]
>
> [Melancholy calculators of human misery,
> Do not console me, you but sharpen my pains.
>
> . . . .
>
> And you compose in this fatal chaos of the sorrows
> Of each being a happiness for all!]

Even the doctrine of Pascal is more consoling than the optimism of Leibniz. Voltaire was repulsed by the bleakness and debasement of the image of man offered by Pascal,[25] and throughout his life he felt a profound need to believe that a rational order governed the cosmos. However, bitter experiences in his later life, crystallized by the Lisbon earthquake, made the ratiocinations of Leibniz seem mere absurdity.[26]

For the most part Leibniz avoids the potential callousness of his theodicy by keeping the distinctions between metaphysical, moral, and physical evil. It is the metaphysical benefits of admitting evil that motivate God's preference for it, not his desire to permit misconduct or pain, which he is morally obliged to minimize as much as possible. In less subtle hands, however, the logic of theodicy comes to seem so facile that it becomes difficult to credit the undeniable force exerted by these ideas over a long period of time. In enthusiastic versions like Pope's *Essay on Man*, the optimism of the best possible leads to an absurd encomium to the cosmic status quo:

> All Nature is but Art, unknown to thee;
> All Chance, Direction, which thou canst not see;
> All Discord, Harmony not understood;

[24] Voltaire, *Poème sur le désastre de Lisbonne,* in *Mélanges,* ed. Jacques van den Heuvel (Paris: Gallimard, 1961), 306–7, 324–25.

[25] It is not surprising that Voltaire, earlier in his career, when Pascal, not Leibniz, was his target, was far more willing to justify Providence than after 1756. In an imaginary dialogue with Pascal, he asks, "Is not the present state of man a benefit from the creator? Who has told you that God owes you more? . . . You complain of a life so short and so unfortunate; thank God it is not shorter and unhappier." *Lettres philosophiques,* intercalated as number 29 in the Pascal chapter in the 1739 edition. *Mélanges,* 1347, n. 2.

[26] Bronislaw Baczko, *Job, mon ami: Promesses du bonheur et fatalité du mal,* pt. 1 (Paris: Gallimard, 1997), describes Voltaire's movement from a relatively sanguine optimism (not "Tout est bien" but "Tout est passable") though the crisis period of the Lisbon earthquake to the modified rationalism of his later years.

> All partial Evil, universal Good:
> And, spite of Pride, in erring Reason's spite,
> One truth is clear, 'Whatever IS, is RIGHT.'
> (1:289–94)[27]

In spite of his many rebukes to human pride, Pope in this poem gives himself license to "Expatiate free o'er all this scene of Man" (1:5). It is a freedom that seems all the more unaccountable and a satisfaction all the more gratuitous as it becomes progressively grander in its declarations of human limit. When we remember that "Hope springs eternal in the human breast," it is important to include the sequel, "Man never Is, but always To be blest" (1:95–96). It is even more important to remember that, for Pope, this is still an occasion for gratitude, hope being one of the important Providential anodynes that keep the life we actually lead from becoming intolerable. Though hope is vain, without it we would be even more miserable than we are. Ignorance is another indispensable resource.

> Heav'n from all creatures hides the book of Fate,
> All but the page prescrib'd, their present state:
> From brutes what men, from men what spirits know:
> Or who could suffer Being here below?
> The lamb thy riot dooms to bleed to-day,
> Had he thy Reason, would he skip and play?
> Pleas'd to the last, he crops the flow'ry food,
> And licks the hand just rais'd to shed his blood.
> Oh blindness to the future! kindly giv'n,
> That each may fill the circle mark'd by Heaven:
> Who sees with equal eye, as God of all,
> A hero perish, or a sparrow fall,
> Atoms or systems into ruin hurl'd,
> And now a bubble burst, and now a world.
> (1:77–90)

The Christian imagery of the lamb finds a strange variation in this passage, where all creatures become lamb-like victims, blessed not in innocence but ignorance, while Heaven surveys each scale of ruin with an "equal eye," insensible of distinction. Hamlet's "special Providence in the fall of a sparrow" has become a general vision of undiscriminating order. Following in Milton's footsteps, Pope sets out to "vindicate the ways of God to Man" (1:16), not by locating human responsibility for the imperfections of the world but rather by replacing the drama of salvation with an exposition of necessity. Because the imperfections of the world are only apparent and relative to us,

---

[27] *An Essay on Man,* ed. Maynard Mack, vol. 3, pt. 1 of *The Twickenham Edition of the Poems of Alexander Pope* (New Haven: Yale University Press, 1950).

while necessary and beneficial in view of the whole, the doctrine of the Fall has been rendered not only untenable but otiose.[28] Our consolation, then, is neither that we are ultimately responsible for our human predicament and can do better with the help of the church, as the Catholic view would have it, nor that God has saved us out of his incomprehensible grace, as for Luther, but that our sufferings are necessary to allow the fullest expression of God's power and to provide him and other observers of the divine order with the most satisfying spectacle of being. There is, of course, a benevolent intention running through the whole, but the ironic limitation of our power to grasp it is central to the design. We are asked to assume the standpoint of a benevolence that is as incomprehensible as the vindictiveness of Calvin's deity.

If it is not comforting for readers of the *Essay on Man* to be told that human distresses are a necessary element of the beautiful whole, it is but a small step to the more disturbing and truly paranoid idea that, from the point of view of higher spectators, our sufferings are actually a pleasure in themselves. The suggestion is latent in Pope's passage about the lamb quoted above, and Pope's expositor Soame Jenyns makes it explicit. As Samuel Johnson puts it in his famous review of Jenyns' book, "He has at last thought on a way by which human sufferings may produce good effects. He imagines that as we have not only animals for food, but choose some for our diversion, the same privilege may be allowed to some beings above us, *who may deceive, torment, or destroy us for the ends only of their own pleasure or utility.*"[29] Johnson confesses himself unable to resist extending Jenyns's argument.

> He might have shown that these *hunters, whose game is man* have many sports analogous to our own. As we drown whelps and kittens, they amuse themselves now and then with sinking a ship, and stand round the fields of Blenheim, or the walls of Prague, as we encircle a cockpit. As we shoot a bird flying, they take a man in the midst of his business or pleasure, and knock him down with an apoplexy. Some of them, perhaps, are virtuosi, and delight in the operations of an asthma, as a human philosopher in the effects of the air pump. To swell a man with a tympany is as good sport as to blow a frog. Many a merry bout have these frolic beings at the vicissitudes of an ague, and good sport it is to see a man tumble with an epilepsy, and revive and tumble again, and all this he knows not why. As they are wiser and more powerful than we, they have more exquisite diversions; for we have no way of

[28] As Lovejoy notes, William King, one of the earliest and most important proponents of philosophical optimism, could only cope with the notion of the Fall by suggesting that the original felicities of Eden had been somehow exaggerated! *Great Chain of Being,* 221.

[29] Samuel Johnson, "Review of *A Free Inquiry into the Nature and Origin of Evil*," in *The Oxford Authors Samuel Johnson,* ed. Donald Greene (New York: Oxford, 1984), 534–35. Johnson's article originally appeared in *The Literary Magazine* in 1757.

procuring any sport so brisk and so lasting as the paroxysms of the gout and stone, which undoubtedly must make high mirth, especially if the play be a little diversified with the blunders and puzzles of the blind and deaf. We know not how far their sphere of observation may extend. Perhaps now and then a merry being may place himself in such a situation as to enjoy at once all the varieties of an epidemical disease, or amuse his leisure with the tossings and contortions of every possible pain exhibited together. (535)

The passage concludes with the brilliant suggestion that Jenyns' call to authorship might itself be the tormenting prank of a higher being. "Many of the books which now crowd the world may be justly suspected to be written for the sake of some invisible order of beings, for surely they are of no use to any of the corporeal inhabitants of the world" (536).

It is important to recognize that, while mocking the brittle rationalism of Leibniz, Pope, and Jenyns, neither Voltaire nor Johnson intended to dismiss the problem they were attempting to solve. It was the facility of the solution and its impotence in the face of experience that made optimism so infuriating, especially considering that indeed no better solutions were to be had. However comforting in a certain sense it might have been for human beings to be assured, in spite of all the sufferings flesh is heir to, that things could not have been otherwise, Leibniz, for all of his ingenuity, could not produce a compelling case that God had no better choice, that the appeal to Necessity was anything other than what Milton called it, "the tyrant's plea."[30] It was particularly egregious that God was unwilling to intervene in mortal sufferings only because to do so would require him to abrogate his self-imposed laws. As Johnson pointed out, the aim of theodicy was consolation and patience, but nothing is less conducive to patience than the idea that we are being made an object of sport, like "puppets, of which some creature not much wiser than ourselves manages the wires" (536). However abstract the logic by which this world must be the best of all possible, there was yet a will involved, a power of agency by which God had chosen the conditions of our existence according to his own values and interests rather than ours. Luther's God was more threatening in his arbitrariness and anger, but he did not claim to be a God of reason in a sense that human beings could understand. Leibniz and Pope had replaced an angry father with a metaphysical mannequin lacking moral engagement with his creation. This abrogation of the moral combined with the claim of benevolence was the crucial gesture that made the vestiges of divine agency and choice unpalatable.[31]

[30] *Paradise Lost*, 4.393–94.

[31] See, however, Charles Taylor's argument that the autonomy of God's created order, which miracles would have impaired, was one of the sources of its attraction. *Sources of the Self*, 272–73.

It is interesting to consider how closely the English defenders of theodicy were connected with that supreme pessimist, Jonathan Swift. William King, the Archbishop of Dublin, whose *De origine mali* (1702) was one of the earliest and fullest treatments of the theme, was Swift's ecclesiastical superior in Ireland; the two men had a long and sometimes difficult association. Henry St. John, Viscount Bolingbroke, whose philosophy was often thought to be the immediate inspiration of Pope's *Essay,* was the presiding genius of Swift's political career. And Pope, of course, was Swift's friend and sometime collaborator over many years; the relationship between the two poets and satirists was grounded not only in mutual admiration for each others' talents but in an outlook deeply shared. Swift was surrounded, then, by almost the entire galaxy of philosophical optimists, but only the most superficial interpreter could take his misanthropy for a reaction to their theoretical cheerfulness. Far more important was the element all of these men had in common, and especially the two great satirists—an utter inability to believe that human beings could be other than what they are. Whereas Swift found the critical distance between the Actual and the Ideal that makes the space of agency and judgment impossible to bridge, the domain of the Ideal having been deflated to nothing or put entirely beyond human reach, Pope found the two realms impossible to separate, there being in existence nothing but the Ideal—or the closest to it that can be had. And yet in this remaining space between the best that is logically possible and what mortals might imagine as the good, Pope could recapture almost the entire ground of Swift's bitterness. The important difference between the two men was that Swift was sincere enough in his disgust with human beings to resent the fact that they are not as unhappy as their condition ought to make them, whereas Pope, from the heights of his artistry, found malicious pleasure in the fact that irrationality and pride are so strong in human beings as to make their delusions of happiness almost indestructible.

> See the blind beggar dance, the cripple sing.
> The sot a hero, lunatic a king;
> The starving chemist in his golden views
> Supremely bless'd, the poet in his muse.
>   (2:267–70)

With gestures of this kind, Pope makes himself at home in the grotesquery of the satirist's world. When Swift includes the satirist in the spectacle of folly, and subjects himself to his own awesome violence, his moralism and his egotism together seem to be striving toward a certain impotent grandeur, with an effect that can only be disturbing to the reader. With Pope, however, the effect has the cleanliness of wit. Egotism and artistry merge in the necessity of Pope's couplet, without leaving a remainder.

The Empirical Self and its Inquisitors

I have been considering the most cosmic dimension of Enlightenment optimism, that dimension in which theodicy and natural theology opened up an
intellectual space between Christianity and agnosticism, a space that could
also accommodate some adherents of both. This space has closed so definitively that it is now difficult for us to appreciate its importance. Insofar as
we continue to share the optimism of the Enlightenment, we must do so without the guarantees of general providence or natural theology. When we look
back to the eighteenth century, we look to the world of practical rationality
to find our origins. The emblematic figure is neither Leibniz nor the author
of the *Essay on Man* but John Locke, who provided the blueprint for the
world that so many people could defend as the best possible here among us.

Locke shared with Bacon, Hobbes, and Descartes what we may call the
founding assumption of the Enlightenment, that the progress of human
thought and the benefits of human life can only be secured by a radical critique of all the notions we have inherited from the past. Locke's philosophy
stresses the mystifications of language and the mythologies that have been
foisted upon mankind under the false pretense of "innate ideas." The *Essay
concerning Human Understanding* is an exhaustive critique of the sources and
modes of knowledge, intended to free the mind from all forms of error and
to give a proper and rational order to thought. Its success and influence have
been extraordinary. In one version or another it dominated philosophy in the
English-speaking countries into the second half of the twentieth century.

Lockean "empiricism" derives our knowledge not only from experience
but also from reflection upon experience and the processes of intellect.
Locke's reflecting agent is a tireless critic of the patterns and associations of
thought, what he calls the "empire of habit,"[32] always looking to separate
connections that have a rational basis from ones that have been unreflectingly
accepted, either at the behest of others or the urging of our passions. "Tem-
ples have their sacred images," he warns, "and we see what influence they
have always had over a great portion of mankind. But in truth the ideas and
images in men's minds are the invisible powers that constantly govern them,
and to these they all universally pay a ready submission."[33] This is a key lesson for education, in many ways the central Lockean concern. Since "the difference to be found in the manners and abilities of men is owing more to their
education than to anything else, we have reason to conclude that great care is
to be had of the forming children's *minds* and giving them that seasoning early
which shall influence their lives always after."[34] It is essential that the "in-

[32] John Locke, *The Conduct of the Understanding*, in *"Some Thoughts Concerning Education" and "The Conduct of the Understanding,"* ed. Ruth W. Grant and Nathan Tarcov (Indianapolis: Hackett, 1996), 218.

[33] *The Conduct of the Understanding*, 167.

[34] *Some Thoughts Concerning Education*, 25.

visible powers" that seek to govern us should be combated as early in child-hood as possible.

For Locke it is not only, or even primarily, the character, then, that must be disciplined and mastered in order to achieve authentic self-possession, but rather the order of intellect itself. This is the positive teaching of the *Essay,* and it is developed further in Locke's subsequent writings. Since pleasure and pain, and especially pain, are the central human stimulates, by governing a child with reward and punishment, "little encouragements" or "the rod," rather than caprice or indulgence, the teacher can set his or her life on the solid foundation of reason.

> Remove hope and fear, and there is an end of all discipline. I grant that good and evil, *reward* and *punishment,* are the only motives to a ratio-nal creature; these are the spur and reins whereby all mankind are set on work and guided, and therefore they are to be made use of to chil-dren too. For I advise their parents and governors always to carry this in their minds, that children are to be treated as rational creatures. (35)

Rationality for Locke is not the renunciation of pleasure and the acceptance of pain, as it was for earlier Christians, but the maximizing of pleasure and minimizing of pain both here on earth and in the afterlife.

Locke's religion is the correlate of this pragmatic and worldly vigilance, the pursuit of reward and punishment on the ultimate scale. While he is no admirer of the vulgar run of mankind, he does not find mankind in general to be in a fallen condition and sees no biblical evidence for the doctrine of hereditary sin. Men and woman have been condemned to death for the sin of Adam, but it has not impaired their natures, which in any case have been restored by Christ. In a work entitled *The Reasonableness of Christianity,* Locke argues that the Gospels contain nothing we need to know about God that reflection upon our experience could not tell us; Christ's coming was a benefit not because human nature needed to be restored but because men so often fail to use their reason as they should.[35] Locke's Christ is preeminently a teacher; rational assent to the fact that Christ is the Messiah is the essence of his Christianity (32). This makes part of the ground for his famous de-fense of toleration—that there is no value in forcing men to practice a reli-gion whose creed they do not willingly accept on the basis of the evidence.

In the sphere of the political, Locke has become the canonical spokesman for the "Society of Rational Creatures entered into Community for their mu-tual good," as he puts it in the second of the *Two Treatises of Civil Gov-ernment.*[36] The interests of the members of this community are grounded in

[35] John Locke, *The Reasonableness of Christianity* (Stanford: Stanford University Press, 1958), 57, 60–61.

[36] John Locke, *Two Treatises of Civil Government,* ed. Peter Laslett, Cambridge Texts in the History of Political Philosophy (Cambridge: Cambridge University Press, 1960), 294.

the natural law that commands each of us to preserve the life God has given us and not to harm the "Life, Health, Liberty, or Possessions" of any of the other rational creatures he has made (271). Locke establishes the government as the protector of private interests and the "Umpire" that settles their differences (324), and he endows the pursuit of private interests with pre-eminent social value, since "he who appropriates land to himself by his labour, does not lessen but increase the common stock of mankind" (294). Self-interest, then, and social interest are naturally aligned. The labor theory of value Locke espouses is a natural correlate of this outlook, a hopeful simplification of the relation between human effort and the achievement of the good. It is also powerfully individualistic. For Locke, each man is an Adam taking possession of his own territory by improving it for his own benefit and the benefit of all. It is this natural right that is protected by the constitution of civil society.

If any philosopher ever succeeded in forging the spirit of his time in thought, it was Locke. He participated in the founding of the modern political and legal-economic orders, gave canonical expression to the key concept of toleration, and shaped views of education, social organization, and social discipline into the twentieth century.[37] Where in his account Locke's predecessors saw a creature bound by the sovereignty of divine right and patriarchal possession, imbued with the fixed knowledge of "innate ideas" and submissive to authority on account of original sin or a fundamental irrationality, Locke saw a rational agent able to control the formation of his own mind, create economic value and social order, and wield political power when the existing order no longer served its function.

We rightly associate Locke with the achievement of many of our essential freedoms. But his vision, hopeful as its tendency may be, also offers natural opportunities for suspicion. Locke's political doctrine envisions the individual's pursuit of self-preservation and self-interest as essentially private and the state as an agency for the protection of the rights of self-interest. Though the sovereign is no longer thought of as pursuing its own interests, as in Hobbes's account, its agency remains essentially negative. Just as it prevents me from interfering with property and interests of others, so it prevents them from interfering with mine. Freedom for Locke is the absence of interference. Such freedom is precious enough in its own terms, but it can leave the goal-directed aspects of social and government activity looking illegitimate and threatening. In defining government activity primarily in terms of potential interference, it fosters a habit of thinking in terms of passivity and victimization rather than action. This habit becomes more significant insofar as political agency provides a model for agency in general. Rousseau was to learn a great deal from "le sage Locke."

I have already mentioned the degree to which Locke was concerned with

[37] On Locke and discipline, see James Tully, chap. 6 in *An Approach to Political Philosophy: Locke in Contexts* (New York: Cambridge University Press, 1993).

control of one's own mind, with giving the proper order to one's ideas and avoiding the manipulations of others—the "invisible powers" that govern. At the same time that he showed how easily the mind can be influenced by others, he also showed the necessity for one's own activities of control. With the recognition of the power that others can exert over the order of our ideas, Locke found it necessary to set up the educator as a countervailing power of equal vigilance and suspicion. Thus he became an advocate both of toleration and conformity, of freedom and manipulation. Locke helped establish the political framework of the public sphere and to define the new, softer but more pervasive forms of influence that would belong to it. His program for the reorganization of workhouses in England was far more influential than Bentham's Panopticon, and he is certainly the precursor of Bentham's magistrate, who, "operating in the character of a tutor upon all the members of the state, by the direction he gives to their hopes and fears," uses pleasure and pain to shape their behavior, "the quantum and bias of [their] moral, religious, sympathetic, and antipathetic sensibilities," thus producing a coalescence of interests for the greatest good.[38] Locke and Bentham added the carrot to Hobbes's stick. We cannot attribute the utopian enthusiasm of reformers like Helvétius and Bentham to Locke.[39] We cannot blame him for Bentham's ostentatiously cavalier reductionism, nor for the bravado that leads the founder of the utilitarian movement to insist that he does not care if his citizens are soldiers, monks, or machines as long as they are happy ones.[40] Locke's detached and frigid manner and his sober sense of the intractability of humankind made him incapable of such flights of fancy. Yet it is to Locke we owe the notion that the order of human thought is fundamentally liable to reconstruction and that one must either find a way of reforming others or be reformed in one's turn.[41]

Locke's epistemology also makes its contribution to the resources of suspicion. In his concern to free the mind from the sources of outside influence, Locke created a model of the psyche that could enjoy only the most tenuous contact with reality. The knowing subject can properly claim access to nothing but its own ideas and their relations with each other. Of the substances that underlie the order of appearance we can have no experience and no real knowledge. Although Locke frequently talks as if these postulates do not entirely cut us off from the external world, he recognizes that his attitude toward knowledge leaves little hope that natural philosophy will ever achieve a serious account of the external world.[42] Even Newton's physics can stand

[38] John Bowring, ed., *The Works of Jeremy Bentham* (Edinburgh: W. Tait, 1838), 1:30.

[39] For a corrective to this tendency, see W. M. Spellman, *John Locke and Total Depravity* (Oxford: Clarendon Press, 1988).

[40] Bowring, *The Works of Jeremy Bentham*, 4:71.

[41] Alasdair MacIntyre argues that the exclusion of non-manipulative social relations was a central contribution of the thought of this period to later modern culture. *After Virtue: A Study in Moral Theory* (Notre Dame: University of Notre Dame Press, 1981), 22 and 66.

[42] *Some Thoughts Concerning Education*, 144.

but on the most tenuous basis.[43] We are essentially prisoners of consciousness. Our condition is one of detachment, and the only remedy lies in further detachment. In the *Essay*, Locke gives voice to the objection that his account of the mind puts the sane person on equal terms with the mad: "If it be true, that all Knowledge lies only in the perception of the agreement or disagreement of our own *Ideas*, the Visions of an Enthusiast, and the Reasonings of a sober Man, will be equally certain." In fact, on these grounds sanity appears to disadvantage. "If there be any difference between them, the advantage will be on the warm-headed Man's side, as having the more *Ideas*, and the more lively. And so, by your Rules, he will be the more knowing."[44] It does not seem to me that Locke has an adequate reply to his own objection, and his attempt to formulate the nature of personal identity within the terms of this model led to notoriously paradoxical results. Centuries of scholarship have only added to the authority of *Tristram Shandy* as the definitive commentary on Locke's *Essay*. If skepticism can lead to peace and withdrawal from concern with the world, combined with suspicion it can create the sense that the struggle to define one's reality against the persuasions of others has no proper basis on which to proceed.

Since Locke must impress all of his readers as the sanest and soberest of men, it is natural to wonder how he could have arrived at this outlook, at once empowering and confining, which seems to produce a nearly intolerable impasse for the rational agent. No easy explanation can be given. I have already mentioned the fact that Lockean psychology was designed with exclusionary aims in mind, the containment of religious mania and manipulation. It also strove to establish the evidence of the senses as the primary source of our knowledge about the world. And insofar as the knowledge provided by the senses may be imperfect, Locke could find assurance in the notion that the faculties we have must be the ones God considered us to need (45). To expect more from him would be presumptuous folly. Locke's theology, then, could in a measure buttress his theory of knowledge. It was left to George Berkeley to introduce an invisible hand into the Lockean model, a divine principle of intervention that could be held responsible for the order and coherence of our experience without resorting to the objectively existing substances Locke had put out of reach. In Berkeley's scheme, if the world is still there when we look for it, it is because God is keeping the appearances in place, and these appearances are all we know. Once again God plays the role of the Cartesian demon, signaling the need of some higher force to restore order in a world of experience that has experimentally been rendered incoherent.

---

[43] Richard H. Popkin characterizes Locke's position as "a sort of semiscepticism that could be read as a justification for empirical science." *The History of Scepticism: From Savonarola to Bayle* (New York: Oxford University Press, 2003), 260.

[44] John Locke, *An Essay concerning Human Understanding*, ed. Peter Nidditch (Oxford: Oxford University Press, 1975), 562–63.

For some of Locke's successors, the blankness and manipulability of the Lockean self seemed to offer a grand opportunity to perfect mankind through education. The spectacle of human flexibility that frightened Pascal proved exhilarating to Helvétius, Bentham, and Godwin. Even Jonathan Edwards recognized in Locke's psychology the potential for benevolent psychological manipulation; Perry Miller tells us that Edwards's reading of Locke was "the central and decisive event in his intellectual life."[45] Modern advertising and publicity would be Locke's ultimate beneficiary.[46] The less sanguine, however, among Locke's readers recognized that the original blankness of the empirical subject might lead to nothing but a Hobbesian contest of wills, with no criteria of truth or value to act as a control.

This concern about the emptiness of the empirical self led directly to the invention of a new inner compass, the "moral sense," in the writings of Shaftesbury, Hutcheson, and Hume, a novel, less guilty, and more naturally benevolent version of the conscience. This moral sense was the most fragile of fictions, for if the Lockean subject could not even confirm the existence of the world beyond the senses, which no one can sincerely doubt as an everyday proposition, how could it lay claim to natural rightness of judgment in the far more controversial domain of the moral? How could such preternatural rightness be based on a faculty of sense previously unheard-of and difficult to credit under any system?

Having reduced judgment to feeling (or, in Adam Smith's case, to "sympathy," a more general form of imaginative engagement), it was typical of these systems to emphasize the development of an inner monitor, an "Inspector," "Auditor," or even "Inquisition," as Shaftesbury variously puts it. By inner interrogation, he argues, this inquisition, "as Cruel a Court as it appears," regulates and confirms us in our desires, opinions, and inclinations, our "Meaning and Design," so that we can make a warrantable claim to be "one and the same Person to day as yesterday, and to morrow as to day" (1:186–87). Smith's version of inner self-interrogation envisions an "inmate of the breast" that can internalize the viewpoint of an "impartial spectator," allowing us to keep our feelings at precisely the pitch and distance that make them appropriate for the comfortable and sympathetic examination of others. As with Hume's theory of taste, to which they are closely related, all of these accounts discover a certain space for the education of our natural sentiments through socialization or experience, while largely excluding the need for intellectual faculties or principles to play a part. It is a space in which our sentiments can mingle in order to find the most civilized and sympathetic balance, the one that accords with the views and sentiments of others.

If the empirical subject, then, always needed some external source of coherence, it is clear where that support was ultimately to be found—not in

---

[45] Perry Miller, *Jonathan Edwards* (New York: William Sloane Associates, 1949), 52.

[46] See Stewart Justman, chap. 1 in *The Psychological Mystique* (Evanston: Northwestern University Press, 1998).

God, as for Locke or Berkeley, nor in the ruler, as for Hobbes, but in our relations with others, guided by a moral sense that has been refined in the process of human relations, as if we were, to recall Shaftesbury's famous metaphor, polished into politeness by "amiable Collision."[47] This image of natural goodness refined through ordinary sociability, underwritten by the freedoms of the Glorious Revolution and the harmonious balance of the English constitution, became the prevailing answer to the egoism of Hobbes and such later interpreters as Mandeville, who kept Calvin's view of human nature alive. The true basis for this confident recourse to the social was undoubtedly the growing political security and economic success of British society through the course of the eighteenth century.

The philosophical rationale for a recourse to the benefits of sociability is given its most powerful expression in a crucial chapter of Hume's *Treatise of Human Nature* (1740). Hume has pursued the implications deriving from the fact that our knowledge consists in nothing other than the more or less vivid impressions of the senses, the mind being a heap of disconnected impressions with nothing more solid than habit and custom upon which to ground the regularity of their connections. Now the philosopher finds himself in a state of intense discomfort both on account of the isolation his philosophy describes and the distance and possible contempt it sets between him and others who have thought upon the same subject.

I am first affrighted and confounded with that forlorn solitude, in which I am plac'd in my philosophy, and fancy myself some strange uncouth monster, who not being able to mingle and unite in society, has been expell'd all human commerce, and left utterly abandon'd and disconsolate. Fain wou'd I run into the crowd for shelter and warmth; but cannot prevail with myself to mix with such deformity. I call upon others to join me, in order to make a company apart; but no one will hearken to me. Every one keeps at a distance, and dreads that storm, which beats upon me from every side. I have expos'd myself to the enmity of all metaphysicians, logicians, mathematicians, and even theologians; and can I wonder at the insults I must suffer? I have declar'd my disapprobation of their systems; and can I be surpriz'd, if they shou'd express a hatred of mine and of my person? When I look abroad, I foresee on every side, dispute, contradiction, anger, calumny and detraction. When I turn my eye inward, I find nothing but doubt and ignorance. All the world conspires to oppose and contradict me; tho' such is my weakness, that I feel all my opinions loosen and fall of themselves, when unsupported by the approbation of others. Every step I take is with hesitation, and every new reflection makes me dread an error and absurdity in my reasoning. (264)

---

[47] Shaftesbury, *Characteristics*, 1:64.

The special terror that plagues the self-dramatizing philosopher in this passage derives from the fact that, "in leaving all establish'd opinions," he has no solid reasons of his own to go on, only "a *strong* propensity to consider objects *strongly* in that view" (265). The fact that these reasons are persuasive to him does not furnish a motive for the belief of others, and yet these reasons are of so simple and fundamental a character that, once he has imaginatively entered into them, they are extremely difficult to put aside. It is only the peculiarity of the fancy that keeps him from entering into skeptical doubts most of the time. When the philosopher truly comes to reckon with his situation, left with the choice "betwixt a false reason and none at all," and having reduced his own being more or less to nothing, he can find an answer neither to his critics nor to his own reservations.

> Where am I, or what? From what causes do I derive my existence, and to what condition shall I return? Whose favour shall I court, and whose anger must I dread? What beings surround me? and on whom have I any influence, or who have any influence on me? I am confounded with all these questions, and begin to fancy myself in the most deplorable condition imaginable, inviron'd with the deepest darkness, and utterly depriv'd of the use of every member and faculty. (269)

In this passage, Hume artfully portrays himself swirling in metaphysical and psychological disorientation, lost for his origins and identity, seeking grounds upon which to establish his superiority to the vulgar run of mankind and, paradoxically, longing for the agreement of others in his solipsistic conclusions. Like Descartes, he is in the grip of a philosophical nightmare, but here it is not a resource of the mind that extricates him from his dilemma, but the mind's very lack of the resources to sustain the discomfort it has wrought. It is Nature that comes providentially to his rescue.

> Most fortunately it happens, that since reason is incapable of dispelling these clouds, nature herself suffices to that purpose, and cures me of this philosophical melancholy and delirium, either by relaxing this bent of mind, or by some avocation, and lively impression of my senses, which obliterate all these chimeras. I dine, I play a game of back-gammon, I converse, and am merry with my friends; and when after three or four hour's amusement, I wou'd return to these speculations, they appear so cold, and strain'd, and ridiculous, that I cannot find in my heart to enter into them any farther. (269)

The skeptical perplexity in which Hume finds himself in this passage is even deeper than the one that bedeviled Descartes at the beginning of his *Meditations,* for there the philosopher finds himself at a disadvantage in power that allows him to take nothing for granted in his particular case, whereas Hume, in the course of his meditations, has undermined the grounds for the possibility of knowledge not just in this particular case but in general. It is, in fact, his own philosophizing that has separated the Humean reasoner from others. His "philosophical enthusiasm" is as much of an aberration as the "religious superstition" with which he equates it.[48] As long as he considers things in a philosophical light he must remain a "monster" among "deformity," a distinctly Swiftian condition. The superiority of the monster among deformity is that he is able to recognize the absurdity of his condition, while they are not. This superiority, however, cannot be separated from the disadvantages of living as a monster among deformity, or rather as a set of impressions of being such.

The idea of his own imperfection led Descartes to the notion of a perfect being and therefore to a resolution of his doubts. Hume too feels most acutely the imperfection of his state, but his solution is to dismiss the standard by which it can be perceived, "that grave philosophic Endeavour after Perfection, which, under Pretext of reforming Prejudices and Errors, strikes at all the most endearing Sentiments of the Heart, and all the most useful Byasses and Instincts, which can govern a human Creature."[49] It is to the "useful Byasses and Instincts" that Hume commends himself, in a gesture that is the opposite and undoing of the philosophical commitment to truth. Nature "cures" the philosopher of his "philosophical melancholy and delirium" by returning him to the pleasures of the club, where he can forget the discomforts of that self he has philosophically dissolved.

The Humean concept of Nature becomes identical to reason because it is that to which our reason naturally leads us once it has been purged of philosophical egotism. It is also a general name for habit and custom (the social twin of habit), which together become the only true arbiters of a well-tempered reason from which higher appeals have been discredited. Nature also very much corresponds with the world as it is given in imagination, for only that which has a natural vividness will be able to motivate our consent, except in moments of philosophical alienation. Hume's conception of Nature, then, represents a remarkable collapsing of distinctions. The space of moral agency and critical reflection have not simply been evacuated but seem to vanish completely. What remains is a philosophically unpretentious form of "philosophical decisions," which are "nothing but the reflections of common life, methodized and corrected" (162). If we do not find it advisable to abandon philosophy altogether, it is only because of the need for an antidote to religious superstition (271). Otherwise, even our skeptical reservations do not survive the cost-benefit test of the utilitarian: "If we believe, that fire warms, or water refreshes, 'tis only because it costs us too much pains to think otherwise" (270). This sentence nicely captures the ironizing ambiva-

---

[48] David Hume, *Enquiry concerning Human Understanding*, in *Enquiries concerning Human Understanding and concerning the Principles of Morals*, ed. L. A. Selby-Bigge, 3rd ed., revised by P. H. Nidditch (Oxford: Oxford University Press, 1975), 343.

[49] Hume, *Enquiry*, 539.

lence of Hume's position, for it puts the believer in a state of naïveté and the skeptic in a state of folly at the very same time.

Hume's form of naturalism was too esoteric, brittle, and strange to become a common way of thinking, but it provides a clarifying example of the enduring tendency of a significant class of people who no longer wanted to be disturbed by social discontents armed with philosophical weapons. It points in the direction of what was to be perhaps the chief intellectual resource of the period, the naturalizing of society. Hume's philosophical drama sets the lonely, melancholy intellectual, agitated by ambition, resentment, irony, and self-doubt, against the healthy, sociable run of mankind. Whereas Hobbes had found man in the mass threatening and the behavior of men in sociable groups to be evidence of our essential competitiveness and violence, Hume sees our social nature as the redemption of the private man and the dynamics of man in the mass as the great locus where the aberrations of the individual can be corrected by the broader drift of society. Thus the solipsism of the empirical subject, augmented by the discovery of the moral sense and the internalization of the gentlemanly spectator, could become consistent with the social optimism of the period.

In the face of reason's limits, the English gentleman, the envy of Europe in the eighteenth century, could put his confidence in the benevolent offices of Nature, in the balance of forces in society and in the English constitution, in the perennial wisdom of custom and the common law, and in the divine order of Providence. As with the Hegelian dialectic, which was a descendent of this simultaneously rationalizing and naturalizing mode, every appearance of conflict only veiled a more general harmony. So for Pope, "Self-love and Social" are the same, and "jarring int'rests of themselves create/Th'according music of a well-mix'd State."[50] The natural balance of the English constitution was ratified by Montesquieu[51] and imitated by the American founders. Edmund Burke stands in wonder before "the disposition of a stupendous wisdom" in the English social order, a system "placed in a just correspondence and symmetry with the order of the world," a mechanism both providential and natural, "the result of profound reflection, or rather the happy effect of following nature, which is wisdom without reflection, and above it."[52] Burke's providential piety has warmth, sentimentality, patriotic fervor, and urgency, all qualities that set it apart from the Augustan mode, yet it is recognizably of the same intellectual stamp. His horror of "metaphysical innovations" and his turbulent reaction to the reforming idealism of the French Revolution shows not only the effects of moral and practical alarm but also the vulnerability of a conservative skepticism that has become dependent upon

[50] *An Essay on Man*, 3:318 and 3:293–94.

[51] Montesquieu's social science in general has an unmistakably normative quality, a sense of Nature as ideal. As Ehrard observes, "The 'necessary relations' that Montesquieu studies are as much relations of perfection as laws of causality." *L'Idée de nature*, 421. See also 371.

[52] *Reflections on the Revolution in France*, ed. Conor Cruise O'Brien (New York: Penguin, 1968), 119–20.

custom and practical consensus and is reluctant to resort to ideals. In all of these notions we find a remarkable capacity to interpret the elaborate contrivances of human ingenuity as natural and to see their efficacy as neither the result of simple insight nor fortuitous adaptation but a hidden principle of order working to human benefit as long as human will can be excluded.[53]

For so many of these developments, the thought of Adam Smith represents a canonical expression. As a moral philosopher, Smith took as his chief principle the notion that moral thinking is fundamentally social thinking and that we have no moral life apart from the image of ourselves we conceive in the minds of others. If we desire wealth or goods or power, it is not for these things in themselves but because they bring us the favorable identification, or "sympathy," of others. The virtue of self-command, which he holds in high regard, derives from our need to moderate our emotions so that we can present ourselves in such light as not to discourage the sympathy of an "impartial spectator." Smith reformulates the golden rule in these terms: "As to love our neighbour as we love ourselves is the great law of Christianity, so it is the great precept of nature to love ourselves only as we love our neighbour, or what comes to the same thing, as our neighbour is capable of loving us."[54] To love ourselves more than our neighbor is able to love us would be to cut ourselves off from the sympathy of others, the sympathy of those "hearts beating in time" with our own that is our true desire.

It is important to understand that, when we take up the point of view of the impartial spectator judging our action, we are not applying the principles of a "perfect being" but those that are actually relied upon by "so weak and imperfect a creature as man" (77n). This means that though we know wealth and power do not necessarily indicate virtue, and though the tendency to confuse them is the greatest source of corruption in our morals, they remain the "natural objects" of our admiration (62). Even the "fortunate violence" of rulers incites our affection and makes us better able to bear the inequalities of society (253), a thought that would have comforted Hobbes. In general, even though we know that strictly speaking it is the intention that tells us about the agent's true character, we are often as strongly affected in our judgments by the outcome of an action as by its original intention. In such cases, we see the natural dimension of moral judgment, a dimension in which philosophy would do well not to interfere, since the unintended practical consequences are beneficial.[55] The secret drift of our moral sensibility

---

[53] The essentially negative and skeptical character of Burke's naturalism and its concern to defuse or contain claims to agency makes it oddly compatible with an intellectual stance and a rhetorical style depending upon irony and theatricality. See Yoon Sun Lee, chap. 2 in *Nationalism and Irony: Burke, Scott, Carlyle* (New York: Oxford University Press, 2004).

[54] Adam Smith, *The Theory of Moral Sentiments,* ed. D. D. Raphael and A. L. Macfie (New York: Oxford University Press, 1976), 25.

[55] Smith is perhaps the first to observe the "irregularity of sentiment" that recent philosophers have discussed under the label "moral luck." See pt. 2, sec. 3 of the *Theory of Moral Sentiments.*

is to admire success. It represents a "great disorder" of our moral conscious-ness (253), but one that we cannot truly regret.

Smith's economic doctrine, of course, embodies a similar trust in the benef-icence of Nature above and in spite of our intentions—if only the sources of interference can be eliminated: "All systems either of preference or of restraint . . . being . . . completely taken away, the obvious and simple system of nat-ural liberty establishes itself of its own accord."[56] Smith was eager to help Nature move in this direction. In launching *The Wealth of Nations,* he in-tended a "very violent attack . . . upon the whole commercial system of Great Britain."[57] Its aim was to free the operations of this system by helping the "natural effort of every individual" in removing the "hundred impertinent obstructions with which the folly of human laws too often encumbers its op-erations."[58] However "obvious and simple" the "system of natural liberty" may have seemed to Smith, though, its operations also famously required a certain indirection, unintended consequences orchestrated by an "invisible hand" which, by a natural mechanism, turns self-interested effort into the benefits of the whole. There is a further irony involved, for the benefits prov-identially generated and distributed by the process of economic exchange are only marginally connected with the actual happiness of human beings.

> The rich only select from the heap what is most precious and agree-able. They consume little more than the poor, and in spite of their nat-ural selfishness and rapacity, though they mean only their own conveniency, though the sole end which they propose from the labours of all the thousands whom they employ, be the gratification of their own vain and insatiable desires, they divide with the poor the produce of all their improvements. They are led by an invisible hand to make nearly the same distribution of the necessities of life, which would have been made, had the earth been divided into equal portions among all its inhabitants, and thus without intending it, without knowing it, ad-vance the interest of the society, and afford means to the multiplication of the species. When Providence divided the earth among a few lordly masters, it neither forgot nor abandoned those who seemed to have been left out in the partition. These last too enjoy their share of all that it produces. In what constitutes the real happiness of human life, they are in no respect inferior to those who would seem so much above them. In ease of body and peace of mind, all the different ranks of life are nearly upon a level, and the beggar who suns himself by the side of the highway, possesses the security which kings are fighting for.[59]

[56] *An Inquiry into the Nature and Causes of the Wealth of Nations,* 2 vols., ed. R. H. Camp-bell, A. S. Skinner, and W. B. Todd (New York: Oxford University Press, 1976), 2:687.

[57] Letter to A. Holt, 26 Oct. 1780. *The Correspondence of Adam Smith,* ed. Ernest Camp-bell Mossner and Ian Simpson Ross (New York: Oxford University Press, 1977), 251.

[58] *Wealth of Nations,* 1:540.

[59] *Theory of Moral Sentiments,* 184–85.

Passages like this one lend to Smith's enthusiastic naturalism a certain unmistakable irony; he slips easily from utopian wonder and hopefulness into optimism of the Augustan kind. While our social and moral natures lead us to seek admiration and the wealth and practical achievements that secure it for us, and while the pragmatic and result-oriented cast of our natures makes us largely immune to perfectionistic moralizing or calls for the renunciation of worldly life, our quest for admiration rarely leaves us in peace, and our conquests rarely set us in a better condition than those far beneath us. Here Smith seems closest to the Stoic philosophy he so much admired, but he cannot endorse the contemplative detachment of the Stoic. While he praises the beauty, order, and harmony of the cosmos as demonstratively as Pope, this vision is for him too distant to make an impact upon a creature so fully absorbed in the spectacle of human life. "Nature has not prescribed to us this sublime contemplation as the great business and occupation of our lives. She only points it out to us as the consolation of our misfortunes" (292). The great order of the world should not distract us from the smallest worldly duty, since it is the affairs of this world to which we are given (237)—even though they cannot make us happy.

There is something contradictory at the heart of Smith's attitude toward Nature, and it appears at every level of this thinking. The impartial spectator, the motivating witness of our worthiest powers of self-command, being often more interested in the results of our actions than in their intentions, is inclined to admire us for what is not truly to our credit and to blame us for what is not truly our fault. Similarly, the wealth that we acquire on account of our aggregate behavior, as the "invisible hand" magically gets the best both of our virtues and our vices, promises a happiness that is really an illusion. And when we turn away from these mundane affairs toward the beautiful and perfect order of the cosmos, that spectacle can offer us only a dim aesthetic pleasure even though it includes us and everything we know.[60]

Smith's "system of liberty" is very much what he said it was, a modified utopia suited to imperfect beings. Its economic mechanism was a natural one but it could not function without the aid and protection of the state. It depended upon the education and virtue of its citizens. And the happiness it provided was of an ironically partial and imaginary sort. Smith always seems to have more sublime conceptions of virtue in view, but he cannot seriously endorse them. What he offered to the time, though, was a mode of initiative that separated agency from idea and therefore freed it from moral control and political controversy, at the same time making this achievement the very basis of practical success. To naturalize agency was at once to explain it and

[60] Louis Dumont observes that Smith was projecting what was originally a scholastic natural teleology onto the economic dimension, but we might choose another metaphor and say that the deflation of the cosmic scale, its loss of vivid implication, enabled the naturalistic scheme to migrate back to the dimension of society, even though in a strangely ironized form. *From Mandeville to Marx: The Genesis and Triumph of Economic Ideology* (Chicago: University of Chicago Press, 1977), 41–43.

to empower it, to neutralize its moral dangers and ensure its success. To take up the social point of view was to see things with the eye of Nature—if not the "equal eye" of the optimist then the equalizing eye of the invisible hand and the sympathizing eye of the impartial spectator. In this way Smith developed a providential form of naturalism far more plausible than Pope's or Berkeley's, and one that could more easily be separated from its cosmic framework. In spite of all the ironies and points of ambivalence I have mentioned, it was in the writings of Smith that the Enlightenment rehabilitation of Nature and human agency reached its most complete and influential form. Some later interpreters of capitalism would sharpen the opposition between the workings of the market and government action, while others, especially in the utilitarian vein, would enhance the role of government in bringing about the "natural identity of interests" and the "spontaneous harmony of egoisms"[61] that underlie the apparent diversity of society. But Enlightenment naturalism would remain central to the culture of capitalism.

Smith's moral philosophy has a far richer descriptive texture than that of any of his contemporaries. He implicitly connects himself with Aristotle's ethics when he distinguishes the ancient philosophers as "critics" of human behavior, as opposed to what he considers the legalistic orientation of Christian moralism. But Smith's systemic attitude, which separates the effect of the whole from the intentions of individuals, not only makes individual agency uncanny but abstracts away from the context of social action itself. The social is only intelligible as a whole. Missing from the account is the dimension Hegel called "ethical substance," or, more simply, the interwoven pattern of roles that constitute an actual society. It is roles that provide a mediating structure between the individual and society. They are the governing frame of socially significant action on an everyday basis, and their generality corresponds with the meaningfulness of the purposes they aim to accomplish. This generality is also what permits those who perform them to be compared with others and, consequently, to establish personal identity in a way that is competitive without necessarily being manipulative. If Hume looks into his mind and cannot find a self, this is in part because he is looking in the wrong place. He has abstracted from all of the social connections that could define his identity. As Alasdair MacIntyre points out, roles, because of their undeniably teleological dimension, remove the gap between Is and Ought, between what we have been calling the actual and the ideal. "It is only when man is thought of as an individual prior to and apart from all roles that 'man' ceases to be a functional concept."[62]

It can barely be a matter of dispute as to what it means in general to be a

---

[61] The phrases belong to Élie Halévy, who pointed out that these doctrines were to remain a shared emphasis of utilitarians and other advocates of free-market economics. *The Growth of Philosophic Radicalism,* trans. Mary Morris (New York: Macmillan, 1928), 1:89.

[62] Alasdair MacIntyre, *After Virtue: A Study in Moral Theory* (Notre Dame: University of Notre Dame Press, 1981), 56. *After Virtue* provides a very striking analysis of the culture of mutually manipulative individuals and the impoverishment of its ethical vocabulary.

good father or mother, a good basketball player, or a good doctor, and few of us would not be shocked to be told by those we respect that we are poor colleagues or friends. The writers we have been studying largely devalued the role-playing, functional dimension of human life, even while they invented new roles and functions for themselves. As a result of their influence, social identity has become in many ways unintelligible to us, even though it remains the central fact of our existence.

Some Further Implications

In many ways, naturalism of the Enlightened kind was an inversion of the traditional sort, and this accounts for some of its paradoxical effects. It re-cuperates self-interest on the private level, but it equally discredits altruism on the level of the whole. It empowers, therefore, the kind of behavior that most schemes of morality have attempted to suppress, and it discourages the kind of behavior they have attempted to promote. Smith did not so much worry that if individuals were able to moderate their private impulses toward accumulation and consumption, the economy would lose its energy; he did not share Mandeville's view of the benefits of luxury.[63] It was rather that if the state, or any other local or private entity, should try to regulate the work-ings of the system for its own gain or for the good of the whole, the entire system would be impaired. Society is, indeed, a natural system that depends upon the serendipity of unintended consequences and effects of composition. It cannot admit a strong sense of social agency—action guided by a rational aim to achieve a benefit. It has the teleological confidence, then, of older types of naturalistic thinking, but the relation between agent and idea has been drastically altered.

It is important to understand the difference this makes in comparison with older varieties of naturalistic thinking and to mark the difference from Aris-totle, not because we can reestablish Aristotle's way of thinking, but because it shows us the structure of naturalism as it was originally designed. Both Aristotle and Smith have a teleological view of society in that they assume a natural good to be the end of human life and of the political or social sphere, but Aristotle goes farther in assuming a rational capacity in human beings—at least some of them—to recognize the good of the whole as well as their own good, and to strive for both of them at the same time. In fact, the good of the individual is good often because of its benefit for the whole or for larger parts of the whole. This is why the horizon of ethics must be the po-lis and why Aristotle considers ethics and politics to be two branches of the same inquiry. In a sense, it is the natural function of rational agency to bring

---

[63] Because of the need for capital accumulation in the economy as a whole, "every prodigal appears to be a publick enemy, and every frugal man a publick benefactor." *Wealth of Nations,* 1:340.

about the fulfillment of its telos through action. Human happiness is simply the habit of deciding and acting in accordance with the ideals of human behavior, and this is the natural function of a human being, its work or *ergon*. In order to act virtuously, human beings must be able to recognize proper ends, to deliberate about the means for achieving them, and to choose to act on the basis of such deliberation. For the systemic teleological model of the Enlightened variety, however, order and purpose belong only to the system. The notion of individual agency in light of the whole becomes a threat. For an individual to act for the good of the system would be to impose a partial and individual notion upon a natural whole that can only thrive by negating the effect of individual interest. Agency must remain on the private scale in order to be properly negated at the next level. To act according to a concept of the whole is to deny one's actual desires and to impair the necessary functioning of the system. No one, then, can be responsible for the functioning of the whole. The invisible hand must remain invisible, its significance being entirely negative. To apply a concept to the whole that is different from its actuality would be to destroy its magic.[64]

Since deliberation to bring about general ends has been denaturalized, it inevitably becomes the repository of otherness and evil. If the system is not what it ought to be, human interference must be the reason. Thus Mandeville's great fear is the virtue-imposing politician, who would keep the dissolute class from its necessary vices. For Adam Smith, government regulation limits economic productivity because it restrains the cumulative effects of private initiative. Protecting the invisible hand from the hindrance of visible human agencies has remained an important concern of political and social discourse in America and elsewhere. In the late nineteenth century, social Darwinism added a biological overlay to the capitalist's invisible hand. It was not only necessary for the economy that some should succeed and some fail in the quest for gain; now it was necessary for the species as well, and liberal philanthropy acquired new dangers. Nietzsche, the most brilliant of Darwin's literary disciples, made history into a great battleground of the strong and the healthy versus the weak and degenerate. Like Mandeville, he saw idealistic conspiracies constraining the energies of the strong, corrupting them with myths of virtue and ascetic ideals.

Now if the economic and biological version of naturalism that I have been describing seems to be the supreme resource of the ideology of capitalist and bourgeois culture, as well as an obvious invitation to paranoia, should we not look to Marxism to provide us with a telling critique? It is often claimed, even by those who are skeptical of the programmatic value of Marx's thought, that it provides valuable insights into the vicissitudes of capitalism. One might

---

[64] Charles Taylor's way of describing the deistic scheme is close to mine. "Living according to nature," he says, no longer means "living according to the hierarchy of goals of (substantive) reason. It means, rather, living according to the design of things," a design that "aims at interlocking purposes." Taylor, *Sources of the Self,* 279.

think that one could rely upon Marxism to show how the idea of capitalism and its all-reconciling system operates to disguise the interests of a particular class, and how such classes benefit from the mythological laws of economic activity. One would also expect such an engaged critique to demonstrate that the social and economic system is the creature of the individuals and classes which sustain it, and that it is up to human beings to take up their destinies in order to achieve change. When Marx tells us that men make their own destinies, but not under conditions of their own choosing, we seem to be in the presence of a sober and clear-sighted pragmatism aiming to locate possibilities for agency.

Unfortunately, though this was undoubtedly his intention, Marx's efforts to resuscitate and invigorate human agency proved inadequate because he retained too many assumptions from the model he attempted to subvert. For scientific materialism is yet another vision of the natural system that moves toward its telos through necessity and in spite of the diverse intentions of the agents and interests that compose it. The difference between it and its "bourgeois" predecessors is that while capitalist naturalism, for example, has already accomplished its goal, making clear, as Adam Smith would have it, the true grounds of economic rationality by which the past and present can be explained, Marx, following Hegel, adds a further and higher phase where present evils, or "contradictions," will become converted into benefits very much in the manner of a Popean theodicy. As is usual in the Augustan mode, if misery is here, that means happiness is elsewhere, not this time in a higher world but in a future one. The contradictions of our world are not accidental but necessary, pointing toward the higher ground of Absolute Spirit or the universal class. One is reminded of Kafka's lament that the universe contains "infinitely much hope—only not for us."[65] It may seem strange to liken Pope with Marx, but both were supreme rationalizers of what must be.

What, then, becomes of human agency in this scheme of things? How can the revolutionary agent conceptualize his or her own activity in bringing about the goal of history, given that the arrival of this goal is a necessary event that has in a sense already taken into account the collective force of human effort? The question has haunted Marxism in all the versions that I know. The problem is that, as in other naturalizing systems, human thought can play its role only in governing the particles of the system. Any attempt to conceive of a social action that effects the whole will necessarily have a false generality. It will be an ideology. Thought in this model acquires its content only from the actual conditions of its emergence. The possibility that an idea stands at a distance from present reality suffices to invalidate it, even though it is only from such thought that a critical perspective can emerge. Criticism, therefore, becomes uncanny.

This dynamic paradox—"Whatever IS, is RIGHT" as a principle of *rev-*

[65] Quoted from Walter Benjamin, *Über Literatur* (Frankfurt: Suhrkamp, 1969), 158.

olution—has made Marxism one of the most productive discourses of suspicion. It specializes in unmasking the thought of others, yet it cannot sustain the discourse of its own agency because rational agency requires a degree of critical distance that dialectical materialism cannot admit. This is why Marxist revolutionaries have always found themselves speaking for the interests of a future which should be as obscure to them as everyone else and for a class that does not yet exist and to which they would have small title to belong.

It is telling that, while Marx betrays a certain unmistakable admiration of the capitalist entrepreneur, who is part of the historically revolutionary and necessary bourgeois class, he sounds like Luther denouncing idealistic social reformers and philanthropists. To him they are cast-offs of history, effete utopians who lead others astray by exaggerating human powers. Their attempts at amelioration would moderate the contradictions that drive the historical process and thereby impose a historically limited and arbitrary ideal. Such Quixotic dreamers seek to exert human control at the level of the system rather than playing the roles given to them by history. Like Smith and Mandeville before him, Marx directed his keenest attacks at other economic theorists who wanted to interfere with his machine.

In the course of this chapter, we have been surveying in rapid fashion some examples of a central structure of Enlightenment thought. What we see is a society that, in its most vocal representatives, can affirm its own goodness, the goodness of the individuals who compose it, and the goodness of the Creator who brought it into being all at the same time. This hopeful note distinguishes it from the contentious age that came before. Yet in spite of all of this hopefulness, and the relentless emphasis upon the goodness of practical life, there is still a powerful mistrust of human agency and power, a tendency to look to unaccountable forces, higher points of view, invisible hands, and an ultimately enigmatic Nature to underwrite the collective benefits of social action.

While such mistrust of human agency sounds like an invitation to paranoia, for the most part it remained no more than that thanks to the relatively calm social and political atmosphere of the period. It was not until the end of the eighteenth century that the closing of the space between actual and ideal came fully into conflict with the reforming impulses of the age. Goethe could look back on the situation with a certain wry amusement at the beginning of the next century. His Faust, having held out for decades against the temptations of accommodation with the world as it is, finally gives in to the demonic temptations of contentment, so that God has to break the devil's bargain and save him at the last minute. Leibniz would not have allowed the intervention.

13

Rousseau's Great Plot

Though Enlightenment culture was founded upon a critique of past and existing societies, with a new focus upon the nature of the individual human being as a key to the life of the species, it maintained, we have seen, a remarkable emphasis upon the centrality and value of social existence. If human beings, the natural order, and the cosmos are all essentially good, as the leading figures of Enlightenment typically assumed, then the idea of a fundamental selfishness of the kind proposed by Hobbes could find little purchase. Thus we see even Hume, the most skeptical of the *philosophes*, escaping from the solipsism of his philosophical melancholy and returning to the warming influence of the club, while Adam Smith finds the touchstone of all ethical values in the moderate pleasures of civilized theatricality. An apparent dissenter like Mandeville could regret the sacrifices that society demands of the individual but nevertheless consider those demands to be in fact unnecessary since, in a less morally regulated society, there would be a natural convergence between prosperity and the consumption of the better classes. Mandeville even defended the value of prostitution and the "public stews" as a safety valve for the Quixotic energies of idealistic love.[1]

Mandeville found a clever way of using an older form of moralism to enhance the temptations of the new social order. Jean-Jacques Rousseau found an even more clever way of using the new, optimistic moralism to combat the temptations of the new social order. His argument was not that vice was necessary for society but that society was necessary for vice and that not only vice but all human evils stem from our social being. But whereas Mandeville

---

[1] *A modest defence of publick stews; or, An essay upon whoring, as it is now practis'd in these kingdoms* (1724; Los Angeles: William Andrews Clark Memorial Library, 1973), 28. Originally published by A. Moore near St. Paul's.

was a cold master of paradoxes, Rousseau was a passionate fantasist who, at a crucial point of his life, experienced an all-consuming revelation that allowed him in a moment to penetrate the false pretenses of civilization. On reading the question proposed by the Academy of Dijon, he "saw another world and became another man."[2] Having staked his fame upon the notion that all of the products of human invention are evil and society itself a curse, he defended his "sad and great System" (3:105) and lived out its consequences for almost three decades. His ultimate accounts of the adventure are those of a paranoid protesting his innocence against his enemies and attempting to outwit their conspiracy, yet his writings stand nevertheless among the key documents of the modern self.

In the course of his career we will see Rousseau reimagining the conditions and context of human agency, unearthing the origins of society, and rationalizing the proper functioning of the state. One of the fruits of his analysis will be the recognition that the return of society to the state of nature is impossible, leading to a second central question: how can the individual be made to resist the corruption of the social world around him? Rousseau's central question thus becomes the question of education. In the last phase of his career, Rousseau turns to a new project, that of personal self-justification, and it is there that we can see most clearly the psychological meaning of his search for truth. The inherent goodness of the human being, as exemplified supremely by Jean-Jacques Rousseau himself, constitutes the dominant theme, but this is paradoxically combined with a vision of the complete corruption of the human past, of the human intellect, and of present society, including Rousseau himself, except that in his case his external behavior belies the true goodness of his heart. Only in the mind of Don Quixote do other-worldly idealism and this-worldly corruption stand so remarkably in contrast, and, as we shall see, Rousseau will have his own swarm of enchanters to help him keep both dimensions simultaneously in force.

In the next chapter we will consider Rousseau's account of the personal circumstances that produced his great anti-social revelation. Here we take up his account of the state of society itself and the causes of its fall into corruption, beginning with the *Discourse on the Sciences and the Arts* (the *First Discourse*). Rousseau's account of the development of humankind has an unmistakably mythic dimension. It is a new version of Eden and the Fall. The myth, though, is not only given a newly paranoid dimension with clear origins, as we will see, in the demands of Rousseau's personality, but it is also couched in the terms of a multi-layered historical causality, in which environmental nature, human nature, and chance all play a role. Rousseau begins with the crystallizing of a central insight—the essential innocence and

---

[2] *Confessions* 1:351. All references to Rousseau's works will be to the five-volume Pléiade edition of the *Œuvres complètes*, ed. Bernard Gagnebin and Marcel Raymond (Paris: Gallimard, 1959–95).

victimization of man—which he then develops with ever more elaborate supporting explanations.

The *First Discourse* concentrates, in response to the question that provoked it, on the moral effect of the "restoration" of science and art, in other words, the postmedieval advancement of learning. Breath-taking, though, is how naturally Rousseau, in his philosophical debut, takes for granted the thoroughgoing suspicion of political society that would become the central motif of his writings. "While Government and Laws provide for the safety and well-being of assembled men," he says, "the Sciences, Letters, and Arts, less despotic and perhaps more powerful, spread garlands of flowers over the chains with which men have been burdened, stifle in them the sentiment of that original liberty for which they seemed to have been born, and turn them into what is called civilized peoples." Due to the sweet regime of art, men are "happy slaves," living in a herd, in "vile and deceptive uniformity," not daring to use their own "genius" or show what they really are. The need for duplicity makes society into a vicious parade of uncertain appearances disguising unknowable characters (3:56). "What train of vices," he asks, "will not accompany this uncertainty? No more sincere friendships; no more real esteem; no more well-founded confidence. Suspicions, offenses, fears, coldness, reserve, hatred, betrayal hide constantly under that uniform and perfidious veil of politeness, under that much vaunted urbanity which we owe to the enlightenment of our century" (3:8–9).

What ensues, both in the *Discourse* and in the replies that followed it, is an attempt to explain the causes of this corruption, not by undertaking an investigation of its particular origins but by showing a general historical correlation between, on the one hand, vice, corruption, social degeneration, and martial weakness, and, on the other hand, the development of the sciences and the arts. Rousseau does not deny that these activities have value in themselves. "In a sense," he admits in one of his defenses of the *First Discourse*, "it is a share of the supreme intelligence to acquire knowledge and expand one's enlightenment."[3] Nor does he deny that there are "sublime geniuses" like Socrates, Bacon, and Newton who are capable of pursuing knowledge while preserving their own virtues.[4] Indeed, it is necessary for rulers to make use of the "Truly Learned" and their gifts;[5] our fallen state makes it "essential today" that we use the sciences and the arts "as a medicine for the evils they have caused."[6] Yet in spite of these concessions, it is for Rousseau a laughable notion that there could ever be a society composed of men wise enough to be capable of resisting the hazards of human invention (3:227). Luxury makes men soft, lazy, and effeminate; medicine undermines their health; dependence upon each other makes them weak and deceptive. Busi-

[3] "De Jean-Jacques Rousseau, de Genève, Sur la Réponse qui a été faite à son Discours," 3:36.
[4] *Préface de Narcisse,* 2:970.
[5] "De Jean-Jacques Rousseau," 3:39.
[6] *Préface de Narcisse,* 2:974n.

ness and commerce teach men to evaluate each other "like heads of cattle" for their market value or power of consumption (3:20). In another work of this period, philosophy comes fully under the indictment. The surest path of corruption, it "loosens all the bonds of esteem and benevolence that attach men to society. . . . The charm of study soon renders all other attachments insipid" and the philosopher's *amour-propre* inspires a general contempt, since "for him, family, fatherland become words empty of meaning: he is neither parent, nor citizen, nor man; he is a philosopher" (2:967).

It is apparent in this attack on the character of the *philosophe* that Rousseau was aiming directly at the project of Enlightenment represented by his close friend Diderot. Just as the first volumes of the *Encyclopedia,* that great repository of the achievements of human civilization, harvested from the ages and purified from superstition, were nearing the light of day, here was Rousseau calling into question not only the benefits of civilization but the character of its defenders as well. He portrays their philosophy as nothing but a grandiose form of self-intoxication, a poisonous influence destroying "that sweet and precious ignorance, the treasure of a soul that is pure and content with itself."[7]

The argument of the *First Discourse* is a historical one. It seeks to establish the constant conjunctions of simplicity with virtue and of sophistication with vice in classical and modern history and to infer a casual connection from each case. Rousseau sees in the intellectual refinements of Athens the source of its martial weakness and in the moral harshness of Sparta its martial strength. Sparta and its virtues were a life-long point of reference for him, as were the American savages, while Rome at different points in its history could exemplify either virtue or decay. In this historical attack upon the refinements of culture, Rousseau was drawing, of course, upon moral strictures familiar from the ancient historians, especially Plutarch and Tacitus, and echoing the Pauline distrust of pagan learning as well. Rousseau's innovation was to apply these strictures to the philosophy of the moment—to unmask modern philosophy as one of the causes of the inequality and deceptiveness of the society it claimed to critique, and to radicalize the critique so that it could apply virtually to all intellectual activities. "Everything beyond physical necessity," he says in defense of the *First Discourse,* "is a source of evil."[8]

Rousseau learned, however, from the replies evoked by the *Discourse,* that the historical issue regarding the connection between weakness and vice and civilization threatened to become an interminable one, for his more able critics found no difficulty either in producing counterexamples to the ones that supported his thesis or putting a different interpretation on the examples he

---

[7] *First Discourse,* 3:54. On Rousseau's relation to the Enlightenment and the *philosophes,* see Graeme Garrard, *Rousseau's Counter-Enlightenment* (Albany: State University of New York Press, 2003), esp. 30–35, and Mark Hulliung, *The Autocritique of Enlightenment: Rousseau and the Philosophes* (Cambridge: Harvard University Press, 1994).

[8] *La Dernière réponse de J.-J. Rousseau de Genève,* 3:95.

had given. In response, Rousseau complains that to resolve such issues, "It would be necessary to argue. . . . Brochures would turn into Volumes, Books would multiply, and the question would be forgotten. . . . It is not worth the trouble to begin."[9] Already one senses Rousseau's characteristic discomfort with issues that cannot be settled upon the basis of his own clear and distinct judgments.

The difficulty of establishing the natural innocence of man and the evil of civilization on historical grounds led to a crucial departure at the beginning of Rousseau's next major treatise, the *Discourse on the Origin and Foundations of Inequality* (the *Second Discourse*), again written in response to a topic proposed by the Academy of Dijon. Here Rousseau argues that those like Hobbes who had investigated the nature of man in history and found him to be an evil creature had made a crucial mistake by confounding man's essential good nature with the competitive and vicious one brought into being by society. This social nature was the only one visible in history or even, for the most part, among the savages. History, therefore, has its limits as evidence in moral questions. What Rousseau proposes, then, is to begin by "throwing out all the facts ("écarter tous les faits"), since they do not bear upon the question. It is not necessary," he continues, "to regard the Researches we can undertake on the subject for historical Truths, but only for hypothetical and conditional reasonings, more proper to Clarify the Nature of things than to show their true origins, as our Physicists regularly do concerning the formation of the World" (3:132). Forsaking origins, Rousseau seeks to clarify the nature of man in itself. He assumes that man's nature is not to be found among the variegated products of civilization but in what he is before civilization can touch him. It is outside of history that we must seek the natural man, in "a State that no longer exists, that probably never existed, that will probably never exist again, and of which, however, it is necessary to have some accurate notions in order correctly to judge our present state" (3:123).

With this Cartesian boldness, Rousseau excludes from man's nature the vast display of human potential in history, and the varying capacities of intellect and invention that make it possible, and by the same gesture he frees his own intellect from the constraints of historical investigation. With considerable shrewdness, he situates his inquiry between Christian history and natural science, warning that reasonings about the state of nature must be considered speculative because Moses, the author of Genesis, has already told us that God removed the first man from the state of nature (3:132). With the appeal to the hypothetical procedures of natural scientists, Rousseau sets his inquiry in line with a method that can start with conjecture but conclude with factual explanation. What is most remarkable about his performance, though, is that, having admitted the speculative nature of his approach and having cast the facts of history aside, Rousseau immediately returns to them

[9] *Lettre à Grimm*, 3:61.

with new confidence and with the rhetorical bravado that is the mark of his personality. "O Man, from whatever Country you may be, whatever your opinions, listen: here is your history, as I believe I was able to read it, not in the Books of your fellow creatures, who are liars, but in Nature, which never lies" (3:135).

What follows is a depiction of pre-social man that is neither the golden age of the Greeks, nor Edenic innocence, nor Hobbes's state of civil war. "Stripping the human being" of all "supernatural gifts" and "artificial faculties" and "considering him . . . such as he must have come from the hands of Nature," Rousseau sees "an animal less strong than some, less agile than others, but on the whole the most advantageously organized of all" (3:134–35), an animal not yet physically enervated by the unnatural strain of cogitation, for "the man who meditates is a depraved animal" (3:138). Man in his natural condition is untroubled by passion, has no use for language, and is free of the torments of love, which depend upon distinguishing self from other.

> Wandering in the forests without industry, without speech, without dwelling, without war, and without connections, without any need of his fellow creatures as without any desire to harm them, perhaps without even any need to recognize any of them individually, savage Man, subject to few passions and sufficient unto himself, had only the sentiments and awareness proper to his state; he felt only his true needs, looked only at what he believed would be of interest to see, and his intelligence made no more progress than his vanity. If by chance he made some discovery, he could as little communicate it as he could recognize his Children. The art perished with the inventor; there was neither education nor progress, the generations were multiplied without purpose, and each departing from the same point, the Centuries flowed past in all the crudity of the first ages; the species was already old and man remained still a child. (3:159–60)

This is the natural state of man, the hypothetical ideal that Rousseau erected as the measure of all things human. It is the state of a healthy animal, innocent of moral distinctions, unaware of self or others, incapable either of sublimity or misery—a condition of bliss entirely negative, a privation of privations. In this negativity lies its happiness, for "what kind of misery can there be for a free being whose heart is at peace and body in good health"? (3:152). Such a happy creature has only one claim to goodness, which lies in his natural repugnance at seeing any other sensitive being suffer, and especially one of his "fellows" ("semblables"). Passionately interested in his own well-being and self-preservation, he pursues it in a way that as much as possible avoids harm to others. Rousseau, like Hobbes and Adam Smith, finds himself reformulating the golden rule of the Gospel on a natural basis: "Do what is good for you with the least possible harm to others" (3:156).

In the state of nature, this rule constitutes a guiding passion. It "takes the place of Laws, manners, and virtues, with that advantage that no one is tempted to disobey this sweet voice" (3:156). In the myth of Eden, Adam was brought into the realm of intellectual and moral being, given a companion to assuage his loneliness, and put in the way of temptation by God himself. In Rousseau's state of nature, however, "everything seems to distance Savage man from temptation and the means of ceasing to be Savage. His imagination depicts nothing to him; his heart asks nothing of him" (3:144). Mother Nature has been kinder to him than God the Father, and he is unaware that things could be otherwise.

The bliss of natural man consists of the absence of all those things that constitute society, all the false accoutrements that Rousseau in his analysis has stripped away. His account of the Fall, therefore, is nothing less than the retelling of the history of human progress, the invention of everything that takes man out of himself and distracts him from enjoying the sensation of his own existence. Private property was a great step in the corruption of the species. "The first who, having enclosed some terrain, thought to say, *This is mine,* and found people simple enough to believe it, was the true founder of civil society. What crimes, what wars, what murders, what miseries, and what horrors would not human kind have been spared" if only someone had protested (1:164). But the invention of private property required a long preparation—the gradual development of cooperation, the division of labor, the differentiation in the roles of the sexes, and, most unaccountably for Rousseau, the development of language, an invention that seems inconceivable as the work of those who do not already possess it. The point where sociability, language, and the family have emerged but not yet the true foundations of civil society forms for Rousseau a second landmark in the development of humankind, an epoch which, he says, "must have been the happiest and most durable." Dwelling at this stage we see the existing nations of "savages," whose life is a "happy medium between the indolence of the primitive condition" and the petulant activity of our *amour-propre.* This happy state, however, "the true youth of the World," could not survive the inventiveness of men. Agriculture and metallurgy exerted a revolutionary influence: they "civilized men, and perished humankind" (3:171). Private property came into being. At this point in the story the development of civilization and the destruction of human nature are almost complete. Rousseau has achieved his goal of identifying the origins of inequality among men though the deployment of a speculative hypothesis developed with visionary confidence.

What then, precisely, were the essential causes that led human beings to be separated from their original nature? The first answer that Rousseau entertains is a familiar one: human beings in the state of nature "act in the manner of free agents," able to choose not between good and evil, which they do not yet understand, but between obeying their natural inclinations and resisting them. It is not that animals are entirely lacking in the capacity to think but that, being entirely under the care of Nature, they cannot oppose their natural impulses (3:141). Rousseau, however, is not content with this traditional way of distinguishing man from animal based upon the freedom of the will, perhaps because it makes man a responsible being right from the start. He sets it aside as controversial and takes up another criterion of human distinction, the "faculty of perfecting oneself." Our capacity for change, our "perfectibility," as Rousseau calls it, "this distinctive and almost limitless faculty," is "the source of all the ills of man" (3:142). It is not that we have used it improperly that brings disaster but that we have used it at all. Whereas the generations of animals passed from one to the next with their natures undisturbed, human beings have surrendered the protection of instinct in order to undertake their own guidance. "Why is man alone subject to becoming an imbecile?" (3:142). The answer is, on account of our "perfectibility"—a new word, and no better could be found to express the aspirations of the "century of enlightenment" or Rousseau's mistrust of those aspirations. "Perfectibility" in his vocabulary is an ironic euphemism for corruptibility and, indeed, evil.[10]

Yet the corruptibility of our nature, though necessary for our departure from the natural state, does not provide a sufficient explanation for the present state of things. There had to be some immediate stimulus to interrupt the natural flow of time and precipitate the fatal denaturalizing step. Here Nature seems to take a different role from the nurturing and tranquilizing one that the author has ascribed to it, for it was in response to natural difficulties that the human instinct for self-preservation, waking from the slumbers of natural indolence, became ingenious and brought the practical intellect into being. The height of fruit-bearing trees, changes in the seasons, and differences of climate led gradually to the development both of the intellectual means to cope with such challenges and eventually to the formation of the family and primitive society. It would seem, then, that Nature itself had set human corruptibility on its course.

Here, however, Rousseau has found a way of preserving the innocence of Nature without entirely reverting to the myth of the Fall, about which he was to observe almost a decade later that original sin accounts for everything but itself since it takes for granted the primal human responsibility it seeks to explain.[11] Before he begins his account of the eclipse of natural goodness, he assigns a general cause—chance. Man might never have developed his potential for civilization had it not been for "the fortuitous concourse of many external causes which might never have come into being [concours fortuit de plusieurs causes étrangères qui pouvoient ne jamais naître] and without which he would have remained eternally in his primitive condition" (3:162). These are key words for understanding Rousseau's thought and worldview.

[10] On the origins of this term, see note 3 to page 142 of the *Second Discourse*, 3:1317–19.
[11] *Lettre à Christophe de Beaumont*, 4:939.

He will repeat many times that our human ills are entirely of our own making; nevertheless it is clear from his account that the conditions under which we make them are contingent ones and that our actions are contingent as well. They are determined by circumstance, "funeste hasard" or "fatal chance," as he calls it at a later stage (3:171). Because history for Rousseau is the history of human invention, it cannot have a logic or a principle of necessity. Yet it bears a form of contingency whose conditions have an aspect of fatality. Once the first steps away from the state of nature have been taken, there is no going back. The emergence of a single civil society initiates a competition in which the protections of group security become compulsory for all (3:178). The progress of perfectibility cannot be reversed, for Rousseau has already given out as a "grand and fatal truth" that, while it was possible to move from knowledge to ignorance, "no one has ever seen a people, once corrupted, return to virtue."[12] In the notes to the *Second Discourse* he mocks those critics who took him to be suggesting we should return to "live in the forest with the Bears" (3:207). It is clear then that the momentum of perfectibility ironically renders human agency unable to address the besetting ills of the species.

If the return to virtue is as implausible to the Rousseau of the *Second Discourse* as living with the bears, it is owing no doubt to the third essential ingredient in the corruption of humankind, the final necessary element that, combined with perfectibility and the workings of chance, was sufficient to undermine our natural good. That element is not inequality but the falsity, artifice, competition, and violence that come to dominate human society once individual differences in talent begin to appear. As languages develop and families begin to form, "People become accustomed to considering different objects and making comparisons; they imperceptibly acquire those ideas of merit and Beauty that produce feelings of preference. Having seen each other, they can no longer do without seeing each other again. A sweet and tender feeling insinuates itself into the soul, and by the least opposition becomes an impetuous fury: jealousy awakens with love; Discord triumphs, and the sweetest of passions receives sacrifices of human blood" (3:169). Idle gatherings, once the occasion of innocent pleasures, now become initiation rituals of inequality. "Each person began to look at the others and to be looked at himself, and public esteem had a price. The one who sang or danced the best; the most Beautiful, the strongest, the most adroit or the most eloquent became the most respected, and there at the same time was the first step toward inequality and toward vice: from these first preferences were born on the one side vanity and contempt, on the other shame and envy; and the fermentations caused by these new leavening agents finally produced combinations fatal to happiness and to innocence" (3:169–70).

From our desire for respect and attention, our "ardor to make ourselves

[12] *De Jean-Jacques Rousseau de Geneve*, 3:56.

the subject of talk" (3:189), Rousseau derives all of our virtues and vices—
but the vices are far more significant than the virtues. Once the will to competition has been unleashed, violence and domination must follow. From
men's mutual dependency in practical things comes their moral and psychological dependency, and with it a fatal loss of autonomy. "The Savage,"
Rousseau tells us, "lives in himself; sociable man, always outside of himself,
knows how to live only in the opinion of others, and it is, so to speak, from
their judgment alone that he draws the feeling of his own existence" (3:193).
To discover one's own being only in the eyes of others, surely this is the most
ironic form of enslavement ever imagined, for the greater one becomes in the
eyes of others, the more completely one depends upon them. Thus the paradox of individual development mirrors that of society as a whole: the wealth-
ier and more sophisticated the society, the weaker and more unequal in its
inner constitution. Rousseau's grand summation of the socially corrupted
man looks backward to Pascal's account of fallen worldliness; it also provided Hegel with the inspiration for his master-slave dialectic. Once all of
our human faculties are developed and in play, establishing ranks among human beings according to beauty, merit, and intellect, Rousseau says that:

> It is necessary for one's advantage to show oneself as being other than
> what one actually is. To be and to appear become two completely dif-
> ferent things, and from this distinction derive impressive luxury, de-
> ceptive trickery, and all the vices following in their train. Conversely,
> as free and independent as man had once been, see him subjected now,
> so to speak, to all of Nature by a multitude of new needs, and above
> all to his fellow human beings, of whom he becomes the slave in one
> sense even in becoming their master [in another]; rich, he needs their
> services; poor he needs their help, and a middling condition does not
> enable him to do without them. . . . Finally, devouring ambition . . . in-
> spires in all men a dark tendency to mutual harm, a secret jealousy so
> much the more dangerous in that, in order to strike its blow more
> safely, it often puts on the mask of benevolence. . . . All these evils are
> the first effect of property and the inseparable accompaniment of
> nascent inequality. (3:174–75)

Rousseau was aware that his account of man extracted from the state of nature hearkened directly back to Hobbes's description of man in the state of
Civil War; but Hobbes, he argues, had given an accurate account of man in
society and mistaken it for Nature (3:132). It is society that makes man a
wolf to man. And this means for Rousseau that human beings, as in the myth
of the Fall, had brought about, through their own actions, the state of corruption, inequality, falsehood, and acute unhappiness that is civil society. It
was a grand assertion of human responsibility despite the note of "fatal
chance" and despite the assumption that human action can only change
things for the worse.

The Social Conspiracy

With this description of sociable man, Rousseau had succeeded in completing his account of the origins of inequality. It is important to recognize, though, that Rousseau was pursuing a second goal in the *Discourse*, one that he most explicitly assigns to himself from the outset as the central purpose of the work: "to mark in the progress of things, the moment where, Right succeeding Violence, Nature was subjected to Law; to explain by what concatenation of prodigies the strong could resolve to serve the weak, and the People to purchase a tranquility in theory at the price of a real felicity" (3:132). This strangely ambivalent and ironic formula is Rousseau's way of referring to the institution of civil society itself. As for Hobbes, it emerges from a state of war stemming from the "perpetual conflict" between the right of the strongest and the right of the first possessor (3:176). In this state of violence and brigandage, the rich, having the most to lose and being without a principle to justify their privileges or sufficient power to maintain them, managed to conceive "the most deeply meditated project that ever entered into the human mind; it was to employ in their favor the very force of those who were attacking them, to make defenders of their adversaries, to inspire them with other principles, and to give them other institutions that made them as favorable [toward the rich] as natural Right had made them unfavorable" (3:177). This agreement, unlike the one envisioned by Hobbes, was not proposed as a sacrifice of power in the interests of peace. It was put forward with "specious reasons" that Rousseau expresses in an imaginary oration in which the voice of the rich offers general security and the conversion of warring interests into a "supreme power" that will govern under "sage Laws" for the protection of all, thus repulsing common enemies and preserving "eternal concord" (3:177). Crude and simple man, "easy to seduce" and already dependent in so many ways, was ready to sacrifice part of his liberty to retain the rest, as a wounded man cuts off his arm to preserve the rest of his body. "Such was, or must have been," Rousseau concludes, with a hesitation that preserves the ambiguously historical and hypothetical character of his account, "the origin of Society and the Laws, which gave new shackles to the weak and new powers to the rich, destroying natural liberty without recourse, fixing property and inequality forever, which made from an adroit usurpation an irrevocable right and, for the profit of a few ambitious men, henceforth subjected all of human kind to work, to servitude, and to misery" (3:178). Society itself at its origins was a great conspiracy of the rich.

Now, in grasping the meaning of this "most deeply meditated project," the substitution of Right in the place of power, it is important to observe that Rousseau does not consider political order to be illegitimate or deceptive by nature. Already in the *Second Discourse* his theory of the social contract, a union of the entire populace into a single will expressing itself in fundamental laws (3:185), is put forward in a skeletal form. This alienation of individual wills into a general will is an alternative to the form of sovereignty by submission advocated by Hobbes and to the patriarchy of Sir Robert Filmer. The *Discourse* leaves, therefore, some space for the possibility of political reform. At the same time Rousseau portrays the stages of corruption that he has described as making an inevitable progress. The motives for which the state was formed are less important for understanding its development than the manner of its implementation and the "inconveniences" it brings about: "for the vices that make social institutions necessary are the same ones that make their abuse inevitable."[13] With this principle in mind, we can now see the necessary course of history, which moves from natural freedom in solitude toward evolving social cooperation and conflict, followed by the eventual establishment of a social order that is prey to all the vices of the men that formed it, being itself a deliberate but covert form of self-interested manipulation. In spite, then, of the occasional and temporary felicity of wise cities such as Sparta, the laws are corrupt in their origin and "restrain men without changing them," leading eventually to a perfect enslavement in despotism. This development is dictated by the internal development of each state and enforced by their conflicts with each other.

In addressing his contemporary moment, then, Rousseau could add a fourth factor to condition our understanding of the corrupt state of society. Once the perfectibility of man, activated by the contingencies of physical need, had brought society into being and put into play both the divergence of our interests, which makes us want to manipulate each other, and our practical and psychological need to appear better than we are, which makes us want to deceive each other, it was not beyond the power of the great to use the ideas of justice, laws, and government to establish a permanent means of enslavement of the rest of society. The difference between being and appearance (*être* and *paraître*), Rousseau was later to say, depends upon the discrepancy between action and speech (*agir* and *parler*).[14] The institution of civil society was a grand action, then, accompanied by a grand regime of speech and rhetoric designed to protect social inequality. "All public instruction will always tend to be lies to the extent that those who direct it find their interest in lying, and it is for them alone that the truth is not a good thing to speak" (3:967). The polite world of society, with all its refinements, its delicate pleasures and social graces, and the commerce and civil institutions that support them, became for Rousseau an elaborate disguise to conceal the true nature of social interaction, which is mutual bondage and exploitation.

We can return now, with deepened appreciation, to Rousseau's formula from the beginning of the *First Discourse*—the sciences and the arts are the

---

[13] *Second Discourse*, 3:187. One of the manuscripts of the *Second Discourse* contains a long gloss of this important maxim emphasizing the unavoidable perils of the self-interested magistrate. See variant (c) to page 187 on 3:1356–57.

[14] *Lettre à Beaumont*, 3:966.

"garlands of flowers" spread "over the chains with which men are burdened"—and we can also see how the grounds of argument have shifted between the *First Discourse* and the *Second*. The *First Discourse* depicts a
difference between two kinds of society: one that is simple, honest, vigorous,
masculine, and virtuous, and another that is artful, deceptive, degenerate,
feminine, and vicious. The *Second Discourse* shows us that this distinction
is a relative and historical one. All societies are already on the path to de-
generacy by a necessary and predictable development because the good of
Nature is so fragile that it cannot endure even the first step into self-consciousness. To become self-conscious is to define oneself in relation to others, and that is to enter the order of violence and deception. Once that order
is in place, the progress from primitive society upward to Sparta and downward to Paris has become inevitable.

The *Second Discourse* contains a ringing and historically important dec-
laration of the historical differences in human nature (3:192), but underlying these differences is the same dynamic, the same inevitable course toward
corruption. Natural man is always good but social man is always evil. Insofar as we can see ourselves as natural and individual, we are not responsible
for our corruption, but insofar as we are social beings, we are too corrupt to
be worth saving. Rousseau claimed that the myth of the Fall began with a
paradox because it assumed the responsibility it was meant to explain, but
his own account follows a similar logic. It begins with an image of merely
animal happiness, one that we cannot imaginatively occupy as human beings, and sets this alongside the image of our fallen selves, which is only what
society, what others, have made us. Man in his social dimension is responsible for his corruption, but as individuals men remain innocent.

Rousseau's system, as he liked to call it, has obvious structural similarities with Quixotic delusion and paranoia. There is the idealizing self-image
(the Golden Age of our natural innocence), the conspiracy to corrupt it (society), alien forces of power and control (the rich, the law, the state), the systematic discrepancy between appearance and reality (the sciences and arts,
the urbanity of the great world), and the demand for a pervasive unmasking. It is a set of general hypotheses rather than an individual theory of persecution, but it licenses and, indeed, justifies each individual in the belief that
he or she is the victim of powerful collective forces that have a direct effect
upon his or her nature, outlook, and situation in life, with malicious intent.

Undoubtedly the design of his system answered the peculiar imperatives
of Rousseau's personality, and we shall see that eventually he made his own
experience one of the chief sources of support for his views. It is important,
though, at this point, to see that the logic of Rousseau's system is no mere
private form of projection, but that its dynamic also springs in large measure
from the mutilated form of naturalism Rousseau inherited and was seeking
to defend. As we have seen, nature is an identity of ideal and actual. What
is natural is always already what it ought to be. There is literally no space,
then, for agency to operate unless the entity in question has as part of its na-

ture the potential for development. In Aristotle's version of naturalism, the nature of each thing is merely potential, and it is the goal of agents to bring this nature to fulfillment. This reaching for the goal is also a fulfillment of the agent's own nature as an agent, which is to say as a knowing being who can act in a manner guided by the nature of the object he or she seeks. More typical eighteenth-century accounts of agency tended, we have seen, to preserve the sense that reason and Nature are the same but to make Nature the primary term, so that reason becomes the "slave of the passions" and can operate in the interests of Nature as it pursues its needs without teleological guidance. Reason thus is thoroughly naturalized, a project that is still being pursued in our own day. Rousseau, however, takes the opposite direction, setting the development of the intellect outside of Nature. With his denial of the possibility of human progress, he reverses the direction of moral development per se. Individual human nature, as he posits it in the state of nature, is, or was, already perfect and complete. The only potential for agency and development, therefore, must come from outside, for the natural being could not be at once perfect and the agent of its own destruction. This is confirmed by Rousseau's definition of freedom, which, he says, "consists less in doing one's will than in not being subjected to the will of another."[15] If the natural being no longer coincides with what it should be, some external agency must have intervened to remove its freedom by separating it from the good of its nature. A naturalist model in which Nature is complete and requires no development necessarily posits agency as external, negative, and denaturing. If we are not what we should be, some other is necessarily to blame.

Many accounts of Rousseau's thought emphasize the powerful sense of injustice that motivates his critique of inequality and the fact that he himself was a socially marginal figure who experienced injustice at first hand.[16] They are right to do so, and no one has contributed more powerfully to the discourse of modern social consciousness than Rousseau. It is in his writings, almost for the first time, that our social arrangements as a whole come to look arbitrary and subject to criticism. This is what made him so terrifying to readers like the later Burke and so enabling to ones like Robespierre and Saint Just. It would be impossible to better, for example, the mordant, unsentimental description of the differences in treatment that a rich and a poor man can expect from their fellows given by Rousseau in his article on political economy, leading to the question, "Do not all the advantages of society belong to the rich and powerful?"[17] Yet the moral force of this question is defused by a certain irony when we consider that, for Rousseau, the advantages of society themselves are largely illusory. The tragedy of our social condition is not that we have imposed inequality upon each other but that we

---

[15] *Lettres écrites de la montagne*, 3:841–42.

[16] See, for example, Bronislaw Baczko, chap. 10 in *Job, mon ami: promesses du bonheur et fatalité du mal* (Paris: Gallimard, 1997).

[17] "Discours sur l'Économie politique," 3:271–72.

have entered the social dimension at all. From the moment that we do so, the love of self that is naturally our primary motive begins to turn from healthy self-love into *amour-propre,* which is our desire to aggrandize ourselves in others' eyes.[18] Social being corrupts our erotic nature.[19] Masters are as much corrupted as slaves, for their very power is a shackle: "Whoever is a master cannot be free, and to rule is to obey."[20]

For this reason, Rousseau cannot be satisfied with denouncing specific abuses of justice. In fact he was little interested in political or social injustice when it was not directed specifically at him, and his essential response to the idea of reform was that "the slightest change" was likely to upset the restraining power of custom, leading to the harm of social mores.[21] Rousseau's program was therefore, as Judith Sklar puts it, an "exercise in indignation."[22] His grandiose rhetorical instincts demanded an absolute betrayal of an absolute innocence, and though there is a gesture toward human freedom and responsibility, from the perspective of each individual that responsibility is always elsewhere.

A New Theodicy

Ernst Cassirer, in an influential essay, has argued that the importance of Rousseau's work lies in its contribution to theodicy—that by making society the repository of blame, Rousseau had discovered a new subject of "imputability,"[23] with world-historical consequences. He quotes Immanuel Kant's enthusiastic judgment that "After Newton and Rousseau God is justified, and from now on Pope's doctrine is true."[24] It is a fact, and an interesting one, that Rousseau's attack upon society did not prompt him to abandon his Leibnizian optimism. In response to the objection that he was impugning God's wisdom by suggesting that society in general should be other than it is, he argues that society would not be able to change if that

[18] See Rousseau's note 15 in the *Second Discourse,* 3:219–20.

[19] Not all readers find Rousseau's doctrine of *amour-propre* to be as pessimistic as I do. Joseph K. Reisert, for instance, sees an important potential for *amour-propre* to be redirected toward socially beneficial ends. See *Jean-Jacques Rousseau: A Friend of Virtue* (Ithaca: Cornell University Press, 2003), 19–30, 185–87. There are, of course, La Rochefoucauldian and, especially, Mandevillean precedents. Reisert's view gives *amour-propre* the potential to play a role something like that of "sympathy" in Adam Smith.

[20] *Lettres écrites de la montagne,* 3:841–42.

[21] *Préface de Narcisse,* 2:971.

[22] Judith N. Sklar, *Men and Citizens: A Study of Rousseau's Social Theory* (London: Cambridge University Press, 1969), 28.

[23] Cassirer himself puts this coinage, "Imputabilität," in quotation marks. "Das Problem Jean Jacques Rousseau," first of two installments, *Archiv für Geschichte der Philosophie,* 54 (1932): 207. The discussion of theodicy appears on pages 71–82 of Peter Gay's translation, *The Question of Jean-Jacques Rousseau* (New York: Columbia University Press, 1954).

[24] *Immanuel Kants sämmtliche Werke,* ed. G. von Hartenstein (Leipzig: L. Voss, 1867–1868), 8:630, quoted in Cassirer, "Problem," 205.

were not also part of God's plan.[25] In response to Voltaire's protest at his attack upon society and progress, he insists that his doctrine is a hopeful one, and therefore both "excusable" and "praiseworthy." "For I was showing to men how they made their miseries themselves, and so how they could avoid them." And whereas natural evils like the Lisbon earthquake disturbed Voltaire's confidence in Providence, Rousseau came ingeniously to nature's defense, and that of Leibniz and Pope, by pointing out that it was not Nature that had "gathered together twenty thousand houses with seven or eight stories in the same place" (4:1061). For Rousseau, Lisbon was a man-made disaster, a symptom of human corruption in the mass.

There is something unsatisfactory, though, about Rousseau's reinstatement of human beings as responsible subjects, something inherently relative and unstable about the new subject of imputability he brings into being, because it fails the demand for universality that we associate with Kant. For that reason, it does not furnish a coherent theodicy. To consider human individuals as innocent but society as to blame is merely to consider the same entity under two different descriptions, with only history and accidental change making the distinction. Or, if we consider each person as the victim of every other, then we are all victims and persecutors at once. If we add to the equation the human penchant for inequality and self-aggrandizement so constantly emphasized by Rousseau, then the question naturally arises as to whether you are as much a victim as I am. From the point of view of each individual, the responsibility of the collective other will always be more significant than his or her own. Since the individual is always innocent, while the other is always guilty, there is no way for this perspective to be generalized. This theodicy is inherently divisive.[26]

In spite of this difficulty, Cassirer's remark has its value. The purpose of theodicy is to demonstrate the blamelessness of God. Rousseau's theodicy accomplishes this and something more: it demonstrates the blamelessness of the individual and gives him or her someone else to hold responsible. Imperfection is always here, responsibility elsewhere. What is even more important, it provides a new dualistic scheme of values. For at least half a century before Rousseau, the goodness of all things had been the general refrain—"All partial evil universal good"—but such moral monism has an inherently unsatisfactory aspect. Its Olympian irony undermines the meaningfulness of human struggle and the power to praise and blame. It recognizes no adversary or adversity and cannot genuinely disapprove, and these

---

[25] *Lettre à Philopolis*, 3:234.

[26] It might be tempting to take the individual/social distinction as being parallel to Kant's distinction between the kingdoms of freedom and necessity, but this temptation depends upon our habit of putting freedom and the individual on one side of the equation (the domain of the will and morality) and necessity and society (the domain of natural causes and sociology) on the other. In Rousseau's scheme, however, responsibility lies in society, not the individual. It is thus divorced from our subjective experience of freedom, relocated to an agency that can only be imagined from the outside.

are minimal requirements for a moral system with practical value. Rousseau, however, for all the negativity of his outlook, does provide a kind of moral duality, a capacity for judgment more discriminating than Pope's "equal eye" or the mild Addisonian spectatorship of the gentleman. After Rousseau it became second nature to distinguish the natural from the artificial and to redistribute many other terms of value—strong and weak, masculine and feminine, good and evil—along this divide. Though Nietzsche was sickened by the sentimental element of Rousseau's thought and identified him as the "moral tarantula" that had bitten Kant,[27] his own moralizing form of naturalism is unimaginable without Rousseau's example.

It would be short-sighted, however, to see Rousseau's system as offering merely a stance of critique and a rhetoric of denunciation. There is a kind of action in view, though a negative one. If agency is always other, and its tendency is always harmful, this gives one something to oppose. One can try to prevent the Tower of Babel. We can see the outlines of this program in Rousseau's reply to a brief but trenchant analysis of the *Second Discourse* written by Charles Bonnet, a fellow Genevan, in a letter published under the provocative pseudonym Philopolis. Philopolis poses the basic logical problem of Rousseau's system in the clearest and baldest possible form: "If . . . the *state of society* follows from the faculties of man, it is *natural* to man. It would also then be as reasonable to complain that these faculties in the course of their development gave birth to this condition, as it would be to complain that God gave man such faculties." Rousseau never sent his elaborate and rather evasive reply to this argument, partly because he claimed not to believe that a true citizen of Geneva could have written it without signing his real name.[28] His irritation toward Philopolis is evident:

> Since you claim to attack me by my own system, do not forget, I beg you, that in my view society is as natural to the human species as decrepitude to the individual, and that acts, Laws, Governments are as necessary to Peoples as crutches to old men. The only difference is that the condition of age follows from the solitary nature of man and the condition of society flows from the nature of humankind, not immediately, as you say, but only, as I have proven, with the aide of certain external circumstances which could exist or not exist, or at least happen earlier or later, and therefore accelerate or retard the process. Many even of these circumstances depend upon the will of men. . . . The state of society, then, having an extreme limit of which men are the masters as to whether they arrive sooner or later, it is not useless to show them the danger of going so quickly, and the miseries of a condition they take for the perfection of the species." (3:232)

---

[27] Friedrich Nietzsche, *Daybreak: Thoughts on the Prejudices of Morality,* trans. R. J. Hollingdale (Cambridge: Cambridge University Press, 1982), 3.
[28] *Lettre à Philopolis,* 3:1386–87, note 1.

This passage illuminates a number of the themes we have been pursuing. It shows those two subjects of imputability—humankind and solitary man—very clearly side by side, each one having a nature of its own. And once humankind, "le Genre humain," is assigned a nature, its internal development acquires a natural course of degeneration, from youth to age, by analogy with the ageing of an individual person. It is only the contribution of external circumstances that makes this disintegratory movement inessential, yet those circumstances themselves are natural even though contingent "at least" in their timing. What is Rousseau's justification for taking the solitary individual as the touchstone of human nature rather than man in society? He does not say.

As for the question of agency, this passage does suggest that even though change for Rousseau has become a negative attribute, the inevitable direction of progress itself being negative, there is a role for social agency if it can produce resistance to change by excluding human self-assertion. The perfectibility of our corruption cannot be avoided but it can be retarded. Agency, then, has become the suppression of agency, of change, and of the morally significant presence of others. Just as Luther found a negative role in fighting decline and the devil, so Rousseau, at a similar impasse regarding his own agency, also comes to embody a principle of opposition. And whereas Adam Smith would see the "natural system of liberty" that produced wealth as requiring protection from human interference because it had a natural functionality of its own, for Rousseau such interference becomes the only hope for restraining a system of collective agency that tends by its nature toward decline. The result in all of these cases is a negative teleology, a form of action that functions in resistance to a prior action and a meaning that comes from elsewhere. By making resistance the central form of redemptive action, Rousseau tapped into deep sources of modernity to leave a profound stamp upon the modern political vocabulary.

Reform and Control

Rousseau's two *Discourses,* along with his attacks on French music and on the moral dangers of the theater, made him a focus of controversy in Europe throughout the 1750s. Having questioned the value of all civilized institutions, he was in a position to suggest reforms, and this became the burden of his middle years. Rousseau disdained the notion that his critique of society pointed toward its abolition. He did tend to see opportunity in the destruction of the social fabric when it occurred by chance; so the effects of war and foreign oppression in Corsica and Poland had put those countries in a position to reconstitute society on the basis of national virtue and agrarian rigor.[29] Rousseau understood, though, that a renunciation of present

[29] See *Projet de constitution pour la Corse,* 3:908, and *Considérations sur le gouvernement de Pologne,* 3:954–55.

prosperity could not be expected of any functioning society. His task, then, was the paradoxical one of discovering how the ills inherent in society could be addressed on a social basis alone. His ultimate strategy was to try to imagine the conditions under which society could achieve the kind of integral unity that belonged to the individual in the state of nature. This led him, in the *Social Contract* and in a number of other works, to advance the notion not of a return to the purity of Nature as it had belonged to solitary individuals, but rather the complete abolition of Nature and individuality in favor of civil society. "Good social institutions," Rousseau asserts in *Émile*, "are those that are best able to denature man, remove from him his absolute existence in order to give him a relative one, and carry his self over into the general unity, so that each individual no longer believes himself to be except as part of the general unity, and no longer feels except in the whole" (4:249). Rousseau had acknowledged, in the *Second Discourse*, that the more you study the natural state of man, the further you set your self apart from it (3:122–23). In his political philosophy he makes this paradox into the beginnings of a virtue.

Rousseau's approach to politics has a distinctive aspect. He envisions the establishment of a regime of virtue, a legitimate political order that will be strong, healthy, independent, equitable, and prosperous within narrow limits. These are the social values that will be necessary for the state to enjoy the loyalty of its citizens. But these substantive requirements—the prosperity of the citizens, the good of the state—do not constitute for him the primary goal of civil society. They are only the signs, rather, of a properly ordered polity. What is essential for him in the good constitution of the state is a psychological benefit—that the citizen should be able to enter into the social order without the feeling of subjection. In order to be happy, the citizen must remain free, as free as he had been in the state of nature, which means that he cannot be subject to any other will than his own. For Rousseau the state cannot achieve its purpose of preserving freedom unless the form of sovereignty satisfies this primary psychological and moral need for each citizen. The benefits it provides in terms of equality, equity, prosperity, and civility are clearly secondary. The issue of sovereignty becomes therefore in large part what we might call a psychological or even a therapeutic one. Sovereignty is not an instrument to achieve the other requirements of happiness; it relates directly to the citizen's sense of happiness and well-being.

How, then, can citizens as a group overcome the dynamics of inequality and *amour-propre,* of self against other, of domination and enslavement, that operate once the state of nature has been lost? The answer is that they should abandon their particular will altogether and adopt the "general will" of the state as their own—"each, giving himself to all, gives himself to no one, and because there is no member over whom one does not acquire the same right that one has given away, one gains back all that one has lost, and has more force to preserve what one has" (3:361). Society, thus, becomes a single will, a "common self" ("le moi commune"), and the problem of the other, by this surprising transformation, can simply no longer arise.

The solution is in some ways close to being a Hobbesian one, and it is among the oddities of Rousseau's intellectual style that the thinker he seems most pointedly to oppose is the thinker he most often resembles. Just as the value of Leviathan for Hobbes lies in its absolute singleness, which prevents divisions of power or thought from coming into being, so the general will can only flourish when it succeeds in replacing the divisions among particular wills. The difference, though, is that for Hobbes the sovereign is an individual, the first and most powerful among others, and the ordinary citizens have ceded their power to him in return for peace. With Rousseau, to the contrary, this pragmatic form of resignation is neither possible nor tolerable. It could only be a rationalization for enslavement. If particular interest is going to be sacrificed, it can only be sacrificed in favor of oneself under another and higher description. The individual will becomes identical with the general will of the state; in ceding his power to it, the individual surrenders only to himself. Just as the solitary individuals in the presocial state have a different nature from humankind considered in the social dimension, now the particular wills that combine to form civil society will have a different nature when combined with the general will, and the loss that occurred in the first transformation will be retrieved in the second. By this strange logic, the philosopher of solitary freedom becomes the philosopher of the "common self." The citizen retains his solitary individual will in the sense that his will stands over against no other, but this will has nevertheless fused with a collective one—the sovereign will of the state.

It is vital in this context to take notice of a second important difference between Hobbes and Rousseau. Both of them seem to uphold the idea that the law is not based upon natural or objective principles and that there is no right or wrong outside of civil society. As we have seen, this attitude is consistent with Hobbes's view of the relativity of moral language expressed in *Leviathan*. Rousseau, however, is not a moral relativist. He believes that there are principles of equity and justice that are the same for all. It is the corruption of the human will that is the obstacle: "All justice comes from God, he alone is its source; but if we knew how to receive it from such an elevated source we would need neither government nor laws" (3:378). Wise men can see the difference between right and wrong, but wise men can never be the measure of the polity.

In the course of his work, Rousseau issues many fervent endorsements of the value of reason and expresses many doubts about it. He was himself a tireless reasoner, and, as his correspondence attests, he rarely missed an occasion to instruct. Yet one of his most consistent teachings is the impotence of reason. The truth is far too weak to set men free because it is the heart and not the mind that governs our actions. As the character de Wolmar puts it in *Julie, or, The New Eloise,* "Reason governs while it is alone," but it "never has the force to resist the least effort" (2:495). Without the passionate guidance of the conscience, says another of Rousseau's spokesmen, we have "nothing to raise us above the beasts but the sad privilege of straying from error into error with the aid of an understanding without rule and a reason without principle."[30] Reason provides only analysis. It observes, dissects, comprehends, revolves, but remains immobile. A decade after he wrote the sentences quoted above, Rousseau told a correspondent that, when a man changes his opinions in response to the arguments of another, "a thing already very rare," it is only because motives other than reason are in play— he "gives in on account of prejudice, authority, affection, laziness; rarely, perhaps never, on account of his own judgment."[31]

Reducing the importance of reason is one of Rousseau's most deliberate points of departure from his predecessors. "The error of most moralists," as he puts it, "was always to take man for an essentially reasonable being. Man is merely a sensitive being who consults only his passions in order to act, and to whom reason serves only to palliate those follies his passions have caused him to commit."[32] It is interesting, then, to see Rousseau the self-confessed sentimental Christian and admirer of Leibniz, Malebranche, Berkeley, and Pope attacking the atheistical, materialist Diderot for his naïve belief that natural law could be the basis of a "general will" grounded for each individual in "a pure act of understanding that reasons in the silence of the passions"; Diderot saw this "general will" as part of the wisdom of all peoples, present even in the compacts among thieves.[33] Rousseau could not glimpse it, but even if he had, he would not have been able to accept it as the basis for civil society because, were some individual to adopt the principles of reason and justice, or even of religion, at the promptings of his own intellect, there would be no guarantee that others would adopt them as well.[34] To be good alone is to leave oneself defenseless. Reason, therefore, recognizing the character of our fellow human beings, undermines the very wisdom that reason would provide. "It is necessary then," he insists, "to have conventions and laws in order to join rights and duties and to lead justice to its object."[35] Rousseau's belief in the rewards and punishments of the afterlife play

[30] The speaker is the Savoyard Vicar of *Émile*, 4:601.

[31] Letter to M. de Franquières of 25 March 1769, 4:1133–34. I am not implying, of course, that explaining the relation of reason to the will is any simple task. It is an ancient conundrum. Hume's view of the matter is as bleak and extreme as Rousseau's. "Reason," he says, "is perfectly inert, and can never either prevent or produce any action or affection." David Hume, *A Treatise of Human Nature*, ed. P. H. Nidditch, 2nd ed. (Oxford: Clarendon, 1978), 458.

[32] *Fragments politiques*, 3:554. Rousseau has often been accused of replacing intellect entirely with sentiment. Robert Derathé's classic study, *Le rationalisme de Jean-Jacques Rousseau* (Paris: Presses universitaires, 1948), demonstrates effectively that this is not the case, but even though Derathé takes the rationalist side of the argument a little too far, he recognizes Rousseau's extreme skepticism about the practical value of reason.

[33] See Diderot's "Droit natural," in *Encyclopédie, ou Dictionnaire raisonné des sciences, des arts et des métiers (articles choisis)*, ed. Alain Pons (Paris: Flammarion, 1986), 1:338.

[34] *Première version of Du contract social*, 3:283–87.

[35] *Du contrat social*, 3:378.

no part in this calculus, and the same work that contains the "Profession of Faith of the Savoyard Vicar" also makes the argument that the golden rule of the Gospel cannot be accepted by reason because it suffers from the same difficulty as the chimera natural right—that it would be naïve to adopt it without reciprocal guarantees (4:523). Because human beings do not respond to reason, to put one's faith in it is actually a form of weakness. As Rousseau puts it, "to reason constantly is the mania of small minds. Strong souls have another language. It is with this language that one persuades and incites action."[36]

It is neither the wisdom, then, nor the justice of the general will but the very fact of its existence as a *general* will that makes for its legitimacy. The integrity of the general will is a constitutive principle of civil society. That is why the "Sovereign, by the fact that it is, is always what it ought to be."[37] There is no space of agency or deliberation that can deprive it of its integrity. It has no inside or outside, and this allows it to recapture the perfect unity of man in the solitary state of nature. The mutual cession of particular wills creates the laws, and these laws govern without consideration of the individual. The general will can decide unwisely but it cannot be wrong (3:380). It can create legislation, in other words, that a reasonable sense of equity would not endorse, but this would not entitle any individual to oppose it; that would be to reintroduce otherness, particularity, inequality, and dependency. Returned once more to a state of opposition between particular wills, the individual, even in prevailing over the general will, would have lost his freedom. Such an individual, Rousseau famously writes, would have to be "forced to be free," a phrase that has chilled many readers (3:364). Rousseau's paradox is meant to emphasize that freedom lies not in having one's own choice but in independence and the absence of subjection. Because submission is less poisonously gratifying than domination, it is better to be coerced by the entity to which one's own will theoretically belongs than to coerce an other to whom one will then be enslaved.[38]

The term general will, or *volonté générale,* has a long history among French thinkers, and was especially important to Malebranche.[39] The general will is God's will as he makes the laws, the purpose of the term being to limit God's responsibility by confining it to general enactments. God does not determine particular cases. His Providence is general. For Rousseau, the concept of general will or will of the polity stands in distinction both to the universal political will and to the particular wills of individuals. There is in

---

[36] *Émile,* 4:645. But cf. 695.

[37] *Du contract social,* 3:363.

[38] It is worth noting, at the same time, that, for all his imperious grandeur, submission could give Rousseau pleasure in other realms than the political. "To be on my knees before an imperious mistress, to obey her commands, to have to ask her pardon, was for me the sweetest pleasure" (1:17).

[39] Patrick Riley's *The General Will Before Rousseau: The Transformation of the Divine into the Civic* (Princeton: Princeton University Press, 1986) informs the following discussion.

fact no universal will (or will higher than that of the polity) because, as Rousseau explains in his work on the Abbé de Saint-Pierre, monarchs will never cede the rights of war, so states will always stand toward each other in Hobbesian opposition.[40] Regarding the proper relations between general and particular wills when particular interests are at stake, however, Rousseau finds himself at an impasse. Just as the concept of general will absolves God of responsibility for the evil committed by individuals, so it apparently deprives the state of its power to act justly when individual interests are involved (3:373–74). It seems that human beings in a group can never be free except in the act of giving themselves the same laws. The moment it is time to apply the law to an individual case the fiction of transindividual legislation threatens to dissolve. In the *Considerations on the Government of Poland,* Rousseau compares the problem of setting the laws above men to that of squaring the circle (3:955), and one is never entirely sure he believes in the possibility of achieving this requirement of social freedom or whether he is simply proving that, if it is possible at all, it is possible only in this way. Rousseau's reform of politics would then have the same outcome as his reform of education—to prove that the thing is actually impossible.

The Hidden Law-giver

Rousseau's inability to imagine that individuals could engage with one another in morally or politically acceptable and legitimate relations as individuals is symptomatic of a general intolerance of otherness. This is one of the key elements of his thinking, visible throughout his work.[41] To avoid the inequality that inevitably arises from dependence and difference, the state must be a single self. Both the individual and the state fare best in real or moral solitude, and Rousseau's notion of love is annihilation of the self in the other, evidence of his will to "fusion."[42] Starobinski attributes Rousseau's fear of otherness to a disappointed desire for transparency related to early episodes in his life when he first experienced injustice.[43] In taking this line, he follows Rousseau's own account and articulates it to great effect. But there is no need for us to overlook the psychological imperatives of Rousseau's personality

---

[40] *Jugement sur le projet de paix perpétuelle,* 3:591–95.

[41] On Starobinski's treatment of this theme, see Robert J. Morrissey, "Jean Starobinski and Otherness," introduction to Starobinski's *Jean-Jacques Rousseau: Transparency and Obstruction* (Chicago: University of Chicago Press, 1988), esp. xxii–xxiii.

[42] Jan Marejko calls it his "fusional drive" ("élan fusionnel"). *Jean-Jacques Rousseau et la dérive totalitaire* (Lausanne: L'Age d'homme, 1984), 126–133 and passim. See also Carol Blum, *Rousseau and the Republic of Virtue: The Language of Politics in the French Revolution* (Ithaca: Cornell University Press, 1986), 86. I have benefited greatly from both these authors' insights into Rousseau's psychology.

[43] Jean Starobinski, *Jean-Jacques Rousseau: La transparence et l'obstacle,* 2nd ed. (Paris: Gallimard, 1971), 20–21.

to see that in constructing his philosophy of alienation and fusion, Rousseau was reiterating or reintegrating patterns of thought that had come to him as part of the intellectual heritage of his time. Like Hobbes, for instance, Rousseau cannot accept the possibility of a rational political procedure that puts aside private interests to an acceptable degree. There can neither be an authority that decides for all on the basis of justice nor can there be a division of sovereignty nor a dialogue among rival interests. Nor can Rousseau be sanguine about the state as a natural mechanism of oppositions that succeeds by the separation of powers, a faith that, of course, does involve considerable suspension of disbelief. For him no situation that involves division or otherness can be anything but a confrontation of mutual disguise and an attempt at enslavement. We see the same anxiety about divisions in the discussions of *imperium in imperio* that preoccupy the *Federalist Papers*. If these are principles of paranoia, they are no private delusion, and Rousseau's struggle with them once they have been adopted represents a search for integration within a moral and political vocabulary that creates unavoidable difficulties.

In Rousseau's political mythology, as in his mythology of Nature, agency is always other unless it is that agency to which I have united myself in a single will, but once I have done so, I can recognize no other. Agency, therefore, becomes unaccountable, and though in his writing about politics Rousseau does seem to recognize ordinary proceedings and differences of opinion, on the theoretical plane these remain unintelligible. How is it, then, that the state can actually come into being and function? It is clear enough from the *Second Discourse* that Rousseau can hardly be called naïve about political realities unless we attribute to him the naïveté of suspicion. He views the state as largely a tool of the rich. Its normal trend of development is toward tyranny. Nevertheless, Rousseau does articulate conditions of hope even if they are uncanny: if virtue is to be brought to the state, it can only be by the hidden operation of a secret influence who works outside its official structure as a lawgiver. Just as the convention of the general will brings the state into being, so the lawgiver instills its character and its mores. He makes men into citizens, lovers of virtue and the polis.

The lawgiver is an other but one that the citizen will never have to confront. In this way he is like God. But he has an advantage over the divine agency and that of the polis, for though he is the real maker of the laws that the people have adopted for themselves, his will is not merely general. He can descend to particulars. His aim is to shape the hearts of the individual citizens, for "If it is good to know how to employ men such as they are, it is much better still to make them such as one needs them to be; the most absolute authority is that which penetrates into man's interior and works upon his will as much as his actions."[44] To accomplish this task, it is best for the lawgiver to be an outsider, though a benevolent one; while he can have no

---

[44] "Discours sur l'Économie politique," 3:251.

official role in the structure of government, he constitutes its practical condition of possibility (3:382).

Rousseau does nothing to conceal the paradoxical nature of the lawgiver. He must be "a superior intelligence, who sees all the passions of men and who experiences none of them, who has no connection with our nature and who knows it to the bottom, whose happiness is independent of ours and who nevertheless is quite willing to occupy himself with ours; who, in the course of time preparing for himself a distant glory, can work in one century and enjoy the results in another. It would take a God," Rousseau concludes, "to give laws to men" (3:381). The lawgiver is in every way an "extraordinary man." Undertaking a task that is "above human powers," he possesses "an authority that is nothing" (3:383). Nor can he use reason to accomplish his ends, for the people are not subject to reason, and, as we have seen, reason cannot motivate the formation of the general will. The lack of other means is what "compelled the fathers of nations at all times to appeal to the intervention of heaven and to bestow their own wisdom upon the Gods, in order that the people, subjected to the laws of the State as to the laws of Nature, and recognizing the same power in the formation of man and in that of the city, should obey with liberty and bear with docility the joke of public felicity" (3:383). The invisible, god-like legislator rules by inventing an invisible god to speak for him.

The lawgiver, of course, is transparently a historical fantasy, a figure already the stuff of legend in the pages of Plutarch, where Rousseau probably first encountered it.[45] As we shall see, the ancient historians were to Rousseau what the books of knight-errantry were to Quixote, the models of a heroic self-image. In his mature system, the Plutarchan lawgiver is the imaginary solution to every logical problem. Where ordinary political agency has become unaccountable, the lawgiver has the power to deceive the citizens for their own good. He has a superhuman knowledge of the human heart and its needs, and he can adapt the race he chooses in response to climate, terrain, and all the other variables that condition society and form what Montesquieu called the "spirit of the laws." The lawgiver's primary aim will be to "change, so to speak, human nature," separating each person from his absolute existence and giving him one defined entirely in relation to the state (3:381). All of his measures are directed at attaching each individual will to that of the state and making each citizen love his or her country.

The state depends not upon good men but upon good citizens, and we see Rousseau, in his role as constitutional advisor to the Poles, insisting that in every way the state must exert itself to make its citizens into Poles. Educa-

---

[45] This does not mean, however, that the idea did not have influence. Rousseau contributed to a cult of the legislator that was a vital element in revolutionary and pre-revolutionary France and whose ultimate beneficiary was Napoleon. See David A. Wisner, *The Cult of the Legislator: A Study in the Political Theology of the French Enlightenment* (Oxford: Voltaire Foundation, 1997).

tion is thus the supreme political necessity. It must "give souls a national impetus, and direct their opinions and their tastes in such a way that they are patriots by inclination, by passion, by necessity. An infant opening his eyes should see the fatherland and until his death should see only this."[46] Like Machiavelli, Rousseau is suspicious of the political influence of Christianity. Such universal creeds hinder the republic and weaken it against its enemies. A society of good Christians would be at the mercy of a single Catiline or Cromwell in its midst (3:466). Though Rousseau insists, partly in his role as citizen of Geneva, on his own sincere adherence to Christianity, he believes that the lawgiver must give the citizens a civil religion that is specifically designed to sanctify the laws and cement attachment to the state. Religion should be part of the national cult. Rousseau advises the Genevans to avoid introducing the vain modern rituals of the theater, where people go only to be alone together and have their already corrupt mores reinforced. Instead they should enhance the cult of the state with public spectacles, an idea that was taken up in the French Revolution, when political festivals often invoked Rousseau himself as a presiding spirit. The ritual celebrations of the state will differ crucially from those early festivals of *amour-propre* described in the *Second Discourse,* where people first acquire their taste for the gaze of others. In the spectacles of Geneva, the people look at each other only as part of the unified whole in which they themselves are included.[47]

The ultimate irony of Rousseau's politics, then, is that, though even its primary aim was to free the social individual from deception, manipulation, and dependency, Rousseau could imagine this goal being brought about only by these very means because only a few men of genius can see the truth of human nature and the human heart and understand where happiness lies. The rest can neither see the truth for themselves nor accept it from others. As a result, they have to be led. Thus we see the greatest prophet of egalitarian values finding refuge in the most extreme elitism.

The egotistical grandiosity of this perspective can hardly be overlooked, though such was the impression of genius which Rousseau made upon his contemporaries that, like Plato, he had his opportunities as a lawgiver. Rousseau was aware, though, that the time for lawgivers and the founding of societies for the most part had passed. It was too late either for perfect innocence or supreme wisdom, nor could the feeble modern instruments of language serve the purposes of the virtuous state. The lawgiver must be able to "lead without violence and persuade without convincing" (3:383). His power is a power over the heart, not the intellect, and in this he partakes of the quality of language as spoken by pre-modern man. Like the lawgiver, it too could "persuade without convincing,"[48] while the modern instrument

---

[46] *Considérations sur le gouvernement de Pologne,* 3:966.

[47] *Lettre à d'Alembert sur le Théâtre,* 5:114–16.

[48] Daniel E. Cullen, *Freedom in Rousseau's Political Philosophy* (DeKalb: Northern Illinois University Press, 1993), 124–25.

of speech has become narrow and rational, unsuitable to music, too feeble to be heard in democratic assemblies and too weak to be the instrument of a lawgiver's eloquence.

Many critics have taken M. de Wolmar, in *The New Eloise,* to be a lawgiver in modern form, and it is true that he is presented as a figure of superhuman acumen. His only passions are, by his own infallible account, observation and the love of order, and he would willingly be transformed into nothing but a "living eye" (2:491). His estate, Clarens, is managed with supreme wisdom along the lines of Rousseau's communitarian anarchism, operating as an isolated economic enclave with almost total self-sufficiency and the minimal use of currency. Clarens is Rousseau's state writ small and de Wolmar its presiding spirit. He is a divine, almost omniscient figure, a cunning master and engineer of souls, who dares to bring his wife's former lover into his home and adopt him into its regime in order to teach him that the woman he once loved is now a creature of the past.[49] No scheme or project is too elaborate or too intimate for de Wolmar, and the letters of the other characters pay tribute to his wisdom and goodness. Unfortunately, in the final analysis the absolute coldness of de Wolmar's wisdom becomes a fatal liability, and with the denouement of his novel Rousseau seems to glimpse the inhumanity of his imaginary lawgiver. De Wolmar has understood all hearts except the most important one, that of his wife, who, with bonds of love, has held together the estate he has attempted to manage on the basis of rational calculation alone. In the end Julie dies as an expression of that forsaken love that de Wolmar has taught Saint-Preux to control.

The lawgiver is the benevolent twin of the all-controlling social other that Rousseau fears and the repository of all of the virtues and capacities he has denied to human nature corrupted by society. He asks nothing for himself, is self-sufficient and therefore free of *amour propre.* He has power but no need for recognition, so he does not corrupt those he controls or become dependent upon those he creates. He is an unmoved mover, and in a world in which reason is impotent and all interaction manipulation, he manipulates only for the good of others and to make others good. Most mercifully, he conceals his workings under the aegis of the gods, so that they have the aura of necessity. If, as Rousseau observes, all wise leaders to some degree conceal their power in order to diminish their responsibility in the eyes of their subjects, the lawgiver's self-effacement is perfect, allowing the people to preserve the illusion of their complete freedom. And yet the general will formed by the lawgiver does not only provide freedom; it is also supremely wise— well-adapted to the demands of Nature, climate, and the nature of men. In all of its features it is the undoing of the cunning invention of the state described in the *Second Discourse.* That scheme produces good for a few, this produces good for all, not perhaps the best that can be imagined but the best

---

[49] See Étienne Gilson, "La méthode de M. de Wolmar," in *Les idées et les lettres* (Paris: Vrin, 1955), 275–98.

possible for human beings. Thus we see that suspicion of other human beings leads Rousseau, the great advocate of human nature, to the same recommendation that it led Luther, Bacon, and Hobbes, each in their various fields—the suppression of human imagination and the surrender of power and responsibility to the agency of an unaccountable other.

14

An Attempted Escape

In the same year he published *The Social Contract,* Rousseau produced a second major treatise, *Émile, or, Of Education.* In it he provides his most clarifying expression of the benefits of the social contract with regard to the crucial issues of freedom and control, observing that

> There are two kinds of dependence, dependence upon things, which is natural, and dependence upon men, which is social. The dependence upon things, having no moral element, does not harm liberty and engenders no vices. The dependence upon men, since they are in disorder, engenders all of them, and it is on account of it that master and slave bring each other into depravity. If there is some means of remedying this evil in society, it is to substitute law in the place of man and to arm the general wills [*sic*] with a real force superior to the action of all particular wills. If the laws of nations could have, like those of nature, an inflexibility that no human force could ever conquer, the dependence upon men would then become once again a dependence upon things: one would unite in the Republic all the advantages of the state of nature and the civil state; one would join to the liberty that keeps man exempt from vices the morality that elevates him to virtue. (4:311)

In this republic of Rousseau's imagination, the law, which is itself local and conventional, would, by achieving complete power, acquire not objectivity but inevitability. It would become unquestionable not as a principle but as a fact. One's relations with others would accordingly become as dependable and predictable as one's relations with things, free of social self-consciousness and deluding fantasy. Is and Ought would become inseparable. The abolishing of individual wills would achieve not only unification but reification, both the idealization and the occlusion of agency in a single stroke. Perfect freedom, in Rousseau's version, is not freedom of choice but freedom from the possibility of choice, not just for oneself but for everyone.

Rousseau recognizes, however, that in the present state of society a general will can never be formed. "The public institution no longer exists and can no longer exist because where there is no longer a fatherland there can no longer be citizens" (4:250). To allow men to develop naturally in the society of the present would only be to give them license for the pursuit of vice. And so, in the absence of an authentic general will and the kind of public education that could form the true citizens of a particular state, Rousseau turns to another aspect of the social problem, an aspect that occupies the middle part of his career and is also at the center of *The New Eloise:* seeing that society cannot be reformed and that it is impossible to return to the state of original solitude, how can the individual be protected from the corruptions of society? In other words, since it is the faultiness of their education that has corrupted them in the first place, is it possible to achieve a natural education that will allow human beings to achieve independence and autonomy in society? To answer the question, Rousseau provides a regime and a dramatic fiction to go with it that are equal in scale to those of Plato's *Republic.* Rousseau takes up the role of the "governor" Jean-Jacques, not so much a tutor as a general guide for life, educating the boy Émile, who is put into his care from infancy until he reaches the married state. The book is a strange and brilliant amalgam of good sense with fantasies of power and an exhaustive regime of suspicion and control. Its guiding premise is the all-knowing, wise, and good Jean-Jacques protecting the innocent child from corrupt society and his own imagination.

Rousseau's fundamental educative principle is that the child has a necessary and natural course of development, so the great danger is for him to be exposed to activities and ideas for which he is not ready. Locke's notion that the child should be treated as a reasonable being represents for Rousseau the perfect recipe for disaster, since the child, as a being of Nature, does not have the power of moral reasoning even in a rudimentary sense (4:317). This attitude is a natural consequence of Rousseau's general view of humanity: if men are so rarely adult, how can we expect children to be? It is only in the latest stages of development that reason comes properly into play. In the meantime the governor must exert every ounce of his ingenuity to control the child's behavior and experience without discussion or explanation. The child must never know he has a choice, never imagine that he or anyone else can be good or bad. His only logic is the logic of necessity. There is no right or wrong, only possible and impossible (4:321). In order to preserve this innocence, everything must be done to keep the child in absolute dependence upon the governor, with a minimum of contact with the outside world. The bond between governor and child must be ultimate, permanent, and unbreakable as far as the child is aware (4:267–68). The governor replaces society for his pupil and guards him from its denaturalizing influence. Whereas the lawgiver's task is to make citizens of men by denaturing them, giving them the beliefs and habits of virtue that will enable them to join their will perfectly with that of the state, the governor's task is to teach his pupil to retain the independence of the person who depends only upon things, even though he lives on the fringe of an imperfect society in which all is a contest of wills.

It follows, therefore, that for Rousseau the governor's task will be to protect the child from social influence while allowing him to benefit from the influence of Nature. The child must be allowed to experience the rigor of the elements and to develop his physical powers, to build Spartan resilience and escape the effeminacy of modern cosseting. *Émile* contains some of Rousseau's bitterest complaints against the deleterious effects of modern medicine, which always makes us weak rather than strong. Émile will be a healthy savage, raised in solitude as if he were "an insensible being or an automaton" (4:325). It is obvious that such an education cannot take place in the city—"The breath of man is fatal to his fellow creatures" (4:277). Urbanity and civilization are the very opposites of education. Instead of developing, the child must be protected from developing. Just as the lawgiver seeks to retard the progress of a nation, the governor practices an "éducation . . . purement négative" (4:323). The governor must learn to "do all in doing nothing" (4:362).

At all costs must the governor avoid the role of the tempter, introducing to Edenic innocence the knowledge of good and evil (4:327). The very notion of truth implanted in the mind of the child will lead to lies. If the child ever witnesses a moral reaction such as anger in others or in the governor himself, it must be made to pass as a natural event, an illness (4:127–28). The harm that can come to Émile from one premature episode of moral conflict could last a lifetime, for this natural savage has a fragile sensibility. An ill-timed burst of laughter in his presence will undo the work of six months! (4:128).

The traditional goals of education are entirely out of place for the natural child. Words, books, languages are foreign to his needs. Émile must be led to discover the truth for himself rather than accept it from authority. His "true masters" will be "experience and feeling" (4:445). Imitation will be deadly for him and the forming of any habit except that of yielding to need (4:421n). He knows nothing of obedience or moral obligation, only "force, necessity, powerlessness, and constraint" (4:316). When the governor finally wants to teach him an idea, he must arrange a charade so that Émile can be guided by Nature and experience rather than by the governor's will. Émile learns the notion of private property by witnessing the destruction of a garden he had planted on land belonging to Robert the gardener. Jean-Jacques the governor then contrives a scene between himself, Émile, and the gardener in which Robert explains his right to destroy Émile's garden (4:331–32). All of Émile's education is covert theater, nothing is what it seems to be, and this is the secret of the governor's success: "There is no subjection so perfect as that which preserves the appearance of freedom; in this way one captivates the will itself" (4:362).

When pronouncing hard truths such as this, a strange enthusiasm often swells in the voice of Rousseau. He never seeks to mitigate the extremity of his solutions but to give his phrases the most violent turn, as if inspired by the justification that comes with impersonating natural force. "Command him nothing, no matter what in the world it may be," he advises the governor regarding his pupil.

> Do not even let him imagine that you claim to have any authority over him. Let him know only that he is weak and that you are strong, that according to his condition and your own, he is at your mercy. Let him know it, let him learn it, let him feel it. In good time let him feel on his proud head the hard yoke that nature imposes on man, the heavy yoke of necessity under which it is necessary that all finite beings should bend. Let him see that necessity in things, never in the caprices of men; may the reins that hold him be those of force and not authority. . . . It is thus that you will make him patient, even-tempered, resigned, peaceful, even when he does not get what he wants; for it is in the nature of man to endure patiently the necessity of things, but not the evil will of others. (4:320)

Thus we see that the governor, by dint of force and the preconcerted manipulation of appearances, has become a kind of Nature to the child, in a way that occludes his own and his pupil's existence as moral beings as well as the existence of any other moral beings.

Eventually it is time to reason with Émile, time for him to go from having *Robinson Crusoe* as his model to Fénelon's *Télémaque,* the philosophical traveler with his guide, Mentor, who is really Minerva in disguise.[1] Émile has long been taught that he should be kind and sympathetic toward other creatures, and especially those less powerful than himself. Now he is ready for books, and history will become one of his great teachers—not those heroic tales out of Plutarch, which incited the imagination of the young Jean-Jacques, but the far more sober writings of Hobbes's mentor, Thucydides, who, Rousseau says, gives the most objective view of the way things are (4:529). At the same time as he is learning the lessons of the Corcyran Revolution and the Peloponnesian War, Émile will be initiated into Rousseau's critique of society and taught to recognize men by their deceptions—"the more they disguise themselves, the better we know them" (4:526). He will be given a précis of *The Social Contract* and, in addition, Rousseau's most ideal version of natural religion, voiced through the persona of the Savoyard

---

[1] Fénelon is clearly one of the models of Rousseau's minimalist utopianism. For an account of their relations, see Patrick Riley, "Rousseau, Fénelon, and the Quarrel between the Ancients and the Moderns," in *The Cambridge Companion to Rousseau,* ed. Patrick Riley (Cambridge: Cambridge University Press, 2001), 78–93.

Vicar, which will show him not only the limits of our knowledge but also the sacredness of conscience, leaving him to admire the beauty and perfection of the creation. Above all, Émile will be taught the key to Rousseau's Stoic conception of happiness—that, since happiness is the excess of power over need, one must learn to confine one's desires to the limit imposed by necessity (4:819). Because he has been raised in dependence only upon things and has learned to define his desires only in relation to his own estimate of their objects, Émile will experience no temptation to seek his happiness in the eyes of others. He will live among them as part of necessity and without dependence (4:856).

By the end of the story, all of these sentiments, and these alone, have become second nature to Émile through rigorous training and constant deception. But when the governor finally reveals the covert means by which he has carried out Émile's education, the pupil does not rebel. He accepts what has been done for him with gratitude and wants to remain what his governor has made him (4:651–52). After this education, knowledge of good and evil cannot spoil him. Émile is like a savage who has learned to think and to judge others yet remain very much himself (4:534). He is free and can be happy anywhere.

From One Master to Another

In the education of *Émile*, then, it seems as if Rousseau has finally succeeded in solving, at least for himself, the problem of how one might preserve the goodness of Nature in a social individual. The education of single individuals is a more hopeful project than the education of a people because individuals can be controlled from birth; hence it is possible for them to become wise, which can never be the condition of an entire people. But even Rousseau did not maintain for long that *Émile* showed anything more than that, if such an accomplishment were possible at all, this is how it must be done.[2] For the extraordinary efforts of the governor, like those of the lawgiver before him, seem to testify not so much to the redeemable nature of humankind as to the practical implausibility of the venture. And even if the obstacles to education could be overcome by a virtuous and wise governor, where, given the already corrupt state of civil society, were such governors to be found?

The practical difficulties raised by the scheme of *Émile*, however, are not as troubling as the doubts that emerge from within the text. Even when the educated Émile is equipped with all the natural and intellectual instruments he needs for freedom, Rousseau still cannot imagine him without a governor.[3] When, near the end of the story, the governor Jean-Jacques takes Émile

---

[2] *Lettre à Christophe de Beaumont*, 4:937.
[3] See Judith N. Sklar, chap. 4 in *Men and Citizens: A Study of Rousseau's Social Theory* (London: Cambridge University Press, 1969).

up on the mountaintop finally to expose to him the methods of his education—to reveal to him the facts of sex, relinquish his authority over him, and become his friend—Jean-Jacques has already anticipated that his pupil will refuse this freedom and ask for continued guidance, and he is prepared to agree only reluctantly so that Émile will later have no doubts about his decision. "It is in this moment," he says, "that reserve and gravity are in their place" (4:652). The governor is still contriving to strengthen his hold on Émile even as he pretends to set him free. He will continue to command, only now he will provide explanations if they are wanted. He will also continue to deceive Émile. He even chooses Émile's bride, Sophie, long before Émile ever sees her, and he orchestrates their courtship step by step, including the requirement of a grand tour that will keep them from coming together while they are still in the first transports of love. At the end of the story, Émile is still begging the governor to continue his reign (4:867–68). It is a strange vision of freedom.

What is still stranger, though, and perhaps even more significant, is that, although Émile is ready himself to become a governor and unite the figure of the father and the governor, he himself will have another governor, for though Jean-Jacques has been able to insulate Émile from unequal relations with society, there is one unequal relation that he cannot do without, and that is his relation with his wife. One of the important tasks of the governor is to keep the child in ignorance of sexual matters until he has reached the age in which he is ready to begin courtship. Rousseau believes that this moment should be postponed as long as possible, and there is deep significance in the fact that the governor takes Émile up on the mountaintop to learn two truths at once—the truth of sex and of their own relationship. It is as if in relinquishing his own governance he is also handing Émile over to his new master. And, as we have seen, Jean-Jacques will preside over the transition.

In the state of nature, Rousseau tells us in the *Second Discourse,* differentiation between the sexes is confined to biological functioning, and only gradually do broader gender differences emerge. The sentiment of romantic love based on them is one of the first products of inequality and *amour-propre,* an "artificial feeling" that women foster "with great skill and care in order to establish their empire, and make that sex dominant which ought to obey" (1:158). Love is a symptom of dependence and a cause of violence. Like the pleasures of the sciences and the arts, its sweetness is a disguise for enslavement.

Rousseau sees the domination of women as one of the essential elements of social inequality. Men are what women would have them be. Woman is the chief witness of male *amour-propre,* and because women are corrupt, men are corrupt. Women's great weapon lies in their weakness, and they do everything to enhance it. By giving men the pride of dominating them, and yielding themselves only unwillingly, they exert a secret control. Behind these feminine arts, of course, lies a profound intelligence, an intelligence that Nature has given women to make up for their lack of strength (4:702). They make a profound study of the men around them in order to manipulate them.[4] That they should do so is necessary because Nature has not given them the means to provide for themselves and their children without the help of men. But the effect is pernicious, since their feminizing influences separate men from the rigors of Nature. Because they cannot become men, women try to make men into women.[5]

Relations between the sexes, therefore, are for Rousseau the very essence of unfreedom. They exemplify paradigmatically the fact that the sensation of power over others is always a disguise for weakness. Woman, as Rousseau likes to call her, embodies, in fact, the paradox of power: behind her apparent weakness lies a veritable strength. If "to rule is to obey,"[6] as Rousseau tells us, then for woman, to obey is to rule. In her charms she has her own special form of violence (4:694). And if freedom lies in confining one's desires within one's means of satisfaction, so that one's power always answers to one's need (4:695–96), then the raison d'être of women is to deprive men of this freedom, for it is in the nature of the relations between the sexes that women incite more desire in men than they satisfy, and that it is in their interest to do so. The great panoply of feminine weapons aims toward this purpose: "Modesty is in their faces and libertinage at the bottom of their hearts" (4:740). Rousseau has carefully observed their seductive ways. They even take pride in kissing each other in the presence of men in order to incite their desires! (4:719). The theater is a great pageant of feminine corruption and so are the salons of Paris. Rousseau's defense of the innocent purity of Geneva against the temptations of the theater is largely a plea for the autonomy of the sexes.[7] Rousseau would like to confine the influence of women to the home, but this is, of course, their citadel. In times when virtue reigns, their rule is benevolent and necessary to the virtue of men. Rousseau admits the ascendancy of women in history, and he pities the century in which "women can make nothing of men." Women are the great movers of history; they were the epitome of Roman and Spartan virtue as they are the epitome of modern corruption. "All the great revolutions were brought about by women" (4:742).

How, then, does Émile's governor cope with the problem of marriage when there is no longer a polis which modern women can inspire their men to serve? Will he create for Émile an enlightened woman who will have her own freedom and allow him to have his, or will he instruct Émile about the ruses of women so that he can avoid the sweet enslavement of sex? Surprisingly, he does neither. Sophie will be a virtuous woman who will love only a virtuous man. Before she meets Émile she is in love with the idea of Télé-

---

[4] It is in a Baconian spirit that Rousseau apportions the labor of developing "la moralité expérimentale" between men and women: "It is for women to discover, so to speak, the morality of experience, for us to reduce it to a system." *Émile*, 4:737.

[5] *Lettre à d'Alembert*, 5:92.

[6] *Lettres écrites de la montagne*, 3:841–42.

[7] See *Lettre à d'Alembert*, 5:92–98.

maque! (4:762). Yet once Sophie has entered the sexual bond she will control her lover, and Émile's governor is determined to help her establish her sway. What the illusory charms of the sciences and the arts do for the ties of civil society, love, that "sweet illusion," will do for the tie that links the married couple—"entwine with flowers and garlands the happy bond that unites them till the tomb" (4:790).

In advising mothers on feminine education, Rousseau licenses girls in the use of a certain amount of cunning. Since "trickery is a natural talent of the sex" and "all natural tendencies are good and right in themselves. . . . It is only a matter of preventing their abuse" (4:711). Having brought Émile and Sophie together, Jean-Jacques watches Émile "drink in long draughts the poison" with which the "girl enchantress" intoxicates him (4:776). As soon as they are married, the governor will use all his influence to persuade Émile that neither of the couple should owe sexual favors to the other, so that Sophie can refuse her husband whenever and as often as she likes. She tests her powers on the very first night, and Émile goes into despair.

The rationale for this regime is that, preserving their freedom, it will allow the couple to go on as lovers in the married state. This liberal idea is a façade. The governor is scheming to help Sophie establish her regime. And this, of course, is his own regime too. He has preached independence and reliance only on things while exercising an absolute personal control. Now, having pretended to expose all of his projects so that his pupil can accept the results of education and make them his own, he is really handing him over to another secret governor. Émile is under supervision and control from the cradle to the grave. His experience of Nature and necessity are contrived from beginning to end. He is a happy victim of control answering to the needs of his inventor, who was an unhappy victim of chance and the gaze of others.[8]

Freedom and the Noble Lie

In educating Émile, Rousseau recognized that he was following in the footsteps of a great predecessor, Plato, author of the *Republic*—"the most beautiful treatise on education ever made," as he calls it. (4:250). The two thinkers have some traits in common: both of them are exemplary in considering politics in psychological terms, both see the problems of political association as an overcoming of private interest and an attachment to a higher good, and both think of the solution as a sublimation of eros toward a new object. Most important for our purposes, both see the establishment of the right relation of individuals to realities outside themselves as a matter of such importance that it justifies any measure, even systematic deception and

---

[8] In *Émile et Sophie, ou les solitaires,* the sequel to *Émile,* composed some time later in the distress of Rousseau's full-blown paranoia, Émile's happiness is destroyed by Sophie's weakness and he experiences all the torments of Rousseauvian betrayal.